Contemporary
Turkish Literature

Contemporary Turkish Literature

Fiction and Poetry

Edited with an Introduction by

Talat Sait Halman

Rutherford · Madison · Teaneck
Fairleigh Dickinson University Press
London and Toronto: Associated University Presses

Associated University Presses, Inc.
4 Cornwall Drive
East Brunswick, New Jersey 08816

Associated University Presses
27 Chancery Lane
London WC2A 1NS, England

Associated University Presses
Toronto M5E 1A7, Canada

Library of Congress Cataloging in Publication Data

Main entry under title:

Contemporary Turkish literature.

    1. Turkish literature–20th century.
I. Halman, Talât Sait.
PL232.C6   1980   894'.3508003   77-74391
ISBN 0-8386-1360-8

Printed in the United States of America

Contents

Part 1: Short Stories

Part 2: Poems

CONTENTS 13

Acknowledgments

I wish to thank the following for having given me permission to quote from published works:

Professor Charles Angoff, Professor Martin Green, and *The Literary Review* for "An Episode of Two," "Baby Born in the Field," "The Address of Turkey," "Lost Thing," "Fadim Aǧa's Mills," "The Resurrection of the Unknown Soldier," "Pity," "The Bosporus," excerpts from *Ortadirek* and *Iron Earth, Copper Sky,* "Dry Beans," "The House on the Border," "Green Gold," "Haney Must Live," "Embellishments," several selected "Aphorisms," "I've Registered for Germany," "The Bedouin," "The Quarrel," "They," "A Mother," "Don't Go, Stay," "Poet," "The Critics," "To Guillaume Apollinaire," "The Horses," "The War of the Houses," "Fringe," "Arrival," "Country," "Teasing," "Guillotine," "After One O'Clock at Night," "The Mediterranean Light," "And Came the Tailors," "Old Broken Glasses," and "The Gate of the Lost."

Mr. Frederick Hetzel and the University of Pittsburgh Press for "Beacon," "Gleam in Time," "Jobless," "Village without Rain," "Sparkle," "Beating," "Audience," "Poems of the Mediterranean," and "Banks of the Red River" (from *Fazıl Hüsnü Daǧlarca: Selected Poems,* translated by Talat S. Halman, Pittsburgh, Pennsylvania, University of Pittsburgh Press, 1969).

Mr. Theodore Wilentz and Corinth Books for "This World," "I Am Listening to Istanbul," and "Tamerlane's Price" (from *I Am Listening to Istanbul: Selected Poems of Orhan Veli Kanık,* New York, Corinth Books, 1971).

Professor Roy E. Teele and *Literature East & West* for "Tragedies," "Poems of Twenty-one and Twenty-two O'Clock," "Today Is Sunday," "Poems from Prison," "***," "My Funeral," "To Be You," "Reflection," "A Corpse Turns Cold," "To Wake Up opposite Forty Thousand Villages," "Beyond," "Our First Bondage," "Different Warmth," "Fine Days," "Echo," "Fellow Citizen," "As Death Approaches," "Tail-Song," "Reply," "Ancient Egypt," "Have and Have Not," "hannelise," "At My Touch It Turns into a Faded Rose," "The Left Ear of the Grand Vizier," "A Docile Dog," "Underdeveloped," "The Dagger," "News Bulletin," "The Carter," and "Geography Lesson."

Mr. Andreas Schroeder and *Contemporary Literature in Translation* for "Thirty-three Bullets," "The Darkness of Daybreak," "The Yellow Heat," "Treadmill," "Bone," "How Bad It Is That a Poem Gets Old As One Reads It," "The Thirty Liras," "Shahan the Smuggler," from "The Turkish Alphabet," "Explanations of the Moon," "The Guest," "Awakening," "Bird Temple," "Shadow," "Unawakened," "Sidewalk Superintendent," "Freedom," "The Rooster and the Stairs," and "All Men Die."

Ms. Sonia Raiziss and *Chelsea Review* for "How Can I," "Different Warmth," and "Hope."

Prof. Rainer Schulte and *Mundus Artium* for "All the King's Men," "A Shroud for My Darling," "Eyes," "The Dead Have Grown Old," "The Wall," "Gaff," "A Camp in Hell," and "Autumn, a Wild Shore."

Messrs. Ted Hughes and Daniel Weisbort and *Modern Poetry in Translation* for "Beyond," *"Perçemli Sokak,"* "Autumn Song," "Arrival," "Istanbul," "Sofia," "Pablo Picasso," "Sonnet," "The City," "Building a Bridge," "Harbor," "Eternal House," "Paris," "The First Half," "At the Inquest," "Poems from *Suite in the Ottoman Mode,"* "Ancient Sea Folk," "The Night of the Stag," "Blood Cities," and "Song about Executioners."

Mr. Charles Humboldt and Masses & Mainstream Publishers for "from *The Epic of Sheikh Bedreddin,"* "Letter from Prison," and "Plea" (*Poems by Nazım Hikmet,* translated by Ali Yunus, New York, Masses & Mainstream, 1954) and for "Song for One Who Has Gone Away" from *Masses & Mainstream.*

Jonathan Cape (Cape Editions) for "Since I Was Thrown into This Hole," "That's How It Goes," and "The Armies of China Saved Me Too" (*Selected Poems: Nazım Hikmet,* translated by Taner Baybars, London, Cape Editions, 1967).

Sylvia and Sam Tankel and *Short Story International* for "Sale of Saltanat."

Prof. Robert Stewart and Prof. Robert M. Farnsworth and *New Letters* for "The Cart" and "Grand Surveillance."

Mr. Erje Ayden and Geronimo Books for "On the Nomad Sea," "Pigeon," and "Like Our Hands."

Dr. Grace Schulman and *The Nation* for "Freedom."

Mr. James Laughlin and Ms. Else Albrecht-Carrie and New Directions Publishing Corporation for "Horses before Troy" (*New Directions in Prose and Poetry 33,* James Laughlin, editor).

Prof. Ivar Ivask and *Books Abroad (World Literature Today)* for "On Victory," "Rose," "A Butt Cast in the Sea," and "November 8, 1945."

Mr. James Fitzsimmons and *Art International (The Lugano Review)* for "For the Fallen at Gallipoli."

Mr. Bryan Healing and *Encounter* for "Free."

Ms. Yvonne Mason and *St. Andrews Review* for "Monte Kristo," "Dead," "Bone," "The Voice," and "Fly," and "The Venue Line."

Osman Türkay and *Weekly Turkish News* (London) for "from *Those Lands Belonged to Us,"* "Fahriye Abla," and "Foetus."

Islamic Research Association Miscellany (Bombay) for "Provocateur."

Ms. Kathleen Weaver and Mrs. Thelma Philip and Penguin Books Ltd. for "Ellas and the Statues" (*The Penguin Book of Women Poets,* ed. by Carol Cosman, Joan Keefe, and Kathleen Weaver).

Mrs. Betty Radice and Mr. Will Sulkin and Penguin Books Ltd. for "Fantasy," "First," "Eyes," "If I Had a Magic Wand," "To a Poet of the Sea," "The Saga of Istanbul," "Fear," and "I Want a Country" *(The Penguin Book of Turkish Verse* by Nermin Menemencioglu).

Prof. C. Max Kortepeter for "Sad Freedom" *(Modern Near East: Literature and Society,* published by New York University).

Evelyn P. Gill and the *International Poetry Review* for "If Only I Could Set Sail," "A Small Spring," and "Oh, Winter Came Again."

Prof. Norman Simmons and *Cave* and *Pacific Quarterly* for "The Phaeton," "Nights in the Shanties," "Vanish," "Hollow," "Its Grief," "Migrant Mustafa," "Beyond the Time of the Birds," "Execution," "The Gazelle," "Blood," "Come So Far As You Can Feel," and "The Bedouin."

The editor is grateful to Dr. Jayne Warner for her meticulous proofreading.

Guide to Turkish Spelling and Pronunciation

For Turkish authors, names of places, and special terms, this anthology employs standard Turkish spelling. The short stories, poems, biographical notes, are arranged in the same sequence as the modern Turkish alphabet that appears below together with a simple guide to pronunciation:

a   (like *gun*)   var. â (like *are*)
b   (as in English)
c   (like *jade*)
ç   (*ch* of *chin*)
d   (as in English)
e   (like *pen*)
f   (as in English)
g   (*g* of *good*)
ğ   (makes a preceding vowel longer)
h   (*h* of *half*)
ı   (like the second vowel of *portable*)
i   (like *it*)   var. î (like *eat*)
j   (like *measure*)
k   (*k* of *king*)
l   (as in English)
m   (as in English)
n   (as in English)
o   (like *eau* in French)
ö   (like *bird* or French *deux*)
p   (as in English)
r   (*r* of *rust*)
s   (*s* of *sun*)
ş   (sh of *shine*)
t   (as in English)
u   (like *pull*)   var. û (like *pool*)
ü   (like *tu* in French)
v   (as in English)
y   (*y* of *you*)
z   (as in English

Of the twenty-nine characters in the Turkish alphabet, six do not exist in English: ç, ğ, ı, ö, ş, ü. The letters q, w, x are not in the Turkish alphabet although they may occur in foreign names. The letter ğ has its own capital Ğ, but never starts a word. The undotted ı and the dotted i are separate vowels whose distinctions are strictly observed in pronunciation and spelling. These two letters have their individual capitals as well: I and İ respectively.

For virtually all Turkish words and proper names, the present text uses the authentic Turkish spellings. The few exceptions include Yaşar Kemal, who is known in Europe and the English-speaking countries as Yashar Kemal, and some words, e.g., *hoca* or *rakı* which have their anglicised versions: *hodja* and *raki*.

Special Terms

A number of words, which appear in Turkish or in anglicised spelling, occur in several stories and poems. Most of these require elucidation:

ağa   (often anglicized in other books as *agha*): a versatile term that is variously used in many stories and poems in this anthology as (a) big landowner in the rural areas; (b) a local feudal lord; c. mister (provincial term); (d) elder brother or paternal uncle; (e) master

bey   gentleman or simply Mr. (used after first name)

efendi   (anglicized as *effendi*) gentleman (In Ottoman times, this term was reserved for notables; in recent times, it is used mainly for men in the lower strata of society.)

hoca (also anglicized as khoja) teacher, particularly a teacher of Islam (also a common reference to Nasreddin Hoca, the legendary Turkish wit and raconteur who presumably lived six hundred years ago)

imam   religious leader, guide, prayer leader

kuruş   (sometimes anglicized as *kurush*) piaster or penny—one hundred *kurush* equals one *lira*

lira   principal denomination of Turkish currency, like the dollar

(The anthology covers a period of more than fifty-five years, during which period currency values have changed drastically. Most of the monetary references, therefore, will give some basic idea to the reader about values, prices, salaries, etc. They provide no specific figures for their dollar or pound equivalents.)

rakı   the most common alcoholic beverage in Turkey

Place names remain in Turkish except for non-Turkish places, and the city of İstanbul is spelled as Istanbul.

Footnotes are provided sparingly—only if their absence will lead to lack of comprehension or clarity.

Introduction:
Literature of the Turkish
Republic

Since I last saw you I found brave new words
To make poetry breathe in a wider sky.

—Cemal Süreya

Out of the ruins and ashes of the Ottoman Empire, as the cliché often goes, the Republic of Turkey came into being in 1923. In that fateful year, the influential social thinker Ziya Gökalp wrote: "We belong to the Turkish nation, the Islamic community, and Western civilization.... Our literature must go the people and, at the same time, towards the West." His summation of the Turkish identity was, by and large, correct in terms of historical realities and the burgeoning impetus for Westernization. His counsel for a people's literature exploring the literary norms and values of the West proved inspiring—and prophetic. The literature of the Turkish Republic has achieved Gökalp's dual objective, but in its versatility it has functioned, with impressive accomplishments, in other spheres as well.

Revolution, innovation, and Westernization have been the driving forces of the Turkish nation in the twentieth century. In the transformation of sociopolitical structure, economic life, and culture, the men of letters have served not only as eloquent advocates of progress, but also as catalysts, precursors, pioneers—and creators of brave new ideas of innovation. Today, as in the past thousand years, Turkish literature seems to bear testimony to Carlyle's dictum—"The history of a nation's poetry is the essence of its history, political, scientific, religious"—and to Professor Gustave E. von Grunebaum's observation that "literature has always been the art of the Muslim world, masterpieces of painting and architecture notwithstanding."

Poetry, or literature in general, has been the quintessence of Turkish culture until modern times and a most faithful mirror of socioeconomic realities in Turkey since the inauguration of the Republic in 1923. Virtually all of the salient aspects of Turkish life, politics, and culture have found their direct or indirect expression in poetry, fiction, and drama, as well as in critical and scholarly writing. The themes and concerns have included nationalism, social justice, search for modernity, Westernization, revival of folk culture, economic and technological progress, human dignity, mysticism, pluralistic society, human rights and fundamental freedoms, democratic ideals, hero-cult, populism, Atatürkism, proletarianism, Turanism, Marxist-Leninist ideology, revival of Islam, humanism—in fact, all aspects and components of contemporary culture.

The function of literature, however, has not been confined to that of a mirror held to society and to intellectual life. The basic genres have not only embodied ideas and ideologies, values and verities, beliefs and aspirations, but have also served as vehicles of criticism, protest, opposition, and resistance. Literature in Turkey is a concomitant and catalyst of change: it strives to achieve self-renewal in aesthetic terms, to give voice to cultural and socioeconomic innovation, to provide impetus to progressive or revolutionary change, and to serve the cause of *propaganda fide*.

Turkish literature is among the world's oldest—and youngest—literatures. Its creative tradition, according to the claims of numerous scholars, dates back to before Christ. It is commonly accepted that its legacy of written works spans at least twelve centuries.

In their long history, the Turks have gone through more changes than most nations, and yet—paradoxical as it may sound—they have preserved most of their basic cultural traits. Throughout centuries they lived as nomadic tribes, built small and big states in parts of Asia, created the Seljuk Empire in Asia Minor and later the sprawling Ottoman Empire, which endured from the thirteenth to the early twentieth century, and finally established the modern Republic. At different stages of their history, Turkic communities embraced shamanism, Buddhism, Christianity, Manichaeanism, Zoroastrianism, and other creeds until most of them accepted the Islamic faith more than a thousand years ago. Their language, one of the world's most regular in grammar, and most agglutinative, has used four separate scripts: Köktürk, Uyghur, Arabic, and (since 1928) Latin.

The lyric and epic traditions of the early centuries led to the masterworks of the pre-Ottoman period: *Divan ü Lugat-it-Türk,* an encyclopedic compendium of Turkish linguistics and poetry; *Kutadgu Bilig,* a mirror for princes; and Yunus Emre's mystic folk poetry which is notable, *inter alia,* for its universalist humanism.

Ottoman literature, which stressed poetry as the superior art, utilized the forms and the aesthetic values of Islamic Arabo-Persian literature. The educated elite, led by the Sultans (many of whom were accomplished poets themselves), produced a huge body of verse whose hallmarks included refined diction, abstruse vocabulary, euphony, romantic agony, dedication to formalism and tradition, and the Sufi brand of mysticism. Prose, although not held in high esteem by the Ottoman literary establishment, accounts for some excellent achievements, particularly the travelogues of the seventeenth-century cultural commentator Evliya Chelebi. The Ottoman Empire nurtured a rich theatrical tradition, which consisted of *Karagöz* (shadow plays), *Meddah* (storyteller and impersonator), and *Ortaoyunu* (a type of commedia dell 'arte).

The oral tradition, in addition to the early Dede Korkut tales, which recount the Turks' heroic exploits, produced a large body of legends and stories. Its principal achievement is folk poetry, composed by minstrels and troubadours, who voiced in a spontaneous, sincere, and simple language the sensibilities, yearnings, social protests, and critical views of the uneducated classes. Utilizing Turkic verse forms and syllabic meters, often extemporized and sung to musical accompaniment, replete with assonances, alliterations, and inexact rhymes, folk poetry harped on the themes of love, heroism, the beauties of nature, and, at times, mysticism.

Classical poetry remained under the pervasive influence of Persian and Arabic verse: it imitated and tried to emulate the same verse forms, rhyme and rhythm patterns, meters, mythology, and even the same *Weltanschauung.* It adopted a substantial corpus of vocabulary from the Persian and Arabic languages.

Until the twentieth century, two literary mainstreams, seldom converging, constituted the flow of Ottoman Turkish creative arts—*poesia d'arte* and *poesia popolare*—to use Croce's two categories. The first embodies elite, learned, ornate, refined literature; the second represents spontaneous, indigenous, down-to-earth, unassuming oral literature. *Poesia d'arte* is almost always an urban, and often upper-class, phenomenon, while *poesia popolare* flourishes mainly in the countryside. The former, as the name suggests, has a strong commitment to the principle of art for art's sake, whereas the latter is preponderantly engagé or utilitarian in function and substance.

The conventional devices—strict formalism, stock similes and metaphors—as well as some of the basic themes and concerns of classical Ottoman literature, may be found in a *ghazel* ("lyric ode") by Fuzuli (d. 1556), one of the greatest masters, in a faithful, but grotesquely archaic, translation by E. J. W. Gibb (d. 1901), the indefatigable British scholar who produced the most comprehensive study of Ottoman verse (*A History of Ottoman Poetry*, 6 vols., London, 1900-1909) but who perhaps did irreparable damage to Turkish literature because of his anachronistic translations:

> Feres are heedless, spheres are ruthless, Fortune is inconstant quite;
> Woes are many, friends not any, strong the foe, and weak my plight.
>
> Past away hope's gracious shadow, passion's sun beats fierce and hot;
> Lofty the degree of ruin, lowly is the rank of right.
>
> Little power hath understanding, louder aye grows slander's voice,
> Scant the ruth of fickle Fortune, daily worsens Love's respite.
>
> I'm a stranger in this country, guile-beset is union's path;
> I'm a wight of simple spirit, earth with faerie shows is dight.
>
> Every slender figure's motions form a stream of sorrow's flood,
> Every crescent-brow's a headline of the scroll that madness hight.
>
> Learning's dignity's unstable as the leaf before the wind;
> Fortune's workings are inverted, like the trees in water bright.
>
> Sore desired the frontier, fraught with anguish lies the road of trial;
> Yearned for is the station, all the path of proof beset with fright.
>
> Like the harp's sweet voice, the longed for beauty bides behind the veil;
> Like the bubbles on the wine, reversed the beaker of delight.
>
> Separation is my portion, dread the way to union's land;
> Ah, I weet not where to turn me, none is here to guide aright.
>
> Tears of cramoisie have seizèd on Fuzuli's sallow cheek;
> Lo, what shades the Sphere cerulean maketh thereupon to light.

Yunus Emre (d. ca. 1321) was the wellspring of Anatolian Turkish folk poetry, and remains its paragon. He is best known for quintessential verses and devotional hymns written in syllabic meters and a simple style. He once cautioned against effusive language: "Too many words are fit for a beast of burden." His message to the rural masses is direct and forceful, full of love and humanism:

> I am not here on earth for strife,
> Love is the mission of my love.
> ....
>
> I love you in depths beyond my soul.
> ....
>
> Come, let us all be friends for once,
> Let us make life easy on us
> Let us be lovers and loved ones,
> The earth shall be left to no one.

The nineteenth-century men of letters inherited the classical and the folk traditions, but turned their attention to the literary tastes and movements of the West—particularly of France and, to a lesser extent, England. The Ottoman state, beset by military defeat and atrophied social institutions, embarked upon a process of transformation usually referred to as *Westernization*. In 1839 the *Tanzimat* (Reforms) Period started to introduce legal, administrative, educational, and technological innovations. Cultural and literary changes followed in quick succession. New genres, adopted from Europe, gained ascendancy: fiction, drama for the legitimate stage, journalistic writing, the critical essay, and others. Translations and adaptations, mainly from the French, gave impetus to the Europeanization of Turkish literature.

When the Ottoman state collapsed after nearly 625 years and gave way to the Republic, Mustafa Kemal Pasha (Atatürk) devoted his prodigious energies to the creation of a homogeneous nation-state dedicated to modernization in all walks of life. The hold of Islamic thought and institutions over the nation was broken: secular education replaced Koranic instruction, and the government stressed nationalism as the official ideology, declaring religious allegiance and practice a stumbling block to progress. The legal system adapted the Swiss Civil Code, the Italian Penal Code, and the German Commercial Law. Perhaps the most difficult of all reforms, the Language Revolution, was undertaken with lightning speed in 1928, and since then it has achieved a scope of success unparalleled in the modern world. The Arabic script, considered sacrosanct as Koranic orthography, used by the Turks for a millennium, was replaced by the Latin alphabet. A massive effort, still maintaining its momentum, has effectively purged the language of the vast majority of borrowings from Arabic and Persian. Atatürk's new Turkey, which he defined as a "Republic of Culture," seemed to uphold the statement made by Dr. Abdullah Cevdet, an influential intellectual, in 1913: "There is no other civilization: Civilization means European civilization, and it must be imported with its roses and thorns." Although the sweeping reforms did not extend into the rural areas, in the urban centers drastic changes took place: political system, religious faith, national ideology, educational institutions and methods, intellectual orientation, daily life, script and language—all underwent transformation. Literature was also caught in the maelstrom.

All stages of modern Turkish history (reforms under Atatürk, 1923-38; consolidation under Inönü, 1938-50; democracy under Menderes, 1950-60; junta, coalitions, caretaker cabinets, parliamentary governments since 1960) have been marked by the thrust of literary modernization. Today's Turkey, where parliamentary democracy was replaced in September 1980 by a military regime, is homogeneous in population (more than 99 percent Muslim) and integral in political and administrative structure—yet pluralistic, full of inner tensions, a battleground of the traditionalists versus the revolutionaries. Its literature is vibrant with ideologies, with a feverish search for values old and new, for diverse styles and tastes, for elements that can be employed to revive the traditional national culture, and for significant borrowings from the West as well as from other traditions.

Since the mid-nineteenth century, the most vital debate of Turkish literature has been between the proponents of art for art's sake and the advocates of commitment to realism and social causes. Mustafa Kemal Pasha himself, in a conversation that took place in 1921, about two years before he proclaimed the Republic, exhorted the nineteen-year-old Nâzım Hikmet, already a famous poet, who would soon embrace the communist ideology and influence the course of modern Turkish literature, particularly poetry, more profoundly than anyone else, to "write poems with a purpose." The advice was heeded by each generation of writers since then, giving rise to patriotic verse in abundance on the one hand, and to socialist realism on the other. Especially since 1950, there has been a massive output, in all genres, depicting the plight of the lumpen proletariat. But surrealism, neosymbolism, theater of the absurd, stream-of-consciousness techniques, hermeticism, black comedy, obscurantist verse, and so on, have also flourished.

The literary tastes of the early years of the Republic were dominated by numerous revered poets who had emerged in the twilight of the Ottoman Empire. These prominent figures included Abdülhak Hamit (1852-1937), who, according to E. J. W. Gibb, inaugurated "the true Modern School of Turkish poetry, and whose elegiac, philosophical and metaphysical poems and stentorian verse tragedies fired the imagination of the Ottoman elite." Mehmet Emin Yurdakul (1869-1944) intoned a mystique of Turkish nationalism: "I am a Turk: my faith and my race are mighty." Ahmet Haşim (1885-1933), under the influence of French symbolists, combined a striking fiery imagery with melancholy sonal effects to create his lyrics of spiritual exile ("We ignore the generation which has no sense of melancholy"), articulated a view that summed up a fundamental aspect of classical poetry, and adumbrated the credo of the neosurrealists of the 1950s and 1960s: "The poet's language is constructed not for the purpose of being understood but to be heard; it is an intermediary language between music and words, yet closer to music than to words."

Mehmet Âkif Ersoy (1873-1936), a master of heroic diction, devoted much of his verse to the dogma, passion, and *summum bonum* of Islam. His nationalism has a strong Islamic content, evident in the lyrics of the Turkish national anthem that he wrote. His elegy "For the Fallen at Gallipoli" is a celebrated expression of the values be upheld:

> Soldier, you who have fallen for this earth
> Your fathers may well lean down from heaven to kiss your brow.
> You are great, for your blood saves the True Faith

Only the heroes of Badr* are your equals in glory.
Who can dig a grave that will not be too narrow for you?
If I say: "Let us enshrine you in history," it will not contain you
That book cannot hold your time of troubles
Only eternity can embrace you.
If I were to set up the Ka'ba as your headstone
If I could seize the revelation in my soul and write it as epitaph
If I could take the firmament with all its stars
And lay it as pall over your bloody coffin
And make a ceiling of purple clouds for your open tomb
And hang the seven lamps of the Pleiades
If, as you lie swathed in blood under this chandelier
If I could detain the moonlight by your side
To stay till dawn as guardian of your tomb
If I could charge your chandelier with morning light
And wrap the silken sunset about your wounds—
Still I could not say: "I have done something for your memory..."

(Translated by Bernard Lewis)

* A place near Madinah where Moslems won a battle in 624 A.D. led by the Prophet.

"I am," wrote Yahya Kemal Beyatlı (1884-1958), "the future with roots in the past."
He was the much-acclaimed neoclassicist who produced, in the conventional forms and
meters, meticulous lyrics of love, Ottoman grandeur, and Istanbul's natural attractions.
His "Death of the Epicures" is a testament to spiritual tranquillity and to the aesthetic
life:

In the garden of the poet's* tomb there's a rose, they say,
Day in day out it blooms anew, its color is blood-choked;
A nightingale weeps all night, they say, till the break of day:
In its tunes, the dreams of the city of love * are evoked.

Death for an epicure is the springtime of calm and peace;
For years his soul smolders like incense burning everywhere
While his tomb lies and endures under the cool cypresses—
Each dawn a rose blooms and each night a nightingale sings there.

*The poet referred to is Hafiz, a major Persian poet of the fourteenth century, and the city is identified as Shiraz.

The heroic voice dominated some of Beyatlı's mellifluous verses. "Raiders" is a widely
quoted specimen of his paeans to the Ottoman martial spirit:

We were a thousand horsemen, merry as boys on our raids;
A thousand horsemen, that day we conquered a giant army.
The silver-helmeted Beylerbey* shouted 'Forward!'

On a summer day we crossed the Danube with our caravans.
Like lightning we struck at a land, in seven columns,
Like lightning, where the Turkish horses had once passed,
One day, riding our horses at full gallop
We rose in flight from earth to seventh heaven.
Even today, when we see the roses bloom in paradise
That crimson memory quivers in our eyes.
We were a thousand horsemen, merry as boys on our raids,
A thousand horsemen, that day we conquered a giant army.

(Translated by Bernard Lewis)

*Ottoman governor-general

Among the dedicated revolutionaries in twentieth-century Turkish poetry Nazım Hikmet (1902-1963) ranks the highest. He has been a modernizing force since the early 1920s, remaining significant in aesthetic and political terms. He launched and popularized free verse under the early influence of Mayakovski. A communist, he spent many years in Turkish jails, fled to the Soviet Union in 1951, and died in Moscow in 1963. His poetry fuses social protest and a lyricism full of rhythmic effects and ingenious onomatopoeia. He practiced functionalism by doing away with the conventional molds, and created formal structures as the embodiment of content. Much of his large body of work laments social injustice, complains of the oppression of the masses, and yearns for revolutionary change. He composed many tender love lyrics, but his followers remember him more for his battle cries—"We can only reach our goal/amid bloodletting"—and for his concern about his comrades in other countries, as voiced in "Angina Pectoris," written while he was in prison in the late 1940s:

If the half of my heart is here, doctor,
The other half is in China
With the army going down towards the Yellow River.
And then every morning, doctor,
Every morning at dawn
My heart is shot in Greece.

And then when the prisoners fall asleep,
When the last steps go away from the infirmary
My heart goes off, doctor,
It goes off to a little wooden house in, in Istanbul.
And then for ten years, doctor,
I have had nothing in my hands to offer my people,
Nothing else but an apple,
A red apple, my heart.

I watch the night through the bars
And in spite of all those walls lying heavily on my chest
My heart beats with the most distant star.

My heart beats with the most distant star.
It is on account of all that, doctor,
And not because of arterio-sclerosis,
Or nicotine or prison
That I have this angina pectoris.

(Translated by Taner Baybars)

Turkey's romantiç revolutionary produced a prodigious amount of poetry, many plays—conventional as well as avant-garde—which have been staged not only in Turkey but also in the Soviet Union and numerous European countries, and several inept novels. His *Memleketimden İnsan Manzaraları* (Human Landscapes from My Country), a sprawling, episodic verse saga of the twentieth century, composed in twenty thousand lines, is often touted as his magnum opus. His real masterpiece might well be *Şeyh Bedreddin Destanı (The Epic of Sheikh Bedreddin),* published in 1936. A moving account of the rise and fall of a heretical sect that preached an incipient form of communism in the early fifteenth century, it contains some of the most poignant poetic narrative passages ever written in the Turkish language.

At his best, Nazım Hikmet has been compared by Turkish and non-Turkish men of letters to such figures as Lorca, Aragon, Esenin, Mayakovsky, Neruda, and Artaud. No other Turkish poet has been translated into more languages nor enjoyed greater acclaim in so many countries. Tristan Tzara, who translated some of Nazım Hikmet's poems into French, paid the following tribute: "The life Nazım led engulfs the experiences of a large segment of mankind. His poetry exalts the aspirations of the Turkish people as well as articulates the common ideals of all nations in humanistic terms."

Nazım Hikmet's innovations, although they struck a responsive chord in poetic tastes throughout his life and after his death, by no means established a monopoly. Most of his contemporaries pursued different courses: Necip Fazıl Kısakürek wallowed in the anguish of his own soul; Faruk Nafiz Çamlıbel combined neoclassicism with urbanized versions of folk verse; Ahmet Muhip Dranas, Ahmet Hamdi Tanpınar, and Ahmet Kutsi Tecer specialized in simple lyrics of genteel sensibilites expressed in tidy stanzaic forms and the traditional syllabic meters.

Asaf Halet Çelebi (1907-1958) introduced his own iconoclasm in surrealistic poems that gave the impression of somnambulistic writing with intimations of erudition. "A poem," he declared, "is nothing but a long word made up of syllables joined together. Syllables by themselves have no meaning. It is therefore futile to struggle with meaning in a poem.... Poetry creates an abstract world using concrete materials—just like life itself."

These theories and movements continued to exert varying degrees of influence on the literature of the later decades, but the themes and the tenor of Nazım Hikmet's verse probably wielded the widest impact. Effective voices have been raised among poets, dramatists, fiction writers, essayists, and journalists against the established order and its iniquities, oppression of the proletariat, and national humiliation suffered at imperialist hands. The poetry of social realism concentrates on the creation of a just and equitable society. It is often more romantic and utopian than rhetorical, with sensual strains, tender sentiments, flowing rhythms, but occasionally given to invective and vituperation.

The earlier novels of the Republic depicted the disintegration of the Ottoman society, ferocious political enmities, and the immoral lives of religious sects, as well as the conflicts between urban intellectuals and poverty-stricken peasants—as in the novels of Yakup Kadri Karaosmanoğlu (1889-1974). Turkey's major woman intellectual and advocate of women's rights, Halide Edib Adıvar (1884-1964), produced sagas of the War of Independence, psychological novels, and panoramas of city life. Her novelistic art culminated in *Sinekli Bakkal* (1936), which she originally published in English under the title of *The Clown and His Daughter* (London, 1935).

The harsh realities of Anatolia found fertile ground in the literature of engagement after World War II. Sabahattin Ali (1906-1948) was a pioneer of forceful fiction about the peasant's trials and tribulations. Two books, both published in 1950, *Bizim Köy* by Mahmut Makal (b. 1933) and *Toprak Ana* by Fazıl Hüsnü Dağlarca (b. 1914), exerted a shattering impact on political and intellectual circles by dramatically exposing conditions in villages. The first, available in English translation (*A Village in Anatolia,* translated by Sir Wyndham Deedes), is a series of vignettes written by Makal, a teenage peasant who became a village teacher after graduating from one of the controversial Institutes for Village Teachers. The book reveals the abject poverty of the Anatolian village:

Quite apart from the trouble of earning the wretched stuff, it's difficult even to make bread here in any edible form.... The women rise at night, knead the dough, and while their husbands are still in bed—that is to say, before dawn—they bake enough for the day. If they get up a bit late, they get no end of a beating from their husbands, and everyone calls them "slatterns".... If you want to know what the torments of Hell are like, I'd say it's baking bread in this village.

Not five per cent of the women in our village wear shoes. All the rest go barefoot. Even in winter they do the same, in the snow and the mud and the wet. The girls all go barefoot.... And in summer these same feet go off to the cornfields to plough, all cracked and cut with stones.

In *Toprak Ana* (Mother Earth), Dağlarca gave poetic expression to the same tragic deprivations, as in the poem entitled "Village without Rain":

> I'm hungry, black earth, hungry, hear me.
> With the black ox I'm hungry tonight.
> He thinks, and thinking feeds him,
> I think, and thinking makes my hunger grow.
>> I'm hungry, black earth, hungry, hear me.
>> One can't hide it when he's hungry.
>
> The wind sleeps on the hills of gluttony
> In the sleep of bird and beast.
> When the fat stars glide,
> Darkness get fed.
>> The wind sleeps on the hills of gluttony.
>> One can't sleep it off when he's hungry.
>
> Hunger is black on our faces, hunger is hoary.
> Meadows and hills hunger.
> Rain falls no more and the crops are scorched.

How did we anger the skies far and wide?
    Hunger is black on our faces, hunger is hoary.
    One can't live on it when he's hungry.

In the mid-1950s a brave new genre emerged—the "Village novel," which reached its apogee with Yashar Kemal's *İnce Memed* (this novel has been translated into twenty-five languages; the English translation by Edouard Roditi is entitled *Memed, My Hawk*). Yashar Kemal (1922-), the most famous Turkish novelist at home and abroad, is frequently mentioned, not only in Turkey but also in the world press and literary circles, as a strong candidate for the Nobel Prize. His impressive corpus of fiction, written in a lithe, virtually poetic style, ranks as one of the truly stirring achievements in the history of Turkish literature.

Dealing with the merciless reality of poverty, village literature portrays the peasant threatened by natural disaster and man's inhumanity. The drama is enacted in terms of economic and psychological deprivation, blood feuds, stagnation and starvation, droughts, the tyranny of the gendarmes and petty officials, and exploitation at the hands of landowners and politicos. The style is predominantly lyrical and dialogues record local dialects with an almost flawless accuracy. A pessimistic tone pervades much of village literature: its delineations are bleak even when occasional flashes of humor, or a glimmer of hope or descriptions of nature's beauty, appear. A great strength of the genre has been its freedom from the rhetoric that has marred much of the poetry of social protest. When presenting deprived men and women pitted against hostile forces, the best practitioners offer an affirmation of the human spirit. Their works are often testaments to the dauntless determination of the peasant to survive and to resist—sometimes through rebellion—the forces of oppression.

A growing body of fiction about the urban poor shares the strengths of the village novel —engrossing plot, effective narration, realistic dialogue, and so on—but, like much of the literature of socialist realism throughout the world, both types suffer from lack of psychological depth and subtlety.

Satirical fiction is dominated by Aziz Nesin (1915-), Turkey's best satirist ever. In more than sixty works, Nesin has provided a strong indictment of the oppression and brutalization of the common man. His hero is the man in the street beleaguered by the inimical forces of modern life. He lambastes bureaucracy and exposes economic inequities in stories that effectively combine local color and universal verities. Sait Faik Abasıyanık (1906-1954) is admired for his meditative, rambling romantic fiction, full of intriguing insights into the human soul, capturing the pathos and the bathos of urban life in a style unique for its poetic, yet colloquial, flair.

An awakening of interest in Ottoman history, after several decades of neglect, has given rise to a massive semidocumentary novel by Kemal Tahir (1910-1973), *Devlet Ana* (Mother State), a saga of the emergence of the Ottoman state in the late thirteenth and early fourteenth centuries, and several excellent works of drama by A. Turan Oflazoğlu, Orhan Asena, and others. The Turkish War of Independence has continued to fire novelists' imaginations since the 1920s.

In sharp contrast to realist fiction, a group of authors, some well versed in English and French, produced stream-of-consciousness fiction heavily influenced by Joyce and Faulkner as well as by the French *nouveau roman*. Their works depict in lyrical, and sometimes turgid, styles man's psychological crises. Some of them offer tragicomic scenes of modern life by means of a decomposed language. The principal themes of modern fiction all over the world also characterize the Turkish *nouvelle vague:* dehumanization, moral disintegration, absurdity, lack of heroism, ennui, futility, hypocrisy. The protagonists are often abstractions of psychic turmoil, and phenomena are presented in terms of transmogrification.

A frontal thrust for modernization took place in the early 1940s when Orhan Veli Kanık (1914-1950), Oktay Rifat (1914-), and Melih Cevdet Anday (1915-) launched their poetic realism. Their urge for literary upheaval was revolutionary, as expressed in a joint manifesto of 1941 that called for "altering the whole structure from the foundation up... dumping overboard everything that traditional literature has taught us." The movement did away with rigid conventional forms and meters, reduced rhyme to a bare minimum, avoided stock metaphors, stentorian effects, specious embellishments. It championed the idea and the ideal of "the little man" as its hero, the ordinary citizen who asserted his political will with the advent of democracy. Kanık's "Epitaph" is precisely this type of celebration:

> He suffered from nothing in the world
> The way he suffered from his corns;
> He didn't even feel so badly
> About having been created ugly.
> Though he wouldn't utter the Lord's name
> Unless his shoe pinched,
> He couldn't be considered a sinner either
>
> It's a pity Süleyman Efendi had to die.

The *Garip* ("Strange") Group, as the Kanık-Rifat-Anday triad is referred to, endeavored to write not only *about* the common man, but also *for* him. In order to communicate with him, they employed the rhythms and idioms of colloquial speech, including slang. With their movement, the domination of free verse, introduced in the 1920s by Nazım Hikmet, became complete. They proclaimed with pride: "Every moment in the history of literature imposed a new limitation. It has become our duty to expand the frontiers to their outer limits, better still, to liberate poetry from its restrictions." Many of Kanık's poems are frequently quoted by Turks, a favorite one being the three-line poem entitled "For the Homeland":

> All the things we did for our country.
> Some of us died,
> Some of us gave speeches.

In the late 1950s a strong reaction set in against poetic realism. Literature of commitment came under fire in some circles. Salâh Birsel (1919-) was writing his "Poetry Lesson":

> Take "Love for Mankind" as your topic
> And free verse as prosody.

> Relevant or not,
> Whenever it occurs to you,
> Insert the word "Hunger"
> At a convenient spot.
> Near the end of the poem
> Rhyme "strife" with "the right to good life."

There—that's the way to become A Great Poet.

Getting away from the easy intelligibility and the surface simplicities of the poetic realists, a group of younger poets proudly championed obscurantism and meaningless poetry. Soon, Oktay Rifat and Melih Cevdet Anday also departed from their earlier convictions and commitments: the former took up neosurrealism and the latter the poetry of intellectual complexity.

A new generation had initiated obscurantism, continuing from where Asaf Halet Çelebi's surrealism had left off in the 1940s. İlhan Berk, perhaps Turkey's most daring and durable poetic innovator, who acted as spokesman for the group (often identified as "The Second New"), pontificated: "Art is for innovation's sake." Turgut Uyar's line "on the shore of all possibilities" summed up the autistic aspect of this new esoteric poetry, which was marked by such wild thrusts of imagination and distortion of language that some critics denounced it as "word salad." "Vanish," by Edip Cansever (1928-), is one of the prime examples:

> I reiterate: your face is a laughter
> Glance and an armada of life marches into light
> A flower that hails from subterranean regions
> An eagle gone starknaked
> Now pink is pursued by three persons
> Upward along your shoulder
> Drive them insane in your hair
> Carnation multiple
> Carnation shrinking shrunk

> Most beauty arises in your most secret places
> Lovely as animals suddenly born
> Glance and I deliver a poem to the world
> A poem is made: red round wide
> Widest reddest on planes oppressed
> A secret is now pursued by three persons
> Inward along your eyes

Inward along your eyes
Drive them insane in my lines
Carnation divided
Carnation multiplied multiple

Know your hands in circles of hope
Hands are gaped at holding the void in balance
An extension from hope to man
A plane muddled known only to sight
Love is close while forging day out of night
Now love is chased
By three international persons
Drive them insane in infinity
A tea has many a name
A table many a round

Ornaments rotten animals ramcrossed
They all compel us to stare
Now a light is arrested
By three persons dressed in white
Drive them insane in the void
A window too narrow
A window vanishing vanished...

This type of self-serving aestheticism represents a "supreme fiction" at its best and sterile confusion at its worst. A leading critic, Rauf Mutluay, deplored its egocentricity and narcissism as "the individualistic crisis and this deaf solitude of our poetry." The language is usually lavish, the poetic vision full of inscapes and instresses, ambiguity strives to present itself as virtuosity, metaphors are often strikingly original, but sometimes run amuck. Euphuistic and elliptical writing is a frequent fault committed by the practitioners of abstract verse. The best specimens, however, have an architectonic splendor, rich imagination, and human affirmation.

In obscurantism, the critic Memet Fuat found the malaise of the age, calling it "the critique of the time we live in—the poems of individuals who are oppressed, depressed, and shoved into nothingness." As a principle of the new aesthetics, the poet Edip Cansever called for the "death of the poetic line," whose integrity had been accepted as a fundamental artistic value for generations of Turkish poets: "The function of the poetic line is finished." Extending this statement to the self-imposed isolation of the obscurantists, Mutluay speculated that "perhaps the function of poetry is finished."

In sharp contrast, village poets, standing *media vitae*, continue to serve their rural communities by providing enlightenment as well as live entertainment. The minstrel tradition, with all its stanzaic forms and simple prosody, is alive and well. Particularly since the 1950s, many prominent folk poets have moved to, or made occasional appearances in, the urban areas. Aşık Veysel (1894-1973), a blind minstrel, produced the most poignant specimens of the oral tradition.

I walk on a road long and narrow:
Night and day, on and on I go.
Where am I heading? I don't know:
Night and day, on and on I go.

Even in sleep I must forge ahead:
No rest for the weary, no warm bed;
Fate has doomed me to the roads I dread.
Night and day, on and on I go.

Who can tell why my life went awry?
Sometimes I laugh, sometimes I cry.
Craving a caravanserai,
Night and day, on and on I go.

The forms and values of classical poetry, too, are kept alive by a group of highly accomplished formalists who are clustered mainly around the monthly *Hisar,* which ceased publishing at the end of 1980 after thirty years.

Among the daring, and quite impressive, explorations into Turkey's own literary heritage have been those undertaken by Turgut Uyar, İlhan Berk, and Attilâ İlhan. Although these three major figures are highly individualistic and their works drastically different from one another, they have all acknowledged the need for coming to tems with the viable and the valuable aspects of the Ottoman-Turkish elite poetry. They have used, not its stringent forms and prosody, but its processes of abstracting and its metaphorical techniques. İlhan Berk's aesthetics strives to forge a synthesis of Oriental tradition and Western modernity. In his *Şenlikname* (The Festival Book, 1972), for instance, he conveys through visual evocations, old miniatures, engravings, and subtle sonorities the vista of Ottoman life and art; yet the poetic vision, throughout the book, is that of a twentieth-century man, neutral rather than conditioned by his culture, in a sense more European than Turkish. Attilâ İlhan, Turkey's most successful neoromantic poet, also a major novelist and essayist, has attempted to recapture the milieu and the moods prevailing during the slow death of the Ottoman Empire.

Standing outside of all groups and movements is Behçet Necatigil (d. 1979), who produced refined poems of intellectual complexity with verbal capers and a subdued tone. Some of his poems could be described as cubistic. In most of them, he utilized the subtleties of the language more effectively than did his contemporaries. With a natural disdain for stereotypes, he created a private poetic universe of delicate delineations.

Since the late 1950s, both Oktay Rifat and Melih Cevdet Anday have abandoned their earlier insistence on simplicity, the vernacular, concrete depiction, epigrammatic statement, and so on, which had been the hallmark of the *Garip* Group. Oktay Rifat has taken up a fertile type of neosurrealism, proclaiming that "poetry tells or explains nothing, because beauty explains nothing." Anday's work has moved toward lucid philosophical inquiry: his new aesthetic formula is, in his own words, "thought or essences serving as a context for arriving at beauty." His long poems of the 1960s and 1970s ("Odysseus Bound," "Horses at the Trojan Gates," (also published as "Horses before Troy"), "On the

Nomad Sea," and so forth) seek a synthesis of universal culture, and endeavor to construct superstructures of ideas, myths, and legends.

The concern for world affairs is an absorption of many Turkish poets. Their motivation may be ideological or humanistic; nonetheless, they comment on international events with telling effect. They have poured out elegiac poems for John F. Kennedy, Martin Luther King, Ho Chi Minh, Salvador Allende, and others, along with indictments of the war in Vietnam, celebrations of man's conquest of the moon, and moving accounts of the tragedies of Algeria and Cyprus.

The most encompassing poetic achievement of contemporary Turkey belongs to Fazıl Hüsnü Dağlarca (1914-), the winner of the Award of the International Poetry Forum (Pittsburgh) and the Yugoslav Golden Wreath (Struga), previously won by W. H. Auden, Pablo Neruda, and Eugenio Montale, among others. His range is bewilderingly broad: metaphysical poetry, children's verse, cycles about the space age and the quest for the moon, epics of the conquest of Istanbul and of the War of Independence, aphoristic quatrains, neomysticism, poetry of social protest, travel impressions, books on the national liberation struggles of several countries, humorous anecdotes in verse, and so on. Dağlarca has published only poetry—about sixty collections in all. "In the course of a prestigious career," writes Yaşar Nabi Nayır, a prominent critic, "which started in 1934, Fazıl Hüsnü Dağlarca has tried every form of poetry, achieving equally impressive success in the epic genre, in lyric and inspirational verse, in satire, and in the poetry of social criticism. Since he has contributed to Turkish literature a unique sensibility, new concepts of substance and form, and an inimitable style, his versatility and originality have been matched by few Turkish literary figures, past or present." Dağlarca's tender lyric voice finds its testaments in countless long and short poems:

SPARKLE
Clearly death is not a loss.
Regardless the brooks
Will flow.

With faith
Weeds will turn green and roses will grow.
Clearly death is not a loss.

Dağlarca's protest poetry, however, can often be described as *a verbis ad verbera.*

BEATING
How about it, let's join our hands.
You hit twice, and I'll belt two.
Has he stolen
Or sucked the nation's blood and sweat?
You belt four, and I'll strike four more.

20 sent abroad to buy ships, 30 to select tea...
Did the Foreign Minister get a cut,
While our hairless children starve in mudbaked villages,
And our baby dolls sell their pure flesh night after night?
You hit seven times, and I'll belt seven more.

How about it, eh, let's join hands.
Has he sold a plate of beans, 8 cents' worth for two dollars eighty,
Or did he shake his camel's head at your petition to squeeze 500 out of you?
Elected to Congress did he invest in his own future, trample on progress?
You belt nine, and I'll belt nine more.

A most remarkable development in the Turkish arts in the recent past has been the explosion of theatrical activity and the strides of dramatic writing. Very few cities in the world have a broader spectrum of plays or superior performances presented than Istanbul and Ankara. Turkish playwrights have turned out a wide repertoire, including village plays, tragedies in the grand manner, "boulevard" comedies, vaudevilles, poetic dramas, musical dramas and comedies, Brechtian "epic" theater, Albee-like black comedy, modern versions of the traditional shadow plays, social and political satire, well-made family melodramas, and dramatizations of mythological themes and legends.

Approaching the end of its sixth decade, the Republic of Turkey could boast of a literature that stands on the threshold of greatness. There are some impediments, however: these could be summed up as *cultural convulsion* (cataclysmic changes in sociopolitical institutions, faith, and technology); *language crisis* (a vast transformation, broader than the language reform undertaken by any other nation; vocabulary that consisted of 75 percent Arabic, Persian, and French words in 1920 increased its ratio of native words to 80 percent and reduced borrowings to only 20 percent by 1970; yet the language functions with less than forty thousand dictionary entries); *critical gap* (despite some fine critical writing, Turkish literature still operates, by and large, without the guidance of coherent aesthetic theories and systematic critical analysis); *traditional lacunae* (the noticeable absence of philosophy, of the norms of tragedy, of psychological analysis in depth); and *imitation* of models, movements, and major works that have evolved in the West.

The dynamism, quality, purpose, diversity, and impact of modern Turkish literature seem impressive. There is a fertile versatility at work. Turkish literature has never been more varied nor more inclusive. Following many decades of conscious experimentation, questing for new values, acquisition of deeper literary and human insights, and stronger expertise in blending form and content, Turkish authors are creating an authentic synthesis of national and universal elements. If the synthesis succeeds, the literature of modern Turkey might well be ranked as a major literature in the not too distant future.

Cemal Süreya's eloquent lines, written in 1966, embody the revolutionary experience, the disorientation as well as the optimism and the stirring search of the "New Turkey":

We are the novices of new life
All our knowledge is transformed
Our poetry, our love all over again
Maybe we are living the last bad days
Maybe we shall live the first good days too
There is something bitter in this air
Between the past and the future
Between suffering and joy
Between anger and forgiveness

TALAT SAIT HALMAN

Contemporary
Turkish Literature

PART 1

Short Stories

Sait Faik (Abasıyanık)

An Episode of Two

Translated by Talat Sait Halman

Dialogues between the lame seagull and the fisherman have been witnessed if not actually heard. I'll bet my life that it was the seagull who first started the conversation. I can't tell what the seagull really said, but it's out of the question that it might have been the other way around. I mean, it's impossible that the fisherman addressed the seagull first.

Now, let's forget about what the seagull said to the fisherman. Instead, let's make the fisherman talk.

The seagull said: "......"

The fisherman said: "You gonna shut up, you lame thing you? Yak-yak at this hour of the mornin' . . . . Patience ain't gonna kill you, you know! We haven't even got to the seamark yet. For heaven's sake, hold your tongue! Look, if you keep quiet, we're gonna get there sooner. What am I supposed to do—keep up with your chatter or row? Never say die and keep naggin' me, eh? Guess you're starved. OK, you win! Now, wait—just a minute. I'm gonna cut up a mackerel for you. Now, stop screamin', sonny! That's enough, my boy! Look, you're goin' too far! Damn it, with all this gabble, you're makin' my head swell!"

He flung toward the seagull the bones of a mackerel, stripped from its flesh from the head down, with its tail limp, almost quivering. Then he grabbed the oars. In a short while, the Oxia Isles, veiled in the fog, came into sight. The gull was now quiet. With a couple of flutters of its wings, it overtook the boat—and with seven flutters, it disappeared, past the fisherman, toward the coast of the Oxia Isles. Then, it came back and perched on the calm motionless sea. They no longer talked.

It was then that the fisherman turned to me: "Whenever I go out to the sea, he spots my boat and follows me. And the way he brings me luck—it's somethin'."

"Why do you call him lame, Pop?"

"He's lame, that's why. Take a good look: He's missin' a leg."

"Whatever happened to that leg?"

"I don't know. Maybe a dragon sneaked out of the water and bit the leg off. Maybe he was born that way. Or maybe when he was a baby, he fell into the hands of some little boy. Who knows?"

We stopped talking. The wind carried the smell of the land. I sensed the stench of watermelons turning sour.

"Gosh, look at that," said the fisherman. "Whaddaya know! Just like a human bein'! He went and perched right on the seamark."

We came to a halt where the bird was perched. The gull flew, then lighted about five fathoms or so from us. It screamed joyfully, thrusting its head forward.

As the fisherman pulled out his knife to cut up bait, it took off into the air and flew away till it was no longer in sight.

"He got away, Pop," I said.

"He'll be back in a minute," said the fisherman. "Guess he's gonna find out if there's other guys fishin' around the Spiked Isle."

"Why's that? Does he have to find out?"

"Not for himself. I gotta know, that's why." Then the fisherman paused.

Neither of us liked to talk much. In fact, he seemed to regret that we had already talked so much. One could say that a fisherman is a man who talks to himself, but this description may be incorrect. Fact is, the fisherman's lot is not talkative. I've never run into a talkative fisherman. Personally, I reached this conclusion: *If a man is a fisherman, he is taciturn. If he is garrulous, then he is no fisherman.* But a fisherman must be able to talk when necessary.

"See the tip of Prote Island?"

"I see it."

"On top, there's supposed to be a white strip of land. Right above the tip—near those round-shaped trees on top—do you see that?"

"No."

He pulled the oars a couple of times.

"Now?"

"Now I see it."

He paused again. From the blue universe, a deafening sound emerged. A sound unlike all familiar sounds—human or animal voices, sound of whistles, machinery, wood, wind, wires, trees, insects—a sound unlike all the sounds of the earth. I heard this sound from the depths, from the fathomless depths: the voice of the blue universe breathing and panting. Just like ants (which sense not our total being, but an infinitesimal portion of our existence), I kept hearing a tiny bit (reduced billions of times) of the deep deafening resonance of one part of that enormous and vibrant and magnificent creature: the Sea. My temples throbbed, and my ears whirred. On the sea, far away from land, I have always feared this voice—unruffled and deep and inaudible. Suddenly, an urge to speak gripped me, a yearning to scream so that I could drown the voice of the sea. Deep down, I wished I could swim to the Spiked Isle (which we were now approaching) and set foot there on the land and sing a song at the top of my voice.

"Pop," I said, "tell me, for heaven's sake, why does this gull fly to the Spiked Isle to find out about other fishermen and fly back?"

He lifted his eyes—the edges of his eyelashes were red—and looked into my face. He had sensed that I was frightened by the sea and the silence and the inexhaustible deep voice of the sea. Before giving me an answer, he glanced at me. He smiled and said: "If there's some other guy there, that guy may come over here to my spot. I get mad at that, and I move elsewhere. But all day long, I'm mad as hell; and he's scared I'm gonna give him no fish to eat. Other guys don't know nothin' about this: they think I run away so that they won't find my seamark. Cross my heart, it ain't that! Has nothin' to do with it. God provides food for all His creatures. There's plenty of spots around here for me to fish. Look, I know the bottom of this sea by heart, inside out. I could give a submarine its whole log. It's just that I enjoy fishin' all alone, that's all. Get me?"

Now the fisherman turned to the gull: "This gentleman wants to find out about somethin': How come you know I like fishin' alone? Go, answer him, damn it!"

The gull said nothing any more. Its circular, unblinking eyes with red rings around them were fixed on the boat. It looked lily-white and immaculate. Its onion-colored beak kept opening and closing.

"Go on, lame gull, answer! Tell him. Say no dice for you if other fishermen come over here. Say you get all peeved and take off. Then you're a nasty guy all day. And I suffer because of that. Say you turn into a pig. You try to scare me with that oar. Say you even begrudge me one measly fish head."

The gull stared, kept quiet. The fisherman said to me: "Throw those heads to the gull."

The way the gull gobbled up those heads was a sight to see. Just as there are gluttonous men, there are gluttonous gulls, too. It's nauseating to see it. I personally like to see people eat their meals unobtrusively. I like those people who sit under the shadow of a tree, open a little package, and eat without being noticed by anyone. Maybe they smack their lips. Maybe they even have a big appetite, too. Yet, if someone happens to pass by, they feel embarrassed or ashamed, as though they were caught doing some mischief.

"He's greedy as hell," said the fisherman. "I don't like that habit of his. But what are you gonna do? He's only a gull, after all. These creatures are never fed up, never."

"Like human beings," I said.

"No," he retorted. "Don't malign human beings. There are all sorts of people. Some people ain't greedy at all."

"But there aren't too many like that."

"There's plenty," he said.

He pointed toward Mt. Olympus, whose crest was still covered with the snow that had not melted away.

"Over thataway," he said.

We slipped our angles into the water. Now the fisherman talked incessantly. He seemed to be trying to disprove my dictum that *if a man is garrulous, he is not a fisherman.*

"I've seen many a peasant blush while eatin'. As if eatin' was a shameful thing. I also saw high-class guys gulping their lobster without openin' their mouths, real graceful-like, but—I'm tellin' you—faster than any gull I ever saw. They ate elegant enough. Without smackin' their lips. Just movin' their jaws. But you'd get scared just lookin' at those jaws. Man, they were dreadful things. Not like jaws, like machines. Not like machines, either; like a treadmill."

The lame gull kept circling overhead, all around us.

"I bet this gull has got other friendly boats, too? What do you say, Pop?"

"Sure enough."

"I guess he knows what each one likes, too."

"Of course he does."

"That's a lot of politics for a seagull."

The fisherman showed his decayed teeth. I almost saw his uvula.

"Stomach ... Food ..." he said.

We hushed again. He was gently weighing his angle. Again I was overcome by the feeling that the hook sank together with me—first bit by bit, then swiftly—till I plunged breathless into the fathomless depths. My mind clamored to escape the torment of this blue creature and to die breathing freely on land. No matter how much he enjoys keeping quiet and just waiting for his catch, the fisherman began to talk with a halfhearted loquaciousness that betrayed that he did not always think of himself alone and that he remembered my presence.

"It's gettin' rough," he said. "And you turn sick fast. We're gonna go back in a short while, don't worry."

No sooner than he said this, he started talking in a different vein. "Odd," he said. "I've grown accustomed to that lame thing. Those days when he ain't around I'm like a guy who knows he lost somethin' but doesn't know what—and yet he keeps lookin' for it. I can't get used to people, but I've sure grown fond of this bird. Look, if I could get used to people, I'd marry. I just can't do it. Bein' under the same roof, in the same bed with someone all night long, would drive me out of my mind."

I thought of the fisherman's ground-floor room. He would seldom stay there. He kept his nets in that room, and usually slept in a corner of the coffeehouse or in his boat.

"Pop Moonsheen," I said, "you just don't care for a home."

"You said it. I just don't. I can't stand a home. My mother died when I was an infant. Father never stayed around the house. I used to spend all my summers on the beach, swimmin'. In the evenings I used to wait for my father's return from fishin', and I would cuddle up to the boat's prow. Father used to grumble and head for our chicken coop, where he would sleep on the fishin' nets. Early in the mornings, he used to come to the boat and wake me up. If he wasn't mad at what he'd dreamed, he took me along to fish. If the sea looked a bit rough, he used to grunt and say: 'Go on, you go play at the marketplace.' With a lump in my heart, I used to go away."

"Going fishing, Pop Moonsheen?"

"That's right. So what?"

"Why don't you take me along?"

He didn't answer. He didn't even look at me. Yet he knew that the tips I always gave him (although I don't even catch any fish) was nothing to sneer at. After all, Pop Moonsheen had a lot of practical needs in this world. So it's no wonder that he took me along to fish once again.

"But," he cautioned, "I ain't gonna go back even if you die in that boat."

"That day, I got sick."

"You're gonna be sick again. Never mind. Anyhow, you're so high-strung that one of these days you ain't gonna relax on land, either. Listen, nothin's gonna happen out there on the sea. Besides, what if you die? When death comes, what difference does it make if you're on land or at sea?"

"Why is it that out on the sea one has an odd feeling—like the fear of death?"

"That's no fear of death. That's a fear of the mind."

"Now, what does that mean, Pop?"

"Mind works different at sea than it does on land. When your feet are on the ground, with a snap of your fingers you can find some help, some cure. But in a boat you're helpless, your hands are tied. If you feel sick, there's no doctor. If you die, no priest, no imam. Not that they help any. If you turn blind, there's nobody to hold you by the hand. No morphine if you go berserk. Best thing is to get a bottle of booze. Hey! Sonny, go get us a large bottle, eh."

I jumped into the boat. Suddenly, I noticed a black ribbon on Pop Moonsheen's lapel—the kind that mourners wear.

"Who died in the family, Pop?"

"Some distant relative."

This time we didn't talk at all in the boat. When we got to the seamark, he said: "Do you see the tip of Leandros?"

"I see it."

"Do you see the red soil, too?"

"I do."

"There's supposed to be a white house there on the beach. Is it right over the rocks there?"

"That's right."

I put the bait on the hook and let the line drop into the water. Just then, I remembered the seagull and said: "Where's the lame gull?"

He said: "He died."

"What? How?"

"I don't know how. One mornin', when I got to the seamark, his tiny body was floatin' right on the seamark—dead."

"Do you think he came and died on the seamark so that you could find him there?"

He didn't reply. It suddenly occurred to me that perhaps he put that black ribbon on his lapel because his gull was dead. I smiled.

He said: "What are you smiling about?"

"Nothing," I answered, "Maybe that distant relative was the lame gull?"

He fixed his eyes on my face.

"Today," he said, "your mind works as if you're on land. No fear in that head of yours! That's the way it oughta be. Your mind oughta work at sea just the way it works on land. There's no cure, no solution for anythin' on the ground, either. We just figure solutions and cures are under your nose. That's wrong! It ain't true! This world is a helpless world."

"It isn't so, Moonsheen," I replied. "There are solutions in the world. Men will always find solutions in the world."

"Wow, you sure made it, sonny boy! Now, that's the way one thinks on ground. One oughta think the same way at sea, too. You're wrong, but who cares! One oughta think this way all the time!"

I was about to say something when he raised his hand, his fingers holding a cigarette. He made a signal to me to keep quiet. I held my breath. He pulled his line and caught a gurnard weighing twelve or fourteen pounds. I felt he was thinking that this fish would be worth about ten bucks. He took the scoop and dumped the fish into the stern. He put fresh bait on the hook. Then he looked at me expecting me to speak.

"Ehh," I mumbled. "What was I saying? Maybe you're mourning the lame gull?"

He pointed to his head and said: "The mind ages, grows old—it even dies before the body dies."

Then he pointed to his heart. "What doesn't grow old or get smaller is right here."

He paused. This old man, cursed with a fiery temper, disliked and dreaded by the whole village, said: "I wept when I found his dead body there. Remember, last time we came out fishin', you turned sick in the stomach. I got sick exact same way. I went back without catchin' anything. My bones ached all over. I went home to bed. When I got up in the mornin', there was a bitter taste in my mouth–like poison. I turned the cupboards and chests inside out as if I was lookin' for medicine. Then I found this ribbon and put it on."

With his hooklike fingers, he ripped the black ribbon off his lapel and threw it into the water.

"This," he said, "is another sort of madness. I guess it's the sea that makes us this way. Open that bottle."

We poured liquor into the cup. A tear rolled down his cheeks and dropped into the limpid, pungent water. With his clenched fist, he struck his chest.

"This heart," he said, "this heart of ours is the heart of a crackbrain."

Oktay Akbal

Lost Thing

Translated by Ünal Boduroğlu

"You have changed a lot," he thought of saying. Nevertheless he said, "You haven't changed at all."

This wasn't their first meeting, but it seemed as if it were. As if he hadn't gazed at these eyes, hair, and the curved form of this lip a thousand times. As if he hadn't lived with her for nights and for days. She sat with her legs crossed—her legs hadn't changed in the least ... their desirable, inviting complexion. Her shoes were her favorite type—the kind she used to like. He would much rather gaze at her through an eye behind the years than from a distance of two feet. If he could only see her on an April evening of ten or twelve years ago—an evening like the present one, the sun setting slowly. If the gray in her hair could only diminish, the wrinkles, grief, and the dreamless expression of her face could fade away. If he could only see her again as the great love of his twenties.

"You haven't changed at all."

"You have changed, though."

She had always been cruel. Didn't mind what she said, did she? Maybe what she said was not what she kept secret, but completely different things.

"You have changed, though."

"How have I changed?"

"I don't know. I just feel that way."

Needless, meaningless words. Unable to find things to say, they kept on looking at each other.

"Shall we sit here?"

The boat had left the wharf. The deck was isolated. A cold wind was blowing. She had a light dress on.

"Isn't it too cold for him?"

"No, no."

He thinks of me, thought the woman. Does he still love me? Sure. He couldn't forget her. It was impossible. He still loved her, as he did ten or twelve years ago. She sought in her memory for his image in his college and university days. Couldn't find it. Formless visions are like photographic plates taken one after the other. No single one can be drawn out. She couldn't reproduce his image of ten years ago. Pieces of a few broken words, some actions—that was all. For instance, they were again near the sea. No, not in a boat; in a small casino by the sea. First, they had drunk Coca-Cola, then coffee. They had intended fortune-telling. Neither of them had tried it before, but they had got along all right through the forms of the lumps of coffee around the cup. He was madly in love. She had thought, then, that she was in love too. She was very young. Eighteen years of age means a lot to every girl. Ways and means of youth lie before her in a manner that will never end. She thought it would go on forever. Tea parties, balls, movies, flirtations, dances. And the great love of a man, on one side. She was like a child, not content with her toys. Let each toy wait for its turn in one corner, so that she could find it whenever she wanted. But these toys were human. The instant they were broken, it was impossible to repair or mend them. She played with them thoughtlessly. And finished with them all. The road she walked from that casino by the sea to this boat seemed horrifying to her. She shivered all of a sudden. And fixed her jacket.

"If it's cold here, let's go down."

He still cared for her. Loved her. Disregarding everything, all the past.

"No," she said. "Tell me about yourself. What do you do now?"

The man offered a cigarette. The woman didn't take it. He lit one himself.

He always smoked his cigarette like that, thought the woman. She used to tease him, telling him he didn't know how to smoke. It was just the same, the cigarette about to fall from his fingers.

"There is nothing much to say," he said. "I work here now. I was away from Istanbul a few years. Came back two months ago. We've settled by now."

Nothing much to say. What in the world hadn't come to pass after their last meeting. He had married, his children were born, had come to love his wife. Forgotten the other. Didn't remember her. For years and years. Sometimes, as a morning breeze, the wind of memories revealed the old leaves. He never remembered her as an enemy, though; he always thought of her as one very close to him. Despite all those events and lies.

"I work for some company, too. We still live in our old house."

She couldn't help asking: "How are your wife and children?" Hesitated a moment, and then said: "Are you happy?"

Happiness. Thinking and longing for it were the favorite pastime of the idle days of the old ages. No more place for it now. No time to look for it either. He was in a continual mess of daily sorrows and gaieties. He had even forgotten that he could have loved his wife some time ago. She was just another ordinary woman for him. They were married incidentally. Maybe it would have been the same if he had married *her*. This couldn't be changed. It was even foolish to think whether happiness did exist or not. There was no such thing. Happiness, as they call it, was an unrealized dream, an unnecessary hope of human beings.

"Sure, I'm happy," he said. "And you?"

"I am happy, too."

She smiled. "I am talking nonsense," she said. "That is, we are talking nonsense," she thought.

How she knew it. Their looks met in space. A feeling left fifteen years behind came over them both, nestled between them, no one can tell how. Her eyes became wet. She turned her head toward the sea waves. The bridge was far away now. Beyoğlu and its surroundings resembled the Manhattan seen in the movies. This had been first said by him too.

"Look at your Manhattan," she said.

The Galata Tower, the Tünel lodgings, wharf apartment houses, boats, ships, trams. Never seemed to know the things that come and go. It was always like that ... No one ever heeded the moving time. Time, on the other hand, never expected heedfulness. Loves, hopes were all left behind, far behind.

The days of their love had surely been beautiful. Was there one single moment when she really loved him? She presumed she was in love. But now the woman felt to her bones that those feelings were nothing but love. She had lost her love in the palm of her hand. She thought she would find it and feel it in any other man.

He threw his cigarette into the sea.

"I desperately missed Istanbul when I was away," he said.

"Which part?"

"The Bosporus, boats, the bridge, Beyoğlu, cinemas."

"Is that all?"

"Those I love, naturally, enter into the category."

What meaningless words were these. They were words of people who have nothing more to say to each other. It would have been better if they had never met again. Then there would be no memory of these dire moments. They would continue remembering each other as people of those old days. This meeting destroyed the spell. It constantly occurred to her to ask one certain question: "What in the world did you marry for?" It wasn't a practical question though. They kept on gazing at each other. Then they looked around. There was nothing more to talk about. They seemed to sit on thorns.

"You look fine, today," the man said. "As always."

"Oh no, this is my old dress."

"But it's nice, suits you."

Someone was whistling a tune below—from a new French song. A song that speaks of the leaves dying slowly. Life always separates those in love, it was saying. "The sea wipes out the trails of departed lovers ...."

Why does he remember the words of this song now? There were other songs in those days. This one was new. Other people, ten or twelve years from now, would remember their adventures through these new songs.

Seagulls were diving into the sea. They watched them for a while. It was almost dark.

"Are you going home?" he asked.

"No, I'll first drop in to see a friend of mine. You?"

"I've got urgent business to attend."

Their conversation seemed to come, not from their hearts, but from a page of a dictionary, the words brought out one after other incidentally. They were empty words. If there was anything real, it would be beyond these looks. Lived there. Dumb, motionless, without breathing. If we never meet again, thought the man. She has changed a lot. Somewhat grown old. How did it happen? How can the endless stream of mornings and evenings, following each other continuously, bring an adored being to this state? Perhaps the woman, too, thought in the same way about him. Where had this fat, businessman-type come from? What has he got to do with that thin boy who lived only for love?

They felt disturbed. Constantly looking at the sea. All of a sudden, the woman said: "How old is your child?"

"One of them is four years old. The other, one-and-a-half."

"You have two children then? Which one do you like most?"

She was trying to recover the mood.

He smiled, said nothing.

What meaningless words, she thought. If the boat could only reach the wharf a few minutes earlier. It was useless to continue this conversation. To remember lost things, to make one remember them. Old relationships have to be broken. One has to get friendly with and love new acquaintances. Old loves have to be kept only in dreams.

It was a perfect Istanbul evening. A crimson horizon. A sky getting dark slowly. Seagulls. Small boats. Sounds of trains. Songs whistled. Familiar laughs of people around. It was the same years ago; it will be the same years later. There is something lost, though. But what? The human mind cannot find it.

"I'll catch the bus," said the woman. "I have to go now. You sit here, if you want to."

She rose from her seat. He was pleased by her departure. Didn't move at all. I can create her within me, he thought. She'd better be off. "Goodbye," he said. "I'm so glad to have seen you again."

"Goodbye, I'm glad, too."

From a distance she resembled the girl he knew. Hair flying in the wind. Walking fast. She was like that when she came to their first meeting too. It was as if no time had elapsed from that moment on. He wanted to call her back, then gave up the idea. "How foolish I spoke," he thought. "Couldn't find anything to say."

His wife and children were at home now. Dinner was ready. This was the real thing. This daily life. Work attended early in the morning. Homecoming every evening. Tired sleeps. Days without love. Nights without rest. This was all that is called life. Everything left behind will be lost, continually. They would be lost things. It was unnecessary to feel sorry for the lost things. Together with loves and adventures, people of those memories and their surroundings were destined to be lost. One should never look for lost things. He should go on living his share of the time. It too will be lost when the time comes. It will be a story in turn.

Sabahattin Ali

The Cart

Translated by Frederic Stark

There was trouble over a field, and Hüseyin Savruk shot Blond Mehmet in Arkbaşı.

The village of thirty homes fell into a turmoil. Everyone was confused, afraid of the guard and expecting it to come. Now the post was six hours' ride from there, and as long as no one sent word of the murder it would be at least two weeks before a patrol came through. The villagers, after some time, realized this. Then the old men collected around Hüseyin's father, Mevlut Ağa, in the café. Blond Mehmet had no one but his mother, an old woman. They called her up and warned her against going to the law.

"Granny," said the imam, "what will you get by taking this to the law? Who's going to witness for you that Mevlut Ağa's boy shot somebody? Even if they do, let's say you go into town twice a month and waste four or five days at a time; who's going to plant your crops, who's going to look after things for you? Two days' ride into town. All right, suppose you manage it. Then your witnesses don't show, they tell you to come back in a week, your case is postponed. Then you forget which day and don't go, the guard comes to get you, and this time you can't get out of it even if you want to. You'll end up losing house and home. Now. What's done is done. An accident. God's will. And who are you to set the Lord's decree against a court of law? Do what you like, it won't get you back your son. Close the case, Granny. What good was Blond Mehmet to you anyway? Always at a wedding party, or a picnic, and if you sold half a bushel of grain he'd spend the money on his women. Mevlut Ağa says he'll take care of you from now on. So what about it?"

The old woman sat listening, her head swaying. Like a tree in grief. Her big-jointed, crack-skinned hands, like gnarled branches, wiped at eyes gummy and red with weeping. When the imam finished his speech she went on in the same grieving sway. Her gray hair, its henna faded, sprouted from under her grimy, patched kerchief like a swatch of hay. She pulled it back from her face and wet cheeks. She muttered something.

A few more of the people sitting came over and squatted in front of her. Half coaxing, half threatening, they spoke to her. "That's right though, isn't it? What the imam says is right. Why don't you answer?"

All this while the dead man lay on a straw mat on a bench in the café yard. They had covered him with an old, filthy rug. Two or three flies were buzzing around his head. A short way off stood a gang of small children, squinting in the sun. They had long sticks, taller than they were, and stood perfectly silent watching this draped body and its feet sticking out at the end of the rug. Through the large holes in the sole and heel of their woolen socks, the feet showed sluggish yellow. They were interesting to watch. Flies would circle over them, land and take off, iridescent green, catching the sun. From time to time one of the children would run off, called by his mother in the distance, then appear again running and take up his former place, motionless.

Gradually, the people came out of the café. The old woman went and sat by her son's side. Her one hand waved away the flies, the other wiped at eyes small as hominy with age and sickness. She might herself have been tending the sick. Her hand moved slowly, keeping the flies away. In an old, choked voice she croaked at the children to go home. The others gradually dispersed of their own accord. A few of the young men came and carried the body to her house, and by evening all was normal again. As quietly as after a long sickness ending in natural death, the body was washed and buried. Just before the call to prayer, Mevlut Aǧa sent Blond Mehmet's mother two milking goats, a sack of flour, and two paper bags full of sugar.

It was a month later that two mounted guardsmen rode into the village. They got down in front of the café, and the *muhtar*'s* heart went into his throat. These men weren't local troops. Most likely, they were in the governor's jurisdiction. One of them got out pen and paper in the café, and, starting with the *muhtar,* took down statements from everybody. The other paced up and down in the village square.

Word got around immediately. Mehmet, nicknamed "Weird," a cobbler in town who had a quarrel with Hüseyin Savruk, had taken news of the murder straight to the authorities when he heard it from the villagers. At first, the public prosecutor was going to come out himself and bring a doctor. But then the prospect of several days on horseback in that August heat hadn't appealed to him; so he sent two guardsmen with instructions to make inquiries. The doctor, with even more foresight, gave these two strict orders to exhume the corpse, if there had been a murder, and bring it back to town.

Blond Mehmet's mother said nothing in her statement, only that she had no charges to make against anybody. When they asked whether her son had died of natural causes or been shot, she answered in the same way. The pain of his death hadn't left her, but getting involved with the authorities would be much worse than losing her son had been. Thirty years before, a villager had a sack of cracked wheat stolen in the town marketplace. He had given her as a witness, and it had taken six months, coming and going to court and back. She remembered how her fields have gone to ruin. She'd been young then, too. And then Blond Mehmet wasn't coming back, and there was no use making enemies with Mevlut Aǧa. She'd die of hunger if that happened. So she just disclaimed the whole case.

Midafternoon came, and the guardsmen went with the villagers to dig up Mehmet's body in the graveyard. The corpse, under two feet of earth, had decayed, and they all fell back from the stink. The guardsmen called Mehmet's mother over.

"Hitch up a cart," they said. "You're taking him into town. Doctor wants to examine him."

She squatted there, beating her sides, moaning how even in the grave there was no peace for her boy. And she wept, barely sobbing, like the women of all Anatolia. In silence. She squatted there, weaving without cease as she brought cracked, dry fists to eyes and mouth. One of the guardsmen touched her in the back with his boot.

"Come on," he said, "get up."

She hitched up the oxen, wrapped the worm-shot body of her son in a ragged blanket, spread an old mattress on the floor of the cart, and laying the body on it, tied down the

* Village headman

whole. In doing all this she would often stop to weep and murmur to herself, then go on with the job. She set out when night had fallen, alone on the road to town. Before this the guardsmen had tied together the *muhtar,* the imam, and Hüseyin Savruk. The Guardsmen on horseback, the other three walking ahead, they had started the long trip.

The oxen that drew her cart were scrawny, small as donkeys. With stick in hand, her bare feet stumbling over rocks in the road, and trying in a voice made hoarse with weeping to coax her team, the old woman made her way along. The squealing of the slow cart under that bright summer moon sounded above the cries of jackals, and the cart looked anything but a hearse. The oxen showed strong and robust in the moonlight on their backs. The patched blanket, the ruin of a cart—both seemed wondrously fashioned of some new and precious metal. The woman and the stick she held cast for yards over the white stones and the bushes a shadow that danced and splashed.

But she was over sixty. The stench off the cart had made her woozy, and she had to struggle to keep up with the oxen, for now and again they would quicken their pace. Her feet began to drag, and with her breast shrunken from all the weeping shed within, she grew unable to draw breath.

She went on further a way, holding to her side of the cart. Her feet kept straying into each other. When she made as if to coax the team, no sound came out. She let go of the cart and went down, rolling on the ground. She got up again, covered with dust, and ran. A cool breeze had sprung up and blew at her, set the three-piece skirts she wore flying, while the legs of her trousers flapped, and her black kerchief, a black flag in the wind. When she fell again, face buried in the white, ashy dust, the cart was still ahead of her.

Knocked as it was by rocks, it jounced its bundle from side to side. Its squealing rose, agonized, and subsided. Leaving behind a thin dust cloud in the moonlight and night's silence, the cart continued on its way.

Çetin Altan

Grand Surveillance

Translated by İlhan Tayar

Why does this clod want me to explain how I killed?

"I admit it," I said. "What do you need details for?"

"Stop acting, smarty, go on, spill it," he said.

"What do you want me to tell, Mister, what?"

"How you killed him."

"I killed him like I killed Mustafa and Süleyman."

"Who's Mustafa and Süleyman?"

"Yesterday, your short, fat friend accused me of killing them."

"Are you cracking, punk ...Here only I do the interrogation. No one else can."

"Then why did your friend ask that question ...?"

"Stop all that nonsense, nobody asked you anything yet ... You'll see what will be asked when the actual interrogation begins."

I'm watching the rusty pistol in my hand.

The fellow snatched it.

"Go on, talk!"

"Let *him* explain first," I said, "how I killed. I don't remember exactly, now."

The lame old man aimed his blue eyes at me. His head was bald, and he was breathing heavily....

It was strictly forbidden for me to go into the vineyard, pick fruits or flowers. Pasha papa could see every corner of the garden from the balcony on the facade of the kiosk. Therefore I usually preferred to play in the backyard. Yusuf Ağa had made a cart for me, attaching four wheels to two broad planks nailed together. Sitting on it, I asked Fehime to tug me. Sometimes Fehime rode on it. But I wasn't strong enough to pull her.

During the hours of Pasha papa's afternoon nap, I climbed the dwarf sour cherry trees in the front garden; filling up a tiny bucket coated with tin I would suspend it by a string into the well to chill.

Grandmama constantly made me scared of the wells saying, "Don't you go near the wells, a well monster comes up and pulls the children in."

Therefore I always approached the well only when Yusuf Ağa was close by.

"Will a well monster come up?" I would ask him.

"Not when I'm here ..." he would reply.

Carefully bending over the wall of the well, I would look into it to see if there were any monsters ... There weren't any. Nothing except the moss hanging over the irregular stones and pitch dark water.

Once Fehime said,

"There's no well monster. They said this to scare you."

On hearing this I said to grandmama,

"There's no well monster, you just want to scare me."

"When you see one coming up, then you'll believe me," she replied.

I wondered if these ogres and well monsters always lived in the dark waters. What's more, Sadakat had really showed me one. Sometimes Fehime, covering her head with black cloths, sticking her little fingers into her nose, pulling her lower lip with her pointers, and baring her teeth, walked towards me saying,

"I am a monster."

And imitating her, I too would say,

"I am a monster too, and I'll eat you."

At times when grandmama would come down to open the pantries and cupboards, running to her and pretending to be a well monster, I would say,

"I'll eat you now."

"Don't, I'm scared," she would reply, in mock fear.

Then she would give me some dried apricots or plums. When Fehime did not wash the dishes on time, forgot to turn off the heat under the pots, or delayed when sent to the grocer, grandmama would thrash her, pinch her arms and legs, pull her ears and shout furiously,

"You bitch, you wretch …!"

Fehime was accustomed to all that. Never crying, she would stick her tongue out behind grandmama and say,

"Stupid old bag."

Sticking my tongue out, I would join her and say,

"Stupid old bag."

In spite of all the dried apricots and plums, and even the visits on which grandmama occasionally took me, I was on Fehime's side.

I felt suffocated when they thrashed her.

The well monsters, the games of "You can't catch me," and sneaky fruit thefts in the garden with Fehime continued. But neither of us made any reference to the incident that had occurred one evening in the garret.

We forgot what happened. But in the torture room, it kept coming back to me. Fehime, leaning against the stack of mattresses in that dark room, had suddenly pulled her skirt up, and slightly lowering her bloomers, said,

"Here's my box."

And the lame old man next to the ape-like fellow was coming towards me, saying,

"He pointed the pistol at me."

I am listening silently. All he said was true. But he too couldn't explain why I killed him.

Interrupting the old man, the ape turned to me,

"Speak up, punk, why did you kill this man?"

"I don't know," I replied.

"Then you'll recall by tomorrow."

Together with the old man, he left the room.

I began my walk in the room again. Probably tonight they'll come with loops, electric gadgets, pliers for pulling nails, and seriously start in their actual interrogation.

Will I stand it? It is obvious that I can't. But what and how am I going to explain? They are not satisfied with my pleading guilty. They insist on knowing why I killed. I don't know how to explain it, and they don't understand.

One evening we had liver stew for dinner. Big pieces of liver were floating on the dark greasy sauce full of onions. I was eating bread only. Pasha papa's eyes were fixed on my plate. I put one piece of liver into my mouth, but it was impossible to chew and swallow it. I was near to vomiting.

Suddenly a roar was heard.

"Swallow!"

Swallow, but how? I spurted whatever I had in my mouth into the plate. I was vomiting.

Grandmama, taking me by the arm, dragged me out of the room, saying,

"Pasha, you see that he cannot eat it."

I know that Pasha was really getting angry with me. In spite of the orders he gave I had neither learnt the multiplication table nor eaten the liver stew. This had never happened to Pasha before.

"This thumbsized bastard is protesting against my orders. He must be squashed to obey."

In my thumbsize, I was protesting, and I should be squashed ...

They were grown-ups, and mighty. I could be measured by the span of a hand and had no shelter besides Fehime's garret or Yusuf Aĝa's servant's room.

The next day for lunch, we had liver stew again. This time grandmama had given me just a spoonful, instead of filling the plate.

"By God, Pasha papa will kill you if you don't eat this," she whispered in my ear.

Pieces of liver seemed enormous in the sauce. I stuck my fork into one.

It was impossible to swallow it. Rolling his blue eyes, Pasha papa was watching me. And once more his voice made a ringing sound within the room.

"Swallow! ... "

I did.

By making me swallow the liver stew, he had achieved a victory. Tears were running down my cheeks. This time Pasha papa stood up, left the room earlier than usual.

"I'm not going to eat any more," I said to grandmama.

She repeated the usual threats, that God would register this as a sin, and that it was a curse to refuse benevolence. I would go to Hell, and be so hungry that I would eat fire.

I was willing to die, to eat fire, but I wasn't going to eat that liver stew.

Pasha papa was educated in Germany. Those who knew him in his youth described him as a very successful, reckless and severe person.... When he rode on a horse, he placed a coin between each knee and the belly of the horse. After galloping for several hours, he would take out and show the coins, so good was his style of riding. For these reasons he had made a great reputation in the German army. Prior to his return to Turkey, he was presented with a bust of Wilhelm II and various medals. We heard about all these things from others. Pasha papa would never say anything in regard to himself. I heard him speak German just once.

One afternoon a German lady came to us for a visit. I had no idea who she was, but apparently she was someone Pasha knew intimately. When she arrived, Pasha ran to his room, took off his pajamas and changed into his suit. Grandmama was not favorably impressed by the visitor. To Fehime, she said,

"An enormous infidel woman came. I hope she'll not use the toilet, because they don't wear the pattens, or wash their asses. It will be necessary to clean up the whole house after her."

On the other hand, Pasha papa was absolutely thrilled. He beamed and spoke fluently in German with great joy.

Grandmama was nowhere to be seen. Pasha papa shouted, and said,

"Where on earth are you, serve us a drink, will you ..."

I was constantly on the go between upstairs and downstairs, watching Pasha papa and the German lady, then seeing what grandmama was doing.

"Let them drink shit," grandmama was saying to Fehime. The liquor was upstairs, and grandmama did not want to go there. Taking out a bunch of keys from her pocket she picked one and gave it to Fehime with a long and detailed instruction to find the place of the liquor in the cupboard. Fehime was going to fetch the bottles and the liquor set. Grandmother was to fill the glasses, and Fehime would take them up and serve the infidel woman.

I accompanied Fehime upstairs and carried the bottles, while she brought down the set. There was a mint liquor in one and rasberry in the other.

Grandmama was wondering which one to serve the infidel woman.

She used mint liquor as a remedy for tummy ache, and always kept it in store. Finally she decided on the raspberry. They placed two glasses with long stems on the small silver tray. Grandmama poured the drink herself.

"Make sure to take it up without spilling," she said to Fehime.

With the tray in her hands, Fehime was walking up the stairs very carefully. And I at her heels. She first walked over to serve Pasha papa, which was the usual procedure. This time Pasha, pointing to the lady, said in a highly polished voice to Fehime.

"Serve the lady first."

The girl turned towards the guest. She picked up a glass of liquor.

Conversation in German was going on. Pasha papa was laughing, and the lady was laughing. Pasha raising his glass said,

"Cheers,"

"Cheers."

Fehime was waiting at the far end of the hall to take back the glasses.

"Bring the bottle over here," Pasha said to her.

Fehime ran downstairs, and I after her.

"Pasha wants the bottle," she said to grandmama.

"Oh my God, they'll be dead drunk upstairs," she replied.

But it was out of the question to refuse anything Pasha papa wanted. She handed Fehime the raspberry liquor bottle. Taking it she ran back upstairs and gave it to him. Pasha papa refilled the lady's glass, and then filled his again.

"Cheers."

"Cheers."

Conversation in German continued between laughter and giggles.

The lady stood up and said something to Pasha papa. He too got up and walked towards the door of the toilet, and pointed to it for the lady. The lady went in. Pasha papa was shouting again,

"Bring up a towel."

Grandmama was lamenting downstairs.

"Just what I feared happened, the infidel woman did go into the toilet."

Taking out a huge, fuzzy towel from some place, she handed it to Fehime, saying,

"Go, wait in front of the door. Listen carefully, hear if she'll put on the pattens. You'll know from the sound of it."

Fehime with the towel in her hand went upstairs again. She stood in front of the toilet door–listening for a sound. Standing behind Fehime, I too tried to hear the noise of the pattens.

After a while the lady came out. Fehime gave her the towel. She seemed to wipe her hands, and said,

"Thank you."

Grandmama was waiting for the news about the infidel's use of the pattens. I hadn't heard a sound. Neither did Fehime.

"My lady, I think she didn't put them on, I didn't hear anything," she said to grandmama.

"She didn't," I added. "I too didn't hear anything."

Grandmama lamented more, saying,

"My goodness, we'll have to clean the whole house up after her ..."

Meanwhile a "Hey there" blasted upstairs. Pasha papa was shouting.

"Where on earth is Wilhelm's bust?"

Probably he was going to show the German lady the gift he received in his youth.

"You see, now they're drunk and Pasha wants the infidel's bust..." grandmother said.

Pasha was constantly shouting upstairs,

"Come up and tell me where Wilhelm's bust is."

Grandmama's face looked distressed.

"How do I know where it is," she was grumbling. "A Moslem's house is no place for a statue."

Sharing her trouble with us, she was saying,

"He brought the enormous idol of the infidel with him from Germany. I don't remember where we put it, in the stable or the basement..."

Pasha papa was shouting louder,

"Will you come up here...?"

Grandmama's hands and knees started to shake.

"I knew something unlucky would happen when that woman arrived. You see, he keeps asking for the infidel's statue. If we don't find it, he'll tear the house down. Run along girl, and tell Yusuf Ağa to look in the stable, basement, and search the cupboards of the outdoor kitchen. Dear God, forgive our sins," she was saying.

Grandmother was on her way up, meanwhile Pasha papa continued shouting.

"Where are you?"

A weak reply came out of grandmama,

"I'm here, coming."

I was going up after her. Grandmama entered the hall. The German lady stood up. Pasha introduced grandmama to the lady in German. Smiling, the guest shook hands with grandmama.

"Where is that statue I brought from Germany?" he said.

"We put it up someplace, but I don't remember where..." replied grandmama.

"Search everywhere, and find it," said pasha.

Grandmama disappeared into one of the rooms. She wanted to gain time until she heard from Yusuf Ağa and Fehime. I remembered seeing that statue someplace, but where? It was a bust with pointed moustaches, austere looks, and medals on its chest. I had not recognized where it was when I saw it, but fearing to be reprimanded I hadn't questioned anyone about it. They resented my fiddling with things. Therefore, I preferred not to ask about the objects I saw in the pantries, stable, outdoor kitchen and the basement. If I saw anything useful, I took it. For instance, once I found a bayonet with a rusty sheath and a curved handle. I had shown it to Yusuf Ağa only.

"It's a French bayonet," he had said.

Tying the string at both ends, I had slung it over my shoulder like a rifle and walked around in the garden until I got tired of it. When we were on good terms with Pasha papa, he had given me the gold gilded ribbons of his old uniform. Tying them around my shoulder and waist I played games, like being strong against the well monster with the bayonet on my back as my weapon.

I had seen the statue some place during my hours of searching around. But it kept slipping my mind. Pasha papa wanted it, now. If only I could find it, his anger about the multiplication table would soften.

I did see that statue, but where?

Suddenly I dashed towards the toilet. The toilets of the kiosk were spacious. On the right wall of each toilet was a big marble basin, with a faucet in the middle. Water would flow on pulling the handle outward. Right and left movements would turn it off. In addition there were two tall copper jugs at the bottom of the basin filled with water. They were kept as a spare supply, when the reservoir was emptied. At such times, Fehime, lifting the jugs, would carefully pour water for Pasha papa and grandmama for their ritual washing before prayers. This section was partitioned from the toilet by another door. The floor was of marble. The pattens were kept behind that door. The washcloths used in place of toilet paper were hung over a string...

Dashing to the toilet, I opened the pot cupboard under the big basin. The statue was there, sitting next to the pot.

It was beyond my strength to take it out.

"I found it, Pasha papa, I found it," I shouted.

Pasha papa came, and standing before the open door of the toilet asked in an agitated voice,

"Where is it?"

"Here, in the pot cupboard."

The lady had got up and joined Pasha papa. Kneeling in front of the pot cupboard I kept saying,

"Here it is Pasha papa."

He walked in, bent down, and tried to take the statue out of the pot cupboard. As the head of the bust came out, the chest got stuck behind the pot. The lady, slightly bending, began to watch Pasha. The head of Wilhelm II was moving in and out of the cupboard. Pasha, leaving the statue, thought of taking the pot out first. Then he grabbed the statue again. And it came out... He blew off the dust from the head and shoulders and wiped the rest with his hand. He tossed his head, resembling a watermelon-sized turnip from the rush of blood, and said something to the lady in German. Then he was shouting at us,

"Who on earth has put it in here?"

He placed the bust on the marble table in the hall. With his upright moustaches Wilhelm II was looking at Pasha papa with the corner of his eyes.

Pasha continued his conversation in German...but I could sense his terrible anger.

A short while later grandmama came out of the room she had entered. She must have heard that the bust was discovered. With an innocence smelling of acting,

"So you've found it, where have we put it?" she asked.

"In Hell we've put it," answered Pasha. "It came out of the toilet cupboard, we were disgraced before the lady."

"Let me tell them, so they won't search for it downstairs," Grandmama said and sneaked away.

I was going down with her.

"So what if it came out of the toilet cupboard, the infidel's statue wasn't going to be found in my breast pocket," she was saying.

After a while Pasha accompanied the lady to the gate of the garden. Early next morning, calling up Yusuf Aǧa, he asked him to roll the Persian rug in the middle of the hall and carrying it on his shoulder to take it to the written address Pasha would give him.

The German lady had expressed her admiration for the rug, so Pasha was sending it as a gift to her.

Grandmama was beside herself with anger. She was going up and down the stairs, clinking her keys, with a frown on her face, huffing and puffing more than usual. In the evening she went to bed early saying that she had a headache. This was her custom every time she was mad at Pasha.

It was already night time in the torture room. The guards at the door have changed again. But none of them was staring at me like the one did last night. He was strange. All along his duty hours he had looked at me like that. The light of the room turned on. Apparently the switch is outside. Shortly, dinner came. Always the same men brought the meal. They filled two zinc plates with chick peas and cracked wheat pilaf each.

Every minute I'm waiting on the alert. Suddenly they'll file in the room and begin: "Spit out, skunk."

What will I tell them? Why and what for I have killed the old man...

Why and what for did I kill him?

Why did I feed mother, father, and Sadakat to the monster, why put the house on fire, why be an accomplice of Fatma or even Fehime? When I killed the old man he was young, but he was dead before I killed him. Like the house was burnt already before I put it on fire, and mother, father, grandmother eaten long before I fed them to the monster.

They are asking me the meaning of the meaningless, and the meaninglessness of the meaning.

The mood in the house had changed after the incident of the statue and the rug. Grandmama was barely on speaking terms with Pasha papa. They were not having tea together in the morning nor sitting on the balcony. Pasha papa seemed sort of lonely. He stopped shouting as much as he used to do. During meals he had given up looking at my plate, rolling his eyes and saying,

"Swallow."

Although neither chocolates nor money were given to me, there was an improvement in small things.

When Pasha papa came to the backyard, he called me to go into the hen pens, although he had strictly forbidden it before, saying,

"Go in and see if there are any eggs in the laying nest."

In the house, he asked me for his slippers, giving me his holder saying,

"Clean this with a hen quill, but be careful not to break it."

All these demands filled me with a joy of being treated like an adult. If I only learnt the multiplication table by heart, and surprised him he would really be thrilled, and love me for it. Occasionally, with Fehime's help, I was studying. Two times two four, two times three six, two times four eight...

Including the fives I did quite well. Whenever I said, two times two four, Fehime rhymed it with another sentence...

One morning standing before Pasha papa I began to count in a hurry!

"One times one one, one times two two, one times three three..." Then passing to the twos, "Two times one two, two times two four, two times three six..." Then I started to count the threes...Sometimes I was stuttering. "Three times seven, three times seven..."

"Twenty-one," said Pasha papa.

Trying hard, I counted up to the sixes. Even that much was a victory for Pasha papa. Finally his order was more or less obeyed. He made me sit on his lap, and said,

"Good for you, that's how it should be."

And I hugged him. Kissed him on the cheeks. He hopped me on his shoulders and made me jump. Beside myself with joy I started to beat on his bald head. Slowly at first, then faster, and faster, like beating on a drum...

Apparently I had gone beyond limits; like an explosion, I heard,

"Stop it rascal...Are you beating me..."

Before I knew what happened, Pasha papa pulled me down by my leg, held me tight under his arm, and took me to his room. Holding me by one leg he suspended me outside his window. Below was the huge basin of the pump that drew water from the well in the backyard. Upside down, I was making convulsive movements.

Pasha papa was asking,

"Rascal, do you want me to throw you down?"

I was screaming,

"Please don't drop me Pasha papa, please don't."

Grandmama, entering the door, cried,

"Pasha, what are you doing?"

Fehime too had run upstairs.

They took me away. Pasha was breathing heavily, and growling,

"You rascal, you...You beat a drum on my head and want to take revenge on me."

I was in a state of shock with fear, sobbing and screaming. They were rubbing my hands and feet with rose water and trying to shake me out of the dreadful fright I went through.

"This man will kill the child," grandmama was saying. "I better write to his mother so she takes him back..."

Pasha papa had decided to have the kiosk painted. Outside, a scaffolding was put up. The painters were standing on the wooden planks to paint.

Mother and grandmama had the mattresses in the garret brought down and, opening the trunks on which they were stacked, inspected the contents.

I was watching them as they were rummaging. Within the trunks there were old woolen jackets, worn out sheets, old curtains. From one of them one or two umbrellas with broken handles, discarded shoes, a few rifle swords and a rusty pistol came out. When I saw it, I said,

"Please give that to me."

At first grandmama protested, saying,

"No, God forbid, but the Devil can load it."

I started stomping my feet and saying,

"Please grandmama, let me play with it a little,"

"It's empty, let him have it," mother said.

They gave me the pistol.

Snatching it, I dashed outside. Yusuf Ağa hesitated at the sight of the weapon. For the first time a grown-up was scared of me. I could feel it when I walked towards him.

"Please don't come closer, there may be an accident," Yusuf Ağa said.

Then I pointed at the yogurt vendor, who happened to be there. He was more scared.

"Who gave him that?" he asked.

Then I held it towards the errand boy of the grocer. Fehime was unloading the full paper bags from the boy's large basket. The boy, pushing my hand, said,

"Hold it in another direction."

"Don't be afraid, it's empty," Fehime said to him.

But the errand boy was obviously scared.

Anyone who saw the gun was afraid. For the first time the grown-ups were in fear. They actually felt fear.

The painters continued going up and down the scaffolding, and painting the house. I stuck the pistol between my waist and slacks. I wanted to climb up and down like the painters did. When one painter standing on the highest plank saw me climb, he shouted,

"You get down there!"

Not paying any attention I went on climbing.

"Get down, or I'll come and spank you," he said.

For the first time outside the household somebody was threatening to beat me. I burnt hot with anger. The painter was shouting,

"I tell you to get down."

I slid down, took a few steps back. Taking out the gun, I pointed it at the painter above.

"I'll shoot you," I said.

He wanted to hide behind one of the posts. I couldn't understand very well whether his foot hit the paint bucket or he lost his balance, but he fell down crying,

"Oh, mother."

Other painters ran. Yusuf Ağa came, then Fehime. Finally Pasha papa arrived. They lifted him, and gave him a glass of water. The painter was unable to walk. He groaned, then he fainted. I ran to hide in Yusuf Ağa's room, and hid the pistol under his bed. After a long while, I came out. They had sent the painter away, in a carriage. Who knows what sort of punishment was awaiting me. But no one said or did anything. Perhaps no one had seen me point the gun at the painter. He had fainted before he could say anything. The next day I heard from the other painters that his leg was broken. Some other painter came in to replace him.

Now the lame old man is asking me for the account of it.

"Why did you kill?"

I killed him because he was a grown up and said he would beat me. Anyhow he was a dead man before I killed him. He wasn't actually living. He was just an insignificant hard worker trying to receive a few pennies.

Pacing up and down the torture room, I'm analyzing myself. Do I regret? There's no such feeling in me...I'm now waiting for the hour of torture...To be thrown on the floor, have my feet clubbed until the skin opens, nails pulled, electrodes attached to my genitals, constantly asked,

"Confess, why did you kill?"

Until morning, I waited for the torturer to begin...but no one came. The guards at the door are no longer interested in me either...

I lit a cigarette.

"By golly," I said, "all of this can be nothing but tricks." The crime that they want to find out about is absolutely a different one. They will eventually make me talk about that.

At the risk of accepting all other crimes, I am not going to talk about that one. I'm determined in this...

Fakir Baykurt

Fadim Ağa's Mills

Translated by Bedia Turgay-Ahmad

Each year for twelve months the two men in Fadim Ağa's service never leave his side. Seven or eight times a day, they put the coffeepot on the fire and, taking sweet milky coffee to Fadim Ağa, they say "Here, Master!" He slurps his coffee; this goes on every two hours till evening.

Sitting on a large cushion stuffed with lamb's wool, leaning back on a high pillow, he sticks the Gelincik cigarette in his silver holder and puffs toward the ceiling. Then he might send for someone from the village to chat with. If he feels like it, he gets mad at one or scolds the other. At times the wild horses are harnessed to the carriage....Gaddap! Where to? He takes a ride to Denizli.

His mouth is full of gold teeth like bulletheads. So what? After all, that's why they call him Fadim Ağa. He can hardly turn his neck to the left or right. His belly? Don't talk about that! He weighs 260 pounds stripped. He gets fatter each day. Fadim Ağa tells a tale about Hamdi Bey, a very famous doctor in Denizli:

"I went to see him one day and said: 'Sir, I am ill.'"

He said: "You're not ill."

"I'm ill, sir."

"You don't look ill to me, tell me, where is your pain?"

"I've no pain. I'm too fat. Give me some medicine so that I can lose some flesh."

"There's no medicine for that," the doctor replied. "We give this or that medicine for it, but don't believe it, they're no use. There's only one way of losing weight, let me tell you: don't eat meat! don't eat eggs! don't eat fat! And go to the john four or five times a day, understand?"

"After this I came back to the village. I told the wives to cook *tarhana* soup and rice without any fat for a week. 'I have a bet with the doctor,' I said to them. 'If I come down to 220 pounds, Hamdi Bey will treat me to a full feast when I go to Denizli next time. If I can't come down to 220 pounds, I'll give him a feast with drinks and all....' For two weeks the wives boiled soup, cooked rice without any fat. Yet soup without fat is no different from dog's food. By God, I couldn't eat it. If you ask about going to the john, only for a day or two I went four times. On the third day I stopped going. It comes through the veins; do you think it's easy? I just couldn't do it. As I wasn't keen to see Hamdi Bey, I didn't even go to Denizli after that."

For a man in Fadim Ağa's situation the easiest thing to do is to get fat and bloated, to let his belly get bigger and bigger. What else can he do? He has three wives. No one knows which is the legal one and which ones are illegally kept. All three of them are very

64

much like Fadim Ağa–fleshy. Some women become dirty and ugly when they get fat. These aren't like that. Each one has a smooth neck. Especially one of them, she is very beautiful. In the five-room house overlooking the plains, three rooms belong to the wives. In turn, each room is lit up till morning.

Goods, property, he has it all. Orchards, vineyards, vegetable gardens, woods, bean, corn, cotton fields....And along the river on both sides are twelve mills, the backbone of Fadim Ağa....

One day Mustafa, a fellow farmer from Haydarlar village, who has eight children and a rotten plot of only six acres, said:

"What sort of God is it? He gave all that there is to Fadim Ağa! We pray to Him in vain. He's got no field left to give us." The villagers who heard him replied:

"Ranting and raving like this, you've gone mad, control yourself," and shut the poor man up.

"I'm not mad or anything, friends! Am I living? Today Fadim Ağa owns half the country! Without any help, he can feed a huge army...."

"Of course...Fadim Ağa is a landlord, owns half the country, can alone feed an army, but don't bring God into this. Don't swear or sin! God gave him all this at one time, if He wished he could give you some, give us some...."

"I'm saying exactly the same thing! Why did God bless him all the time? Why did He always choose him? Why didn't he see us too? Have we worshipped false idols?"

"Ee, that's His own business."

The peasant Mustafa from Haydarlar village had exaggerated, but he had also spoken some truth. Fadim Ağa is one of God's chosen. Never mind the rest, those twelve mills alone are worth a fortune. Flour, cracked wheat, pealed wheat, the food of the village people from the plains and from the hills, from exactly forty-eight villages; coarse wheat, the food for the animals of these forty-eight villages–all go through his mill stones. Furthermore, the merchants who sell flour to the villages all along the railway line from Dinar to Aydın, which don't grow dry crops, have their wheat ground in these mills. A lot of customers those mills have! In front of them stand plane trees with thick leaves, colored with the most beautiful shades of green and those fine mills keep on thundering! Yet the roads to them are a bit rough....

Yeleme, Dirice, Çakırlar, İmecik, Yazır.... The people of all these mountain villages spend at least three days having a load of wheat ground there. They tie the sacks onto donkeys, urge them on crying *"deh cüş! deh cüş!"* If they start out in the morning, they reach the mill in the afternoon if they are lucky. They wait in line for a day; next day they grind the wheat, returning on the third day. Those poor donkeys go through all that on those rocky roads! The stones are large, and donkeys aren't shod. The saddles open wounds on their backs. Their withers smell.

After the harvest, the villagers of Yeleme elected Lame Ali as their *muhtar*. * Lame Ali limps and all that, but first he gave a short speech and said:

"I will improve this village."

Then he called Ahmet, Mehmet, and the whole village and said:

"It can't go on like this, friends! What the donkeys have gone through, what we have suffered is enough! Listen, I have an idea. Our village has ninety houses. If each house

* Village headman

gives a sackful of wheat, and each sack sells for fifty liras, it will bring nearly five thousand liras. Those neighbors who aren't so well off can give half a sack each. We can buy a power-mill for four thousand. Come on, let's do this. Let's put the power mill in the middle of the village and stop going to Fadim Ağa's mills. What do you say, can't we do this?"

The villagers at first didn't understand what Lame Ali was talking about. "A mill doesn't turn without water," they said. Lame Ali: "I saw it, friends, I saw the damn thing in Dutluca village, it turned perfectly. It worked nicely, giving fine flour. If I put the four thousand liras in my pocket, I'll be back with the mill in less than five days. Cheap, clean! Everybody will grind his wheat in front of his door. The donkeys will be saved, we will be saved."

He explained the matter to them again and again. The villagers understood. There were those who wouldn't agree. But Lame Ali said: "Let's sell our food and do this!" Urging them this way or that way, he made them accept it. One day, in the afternoon, the power mill entered the village from the direction of the graveyard, with an army of children behind. Apart from women, all the villagers, young and old, gathered around it. Those who saw the engine for the first time looked at it, puzzled. Turning round and feeling here and there, they examined it over and over. Those who had seen such a thing before told the others:

"These are the spark plugs."

"This is the pedal."

"This is the tank."

"This is the break."

Fifteen minutes after the arrival of the power mill the villagers, gathering in twos and threes, began to argue:

"They say this is better than twenty water mills...."

"These clever Christians! First insecticides, then this. Instead of making weapons, why don't they make things of this sort?..."

"Hey, didn't our Muslim brothers make this, then?"

"Have you ever heard of our Muslim brothers making such a thing? They eat, drink, shit, and sleep with their women...."

"Which infidel made this, eh?"

"The German, German, the clever German!"

"We never hear a Muslim's name in these matters!"

The *muhtar* had a brother-in-law, Nuri, who had come first in the driving course during his national service. Then he had also become the general's driver for a few months. He worked the engine, fiddled with the screws, ground very fine flour, cracked the animal fodder, and did a better job than they had all expected. The cost of running the mill was also very small. This was what all the people had looked for but had never found. The villagers said: "We harvest the crop with a plough and it drops into our stomachs after it's cracked by an engine."

After finishing the village's work, the power mill went to the nearby villages like Armut and Akellez for two days a week. The success of the Yeleme people influenced the other villages. They still didn't get together and buy a power mill like the Yeleme residents, but they unanimously decided to do so.

As for Fadim Ağa, he brought down the charge from eight to two *okkas** per

*_oke_, about 2.8 lbs.

donkey-load. He waited long in his house overlooking the plains but didn't hear of a villager from Yeleme or the neighboring villages who had come down to his mills.

"Not because of the income or the charge or the money," he said, "a devil like Lame Ali thinks he's—" but he couldn't finish his sentence.

One day in our village coffeehouse they said the villagers from Dirice and İmecik got together and bought a power mill. Those who were angry at Fadim Ağa threw their hats in the air with joy and danced.

The next day those who came from the plains told the news that Fadim Ağa had gone mad: "Among girls and women, he pissed into the fire where the acorn branches burnt in crimson flames," they said.

Kemal Bilbaşar

Sale of Saltanat

Translated by Esin Bilbaşar

Saltanat, the miller's daughter, was twelve at the end of threshing time. Although her peers were still as lean as a branch whose leaves had fallen, the concealed femininity of her body had suddenly sprouted. The girl had blossomed like an autumn flower.

Hasso, as he watched the sacks of wheat being piled higher than ever before, thought that this must have been a prosperous year. Had the two young men not fought over Saltanat, Hasso would not have recognized his daughter's matured form. One of the young men had seen Saltanat's fresh, rounded body tight as a bow, as she was washing her father's sweaty shirt in the water flowing through the mill wheel. Entranced by her beauty, he had attempted to drag her away by her braided hair as though he had been in a delirium. The other, while loading his donkey with sacks of ground wheat, had seen this and had tried to save the girl. Thus, the two had started to fight.

Hearing the panting and the swearing of the young men, Saltanat's screams, and the cries of the dog, Karakurt, straining at his leash, Hasso and the villagers, who were waiting for their wheat to be ground, ran into the courtyard. At one glance Hasso grasped the situation. The cause of the fight was apparent. Saltanat was standing with her hands pressed upon her cheeks, framing her sparkling coal-black eyes, opened wide with fear. A rip in her blouse revealed a soft, round shoulder.

The deep furrow between Hasso's bushy eyebrows gradually vanished. A smile flitted across his face. Yeah. She's come of age to be sold! At this age, to make her young father a father-in-law! . . . He eyed his daughter from head to toe. A joy began to rise in him. He had brought her up to this age without the help of a mother.

Look at those eyes, brows, that build! D'ya get that pep with the ones brought up by both parents?

Then one of the young men threw the other into the millstream, and the soaring joy in his chest turned into a flood of laughter. Hasso's mirth infected the others. This revelry slowed down the fight and the two young men finally stepped aside. One was wiping the blood off his nose. Saltanat fled into the house because of a shyness she could not understand.

"You dogs," said Hasso finally. He was not laughing anymore. "You hounds, you! Ain't she got a father? You've completely forgotten the custom....Why did you try to break your necks instead of asking me to sell her?"

The two young men bowed their heads guiltily. As Hasso continued, a fury began to rise in his chest.

"By God, both of you need a good beating! Or did ya think I'd ask too much? Ain't it clear that I wouldn't charge a brave man money? If Saltanat's come to the age of sale, well, jus' gimme an ear and let everyone hear this: Whoever wants to get Saltanat should be ready to show his bravery at Karga plains on the first day of snow!"

Such situations expand rapidly. By sundown the young men of three neighboring villages fell madly in love with the coal-black-eyed daughter of the miller. Deep inside of all these men a suspicion was slowly beginning to brew. What kind of bravery will Hasso want for his daughter? This question became the topic of conversation in all the village coffeehouses. Every day new suggestions were made about the kind of bravery Hasso would want from the candidates who wished to become his son-in-law. Most of these guesses centered on robbery. It seemed to them highly probable that Hasso would have them steal horses from neighboring tribes. The one who stole the horse would clip the mane and the tail of the animal in such a way that the owner would not recognize it after trailing the hoofmarks to their village. Hasso, they reasoned, would then sell the horse and make enough money for the sale of Saltanat.

Or perhaps he would have the gold teeth of a newly buried rich man brought to him from the city cemetery.

As the days went by, the kind and the degree of bravery they predicted changed. Now the bravery of the characters in fairy tales was expected. One of those who remembered the lack of water the mill faced during the summer days introduced the idea that Hasso would have water brought from the mountains; and so these guesses reached a peak.

And as yet, Hasso had not moved a finger. Whether day or night, he kept grinding the wheat and the barley, sharpening the stones once every three days, and ignoring the coming competition. On the other hand, he had increased the food fed to Karakurt, the dog. At each meal, he cut up a loaf of bread and soaked the pieces in a bucket of milk and fed it to the animal. As Karakurt grew fatter, his black fur began to glow, he barked with greater ferocity at the villagers who came to the mill, the donkeys, and the mules, and as he attempted to attack the people, he tried to break the chains that were holding him.

When the Süphan mountain became hazy and the snow came down to its skirts in a bluish whiteness, the wolf howlings covered the Karga plains. For three days the villagers had to give an intermission to their daily duties. One morning they woke to a white gleam. The children were happy because they could go sleigh riding and the older ones because the contest day had arrived. The sun was barely up when a voice echoed over the roofs:

"The Hassos are comin'."

Leaving their unfinished milk and tarhanas, women, men, the old and the young ran outside. Hasso appeared in the mill's path. Wrapped in his sheepskin coat, he had perched on his donkey. As he smoked his pipe, he looked satisfied. Behind him walked Saltanat. She wore knee breeches and, on her shoulders, a wolfskin as a robe. She had wrapped around her head and neck long, red wool scarves and her wrists and arms were covered with bands of felt. She was holding Karakurt by a thorny wolf-leash looped around his neck. He was walking rapidly, as if he were trying to drag Saltanat along. Over his spiky teeth a red tongue hung and vapor gushed forth.

They stopped in the village square. Hasso scanned the crowds of people who were clustered in front of the doors and on top of the roofs. He put his hand next to his cheek and yelled:

"Listen, you guys! I'm taking my daughter up to Karga plains. Whoever is sure of his bravery can come over and get her!" Without waiting for any replies, they left the village square and went toward the Karga plains, their feet crushing the snow in their path.

They had finally found out the thing about which they were so curious. Whoever could take Hasso's daughter away from Karakurt could have her. Suddenly, the fever of competition seized Karga plains. The young men who were sure of their dogs began to wrap themselves in felts and rags. Those who had finished their preparations put thorny wolf-leashes on their dogs and trod proudly toward the contest ground. Each one was followed by his coterie of friends and relatives.

Toward noon, the green, yellow, red knee breeches and the baggy trousers slowed down their pace and the spectators formed lines to watch the competition. While holding the dog's chains in a clearing void of snow, Saltanat was waiting for the brave man who could fight to win her. Karakurt lifted his head up and pointed his ears. He was pawing the ground with his hind legs impatiently. The brave men who would be fighting squatted under the trees that covered a part of the plain. So that their dogs would not brawl and bite each other, they were situated apart.

The young men were going to Saltanat one by one. Many, before having the chance to encourage their dogs to attack, realized that they had lost the fight. Not so much from Karakurt's wild attacks, but, once the dogs smelled the wolfskin on Saltanat, they tucked their tails between their legs, folded back their ears, and began backing off. In spite of the insulting outcries of the villagers, the young men were withdrawing from the contest ground. Neither the owner of the dairy farm, Ali Aĝa's son, nor his bloody-eyed, pierced-eared, tailless sheepdog, Kuyruksuz, who had fought with real wolves numerous times, could take Saltanat from Karakurt. Kuyruksuz, bleeding from his throat and bleeding from his feet, left the contest field. Hasso laughed at the Aĝa's son and, in his roaring voice that shook the plains, shouted at all of the defeated young men:

"You dogs, you! Shame! You've left this girl without a husband. There mustn't've been any brave ones on Karga plains!" The audience was listening silently to Hasso's roaring laughter and boasting words. The relatives of the defeated men set their jaws and swore under their breath at those who were withdrawing.

The people moved slightly, getting ready to go away. Suddenly, a whinnying and a growling echoed from the grove of Bitim trees on the right of the Karga plains. The noise and the restless moving ceased. Everyone looked in the direction from which the sounds came. A little later, Ali Aĝa's underservant, Memo of Van, appeared, dragging a female wolf by a chain.

When Memo had discovered the type of contest it was to be, he jumped on his horse and rode into the forest where the howlings of the wolves could be heard. He had frightened a pack of wolves with his gun, separated a female wolf from the pack and chased her until she had collapsed. He then looped a chain about her neck and dragged her for Karga plains.

Hasso stopped his laughing and fixed his eyes on Memo. The way the young man climbed off the horse in one jump and the firm control he had of the wolf, using its chain as a whip, made Hasso envious. This man didn't resemble any of the others.

Seeing Memo drag the wolf into the contest ground, Saltanat's eyes opened wide with fear. Karakurt pointed his ears as if he were seeing something unusual. Curiosity instead of malice was in his eyes. The wolf saw Karakurt with his black fur and sparkling eyes. Most of the audience wanted to see the wolf run away. Not because they favored Karakurt but because they did not want to let both the girl and the reputation for bravery be snatched away by a man from Van. They started to goad the dog on. As if he understood what was being said, Karakurt began to paw the ground with his hind legs and bark. However, he was not showing his teeth while barking. He was slowly approaching the wolf in the manner in which a male shows off to a female, rather than to scare her off. Unwilling to bow to this determination, the wolf showed alarm mixed with fear. As if she were aware of the fact that there was no one on her side, that she was alone and a stranger, she hunched up her body. But she stood her ground, not taking a step backward.

Saltanat and Memo were looking into each other's eyes. Memo's fiery dark pupils had made Saltanat's heart beat with a thrilling fear, something she had never felt before. She had a sudden urge to run away from him, but, at the same moment, she felt like leaning on his broad chest and crying. A self-confident smile had softened Memo's face.

Karakurt, as he came near the wolf, began to sniff her while wiggling his tail slightly. The wolf understood that the dog had no malicious intentions. She was not showing her teeth anymore. She let him smell her body while she growled softly. The two animals continued to smell each other in spite of the children's shouts:

"C'mon Kara, c'mon! Get 'er!"

Her tail, still between her legs, showed that the wolf was afraid. The grown-ups were watching the animals breathlessly. No one even thought of urging Saltanat to goad the dog on.

Memo and Saltanat kept studying each other. Memo's eyes now looked softer. Saltanat felt first a calmness, then a wild joy replacing the fear in her heart. Both let go of the animals' chains unconsciously. As soon as she felt free, the wolf dashed forward, made strange sounds as she ran toward the Bitim grove. Her head was turned back. She looked as if she wanted the dog to follow her. Karakurt was trailing his female, leaping now on her right, now on her left.

Memo and Saltanat looked after the animals for a second, then smiled at each other. Then Memo grabbed the girl by her wrist and led her, willingly, toward the whinnying horse.

Tarık Buğra

Our Son

Translated by Robert P. Finn

My wife was sitting in front of the window, which was just becoming visible. She'd spent the whole night there.

"You still won't go to bed," I said.

She sat up straight. She was only a shadow in front of the ash-gray window. But in this shadow there was something of each day from the more than twenty years we had spent together.

"They're reciting the call to prayer," she muttered.

Her voice upset me. Our room seemed so removed from the outside world, as though emotions couldn't penetrate it; yet my wife was sitting there, fruitlessly awaiting the happiness promised by the Koran. She spoke as if she had been there for centuries.

In her actions and motions, she had the strained silence of a prisoner who accepted defeat. She went into the kitchen. I saw her as if in a dream: she put the coal in the brazier and the samovar, washed her hands and feet, then spread her prayer mat in the hall and began her morning prayers.

The window was quite light.

It was the colorless, soundless time before dawn. The warmth of the bed, confused feelings, avoiding thought....I dozed off.

"Hey."

"What's the matter?"

"He's here."

"Well, good."

But this wasn't the problem. My wife thought I was being too easy and was disappointed.

"Aren't you going to say something? This is the third time.... Well, what are we going to do?"

How the hell did I know? But I said to her:

"I'll do something tomorrow."

"Which tomorrow? The sky's all blue already." My wife was right. I had to make something out of this. My son had just gotten into bed. I had to tell him that what he was doing was hopeless rebellion. I suddenly jumped out of bed. My wife got excited:

"Don't be too hard on him. What's the use now?..."

She couldn't go on. I looked at her. She looked nervous.

As I went out, I put my robe over my shoulders.

His room was on the side where the sun came up. Its windows looked out on a good-sized garden. The sun, about to escape from behind the house across the way, had made the walls of the room slightly pink.

And he, he was asleep.

He had flung his clothes on top of the table and not bothered to put on his pajama top. I sat on the edge of the chair next to his bed. My insides felt funny. I couldn't look at him, but I was filled with him—once more, just like he used to be. He was smaller then. He had contracted typhus, had a fever, and he was delirious. But he wouldn't remember this now....

He was born on a snowy night in February. I felt so strange as I placed him in my father's arms....When I looked for a name, the dictionary seemed so empty to me. I wanted to find him a shining name, a word that meant something like Creation. In the end, we called him Ömer, which means "life." This suited him well, too. I saw him as destined for the heights and for great successes, like all those Ömers who have gone before him into history.

The first laugh...the first tooth...the first word...the first step toward his mother—his young, lovely, and happy mother.

Then, his sixth birthday.... He cried so much the day I took him to school. It was as if he didn't want to accept any other relationship than those in his home. But this was the way it had to be. He was like any other boy, and would eventually be lost to us in the school, in the streets, in the marketplace. It couldn't be prevented.

And his thirteenth birthday: Bad temper, indifference.... A new relationship for us, and the most difficult.... My wife's flushes of pride and my own first concern...

He finished his lycée and, later, his university education. At this time, to give him a little extra, my wife sold the three five-lira gold coins she still had left from the wedding. And he, he was overwhelmed by the misfortunes of first love, and he destroyed us as well.

Thus, as we became more hopelessly tied to him, he gradually began to draw lines between his world and ours.

You've split yourself off from us. As our affection grew, you became a little more discontent. I understood this: You found some kind of attack on your freedom in this. But your mother...

I know: You no longer like the way your room is furnished or even this house.... You want something better, something different, but you've had bad luck so far.... But don't be sad; it's not in your hands; that's life and you can't do anything about it....

I know what you expect in drink, and I'm sure you won't become an alcoholic....But, your mother...

And I know why you run out of the house and what you're looking for out there. Maybe a little whore. I'm not opposed to them; in fact.... But your mother.... The poor woman trembles at the thought that you'll fall into the hands of one of them. When you spend your nights out like this, her suspicions turn to the bright avenues and those stories she's heard about secret rooms in nightclubs.

But what's the use of all of this? Don't you know this already? Don't I know how much all of this stuff has made your heart ache too? Your mother, me, don't pay any attention to us. All of this foolishness is just stuff we've made up. It's as though we were just waiting for you to get sick again. We still want you to remain just as you were when you needed us most. We don't stop to consider that you can change. See, I can't even lay my eyes on your face, can't look at you. Your mother's the same way. Now we can't even wake you up, because we know, without even daring to think about it, that your sleep has changed too. You used to sleep as if you were waiting for us to come into your room. Yes, your sleep has changed too. In fact, the real change has been in your sleep; you've grown apart from us in your sleep.

I turned my head. I looked at him. I did this as though I were forcing my stiff arm to move. But I suddenly became happy inside—as if I had found a friend I had been looking for for years. I felt like whistling. I drew the curtains; the sun would disturb him. His strong, black-bearded face looked like my family. I kissed him lightly and went outside.

While we were drinking our tea, my wife was a little depressed. I secretly put some lemon in my youngest son's tea. He hates lemon.

Cengiz Dağcı

from *Those Lands Belonged to Us*

Translated by Osman Türkay

It was just before daybreak when they arrived at Küçükyanköy. Selim and Hauptmann Schreiber stopped near the village. Muzaffer looked around cautiously and found the man who was called Gani. The two men passed under the huge walnut trees on the outskirts of the village and turned toward a mountain path, both sides of which were overhung by thick boughs.

Gani was a tall, strong, heavily built man with a dark complexion. He greeted Selim Chilingirov, who was the first to speak, and shook hands with him. When Selim said that Lüba was looking for him, Gani's face became somber and sulky. Gani, after scrutinizing Muzaffer from head to toe, led the way angrily until they were two kilometers distant from the village. Then, as they were climbing the mountain path high up on the hill, he grasped Selim by the arm, and, pulling him to one side, murmured:

"Why did you bring this boy here?"

"Boy?" said Selim. "Are you talking about Muzaffer?"

"I don't know whether he's Muzaffer or not. But whoever he is, you shouldn't have brought him here."

"Why shouldn't I?"

"You'll find out soon enough."

A penitent note sounded in Selim's trembling voice.

"*I* didn't bring him—he came by himself."

"Hasn't he got anywhere else to go?"

"No. He wants to fight against the Germans."

Gani smiled without mirth. He looked down at the ground and, stretching out his hand, took Selim by the sleeve of his jacket.

"Well, you go on. I'll go back to the village."

"But what shall we do?"

"Carry on along this path. At the end of the third kilometer you'll meet Lüba. Be careful you don't stray from the path—that's very dangerous."

Before leaving Gani, Selim gave Muzaffer a thoughtful, uneasy glance. Then, after a moment's hesitation, he turned back to Gani and asked:

"Do you know anyone called Şamil A.?"

Gani did not bother to look in Selim's direction. Shrugging his shoulders as if to say "Who cares about your Şamil now!" he set out in the direction of Küçükyanköy....

At the end of the third kilometer, they met Lüba. Here on the slope, where the path curved, there was a large lead-colored rock. A woman came out from behind it. She looked thirty, perhaps thirty-five years old. She was wearing a short leather jacket and boots and an astrakhan cap tilted toward her right ear. She had a white face, black eyes, and reddish cheeks. Her jacket was entirely unbuttoned and open, revealing the long gun under the German belt she wore around her waist.

Selim came forward and stood in front of the woman.

"Are you Lüba?" he asked.

"I'm not sure," she said, raising her arms to her breasts. "For some I am Lüba, for others I am not.* Have you come from Küçükyanköy?"

"Yes," said Selim.

"Who did you meet there?"

"Gani."

Three men now came out from behind the rock, one of them wearing a German helmet. They scrutinized Hauptmann Schreiber first, then turned their cold eyes on Muzaffer. There was a long silence that seemed to separate them from one another. The woman watched Selim intently, then fixed her eyes on the ground for a while before lifting her head again and looking at the German officer.

"Is he a German?" she asked.

"Yes, he is," said Selim.

Smiling, she took Selim's arm, and together they walked away from the others, disappearing from sight behind the rock. Ten minutes later, as they came out, the smile on her face was warmer, the light in her eyes brighter. She spoke hurriedly, looking at the man with a German helmet on his head.

"You, Grisha, take the German to Kozlov. I'll give you a letter. Deliver both the German and the letter to him. Take ten men with you and guard him carefully. Don't let him get away. Go immediately."

Her eyes rested on Muzaffer.

"And you, Nicola, take this hero to Pachenko's group."

Nicola was scratching his beard.

"Is he one of ours?" he asked, looking at Muzaffer's German uniform.

Selim replied instead of Lüba.

"Yes, he is."

"And who might you be?"

"My identity is none of your business. We didn't eat soup from the same bowl. Haven't you received an order to take him to Pachenko's group?"

"Yes, I have...."

"Well, what're you waiting for?"

"Who are *you* to be giving me orders?"

Lüba gave him an angry look, and Nicola fell silent.

Muzaffer seemed very happy to be leaving. Putting his hand on Selim's should, he said: "It won't be for long. I'll be back at Çukurca by harvest time. You must be best man at my wedding. Don't forget."

Selim and Lüba were alone. A wagon stood at one side of the rock. Smoke came out through its rear wheels from a boiler on a fire behind the wagon.

*Lüba, a Russian feminine name, also means "lovely."

Selim and Lüba crossed to the wagon. Lüba hesitated briefly, then looked at Selim, saying: "Are you tired?"

"Yes, I am."

"Why don't you lie down and sleep then. Don't worry, the Germans won't come here. And if they did, I'd wake you up."

"I have never in my life been protected by a woman before. But I guess I'll sleep easy. What happens after that?"

"Then we shall join Pachenko's group."

Selim frowned. "Why didn't we go with the others in that case?"

"Because I wanted to be alone with you. Do you mind?"

Selim did not answer. There was a short silence, and then he said: "Very well. I really must get some sleep. I'm tired."

"Go ahead and sleep. Get in the wagon. There isn't a pillow, but if you like, you can rest your head on my knee."

His eyes closed slowly, and he fell into a deep and heavy sleep. It was almost night when he woke up. The sky was overcast and the air chilly. Lüba had harnessed the horse to the wagon and was now standing next to Selim. He yawned and smiled, rubbing his eyes.

"What's the time?"

"Night isn't far away," replied Lüba.

"Did I sleep?"

"Like a child."

Selim looked up at the wagon.

"Are we off now?"

"Yes," said Lüba.

"Are you ready?"

"For what?"

"To set out."

"Yes, I am ready."

Lüba drove the wagon as they raced under the huge pine trees. She had taken off her leather jacket and laid it at her side. A strong stench of sweat from her perspiring armpits came to Selim's nostrils as he lay on his back in the wagon. He watched Lüba's bra, visible through her transparent blouse, her round shoulders, and her newly washed and combed black hair, and, as he watched, he thought of Natalia.

The pine trees seemed to cover and hide them from the rest of the world. There was no wind, no birds anywhere in sight, and the sky, which could now and again be glimpsed through the trees, grew darker and darker.

They did not speak for a long time. Then Lüba turned her eyes on Selim and smiled.

"What is your name?" she asked

"Selim," he muttered.

"That's a very nice name. How old are you?"

"I'm an old man, honey."

"Are you really? Where have you grown so old?"

"First on the *kolkhoz,* then in the war."

"Are you married?"

"What do you mean?"

"I want to know if you sleep with a woman in your bed."

"Without a woman," said Selim.

Lüba became silent. Then, without looking at him, she said:

"Don't you fancy anybody?"

"Do *you?*"

"You shameless creature!"

Another long silence followed. This time it was Selim who broke it.

"Have you got friends of the opposite sex? What I mean to say is, have you got a boyfriend?"

"No. Oh, there are many who'd like to be, but I don't encourage them."

"That's right. If the bitch doesn't fawn, the dog..."

The wagon stopped. Lüba swiveled round to face Selim.

"You said you weren't married, yet you seem as experienced as I am on the subject."

"I didn't say I wasn't married. I said I sleep without a woman. I've got a houseful of children."

"Who cares what you have and what you don't? It's of no concern to me. But I like you."

"Do you really?"

"Yes, of course I do. Come and sit by my side."

"Only by your side?"

"What else?"

"Look, darling, you drive on—it's getting late."

"You are right. It *is* late, but we shan't go on now—we'll sleep here."

"Where?"

"In the wagon, of course, where else? Know of a bedroom that's handy?"

Lüba stood up and threw her leather jacket in with Selim.

"Make room for me," she said. 'Can I lie down with you?"

"Yes, why not," he replied.

But as she stretched out next to him, Selim got up and, after watching Lüba for a short while, jumped down from the wagon. He stood there holding on to the wagon and looking at Lüba's face.

"Don't be ashamed," she said. "Go ahead and pee—I shan't look." Selim went off through the pine trees. When he returned, darkness had enveloped the wagon and the road.

The wood was silent, brooding. They could hear the dry twigs falling off the pine trees.

Selim remained standing by the wagon, listening to the sound of the falling pine needles. Then, still lost in thought, he crawled under the wagon and lay down on his back. After some time, he turned on one side, using one of his arms to cradle his head.

He just lay there, staring into the darkness, and, as he stared, tears ran down his cheeks.

He stretched out his hand and caressed the breathing earth in the soft spring air.

Long minutes, maybe hours, passed. Lüba knelt inside the wagon and bent over the side.

"Have you been sleeping, Selim?" she asked.

"No, I haven't."

"Don't you feel cold? The weather is chilly."

"Yes, it is, but I don't feel cold."

"Let me feel your hand then."

Stretching out both her arms, she took Selim's hand between her palms.

"Your hand is cold. Come, let me warm you. Get in the wagon. I too feel....It really is cold."

Selim was silent.

"You told me you weren't married. Don't be scared—I have no disease."

Selim's face looked mournful. Withdrawing his hand, he stroked her arm respectfully. Then, speaking in a soft murmur as if he were addressing himself to a remote past or to a near future, he said:

"Forgive me, Lüba....I *am* married."

Letting go of Lüba's arm, he again crawled under the wagon and lay down. Possibly for the first time in his life he wept, silently and painfully. He wept and wept.

The hills and the pine trees were shrouded with a heavy darkness. They were completely silent and still, as if listening to his beating heart.

On the macadamized road between Yalta and Akmesçit, there were no longer any German soldiers to be found. Guerrilla groups, each composed of ten men, which had been in the mountains these past two years, now raided the villages, looting everything they could lay their hands on, including livestock and movables. Armed men raided the towns, too. By mid-April the news that Kerch, Kefe, Sudak, and Karasupazarı had been retaken by the Russians had reached the partisans. The large guerrilla groups organized by the Red Army Commissars left the hills for the towns, but others came to take their place. At this time, when everyone thought that the war on Crimean soil was over, people speaking different languages appeared in the mountains. Most of them were Tartars and Russians, but there were also Greeks, Armenians, Germans, and Jews among them. They were unarmed and would pay thousands of rubles for a pistol and a little ammunition. Why they should be arming themselves was a mystery. They were quite unlike the old partisans. They did not raid the villages and towns; they did not loot the peasants' animals and property. They were a silent lot, sometimes spending days without saying a word. Some would go down to their villages once or twice a week and take the food left for them by their relatives. All of them were unshaved, their clothes were shabby and worn, their faces dirty. They were weary and desperate.

Selim lived three weeks among these people. He looked for Muzaffer everywhere but did not so much as hear his name mentioned. It was now two months since he had left the village of Çukurca with Hauptmann Schreiber, and he felt that he had grown old in that time. His beard had grown longer, his eyelids were red, his eyes were sore. He slept day and night, or lay on his back and watched the sky. Sometimes he just sat idly and killed time by thinking of his son Alim and Bekir's daughter Ayşe.

He started climbing the slope. A man from one of the coastal villages came up to him.

"Where are you off to?" the man asked.

"To my village, of course," said Selim.

The peasant looked at him in astonishment.

"Where is your village, sir?" he asked. "Is it in Anatolia? The Russians are hanging our people on the telegraph poles and bridges. Blood's flowing in our villages."

"What's that you say?"

"Yes, what I'm telling you is true. So what will you do now?"

"I want to go and see for myself."

"Don't be childish. Be patient. We didn't escape to these mountains because we like them so much. But if the Germans recapture the Crimea, we may be able to go home again."

"You stay and wait if you want to. I am going. I'm not waiting here for the Germans to come. If they do come back, do you think they'll pat us on the back?"

The peasant shrugged his shoulders and said nothing. Selim made his way to Çukurca.

As he passed under the huge walnut trees on the green slopes at the back of Küçükyanköy, Selim saw neither man nor beast. He would have gone into the village to look for Gani, but then for no apparent reason he gave us the idea. The sun was setting by the time he approached Tavşanpazarı and the scattered houses were engulfed in a dead silence.

At the side of the road was an overturned wagon surrounded by broken objects. Passing a wooden hut, Selim walked down to the road. He caught sight of four corpses lying one on top of the other in the shade of a mulberry tree. Three of them had shabby peasant clothes, but the fourth was stark naked. Their coloring told him they had been for a long time.

Selim came closer. When he realized that one of the corpses was that of Muzaffer Biber, he covered his face with his hands and retreated to the middle of the road. As he stood there, bewildered, a man came out of the wooden hut. He was an old, thickset Russian, probably over eighty. He came up to Selim, and they both stood there, looking at the dead bodies. Then the old man turned toward Selim and, pointing to the corpses, said:

"Tartars."

Selim stood silent, and, after a short pause, the old man went on:

"War is no good, my son. War is dreadful. These are what it leaves behind. I'm an old man, I've seen too many of them. I also fought. Do you know that my older brother fell in Plevne while fighting with the Turks? Yes, yes, we too have fought. Sometimes we attacked the Turks, sometimes the Turks attacked us. But the Turks are a good and brave people. Now everything has changed—brothers are killing brothers, Russians are shooting the Tartars. I've been living in this hut for twenty years. Do you want to know the truth? The Tartars never did me any harm, that's the truth. They were indeed Muslims like the Turks; but God is my witness, they were kind people. And what have we Russians done to the Tartars? In Yanköy we shot them and hanged the rest on the trees. I keep looking at these corpses from my window and saying to myself how unjust and cruel we've been to carry out this massacre."

The naked corpse belonged to Muzaffer. His young, handsome body was scarred with numerous bullet wounds.

Selim was no longer listening to the old man. He walked slowly toward the corpses and, taking off his jacket, covered Muzaffer's body with it. Just beyond the mulberry trees were cornfields, and he flattened the corn to make room for a grave. The soil was dry and loose. He knelt down and began to dig the earth with his dagger. He wept as he dug, shoveling the soil out with his hand.

Soon he made a shallow grave. Grasping Muzaffer's body with one arm, he carried it across to the field and laid it in the grave. He could not cry any more, as if he had expended his last teardrop. He plucked some green grass, leaves, and acorns and covered the dead face of Muzaffer. Then he scooped back the soil until the body was completely hidden. He stood up with the last handful of earth pressed in his palm and set out toward Çukurca.

He was not in a hurry, waiting for the night to fall. His steps grew slower and more weary. He kept looking at the western horizon, but the sun did not seem to want to go down as it sent its fading rays over the cornfields.

When he was some two kilometers from Çukurca, a young man came out of a nearby orchard. The young man stopped and gazed in his direction, then started running toward him, opening his arms as he ran. He threw his arms round Selim, weeping as he kissed his dry cheeks.

When at last the young man had calmed down a little, they sat down side by side in the field. Wiping the tears from his son's cheeks, Selim asked:

"Tell me, Alim, what's happened in Çukurca?"

Alim stared at him in silence like a dumb man.

"Who is there in Çukurca, Alim?"

Alim shrugged.

"Nobody."

"What about Bilal Ağa?"

Alim turned his eyes on the ground and began to speak in an anguished voice.

"Two days ago the Russians came to the village. They hanged Grandpa Cavit and Kaytaz on the tree by the mosque. They shot fifteen people including Hasan Ağa, lining them up against the mosque wall. They killed some others too, but this I didn't see. Then they gathered the people in the village square. I stood near Bilal Ağa. He whispered in my ear, 'You run away, Alim. Run away to the mountains, look for Selim, find him and tell him what you've seen. Tell him to stay in the hills. You too stay there, don't come back to the village. Because this village isn't ours now.' "

Ferit Edgü

The Lost Day

Translated by Talat Sait Halman

My wife furiously pulled the quilt off me saying, "You're late."

"Could be," I replied. She looked at me with anger. "What if I didn't go to work today?" I asked.

"Stop talking like a fool," she retorted.

I complained: "But I'm bored. Day in day out..."

"Enough of that. I have your coffee ready. Come on, get up."

I gulped my coffee without sugar—I never have breakfast, just coffee without sugar—and dashed out.

I heard the rustling of the sea trickling inland through the trees. The waves were buffeting the pebble stones. Softly. I gather the sea must be a bit choppy. Not a cloud in the sky. I didn't look, but it must have been cloudless. Cool air kept stroking my face, invigorating me.

I was probably late to work at least half an hour. When I get there, the Chief would look me over from top to toe, and say: "At least today you should have been on time. Payday, you know."

Would I ever forget it's payday? I'll sign the voucher and collect my salary. The cashier, who is a lethargic blond spinster, will hand me an envelope with my name written on it. I know it contains exactly 167 liras and 95 cents.

"Payday, my ass," I muttered. "I won't go to work today."

I started going in another direction—to the shore.

A woman was washing the laundry by the shore. I noticed when I came near her that her legs were apart and her panties clearly visible. Pink panties made of coarse cloth. My mother's panties were made of the same material, but they were never pink. All of a sudden, I recalled all this.

Standing there, I looked alternately at the woman and at the sea. She rose to her feet and began to spread the wash on the pebble stones. I noticed that everything she had washed was lingerie. She became aware of my presence only after she got through. From over there, she kept staring at me without blinking an eye. Then she walked up to me: "You have no job?" I said: "I do."

"In that case," she snapped back. "Why do you pop here every morning?"

I made the mistake of saying "You're wrong."

"Wasn't it you," she blurted, "who sat here yesterday morning staring at my bottom?"

"No."

"Embarrassed, huh?"

(I guess I had blushed.)

I said, "Nothing of the sort." And I told her this was the first time I had come to this spot, and that I hadn't stared at her bottom or anything like that.

She smiled. "Fine," she said. "Whatever you say."

We stopped talking. For a moment, she stood motionless and looked right into my eyes. Then, pointing to an indeterminate spot she said: "I live over there, at that cottage. There. Can you see it? Among those trees."

"I see it," I answered although I saw nothing. Just the deep dominant green of the forest, and a tree decked with lilacs in the midst of all that green. That was all I could see. But I said "Yes," and added: "There?" pointing to an indeterminate spot. She said "Yes."

Then she turned to take another look at the wash, and without uttering one more word to me, she walked, raising her skirt up just a little bit at each step, as perky as a young girl, towards the tree decked with lilacs (I think).

I looked at the sea and saw small waves which hit the shore one by one and receded leaving behind them a rustling sound. For a while, this regularity held me spellbound. I had sat down on the pebbles. Cool. Remember, I had thought the sky was cloudless, Well, it wasn't. In the distance, where the sea and the sky blended, there were heaps of white clouds. A cotton field. Cotton field in the sky. The cotton flowers that had burst open stretched towards the green trees. I felt joyful.

I took my jacket off and dropped it on the pebbles. Loosening my tie, I took a long deep breath. Then I turned my back on the sea and glanced at the grove, where the trees were swaying gently. The lilac tree stood erect in the midst of all that swaying green, almost stripped from it—poised like a world unto itself whose gates had not yet been opened by any human being. I thought of nonsensical things like this. Then I said to myself: "That woman with the pink panties is probably waiting for me there." I took my shirt and my shoes off. Meanwhile I kept thinking of the Chief and how he must be saying: "That bum, I bet, will show up at five o'clock."

Well, it's true that I'll show up at five. It's my right, after all, to pick up the envelope with my name written on it which has exactly 167 liras and 95 pennies. The wages of one month's work. The rent. Clothing. Food and drinks. This sum of 167.95 covers it all.

I didn't think of the rest of it. I thought of nothing. Just kept walking by the shore. Stopped. Took another look at the sky. The sun was high up in the sky. I got undressed and ran into the water.

The foams of the waves fondled my feet. I took a few more steps. A chill went up from my legs to my torso. I plunged in the water. It was cold. Fields of white cotton seemed to be marching from afar. I walked towards them.

When I lay down on the pebblestones, the sun was already right over my head. I took off my underpants to wring them. Then I put my shirt and trousers on and began to stalk towards the lilac tree.

She had blue eyes. Light blue like cut glass. With those eyes looking straight into my face, she asked: "Were you swimming?" I nodded: "Yes."

She said: "You're shivering. Where's your jacket?" "Over there," I replied. "I left it on the pebbles."

We went into the cottage. She had already set the dishes on a coarse mattress. "Sit down," she said. I did. She broke a loaf of bread and gave me half of it. There were green vegetables in one of the plates before me, and fish in the other. She picked up the big earthenware pitcher and took loud gulps of water. She said: "This should've been liquor, huh?" I replied: "Oh, yeah."

I put my hands right in between her warm legs and pressed. "Yeah," I said, looking her straight in the eyes, lustfully.

"Stop fooling around," she said. "No hanky panky during a meal."

I pulled my hand back. She had a big appetite. She was devouring her food. I kept staring when suddenly she noticed: "Eat your food," she said, "instead of looking at me like that."

I took a fish, and broke a bit more from the loaf. "Have some of that green stuff, too," she said. "I picked it with my own hands this morning." I took a little bit of that too. But I already had enough.

"Go on, eat," she said.

"I'm full," I answered.

"My, you got a real small appetite."

I felt like saying that I loathed eating, but didn't. I just said: "How about removing the plates?"

"You better take a look at your hair first," she said. I shoved my hair back with my fingers. My hair was still wet.

"Was the water cold?" I said it was.

She picked up the plates, took them out, and left them in front of the cottage door. Then she returned. No sooner than she was back I grabbed her by the waist and pulled her to me. We stumbled on to the floor. As she fell, her head struck the earthenware pitcher which didn't get broken, but all the water in it spilled out, getting the wicker mat all wet.

"I wish we had liquor," she said. "Huh?"

"Yeah," I answered.

She asked me: "You drink?"

"Sure enough," I said.

I leaned over and kissed her neck.

"My husband used to finish a bottle every night."

"Who?"

"My husband. The fisherman. Didn't you know him?"

I unbuttoned her dress.

"No," I said. "Never met him."

She looked at my left hand, at my wedding ring.

"So you're married too," she said.

"Yes."

"I wonder what your wife would do if she saw us like this?"

"Nothing," I said. "What could she do?"

Nothing, my foot. She would leave me. She's been grumbling quite a bit recently, anyway. She keeps saying I'm going to leave you, you'll be left all by yourself, all alone like dogs. As she says these things I keep wondering if dogs are really alone—and how could she leave me, in the first place, where could she go? Then I say let her go if she wants to. Go. Go to hell. Go wherever you want to. Suit yourself. To hell with you. Go and never come back.

"Attaboy," she said.

"She can do nothing," I repeated. "If she sees us, she sees us. What could she do?"
She held my shoulders and pushed me away from her.

"But..." I protested.

"What do you mean but?"

"We were going to..."

She buttoned up. As if she hadn't heard me, she said: "My man drank a whole bottle every night. He made me drink too. My husband. The fisherman."

"Where's he now?"

"Gone," she said. "One morning he left in his boat. Hasn't returned yet. He's been out fishing for the past three months."

I smiled and said: "He must be dead."

"What can I do?" She shrugged her shoulders. She didn't care. "If he's dead, he's dead."

I looked. Her eyes were blue. Blue like cut glass. Twinkling. Vacant. Deep.
She said "I'm going out to get the wash."

"I'll wait here," I said.

In a moment, she was lost among the trees. I went back into the cottage and stretched out on the wicker mat. I stared at the ceiling where a bunch of corn was hanging, and a winter melon beside it. It couldn't be ripe. It must be awfully bitter. I took the little jug near me, and upended it. The water was ice-cold.

I wished she were right here now, with me. Those firm, large, vibrant teats of hers. And her eyes. Her tanned face. (My wife: pale and sickly.)

I rose to my feet and went out. I too got lost among the trees.

She was sitting on the pebblestones on the beach. She had stacked the wash next to her. She was talking to the kids that had gathered round (I think).

I went over. "Why did you come?" she asked.

(When the kids saw me, they stopped laughing.)

"I came," I said. "When you didn't come back....What else could I do? I waited all this time. I got bored. So I came over."

The kids ran into the water.

I sat down next to her. I grabbed her hair, forced her to face me, and kissed her. The kids saw us and giggled.

"Come on," she said. "Take your jacket, let's go home."

"No," I said. "It's nice here."

"Can't do it here," she answered. "There are kids here. Besides, you never can tell, my husband might show up."

I didn't want to repeat that he's dead and will never come.

"Come on," I said. I held her by the hand. We walked towards the grove.

I must have left my jacket behind. When I got back, it was already dark. I kept looking for the jacket, but couldn't find it. The sun was down. The scarlet patch on the horizon was on the point of vanishing. I thought I should go to the factory and collect my salary, give it to my wife—and go to sleep without any further thoughts.

My head was reeling. I was beat. I looked in the direction of the lilac tree. It was pitch-dark everywhere. Nothing was visible.

The guard at the entrance to the factory asked me: "What's up?"

"Nothing," I said. "I'm here to get my salary."

"Didn't you get it yesterday?"

(Yesterday? It wasn't the first of the month yesterday. Not payday.)

I didn't answer. I just asked: "No one in there?"

Shaking his head he said: "No." He pulled out his watch from his vest pocket. "Who could be here at this hour?"

"OK, then" I said. "I'll be seeing you."

Staring after me in astonishment he said: "So long."

Before going home I stopped at the coffeehouse. Anastas and I played cards. He turned sour in the middle of the game: "Just like yesterday," he said. "You're setting up the cards. You try to pull the same trick in every game."

"But, Anastas," I protested. "We didn't play cards yesterday. Neither yesterday nor the day before. It's been a week or so since I was here at this coffeehouse."

"Who do you think you're kidding?" he said. "Yesterday we played right here at this table. At this same time."

"Anastas, you're putting me on," I said.

"Ahmet," he snapped back. "You're putting me on. And each time you try to pull the same tricks with the same cards."

"Don't make things up."

"Yesterday it was the same trick. Today it's the exact same trick." He banged on the cashbox and got up.

Same tricks all the time...same thing yesterday same thing today. After Anastas, I too got up.

I went home. Rang the bell. No one came to the door. I thought my key was in my left pocket. I put my hand into the pockets of my pants, but couldn't find it. It must have slipped out on the pebble stones.

I called to my wife at the top of my voice. Got no reply. She must be asleep, I thought. I managed to go in through the kitchen window. A rope was hanging above the table in the living room. There was a piece of paper on the table with a few shaky lines on it. Faded. A few words. A slanted handwriting. Scribblings with a lot of dots:

"The lilac tree...the cottage...her blue eyes...last hope...the sea was cold...glass blue...open...last hope...Anastas...the jack...the jack...I was playing cards...I did play...It was my last hope...the king with the black beard of a priest...last hope...my legs...I can no longer endure it...last hope...gone...finished...all over...everything's gone...money...belongings...salary...weekly wages...the butcher...the grocer...pots and plates...my wife...it's all over...finished...hope...everything...I cannot bear it anymore...I have exhausted all possibilities...There's no way out...other than...in this blind alley...for me...for me...With ease of mind and a weary heart, with disgust and shame, I am killing myself.

October 1st
Ahmet Hırçın"

I tore the paper up and threw it away.

For a while I paced around. Got bored. It was suffocating. I looked for the daily newspaper. It wasn't around. The delivery boy must have brought it. I took a look. Sure enough. There it was, by the door. It was slightly soiled. I took it: on page one, the upper right corner had a big headline–SUICIDES INCREASING. (This is what I hate most about small-town newspapers: When they can't find juicy news items, they carry silly headlines like this.) Underneath this headline I saw my own name. In smaller type but still fairly big. AHMET HIRÇIN COMMITS SUICIDE. HANGS HIMSELF AT HOME LAST NIGHT. And a photo of mine. No, it isn't. That's not me. I held the paper right to my eyes. No, no, that isn't me. The eyes, the mouth, the nose or anything else has no resemblance to me. That's not me. It must be a case of similar names. Or maybe a tasteless joke.

I crumpled the paper and threw it away. I raised my head: The rope over the table was gently swaying back and forth.

It was like being choked to death. I found my jacket on a chair. I put it on and dashed out. I started running towards the cottage under the lilac tree which was glittering in the moonlight.

Nazlı Eray

Monte Kristo

In the district of Ayrancı, on the second floor of 51 Orange Blossom Street, there lived a housewife who wasn't happy at all with her life in her four walled world. Her husband came home tired every evening and couldn't give her enough attention. Anyway, he was a dense guy who often hurt her feelings. The narrow spaces of her house, her daily housework, taking care of the children, had tired and depressed the poor woman. Her name was Nebile and she had secretly started to dig the wall of a little store room with her nails, where the brooms, wax polish, dustbins, mops, soap, and detergents were kept. Her aim was to dig a tunnel and reach out to freedom. Now and then she could hear voices from the other side of the wall.

She usually dug towards evening, her housework done, her children at school and her husband at his office. At first she dug with her nails; after a while she dug with the broken handled tin fork. Every evening she put the debris that came from the wall into a plastic bag. Every night she secretly poured it into the dustbin. She was up early every morning at the usual time. She laid the table, prepared breakfast, washed the dishes and put the house in order. But for two days since she had started the digging she felt sudden flashes of happiness and hope. Her house work seemed suddenly easier to her.

Nobody except her entered the store room where the brooms, wax polish, dustbins, mops, soap and detergents were kept. Nevertheless, Nebile hid the hole with the big laundry basket every day. She also hid the broken handled fork behind the yellow bread box.

Every morning she left home to do her shopping. She went to the butcher, to the grocer and the green grocer.

Then she could have entered into an unknown street and gotten lost. But she didn't want this kind of freedom. Her arms and hands were always full. For instance, one morning she had a big cabbage under her arm, her grocery bag was full of oranges, potatoes and minced beef meat. At that moment it occurred to her to get into a street and get lost. She couldn't do it. Instead she went home and cooked stuffed cabbage.

From the other side of the wall, murmurs of a happy and orderly life came to her ears. At first it had been those voices that had attracted her attention to the wall. She had decided to enter into the happy life on the other side of that wall. "If I miss my children too much, I may even take them there later," she said to herself.

She couldn't concentrate on her housework anymore. In the old days she could immediately wipe away the cobwebs dangling from the ceiling. Now, she didn't care anymore.

That morning, her husband, while going to his office shouted,

"Another button is missing from my light blue shirt. God dammit, I'm late again," he said.

"For god's sake, whatever you cook, don't let me eat stuffed cabbage again. I've had enough of it"-

"Why don't you go to a hairdresser, your hair looks awful. Well, goodby," he said.

When the children left for school. Nebile washed the breakfast dishes, took her grocery bag into her hand, and went shopping. From the butcher she bought a pound of lamb chops, from the grocer she got some margarine and a bag of bow-shaped noodles and from the green grocer she bought a medium sized cauliflower. When she got home she hung her coat on the hanger by the door. She took off her shoes and put on her slippers. She boiled the cauliflower, cut it into small pieces and made a sauce of oil, lemon and salt. She left it to cool. She boiled a pot of water and poured the bow shaped noodles into it.

Then she went to the mirror. She combed her hair with her fingers.

"Tomorrow I will go to the hairdresser," she told herself.

Later she said to her husband:

"Shall we go to the movies tonight? There is a French new wave film."

Her husband looked at her in a stupefied way.

"My God, Nebile, do you think I have time to scratch my head? I come home dead tired in the evening and you expect me to go to a movie. What is the television for?"

He knotted his shoe string and went to his office.

Nebile washed the dishes. She put the leftover cauliflower salad into the refrigerator. She took the broken handled fork from behind the breadbox. Then she went to the store room where the brooms, wax polish, dustbins, mops, soap, and detergents were kept. She pulled aside the laundry basket and went on digging from where she had left off. Nebile was digging a hole big enough for her to pass through. It wouldn't take her long to get to the other side. When the hole opened it would be possible for her to crawl through it.

She heard the click of high heeled slippers from the other side.

"The slippers that the woman on the other side is wearing must be the kind that are adorned with ostrich feathers," thought Nebile.

She also heard the pattering feet of a child and his talking.

The doorbell rang.

Nebile stood still. At first she thought everything was over. Her hands got moist with sweat. Then she pulled herself together. She closed the hole with the laundry basket, dusted herself with her hand and went to open the door.

It was her friend. It was obvious that she had just had her hair set. Her name was Güzin.

"Did I wake you up, Nebile? I was just passing by. I'll drink a cup of coffee, then leave."

"Of course I wasn't sleeping. I'm bored to death. How good of you to come." They sat opposite each other.

"Do you know, Nebile, now that the spring is here and the days are longer I don't feel like sitting at home. After I do my housework I throw myself into the street."

"I feel depressed at home, too Güzin. Just a minute, let me make the coffee."

"Today I cooked a roast. It was delicious, with garlic. I garnished it with potatoes and carrots. I made a soup out of its stew. Hilmi likes variety in his food. But don't ever cut the roast while it is hot. It all comes to bits. Never forget that. Wait until it gets cold."

When Nebile finished her coffee she neatly turned her cup over on the saucer to read her fortune in the pattern the dried coffee would make. She said,

"Güzin, I'm closing my coffee cup."

"Nebile, how do you wash the curtains?"

"The night before I put them in sudsy water. The next day, I change the water three times. I put four lumps of sugar in the last wash. Then they look well starched."

"Nebile, there is a road in your cup. I swear, look here. A very short road. It's about to open."

After Güzin left, Nebile washed the coffee cups and put them in the cupboard. Then she went straight to the store room where the brooms, wax polish, dustbins, mops, soap, and detergents were kept.

She began digging.

From beyond the wall came the sound of chamber music. The woman in the house was moving, clicking her slippers, and saying:

"My son, wash your hands. Your father will be here in a minute. You must be clean for him!"

Nebile gathered the debris coming out of the wall into a plastic bag. Once more she closed the hole with the laundry basket and went out to the room.

The children came home from school. Then her husband came. In the kitchen Nebile was preparing the evening meal.

"I'm going to have a hot bath tonight and go to bed," said her husband. Next morning Nebile went to the hairdresser.

"Trim my hair without shortening it. Wash and set it, please. I want a manicure and a pedicure too," she said.

While she was under the dryer, her feet in the hot tub, she thought a lot.

When she got home, she heated the meal and set the table.

In the afternoon, after her husband left, she put on her sleeveless black dress. It was a nice dress. She usually wore it at engagement parties and on new year's. It was tight. She wore her smoke-colored panty hose and high heeled black shoes.

She looked quickly in the mirror. Then she filled the tea pot with water. She watered the plants in the sitting room. The camel's foot plant was thriving. It liked its place.

She wound the clock on the sideboard. She straightened out the fringes of the carpets, gave the right shape to the drapes. She looked at the children's room. Everything was in order. She drank a glass of water from the refrigerator, she rinsed the cup and put it on the shelf. She wondered if she ought to leave a note to her husband. She thought it best to leave nothing. Maybe nobody would notice her absence anyway.

Nebile dug at the wall once or twice with the broken-handled fork. The wall was already thin as paper and a hole opened. Silently, Nebile widened the hole. When the hole was big enough for her to go through, she crawled to the other side and pulled the laundry basket back in its place.

From now on nobody could see the hole in the store room where the brooms, wax polish, dustbins, mops, soap, and detergents were kept.

Nebile found herself in a very dark room. When her eyes got used to the dark, she looked around. It was the same as the store room, though probably used for another purpose. There were no signs of mops, brooms, or dustbins. In a corner there was a water tap. Nebile went near the door and tried to listen. The lady of the house sometimes passed in front of the door. Time passed. The doorbell rang. The lady of the house opened the door.

"Welcome, dear Selahattin," she said.

"Take my bag. I'm dead tired today. What do we eat tonight?" Selahattin said.

Nebile crouched in a corner of the dark room. From her own household she could hear voices coming too. She didn't give them an ear.

After a while the door of the room opened. Somebody turned on the light. It was Selahattin Bey. Nebile straightened up from her crouching position. On seeing Nebile, Selahattin Bey was astonished. He stood rooted to his place.

"Excuse me, I have left my house. I have taken refuge here."

"This is my darkroom where I develop my photographs. No one else can come into this room. On weekends I develop my photographs here. That's my hobby," Selahattin Bey said.

Then something occurred to him.

"Did you have anything to eat?" he asked.

Selahattin Bey was tall with a mustache. He looked at Nebile through narrowing eyes.

Selahattin Bey secretly brought Nebile two loaves of bread with some sliced cold tongue. He had wrapped it in his handkerchief and hidden it in his pocket. While Nebile was eating her sandwich, Selahattin Bey watched her. Nebile felt a strange excitement, a fluttering in her heart from those looks Selahattin Bey gave her from his narrowed eyes.

From then on Selahattin Bey spent most of his time in the darkroom. He brought Nebile food and water. They sat together and talked for a long time in a murmuring voice.

Nebile told him all about her old life beyond the wall. She felt very near to Selahattin Bey. It pleased her to be fed and looked after like this. Selahattin Bey said:

"I've been married fifteen years. Feriha doesn't understand me. We live in different worlds. When I come home tired in the evening, she wants to go out. When I feel like going out, she is tired. Every morning she takes Ömer, our son, with her and goes out shopping. It is then that you can go to the toilet."

Gradually, Nebile had become Selahattin Bey's intimate friend. Selahattin Bey secretly brought her the latest fashions in dresses, perfumes, sheer ash-colored stockings, cork heeled shoes, birth control pills, and sometimes flowers.

Nebile stretched a rope from one corner of the dark room to the other and she hung her dresses on it. They put a mattress on the floor in the other corner. They were happy.

During the day, Nebile lay on her mattress and listened to Feriha doing her housework. She got up late in the morning. She was with Selahattin Bey until late at night. Selahattin Bey took poses and poses of Nebile with his flashbulb camera and developed them in the darkroom. The pictures were in color.

Nebile was very jealous of Selahattin Bey's wife. When Selahattin Bey left her to be with his wife, Nebile put her ear to the door and tried to hear what they were saying. But the bedroom was far away. There was a corridor in between. She couldn't hear anything.

Selahattin Bey said to Nebile:

"Our marriage has been dead for years. I feel alive only when I am next to you. I don't understand why you keep worrying about nothing."

Nebile was very curious about certain things concerning Feriha. She kept thinking and making up certain things in her mind. At last she couldn't resist and asked Selahattin Bey:

"Selahattin, I am full of curiosity. What does your wife wash the dishes with? What brand of dishwasing soap does she use? Is it Citi or Pril? For heaven's sake, tell me, or I'll get mad."

Selahattin Bey didn't know what soap his wife washed the dishes with.

"Is this so important to you, Nebile? Why do you think of these things?" he asked. Nebile said:

"For me those are most important things: The brand of the product which the dishes and laundry are washed with, or the kind of margarine and butter used in the kitchen is most important. You can't understand this. These things were my whole life. I can never escape from them."

Selahattin Bey couldn't bear Nebile to be sad. This woman's deep thoughts fascinated him.

He learned all the names of the soaps and detergents and food products which his wife used and told Nebile all of them.

There were also times when Nebile shed tears because of Feriha.

"Ah, Selahattin," she would say. "Is our love always going to remain in the dark?"

Then Selahattin Bey would say to Nebile:

"Believe me, Feriha and I are so far apart, we are not even on talking terms. I haven't even touched her for three months. If she learns of this, she will never divorce me, we will suffer endlessly. She is already suspicious, we must be careful. Be patient, Nebile."

As time passed by, Nebile had little by little forgotten her old life on the other side of the wall. Sometimes, usually at night, she could hear voices coming from there. Usually it was her husband's loud voice.

"Ah!" her husband would say to his visiting friends in a suffering voice.

"Oh, what a good woman she was. She seemed very content and happy too. She loved me very much. Mind you, very much. Every morning while going to the office, she rushed behind me, bringing me my clean handkerchief. 'Don't forget your clean handkerchief,' she used to say.

"She was an honest woman. They probably tricked her into leaving me. I put an ad in the newspaper saying, 'Nebile, come back home.'"

"Maybe she'll read it and come back."

"Ah, my Nebile, ah!" he would say.

Her children went back and forth to school. Housework was done as before. Her husband had hired a charwoman.

Nebile was as happy as could be. She rested all day long, she creamed her face, she filed her nails, she wore the black silk nightgown that Selahattin Bey had given her as a present, she stretched out on the mattress. She waited for the day when she would come out of the darkroom, and enter into the house.

Füruzan

Knowing How to Play the Piano

Translated by Ellen Ervin

"It's sinful for them to do the laundry on Saturdays," my mother said. "Not to mention just dumping the dirty water out front at night!"

I was sitting stiffly on the doorsill in my holiday clothes sewn by my mother, with sturdy boys' shoes laced at the top, and a huge satin bow in my hair.

[Being womanly isn't easy. Making something that looks well on you out of nothing. Look what I paid for that print material from the wholesale dry goods store. I rinsed it and got out the stiffening. Then I ironed it. Sewed it quickly in time for the holiday. These people don't even wipe their children's noses. I grew up in mansions. Go and tell that to these common women. My lute, my piano, what beautiful hands I had....]

Down below they had sprinkled the ground in front of the Kurd's coffeehouse. The earth smelled fresh. At the end of every *Ramazan, * they played dance tunes in the coffeehouse.

My shoes had gotten a little smaller this holiday.

"See, *Ramazan* Holiday this year, it's already summertime," said my mother. "God sent us a mild winter."

We had one room. You entered the room right from the door. There was no kitchen; the corner table was used for meals and a kitchen. The dirt on the whitewashed walls showed when the weather got warm enough to open the street door. The window in the corner barely existed. Why does my father work on holidays too? Is there anyone who buys liver for their cats on holidays?

"Mother, when is my father coming?"

"He'll come home around noon. Maybe the end of the afternoon. If they get to talking about their own village. I'm sick of their village, and their beehives. They still haven't gotten rid of their accent. Because they always get together and talk....I'm not the right kind for your father, but what can you do, it's fate."

[Oh, Demir really had some beehives, my child, among the knee-high grass. It's mountain country, our place there, and the air is healthy, the people well-built. But my old man insisted on going away because the government had changed in these parts. Nothing but land and fields and gardens left behind there, in his view. We sold them, but our men spent it all right away among strangers. Whatever I said was no use. You're a woman, you don't know anything about it, they said. Three of my sons gave up and died. They were mountain men and couldn't adjust to the city. Our honey smelled of clover; the breezes rustled through the clover.]

---

*Muslim month of fasting, followed by a three-day holiday.

"Mother, aren't we going to pay a holiday visit to Grandmother?"

"I'm sick and tired of your grandmother's crying. She'll start right in with her three sons who died and she's eighty and still living."

[Ah, daughter-in-law, why did we ever come to these places with huge houses? My sons are gone—only Demir Ali is left. You should appreciate your husband....On holidays everyone used to come and say, "Let me kiss your hand." They drank mastic sweets and spring water in delicate glasses. While my daughters-in-law busied themselves with the sweets, a pleasant scorched smell would come from the stove. My sons would go out in the yard in their serge suits and talk at the top of their voices. Rifles would shoot off in the distance. We had my grandchildren's hair cut very short. My only girl grandchild is this one. And she was born away from our village. They used to wet down the ground before the front door and in the yard. The children ran every which way.]

I'm a city person. It would never have crossed my mind in a million years that I would marry your father; I was fifteen when I married my first husband. In Istanbul there was typhus. Wouldn't you know, my hair fell out all of a sudden and I was left bald on my wedding night. I was still so beautiful, though! I was tiny but I had skin like taffeta and almond-shaped hazel eyes. When Madam Kalyopi was sewing my wedding dress, she said, "What arms you have, what wrists!" A set of rose-colored bed linens were made for me. On the wedding night I kept saying, "I want my mother." I always used to sleep with your grandmother. She had asthma. I got so scared at night, thinking she was going to die. She seemed unable to breathe. We would burn apple peels on the tile stove. Those were the winters in Acıbadem. The Germans were building the Haydarpasha railroad station. The German engineer and his wife lived in the house with a tower, next door to us. The woman's cheeks were all covered with red veins. Your grandmother used to say it was from eating pork. Those people always get like that. Summers we made rose jam; it smelled of roses everywhere. We would go to Necipbey garden by carriage. White grapes, muscatels, and Chasselas grapes from the garden, all heaped up on plates, glistening with dew. Rasim Pasha's daughter used to come in her landau. She wore pistachio green dresses because she had green eyes. Her hair was tighly wrapped up in a scarf. Her long locks were golden yellow—you could see them at her temples. They said she had become bad, the great pasha's daughter. She took Italian and French officers into her home, it seems. People saw their wide greatcoats and white gloves in Rasim Pasha's mansion often. Autumn turns very beautiful in Küçük Camlıca. Everything was covered with dark, quince-colored leaves. At that time they were making bread out of leftover corncobs in Istanbul. I married my first husband through a go-between. She apparently saw me shopping with your grandmother in Orozdibak. They put a diamond ring on my finger as my unveiling gift. My mother-in-law bought my drop earrings at an imperial auction. That year ice came down to the Bosporus from the Black Sea. On the wedding night, the tile stove burned till morning. I already told you that on my wedding night I said, "I want my mother."

My mother was always telling me things, and now she was telling me things again. I found her quite a stranger. What she told me was completely outside our life. And as for that bit about playing the piano, that was what frightened me most. Because I knew what a piano was. In our neighborhood movie theater, the Yavuz, I had seen from beginning to end a film about a man who played that object called a piano. It was a large musical instrument. Some of the things my mother told me I believed—after all I don't know what the other things she mentioned are—but playing the thing called a piano just couldn't have happened. She must have seen it in a movie theater too. Actually, she couldn't have gone to the Yavuz Theater. Because we didn't have the money for films. The bald man at the door would let in the local girls. According to what the boys said, he was a bad guy, up to no good.

"Mother, can I wear my clogs this afternoon? These shoes are too heavy, I can't run in them."

"What else can we do? Look, you've worn them for two years. It's better than going around in clogs on holidays. In my time I had antelope skin shoes. You don't even give an imitation of gentility anyway. Somehow you get by with it. You turned out to be like the mountain people."

[The Istanbulites made fun of us, daughter-in-law. It seems we put embroidered covers on everything. In our village my daughters-in-law would embroider the cloths in summer under the grape arbors. They even embroidered my grandchildren's underclothes. In our place children were very much appreciated. They ran around the yard like little colts. When their fathers returned from work, even the edges of the rough cotton shirts on their sweaty bodies were embroidered with carnations and roses. Everybody worked. In autumn when my sons and their wives went to the plain, I heated the milk fresh from the cows that morning and put it on the table with corn bread. They would dunk the bread in the milk. They all laughed a lot together. Demir Ali, in the honey-gathering time, took along the kids. They went out when they weren't even green yet. But you should have seen our weddings there, daughter. As soon as the young men and fresh young girls joined in the dancing, the skies rang. Weddings began after harvest time. Before the wedding we used to smear butter on the burned noses of our daughters-in-law working hard in the fields. Their poor noses peeled off entirely. When the men had drunk their plum raki, they threw themselves completely into the dance. Round and round they made the girls fly; when they got sweaty they took off their serge jackets. Silver watch chains gleamed on their shirtfronts. They were brave and manly. Well built. Weak people don't last there anyway— I've buried three sons, and I'm still alive. Ah, why should I live and why should those beautiful young men go? They couldn't stand it here. I told them, "Let's not go." "The government is going to change here," they said. And we had to live in exile. Ah, daughter, what are governments to us? Whoever saw the government in the courtyards, the fields, the mountains? These male folk think they know a lot; they're wrong a lot. Only Demir Ali was a bachelor when we arrived. There was a Bulgarian here, Kozma. He had come earlier, he knows us. He sent for my oldest son and told him, it's thus and so here; you'll be a street peddler; you won't be able to find any other kind of work, your brothers won't either.]

My father took me once to Kozma's dairy shop. It smelled of boiled milk everywhere. He had white teeth when he smiled. He said to my father, "Demir Ali, you're welcome here I'm sure." "We're glad we've come, I'm sure," said my father.

"This your daughter, huh?"

"Yes."

"She's grown."

"Yes, she doesn't go to school yet. She knows how to read the paper. She reads the local papers."

Then Kozma brought milk, butter, and fresh bread. He put it on the marble table. Both of them began to talk their native dialect. They forgot me. Across from the shop was a barracks. The barracks had so many windows! I couldn't figure out how they could heat it. Sailors were coming and going on the street. Then the bugle sounded. I thought about the fact that my mother was in a place so far off that no one could return from it. As if she had gone off with the mixed-up things she talked about. I was very sorry for her. I looked at my father. He and Kozma weren't talking. Father was resting his great hands on the tabletop. We got up.

"Demir Ali, I'm glad you came," said Kozma.

"We're glad too," said my father.

The sailors' footsteps could be heard from the barracks. When we returned home, my mother was darning stockings. Father put the change down on the chest of drawers that belonged to mother.

"We went to see Kozma. The girl is stuffed. I'm going to buy a portable chest. Kozma said that up there above, liver and lung sellers make a lot of money. He's going to get our Fazlı into the slaughterhouse. It's at Sütlüce. Near here. I'm going to buy a portable chest. There's money in liver and lung selling. 'Go into the slaughterhouse if you want to,' Kozma said. 'If you want, work with me.' He asked about my bees. We laughed. Then he asked 'Is anyone of you left thereabouts?' I said, 'Aunt Pink is left. She didn't come. Her sons didn't come either. In our family you can't oppose your elders,' I said. Kozma also said that you can't oppose them. I'm going to get a portable chest today."

My mother never raised her head.

"Only God neither falls nor rises," she said.

"I'll earn money in this place too, by my honesty," said my father.

My mother, still without raising her head: "What difference is there between what you do and begging? How will I tell it to the people at Kadiköy?"

"Don't get me started on their book, their idol, their prophet for discussion," said my father.

Infidel! They don't have an idol. Worry about yourself, you haven't learned how to talk correctly yet.

My father got up and left.

I was in front of the door, eating the fresh bread my mother had given me. She had spread it with fat and sprinkled red pepper on it. If only I could have run off to the field.

[Your father doesn't understand anything about holidays or excursions. What has become of refined and educated people! We all studied with İhsan at Acıbadem. When your grandparents set off on a tour of the Kuşdili meadow, we stayed home and devoured all the novels. Where have those days gone! Everything is over and done with. For lack of money we married off your sister when she was young. And, moreover, she was well born. Your sister was from my first husband. I was fifteen years old when I gave birth to her. It was winter, February. The stoves were burning constantly. They said that wolves came down to Ziverbey. My milk didn't come. I had very tiny breasts; there wasn't anything I could do about it. We hired Nazire as wet nurse. Nazire is black. She raised my older sister, İhsan. How many times your grandmother pulled her out of your grandfather's bed! She had such breasts, this big. So short and those breasts! The wisdom of God can't be questioned. One morning we were in bed. Your sister with her black hair was sleeping like an angel between the white bedsheets. Hamit had put on his uniform. He used to

have his clothes made by the most expensive tailor. All the girls were crazy about him.
Especially when he walked around wearing his sword. But he liked me best of all and took
me. My sister-in-law came inside. "Hamit! Hamit! War has started in Anatolia," she
said. I ran to the window. As if the war were outside. My heart leaped into my mouth.
Your sister Muazzam's father left and went away. I was left all alone. My sister-in-law
took Nazire into her room. I was very frightened at night. I kept waking up whenever I
was about to fall asleep. I thought I would get tuberculosis and die. One day the bath was
heated and I was washing myself. All of a sudden the door opened. It was my sister-in-
law's husband. "Oh, please excuse me," he said. I didn't know what to do. I was stark
naked. He closed the door. He went away. I was so ashamed I couldn't look anyone in the
face during dinner. "Why don't you eat?" asked my sister-in-law. My brother-in-law was
very quiet. A few nights later when I was half asleep I heard someone opening my
bedcovers. I was so happy—I thought Hamit had come. I threw my arms around his neck.
There I was, nose to nose with my raki-smelling brother-in-law. I rushed out of bed. I was
so cold I was shaking all over. "I'm going to scream now," I said. "Get out of my room
quick." He said, "Dear, Hamit won't return any more, he's either passed away or about
to." Next day I went back to my mother's house. I was going to wait for my husband
there. I took your sister too. In your grandmother's room I put your sister's bed at the
head of mine. Hamit never did come back again. We heard that he had escaped to Russia.
To join Enver Pasha's army. I still thought he would return. He sent me a picture of
himself in a kalpak from Batum. How handsome he was in that picture! I was a child. My
face was no bigger than a spoon. Around my neck was a gold watch that Hamit
bought—he gave it to me as a present when I became pregnant with your sister. Everyone
felt sorry for me. No one went to Kuşdili anymore. The day when my older sister İhsan
died, your grandmother's asthma got worse. We sent for Dr. Ben Habib quickly. At
home only your grandmother, your sister, my uncle, and I were left. We rented out the
guest part of the house. To three or four families. We closed it off with a barrier between,
but we were tired of listening to their noise every day. Nazire came later on and moved in
to look after your grandmother. They got so fond of each other you would have thought
she had never climbed into bed with your grandfather and the other one never had to pull
her out. At night they talked about their passion for your grandfather's woolen wraps, and
the delicate glassware. "My dear lady," Nazire would say. "In *Ramazan* the whole
mansion used to quarrel over the preparation of the rose-flavored desserts, the Circassian
chicken, the strained pilavs in shiny tinned saucepans. At breakfast if we didn't serve
watermelon jam and unsalted olives, it was unacceptable to the master, no matter if we
had birds' milk. Everything for the mansion was bought by the hundredweight. What
days of plenty they were! May he rest in peace." Then they would begin to sob together in
unison. "That such a man should die." "And yet," my grandmother would say, "what a
good thing that my master didn't live to see these days, when everything is turned upside
down!"

My days passed that way. Thinking news would come from Hamit. One day Hamit
and I went up to the top of Küçük Çamlıca by carriage. There's still a summer coffeehouse
up there. "Müberra," he said, "I might leave this earthly body behind me, but my love for
you will shine in the heavens till judgment day." He said this looking up at the sky.
When your sister was three, we learned that your father had died in Batum of venereal
disease. Your grandmother was already senile. She understood nothing. Nazire didn't

show any lack of respect for her former mistress. She collected the monthly rents. My uncle had been let go from the Public Debts Administration. He found a job as accountant with the Tobacco Monopoly in Üsküdar. He went back and forth to it. To save money, Nazire would fix him three meals to take along. In one part bread, in one part a cold dish in olive oil—mostly eggplant or noodles and cheese. By then we had meat just a few times a year. Your grandmother wouldn't hear of artichokes. Every time she served them, Nazire would say, "Dear lady, this is eggplant." I don't know what we would have done without Nazire. I had never in my life gone down even to Üsküdar alone. Your grandmother would say, I won't eat any other kind of bread than French bread. Maybe she didn't see well, I don't know. She saw everything as it used to be. Later on she began to think your grandfather was still alive. Your grandmother would say, "Go on, Müberra, go to the piano." While I played the piano, the roomers were saying, "The crazy palace set are having fun again," I knew. One day my uncle went to bed with fever. Nazire ran and fetched Dr. Ben Habib from Mağlarbası) The doctor kissed your grandmother's hand. They said that when the master returned in the evening, they would tell him the doctor had come. The doctor was a tiny little man. He listened to the two women and me with love and pity. He didn't take money. A week later my uncle died of pneumonia. Nazire tied up his jaw. They sat up a huge cauldron outdoors. It was the beginning of summer. The month-long rainy season had begun. Your grandmother said to me as if nothing had happened, "Here, this was my burial money, take it for the household expenses."

The last night the dead body was in the house, Nazire scrubbed the floors. She cleaned everywhere. Your grandmother said, "What customs these blacks do have." My uncle's room was closed. They were reading the Koran over him. The reader was the local imam. It seemed as though no one was home. Didn't your grandmother know her brother had died? No one came to his burial. Which means he had no friends where he worked. Nazire sold my uncle's clothes to the secondhand dealer, after a lot of haggling. In his walnut chest they found layers of Damascus silk underwear and nightclothes. "This was for his wedding, but it never came about," said Nazire. Your grandmother said, "He was not masculine, my brother, but he was a good person. He never touched women, drink, or gambling. We are sinful slaves of God. We had more than a few sinful desires." That was the first time I ever heard your grandmother talk that way. We sold the piano too. Nazire got a cataract in one eye. It was just roasting hot that summer. Not a breath of air. The piano money made the house relax. It was a French piano.

Your grandmother called us to her side one day. Her curtains were tightly closed. "I've found out that my husband died. It was he they buried the other day at Karacaahmet. You hid it from me. You weren't ashamed not to have a viewing. The dead man was a devout man who went on the pilgrimage, a great gentleman. I don't want to see anyone. I'm going to retire to a separate room. Prepare my room." She pointed to the bedding cupboard. I began to cry. Nazire took the bedding from the cupboard. She spread out the pillows and the rug with blue roses on it and the nap all worn. She took your grandmother by the arm and led her to the bedding. "The piano will not be played in this house any more," said your grandmother. "We are in mourning. The man of the house is dead." She tucked in the bedding. "Don't grieve," Nazire said. "He no longer belongs to this transitory world." I grew old at age sixteen, my child. I lived through so much then, and I'm living through so much now. How can your father sell innards on the street, how can he! An Armenian woman used to come and give me piano lessons. She used to say, "You have a refined feeling for music." Where we're living now not even the doves coo.

When we were first married, your father and I, we had no money at all. I was ashamed to be seen by people. I didn't have a coat to wear.

"Mother, is my father taking me to Kozma tomorrow?"

"Tomorrow perhaps we'll go to Kadiköy," she said. "Besides, you weren't born here—you were born is Kadiköy."

"I know. I want to go to Kozma's place tomorrow. I don't want to go to Kadiköy."

"You don't love me either," said my mother. "I'm an unlucky woman."

Halikarnas Balıkçısı

The Resurrection of the Unknown Soldier

Travelers flocked from all four points of the compass to assist in the Great Wreath Laying Ceremony, which was to take place the following day. Hotels, motels, inns, and lodging houses were all full to the bursting point. A multitude of tents were even set up around the suburbs of the capital of Gensiania.

At last the much-awaited day dawned. An hour after daybreak the solemn procession assembled, composed of ministers and heads of many states and their vassals and protectorates. There was no lack of democracies at that time; there were democracies of all sorts, advanced ones and retrograde ones, all working for the liberty and prosperity of the human race. The representatives of these mingled with the envoys of the kingdoms and empires. Every delegation was carrying many-colored wreaths to be placed on the Tomb of the Unknown Soldier.

Conspicuous among those who marched was the Great Hurlothrumbo of martial fame. Near him strutted the not-less-warlike two African chiefs, Dindingo of Dululu and the ebony Agiapambo of Farafangana. These had painted their noses with white peace paint (red being the war paint).

The supercilious British envoy, Lord Swig of Swig, earl of Workworthsly, officer of the Order of the Carter, in his red coat contrasted with Sheik Abdullah Eldibbly, who swept the avenue with his flowing white cloak. While Lord Swig was shaven all red like a tomato, the grim-visaged Sheik was black-bearded right to his lower eyelids. He was much revered because his desert territory contained a lot of oil.

Those who most attracted the attention of the crowd were Germany's Baron Mulbach von Kernsdorferhöhe, so stiff in his austere formalism that he must have been poured into his uniform through his collar, as liquid is poured into a kettle; Japan's diminutive and authoritative Tagazaki Kagoshiyama; Hungary's Gyongyos Keszethely; Ukraine's ponderous Rosinsko Warwarofsky; and Italy's goateed, slender Conte Sacarello di Montefiascone.

But before going further with this description, let me mention the tunnel that was being dug beneath the Mount of Glory.

It is not known precisely for what purpose that narrow passage was being excavated. It may have been for laying pipes or cables. But that doesn't matter the least.

The diggers had dug to a point just underneath the Tomb of the Unknown Soldier when a huge mass of earth tumbled down, blocking the passage and shutting in a worker named Jack Legamin, who had loitered behind when the other workmen had departed.

As it was Saturday afternoon, and as the next day was Sunday—that is to say, when no one would come and see that the tunnel was blocked—Legamin thought that he had to dig himself out or suffocate from want of oxygen. Groping around and feeling for an implement, he found neither spade nor shovel. The only thing his hand met was a bar of iron.

He judged that the best thing to do was to poke directly overhead, while standing aside to avoid the falling lumps of earth. He dug about a yard with great difficulty, and his iron lever scraped against a stone. When he struck it, it sounded hollow, whence he concluded that the slab of stone wasn't very thick and that there was nothing above it.

This augured well and, although exhausted, he fell to work with renewed vigor, striking and poking, unaware of the passing of time. At last he succeeded in driving a hole in the stone. He then widened the hole so that it would allow him to pass through. When he had widened the gap he tried to squeeze himself through, but he had hardly shoved himself up to his abdomen when his head bumped against another layer of stone.

He laid his head on the first layer of stone and pushed himself through, lying flat on his back so as to have his hands free to work on the top layer. The slab was quite flat. It was fastened by its edges with concrete to the lateral slabs. He knocked at the concrete so as to unfasten the slab.

Up above, the ceremony of wreath laying was proceeding magnificently. Those who were so fortunate as to be spectators of that unforgettable ceremony were unanimous in stating that such pageantry hadn't been seen for centuries. There were even some who, wishing an extension of the ceremony, cried, "Do, please, imagaine that the Tomb of the Unknown Civilian also lies alongside the Unknown Soldier, for the civilians are killed as much as, and even more than, the soldiers!"

The procession was led by the African emperor of Epithosia. The crown he wore was profusely adorned with the choicest feathers plucked from the sterns of ostriches, which abounded in the sandy wastes of his realms. His most august head resembled much more the Hanging Gardens of Assyria, reputed to be one of the seven wonders of the world. His robe of state, woven from the fur of the tropical fox—an animal long since extinct—trailed full ten yards behind him. Thereupon the names of his illustrious ancestors and their warlike exploits had been woven by the sacred scribes of the chief temple. It was as if the emperor dragged a goodly portion of ancient history in his trail.

After him came His Royal Highness Kiandra the Hundredth, maharajah of Mindir-lala, who had for this occasion donned all the insignia of his royalty. He wore his ponderous and majestic round turban, which symbolized the terrestrial globe as carried by Atlas of mythological fame. The three plumes that shot geyserwise athwart the skies stood for the three principal gods: Brahma, Vishnu, and Siva. On his breast shone the greatest diamond of the world, called the Diamond of Pishar. Behind his highness strode his retinue, including the carpet bearers and the ewer bearers, the ewers being full of the sacred waters of the River Ganges.

Close on His Highness's heels strutted with goose steps the minister extraordinary and envoy plenipotentiary of northern Polygonia, Colonel Techsky, in flowing cordons, ribbons and decorations. On his helmet crouched a huge mythological Tuntunga bird with extended wings.

Beside this Goliath of a man skipped the Lilliputian minister of Belgonium, Monsieur Coceaux de la Trémaillière, with his feathered diplomatic cocked hat, sword, and spurs.

It would be tedious to mention by name every illustrious person who was there. Suffice it to say that the flower and the pick of civilization and the world had gathered at the spot on that memorable day.

Each envoy had to lay the garland on the Unknown Soldier of Gensiania, a country that represented the height of European culture, and then each in turn performed the time-honored rites that had been consecrated by his national tradition.

First, the emperor of Epithosia laid his wreath without uttering a word, and then he performed three somersaults in the air, shrieking as a cat whose tail is being trodden upon.

When the emperor was through with his time-honored ritual, Colonel Techsky of Polygonia came forward. He forthwith shot forth his right arm and, holding it stiffly level, roared thrice: "Tula! Mula! Fula!" in long-drawn martial tones. There was a mighty flourish of trumpets and a thunder of kettledrums, for Polygonia had asked from Gensiania that its delegate's performance should be accompanied by military noises of the most warlike description. Gensiania had readily acquiesced, for it was known that the military preparations of bellicose Polygonia were far in advance of those of Gensiania. Therefore Gensiania firmly believed that its interests lay in the direction of hearty and jolly amity and sincere peacefulness. The noise of the drums was so sudden that some pregnant women were frightened out of their wits and had premature deliveries.

After Colonel Techsky had duly laid his garland, the attendants of His Highness Kiandra, maharajah of Mindirlala, stepped forward and laid a carpet on the avenue. The carpet had been woven by the vestal virgins and religious prostitutes of Mindirlala. As His Highness's sacred feet had been polluted by contact with the avenue that devils of lower castes had trodden upon, and his hands unsanctified by shaking hands with the same, the ewer bearers washed His Highness's hands and feet with purifying Ganges water.

Then His Highness walked to the edge of the carpet and taking from his pocket bearer two pills of nearly the size of walnuts, offered one to the master of ceremonies of Gensiania. The pills were rounded from the sacrosanct dung of the Sacred Cow or Apis of Mindirlala. As Mindirlala was very rich in cotton, and as all the cotton by virtue of the newly signed treaty of commerce had to feed the spinning industry and cotton mills of Gensiania, the master of ceremonies swallowed the pill and remained smiling as if ravished with delight at the honor done him. Then His Highness, turning toward the Tomb of the Unknown Soldier, pronounced the three sacramental grand names: "Brahma! Vishnu! Siva!"

A whisper as that of a wind-touched forest ran over the hushed crowd, for what mortal can hear words of so transcending a spirituality and not be hushed into profound reverence?

But lo! the slab of marble covering the Unknown Soldier's Tomb began slowly to rise as from beneath—O, ominous spectacle—there appeared the uncanny face of the Unknown Soldier! He was most naturally deathly pale, and he looked in wild-eyed amazement at the crowd that surrounded him.

His Highness of Mindirlala, paralyzed with awe, paused stock-still in the very middle of his incantations.

Many in the crowd rubbed their eyes and thought themselves troubled by a vivid hallucination. But the Unknown Soldier continued to emerge inexorably, and, as he did so, his head and shoulders caught at the garlands of flowers, so that when the Unknown Veteran towered to full height above the live human beings, he seemed to be crowned, coated, belted, and petticoated with a variety of flowers.

A sensation of bloodcurdling fear passed over the amassed people. All faces went white as they gaped aghast at the Soldier. No sound was heard except the occasional clang of a death knell that had been ringing for the Unknown Soldier. The very sky seemed to pale as it beheld the Unknown Warrior.

The only people who remained undeterred were, of course, the staunch soldiers and their ebullient officer, whose vocation it was never to be afraid, come what may.

The master of ceremonies also was full of courage. He looked at the Unknown Soldier with considerable wrath and annoyance because of the latter's insolence and his interruption of an officially negotiated, codified, arranged, agreed, recorded, signed, and countersigned social function. What impudence wantonly to disturb the ceremony with such a preposterous item as his resurrection! His sacrosanct duty was to remain dead until Kingdom Come.

The undaunted soldiers were expecting orders to fire at the disturber of the celebration, and were on the verge of action. The commanding officer, who now had to deal with an unprecedented emergency, snatched out his pocketbook of regulations, exclaiming, "Damn him!" He hastily turned the pages scanning the contents. But he found no mention of the steps he had to take in such an occurrence.

What had happened in the Unknown Soldier's grave was this: Legamin was dead tired after his long exertions. He lay motionless in the tomb. But the martial noise that had put a resounding finale to Techsky's performances startled him to new action. Gathering all his force, he pushed the marble slab and succeeded in lifting it. And, dazed as he was, he pushed his head out of the opening.

Legamin, ignorant of his point of emergence, was much awed by the splendor and pomp that surrounded him, the more so when he beheld the looks of horrified astonishment focused upon his person. Being unsteady on his legs, he stumbled a step or two toward His Highness of Mindirlala, who, topped by his huge turban, was standing right in front of him.

His Highness of Mindirlala thought he was being punished by the angered gods for having offered pills of the sacred dung to a low-caste infidel, and that therefore the spirit of ever-young, always being-born Brahma had passed into the corpse of the Dead Soldier, resurrecting him to smite him there and then. His Highness wavered uncertainly, unable to move, speak or cry.

Meanwhile, the commanding officer closed the instruction booklet with a snap, exclaiming, "Dammit! What the deuce have I now to do?" He forthwith turned to his privates, realizing there was nothing so effective as prompt action in all emergencies, and furthermore, since immediate action meant starting to shoot, who should be shot?

The instruction book said nothing about who the enemy was. Had they to shoot at the Unknown Soldier, at the crowd or at one another? That was the question. But since he could find no answer, he took what seemed to him the best course—to wit, the course that seemed to him to carry the least responsibility.

He roared, "Fire off! Volley forth into the skies!"

Then came the question when to stop firing. He couldn't make up his mind. But after a while he was saved the difficulty of deciding upon a course when his soldiers consumed all their ammunition.

When the first volley thundered, His Most Gracious Highness of Mindirlala emitted a heartrending shriek and took to his heels. Everybody's nerves were on edge. The deafening reports were a signal for a general stampede downhill. The Unknown Soldier, whose teeth chattered from fright, bolted and dashed after His Highness of Mindirlala. People were running and screaming, thinking the ghost of the Unknown Soldier was trying to catch them.

The firing of the rifles and the whizzing of the bullets transformed the disarray into a wholesale rout. As the surging mob tore through the streets with the ghost of the Unknown Soldier in close pursuit, an American who was sedately sipping a martini in a bar said, "What's all this noise about? Probably a Hollywood movie mogul is on location for a new burlesque film." And he ordered another cocktail.

Orhan Hançerlioğlu

Pity

Translated by Gönül Suveren

Recep sat up in bed and looked down at his wife, who was sleeping beside him, stretched out on the couch like a patient about to expire. He listened to her tired breathing interrupted by deep sighs. Her fists were closed tight on calloused palms. Sweat streaming from her forehead dissolved the dirt caked on her weather-beaten face and ran down to her sunburned neck, where it gathered in the pits of her shoulders and from there spread over her body. As she breathed, her bosom rose slowly as if it were being thrust forward from within. Her heavy and deformed breasts, like overturned cups, seemed to struggle against the weight of the darkness. Looking at his wife for a long time, Recep grumbled: "One would have to be blind to call this a woman!"

Though the night was far advanced, the air was not getting cooler. Recep felt for his shoes in the dark and put them on. Habit guided his steps as he walked in the heavy darkness. He left the house to lie down on the ground outside.

The village seemed to have melted away under the hot and black night.

To pass the time, he opened his wooden tobacco box and rolled a cigarette. He had a strange feeling of uneasiness or oppression in his heart, one which couldn't be compared with the grief he had felt the day he had lost the election for village alderman, or with the sorrow he had suffered when he had been thoroughly beaten by the police, or with the pain he had known when he received only fifty liras for a cartload of melons and for which seventy-five had been offered only an hour later. During the last few days, nothing but nothing had happened to upset him. The beets had been planted in time, the injured foot of the ox had healed, the cow had calved, the police sergeant had played cards with him in the coffeehouse. There was absolutely no reason for him to be discontented with his life. He turned restlessly from right to left on the cool earth. Then he gave up thinking and fell asleep.

When he awoke, the sun was quite high. His wife and daughters had gone down to the plain long ago. Stretching himself lazily, he got up, walked toward the brick cottage, crumbled some bread in a cup of buttermilk he found by the fireplace and satisfied his hunger. His wife had folded the bedding and piled it in a corner. He had nothing to do but go the the coffeehouse and play cards, though he was not inclined to do so today. The uneasiness in his heart had seized his whole body. By God, what was it? No rain, which had always made him uncomfortable, but not like this.... When the earth had not given back the seed that had been planted, Recep had always felt uneasy, but not like this...When the tax collector had knocked on the door, Recep had felt uneasy, but not like this...

"Let me go to the fields," he thought. "That might change my mood...and it would let me see what the women have done."

The good rains had ended long ago....Now a burning heat scorched the earth. A heavy smell spread from the dunghill in the yards of the brick cottages. Under the sun the village was like a body in a trance, soundless and motionless.

After passing the last houses in the village, Recep stopped for a moment. He mopped his sweat with his handkerchief, muttering, "If hell is so hot, one must find a way to Heaven." Blinking in the sunlight, he stared at the plain. The beet fields were filled with women who looked in their large purple trousers like huge red cabbages. His eyes smarted from the sweat trickling from his brow. The fields that he saw through his eyelashes seemed to lie far away, vanishing like a dream. The plain from end to end was in feverish activity. The hoes toiled incessantly, the soil, baked and cracked by the sun, fell to pieces; the roots of the beets took a deep breath of fresh air.

With a last effort, Recep reached his wife and stood before her.

"Are you now half through?" he asked.

Bowing her head to the ground, which was sprinkled with her sweat, she whispered in a voice not unlike a moan, "There are still twenty acres left."

"Then what have you been doing all these ten days?"

The woman continued her work without reply.

Recep, with the conceit of one who has been created a male, cried out harshly, "I am speaking to you, woman, damn you....Are you deaf?"

The woman raised her head slowly...looked at her husband without uttering a word. She was panting like a dying animal. Her eyes, inflamed with sweat and dust, were as dark as a cloudy night. Her face reflected all the misery of mankind; the whole humiliation of life quivered on it.

Recep suddenly felt confused and shaken. At last he knew the reason for the uneasiness that had crushed his heart: he had pitied his wife.

The next evening Recep returned from the marketplace with two ship's lanterns in his hand and said to his wife, "Take these lanterns. It is too hot in the daytime—you get too tired. You can work at night from now on...."

Yakup Kadri Karaosmanoğlu

from *Mansion for Rent*

Translated by Robert P. Finn

Naim Efendi's family had not moved to Kanlıca this year. Most pleased of all about this were Servet Bey's children, because that particular corner of the Bosporus was not suitable for any modern amusements. During the months that they stayed in Kanlıca, they had to take a lengthy break from their pastime of walking by the shop windows of Beyoğlu–a pastime that offered a thousand chances for love and romance in each step. Servet Bey's son, Cemil, in spite of being only a twenty-year-old student, was a faithful client of the great restaurants, nightclubs, bars, and certain of the houses of pleasure in Beyoğlu. At this young age, he had already a number of fixations, certain habits he could not give up and pleasures and enjoyments that had become second nature to him. He occasionally spoke to his sister about one of his mistresses, whom he loved madly. Naturally, this mistress of his was one of those people who stayed in Beyoğlu both winter and summer. So for Cemil, country life had become an unendurable affliction, because of all these inconveniences. One of his most unpleasant duties was to either run across the Karaköy bridge and catch the last boat just at the hour when everything was beginning to happen in Beyoğlu or else, having missed the boat, whether by accident or on purpose, to get involved, at great moral and financial cost, in methods of making things right at home by showing some reasonable cause for his nocturnal flights. His father, who was a freethinker in everything else, never showed himself amenable to his son's spending nights away from home. Servet Bey, whether from convictions concerning domestic life and propriety or merely from a paternal feeling, united, in this matter, with his father-in-law, and found the anxieties of his wife justified.

"I don't say that he shouldn't go out and enjoy himself," he said. "He is young and can take care of himself. He was brought up according to modern, up-to-date standards. Naturally, he will go through many phases in life. However, this existence must at no time come to a point where it infringes upon his health. I don't say that he should hide himself in the house at dusk, like the common people of Istanbul, and go to sleep as soon as he eats his food. No, no....But he must at least be in the house before midnight, and when that is absolutely impossible, return home before dawn."

When her father spoke this way, Seniha, who was well-acquainted with her brother's little secrets, would laugh mischievously to herself, but then, every word and action seemed comic to her. Her father, in his opinions and even in his movements, seemed particularly primitive, old-fashioned, and strange to her, as did her grandfather's personality and her mother's mannerisms. She was, really, what the French term a *fin de siècle* girl–*fin de siècle,* the symbol of a new kind of society, free from any restriction of the present or the past in both her external and internal behavior and subject to the dictates of a future that was only then beginning to take shape. Seniha always resembled the pictures in the latest fashion magazines. Her thin, supple body was in constant tranformation, like that of a silkworm. The timbre of her voice, the harmony of her movements, and even her shape continually changed, the color of her green eyes altered according to the brightness of the sunlight. Her personality remained the same. She had a spirit just like the color of her eyes—sometimes rebellious, afflicted, overcast, and malevolent, sometimes sparkling and sweet. But this small, devilish person had one unvarying characteristic, and that was her playfulness and coquettishness. The literary material from which she derived the most pleasure were the novels of Gyp, new plays, and Parisian humor magazines. Gyp was a second mother, a second governess, to her. The half-male, half-female young women in this author's novels, with their free manners and free spirits, were the models she followed. It may be said that her only occupation all day long was bringing these characters to life.

One rainy day Seniha was wandering around the house in a very bored mood, swinging the small ship she had in her hand back and forth, hitting the doors and furniture. She was fidgeting in the house, going now upstairs, now down, as if she were some great bird confined to a narrow cage. At one moment, her grandfather, Naim Efendi, appeared in front of her. The old man was passing from one room to another. He was enveloped in a fur coat and had a volume with a thick cover in one hand. Seniha leaped at him like a greyhound waiting for its prey and, hitting a few strong blows on the thick binding of the book with her whip, said:

"Grandfather, you are as suffocating as life itself!" Then she went away, whistling like a street urchin.

Naim Efendi looked after his grandchild for a while in a daze and then said to himself, "My goodness!" What a strange child!"

However, Naim Efendi called whatever happened "strange." His feelings never descended to the level of anger. In fact, everything he heard and saw was so extremely odd to him that none of it reached a level of reality capable of his comprehension. To be angry or offended one must necessarily understand a little. But Naim Efendi was unable to understand the meaning or the manner of life of either his son-in-law or his grand-children. *Alla franca, the needs of the age*—the new usage of these words in the mansion had not sufficiently illuminated them in his view. Sometimes there were slight quarrels with his son-in-law and, more frequently, with his daughter. Naim Efendi would say to her:

"My dear, I'm not at all pleased with your children's manners and behavior. I believe this Polish woman has given them an improper education. Seniha is almost eighteen, but she's still as flighty and naughty as an eight-year-old. Cemil's not even twenty, but he leads the life of a man of thirty. How dare he come and stand about in front of you after dinner, smoking cigarettes? He listens to neither you nor his father....As for me, I pretend to see nothing. I'm afraid to open my mouth and say anything to either one of them. God forbid they should be disobedient to me. I'm afraid they would answer me back...."

In spite of everything, Naim Efendi was still the only authority who inspired fear and respect in the house. If he showed a little force, it was still likely that everything would go on properly. But, unfortunately, he was a softhearted grandfather. Then too, the manners he had received didn't permit him to speak with anyone—no matter whom—in a loud voice. One day–it was in the first days of the revolution–he entered into a political discussion with his son-in-law. Naim Efendi was complaining about the newspapers.

"Sir, all well and good....But these newspapers are being very forward," he said. "They have no respect toward anything in the country. They aren't embarrassed to use the coarsest epithets against the Sultan and his ministers. They call it public life, and then they begin to attack everyone's private life. The other day I visited Hasip Pasha in Erenköy. The poor man was in such a state that I felt sorry for him. It appears that the newspaper *Tanin* is talking about some embezzling and misappropriation that occurred when he was minister, however..."

His son-in-law, Servet Bey, interrupted him with an impatient gesture:

"However...no, Sir, when one regime leaves and another regime takes its place, quite naturally, the men of the new regime will ask for an accounting from those of the old. Besides, you know better than everyone else what kind of regime the old one was."

Naim Efendi was as embarrassed as a child.

"Don't get angry," he said. "I didn't say that an accounting shouldn't be asked for. God forbid! Only, think for a minute. I appeal to your conscience. How can an accounting be asked for from such an upright person as Hasip Pasha?...I assure you, he hasn't five cents to his name. He gets by on his wife's money."

Servet Bey said, with the inner boredom of someone who is speaking to a person who does not have to account for himself or his own actions:

"Sir, there is a court and portal of justice in this country. Hasip Pasha gets taken to court, surrendered to justice. If he's innocent, all well and good, if he's not....The guillotine, sir, the guillotine cleans....All the old heads must be cut off, not just those of the dishonorable!"

Naim Efendi felt the savage allusion in the last sentence, but couldn't find the strength within himself to answer. He lowered his eyes to the floor and pondered deeply.

Bilge Karasu

The Bosporus

Translated by Frederic Stark

I

It must have gone WOOM, vibrating and rocking; and that marked the end of the small world of bouncing legs, fleeing, lithe bodies, stealthy paws, and sharp teeth exercising their absolute sovereignty in their respective areas of shrubbery, undergrowth, high branches, and tall tops of

the most ancient agglomeration of vegetal life—vulgar, similar to all other forests east and west—the first distinctive quality of which must have come with its utter destruction and disappearance into the bottom of a new sea,

which, at the intersection of the two bodies of water, one deadly salt, one mortally sweet, came into being in the awful clash that followed

the Collapse.

This is how I like to imagine, without the slightest regard for geological truth or paleontological accuracy what must have been

hundreds of thousands of years ago at the origin of the Bosporus, Bosphorus—in Turkish, the *Boğaz,* meaning "strait," "channel," and, also, "gullet."

And then, came the reign of the Fish.

The Fish, the drifting, streaming, swarming, jumping streak of light and darkness

(as seen from a second- or third-floor window, a half-attic, half-top-floor balcony, overlooking the stream, which reflects all the hours of the day in its colors, where the schools of silvery-scaled or skinned fish, swarming in from either of the seas north or south, will be followed by the black dolphins, swimming right under the surface, becoming the light itself or diving into the dark waters, and then, there is nothing left),

and of

the Gull, the death, or, at least,

one of the faces of death, white, plunging and soaring, croak-voiced, glutton;

and later, much later,

the reign of Man, king and subject, lord and slave, fed-full and food.

(All monarchs, kings, emperors, sultans, tyrants seem to have had a particular devotion to the fish, settled or stray, giving them their feed every now and again, sacrificing for them their best rebels, their most disobedient subjects, their finest flesh of dissent. Lovers have been seen floating gray-green-white, continuing their purposeless pursuit along with swollen sheep and watermelon refuse; but only occasionally, since they still prefer wells, revolvers, or sleeping pills. Mothers with child, children, fishermen will now and then offer themselves. Voluntarily. Drunkards will slip and sleep or sleep and slip,

> whichever,
> and the fish will delight on eyes, sexes, lips, and nips.)

(And, of course, to have another parenthesis, we must speak of Man feeding, *viz,* catching, frying, boiling, grilling and eating because he needs, because he has to, because of what other people will think, because it is or is not fashionable, because to drink one must have some fish, because fish helps in the dark, cool beds. But of that, later.)

Of Man, I say,

> who no matter what the period, epoch, age, year,
> no matter what state, army power, and direction of expansion, killing, plundering, burning down, or building,
> no matter what faith, truth and lie, greed or self-effacement, belief and illusion

may have been his case,

> continued, endured, adventured, stayed, and died on these shores, on this stage
> (this immense stage where puppets are still puppets, not a bit grown out of their

undersized universe,

> where the strings are no longer visible against the intemporal background and

where the play

> with infinite and infinitesimal variations has been progressing for a few thousand

years past

> for the benefit of no spectator
> but the stage itself.)
> Man, for whom stands the Fish.

I've had more than enough of those ninnyish tales for turbulent young tribes and nervous or sensitive children of the last twenty-five centuries, those legends of barks and boats and sailors, of fleets and fleece and rocks and what not, appearing to think of the strait as the way to Heaven and Hell, although they pretty well knew, those people, that it was nothing but a path conducting into a large, enclosed garden.

I shall still think of (and imagine) the two seas when they clashed and caused the death of all the ancient fish

> another legend, this, but more attractive,
> the ancient fish of the ancient Euxine who,
> fleeing away from the atrocious suffering of the salty death brought in by the waters

of the Mediterranean, rolled over each other and tumbled, in a huge ball, crashed, broke

> into what was to become the pit, where, even today, it is said, there can be no life,

the pit no living thing can cross the border of

> with impunity.
> Putrefaction solidified.
> But tamed. Tamed, circumscribed, turned into a burnished antique to keep

forever silent in its half-smile, open only to endless conjectures,

> price and counterweight of life.

The pit no living thing can cross the border of, because there is no escape from death, and the Fish know it well now but still fail to teach it to Man.

So, when the fish of the Mediterranean, clever and cunning, must have invaded by stages, and, taking their time at that, the ancient grounds

(or should we say "waters"?)

of the fish that were no more, in prefiguration of the columns of humans who were to cross this new path of water into what was now the Other Continent,

continuity entered the stage against eternity.

The City followed.

But man—as well as beast— must eat, and now the sea fish was a new variety to men who had come a long way, inland, eating, whether smaller or larger, nothing but land food, including lake and river fish. Now they would be able to acquaint themselves with the supreme contradiction, the resolution of so many contradictions that it became outright outrageous, the

Sea Fish.

Paleontology, Darwin, and molecular biology were still a bit far-off in the dark distance. Poor, poor creatures, who didn't know!

Strange or not, food is supposed to be eaten and, once eaten, taken for granted with no attention whatsoever paid to its origin.

Therefore, no wondering any longer. Fish is there to feed on and catch as catch can.

II

Gods must have played with the idea of Triskelion long before any human artist distilled the perfection of movement within an absolutely still disk, when,

thrusting their thumb into the thick paint of the earth, and, wriggling it downward, as it were, caused the

the Collapse.

Causing thus the Triskelion to take shape as can best be seen from either of the three promontories on the outer ridge of the central sea, holding apart the three capes that *are* the City.

Humans had to be more rational and select one of those promontories to make into an acropolis, building their city behind it.

So that whoever goes there will see the three legs of sea, each with its philosophical implication:

1. blind alley, ending in ever-increasing, cannibal mud;
2. open sea—although deceitfully so, since there will be a chain of seas opening into each other through more and more ridiculous straits, while the seas will become larger and larger; and,

3. the Strait, the Gullet, opening into the fiercer and sudden storms of the Enclosed Garden.

Here we dwell today.

To my mind, all beginnings are in the City.

To take which, warriors built fortresses right at the midpoint of the channel. The only things that remain from the past, the only buildings considered important enough to be made strong. None but the warriors have ever been able to mark their passage across the Stage with enduring stone.

All the other humans, conscious, obviously, of their mortality as well as of

their own mortality as well as of

everything else's, contented themselves with flimsy structures, great or small, which,

no matter how imposing or charming in their youths, were slowly conquered and defeated by rot, by salt, by air, by fire.

The Four Elements in their sway.

The last of the Great, an engraving of which, made barely a hundred years ago, shows a most magnificent structure of beautifully carved, painted, designed wood, peacefully mirroring itself in the quiet water under the embankment, peacefully dying away until a few years ago, still carrying the ominous name of Snake Mansion into its grave, its dust and ash

that is to say, into a host of smaller dwellings, with hens and cocks soiling its patch of grass just in front of its door as well as the floors within,

and the cats darting from its threshold to the wild fig tree

grown there to mark the end of its splendor

(fig trees are always one of the masks of death for walls in the City)

and back,

finally,

one winter night a few years ago,

merely turned into a large, single blaze hardly reflected by the water below (because the road running along the line of the shore had long since cut it from its basic element) and disappared into a heap of black nothingness, burying for eternity the legend of its secret passages, devised to allow the conspiring owners to escape any raid of the imperial police.

There will certainly be a block of concrete, some day, standing where the fig tree used to stand, catless, henless, vibrating in the flow of cars on the road.

Palaces were built, and schools, and warehouses, and hospitals and landings and, in greater and greater numbers nowadays, blocks of concrete to accommodate city people, foreigners, the sick rich, and the sick poor. But, apart from the sick, all the others will go down to the sea to swim, to sail, to eat, and to fish,

then up, back to their rooms, to make love.

The rich will fish, and the poor will fish, and, occasionally, a cat will fish, using its paw to retrieve what it considers to be its right and its share from among the still-tail-swishing half-corpses on the flags of the embankment.

(Yes, there are rare cats, robust gray tigers, typical citizens of this fish country, never hungry because so cunning and quick and nimble, who will come down to the shore with their masters, watch them throw their lines, watch them fail or succeed, never touch a fish, but only wait for the first freak to be given to them. Then they will play with it, for hours on end as it were, without so much as tearing the fish apart or making it bleed, although they appear to use fang and claw. Such artistic cats, and yet, they exist; they are the most ferocious bird hunters in their gardens, the bloodthirstiest rat killers in the attics and closets and boathouses of the old mansions.)

And, as all beginnings are in the City, the fishing lines and the fishing rods will begin to give a display of their skill or their foolishness in the heart of the City,

at the Point of the Seraglio, first,

on the south bank of the Old City, toward the largest and the longest leg of Triskelion,

on the north, at the Bridge, flimsy, tattering old structure bridging over the muddy estuary, most unwashed leg of the Triskelion, the Old and the Newer Cities, suspended, as it were, between the New Mosque of the seventeenth century and the old Genoese Tower,

(Genoese? Hardly....Twelve times a hundred years

old, rather) —

the Bridge, we were saying, parting, in a way, the muddy sea arm from the clean, the stale waters from the fresh, thus making a clean start for the Bosporus,

the Bridge, then, with its hundreds of fishermen, professional or not, with its scores of kitchen boats which, in the proper season will be frying the freshly caught fish into a coarse-shaped sandwich to end, then and there, in the greedy blank mouths of the time-pressed crowd

and its real kitchens, which, all the year round, will serve the fish still sizzling. (Is it life still sizzling in them?)

Far up the Bosporus, in posh restaurants, customers will watch the fish (swimming the more furiously, in their small glass cages, for being watched) to select the bite they would like to have. Bitter for the fish and

bitter for the man who pays to eat a prisoner.

Forget the fish for a moment, it will come back of itself, anyway.

Back in the tea gardens, whether spreading on plain earth, under the shade of trees that must have been standing at the same place before the great revolutions, French or industrial, perhaps even before the idea of any decline ever so much as flashed in the minds of the emperor's subjects, old people basking in the afternoon sun, having their tea, younger men playing endless games of backgammon (perhaps even now, in some of those gardens, having the set of the game brought with a prize Turkish delight to be eaten by...

that was one of the great mysteries of my childhood
since I could never understand who was supposed to eat
it, the winner for having won or the loser for having
let win? It was always the child or children hanging

around the players who would be offered the Turkish
delight....),
also women, old and young, with a hoard of young children running, romping, crying,
falling, all having tea and an occasional *simit* *

or on half- or all-concrete floors, sometimes on boards extending over the sea, still
tea gardens, the gently waisted, small tea glass and the hookah being the common
features,

or, in the winter, in smoky teahouses, forcing the customers to society, elbowing
each other, making their talk become unrealistic with noise and interference,

the sound of dice and the clack of backgammon punctuating the din,

or at one certain spot, where some of the best yogurt can be eaten,

people will be sitting, relishing the particular cult of that place, whether it is tea
or water drinking, yogurt eating or, even, stately-indian-corn-gnawing.

For years innumerable people from the city have come, and will come, to this or
that spot to have the particular thing one should have there.

And this is not simple fashion or snobbishness

It is part of life.

Nightingale-listening is not to be found only in books of sixty or seventy years
ago. People will still rush to listening posts, in the mating season, after late parties, in
their blood to hear the delicate trills. Only now, and that also is becoming an institution,
they will go there in cars, while in those days scores of slender elegant boats would nudge
each other in the stream, the rowing slow, the pleasure longer, the talk hushed.

Nowadays, boats will crowd on the black waters at nightfall or much later, just
before daybreak, for a much more silent ritual. Only now and then a jagged voice will
shout a command, the only sound to make the lantern-speckled dark vibrate, apart from
an occasional siren of a late or early ferry and the far-off beeping of cars on both coasts.

This is sport to a few, earning a living for most.

In the evening the smell of fish will become more intense, more piercing. The
wind will carry away the smoke and bring a whiff of aniseed-flavored alcohol. Cats on
doorsteps will sniff, motionless.

And in the continuous stream of the fish and the fishing, of Man eating and dying
and being buried, old or less old, in
the graveyards, old or less old, on
the hillsides, overlooking in their
stillness the crowding life below—
Man, then, eating and not remembering that he will die, drinking instead,
tearing into shred the fish caught the night before or even a few hours previously,
discarding the bones
and feeding every hungry restaurant
and drinking-house cats, tabby, skinny,
yet strong and cunning,
in the cheaper places, and

*A bagellike sesame ring.

discarding bone, skin, and head, but tearing the fish into shreds, all the same in Sunday "in" places,

cats, again, will be the first, if not the only, witnesses of the return of the boats in the morning mist, black against the fainter black of the sky, loaded with fish life,

with fish life that was

and will become again,

while the streets, paved, cobbled, straight, tortuous, flat or steep, will still be asleep.

Refik Halit Karay

The Gray Donkey

Translated by Robert P. Finn

The children carrying water from the river brought the news that there was an old man lying on the mountain road. There was a gray donkey there, too, wandering about by himself. Hüsmen Hoca* said:

"Let's go and see."

It was near evening. A thick, pungent cloud rose from the rice fields and spread toward a swampy, malaria-infested hollow where two creeks united. From behind the split, charred trunks of five or ten old, lifeless willows, the sun extended a dim light that glinted here and there on the stagnant waters. These lighted patches looked like open stretches in a cloudy sky above the middle of a gray, damp plain. Slowly, they became cloudy and closed and were swallowed up.

Three villagers climbed up the broken, muddy footpath with difficulty, one behind the other. One of them coughed very heavily, like a horse with parasites.

First they saw the gray donkey. It was standing in the middle of the heath, in a dirty, dusty spot. No doubt it had been jumping about, rolling, and playing; now it was taking its ease with a pleased expression, nonchalantly surveying the setting sun.

The Hoca called out:

"Well, where are you, traveler?"

On the other side an old, exhausted man was sitting with his back to a tired-out wild pear tree and breathing heavily. He looked at the newcomers with lusterless eyes and pointed with his hands to his chest. He answered the questions "What's the matter?" and "What's wrong, Pop?" with incomprehensible answers in a gasping rattle that resembled breathing or sighing more than speech.

The villagers, thinking that he was dying, sank down beside him and waited all together. But the sick man was recovering and becoming more lively. He was poorly dressed, with a cotton turban and a purple robe. The part of his face that was left uncovered by his rough, gray beard had been roasted by the sun and was covered with wrinkles and folds. Underneath his loose, thick eyelids, his small eyes were such a light shade of blue that they were almost white. They stared out at people with the openness of a child's glance. Gradually, color came to his face and brightness to his eyes. At the same time, he said some things in an exhausted voice with his back still supported against the pear tree, no doubt relating how he had come from great distances and would travel on to the same. At Hüsmen Hoca's proposal—"Take him to the guest room, and let him lie

---

* A Muslim teacher similar to a rabbi.

there!"–they all helped him to mount the donkey. They descended with a thousand difficulties, sliding over stones and earth and holding on to both sides to give him no opportunity to fall.

The sun had gone, and the waters behind it shone no more. Putting their giant heads wrapped with smoke and clouds toward one another, the large, sheet mountains surrounding them had long since gone to sleep.

The village lay buried in layers of shadows of cliffs, waiting for darkness, with neither a light in a window nor a sound in the road.

An occasional face extended itself from a window in response to the uproar of those arriving. The oxen were lowing in the stables. Hüsmen shouted the news:

"Where are you, everybody? Come on out, we have a guest!"

Then a number of people, wearing their white underwear, emerged with illuminated lamps in their hands and went straight toward the guest room of the village. They moved puzzledly in a haze of smoke and light, sending flashes of light into darkened corners with their lamps and, inadvertently, kicking hardened lumps of manure. This was one of the naked, trackless, wretched villages of Anatolia, two days by road from the nearest town. Sometimes, when the weather was very dry and allowed the opportunity to ford the Kızılırmak, travelers passing on foot from one province to another would leave the highway, pass by this village, and thereby save themselves two days' travel. By this means, then, five or ten people in a year–five or ten poor, exhausted strangers–would come at a dismal hour like this and knock at the doors of the villagers. At that time Hüsmen, the headman, would send word to the person whose turn it was to put up the visitors and that person would settle the travelers in his guest room, where, whether it was winter or summer, an oven would be burning seemingly inexhaustible chips of fuel. The village would learn of the state of the world from the lies and misinformation brought by these arrant, ignorant people.

The sick man quieted down.

"It's the chest," he said. "Every once in a while it pulls."

One of the villagers hung a copper bucket filled with milk on the hook of the fireplace. The flames of the chips beat on it, and the liquid inside began to rise in colors like a soap bubble. The villager took it down and gave a cup of it to the old man. He drank it greedily, blowing on it as he did so. As soon as the milk was finished, the old codger began to cry. His whole body was shaking. The villagers sat cross-legged across from him and waited impatiently for an opportunity to speak. The young men stood in front of the door, their eyes narrowed with sleep. They could understand nothing of this silent, sick guest. His crying didn't stop. On the contrary, it became more frequent, and deeper. At one point the sick man motioned with his hands for the men to come nearer. With Hüsmen first and the other, older men behind him, they surrounded the old man. The youths remained at the door, full of curiosity but not daring to approach any nearer; the traveler was probably relating some problem with difficulty. Perhaps he was making his will. Every once in a while, they heard Hüsmen say:

"Don't worry. Relax, we'll take care of you." Suddenly the old men quickly bent down to the floor. Then they suddenly stood up, Hüsmen muttered:

"He's gone to his rest!" One of the logs in the fireplace fell and illuminated the face of the dead man with a sharp light, then went out. Outside, a donkey brayed continuously.

The traveler had found time to make his last request. He was donating the eight pieces of gold he had stuck in this belt, together with his gray donkey, to the Hejaz.*

The villagers, returning from the cemetery couldn't figure out what they would do with the donkey and the money remaining in their hands, or how they would carry out the old man's request. They stood discussing this under the grape arbor. Finally, they decided to go to town and seek information from the judge. Within the week, Hüsmen would take the donkey with him and set off.

The animal achieved some importance; generous supplies of grain were placed in front of him, and corn husks spread for him. This was done uncomplainingly, respectfully, promptly, as if it were a religious duty. The villagers would frequently remember and ask one another, "Has the gray donkey been taken to be watered? Has he been given barley?"

One morning, at first light, they all accompanied Hüsmen Hoca as far as the mill and bade him farewell. The gray donkey, tied to the Hoca's donkey, went happily, unburdened, his tail waving. The silver rays of the sun made Hüsmen's faded felt sheath glow like velvet.

The road was a long and boring one. Once the blades of rice protruding from still waters and the green of the reeds growing along the banks of the ditches were hidden behind the slopes, the dry and straight way continued, desolate and scorched, for over two days, without passing by a village, a mill, or even a waterhole shaded by two undersized willows. Then an ascent with steep cliffs and a fearful pass presented itself. At the top of the hill, a cool breeze and a pleasant view appeared. A narrow creek gleamed like the back of a short sword from the middle of the groups of quinces and apples; it seemed lush, green and fertile. The white, flat road, outlined by telegraph poles, stretched in coils toward the mountains.

Hüsmen set out early for the government building in the morning, after he had spent the night in an inn.

The tiny town had a mansion with balconies and towers that looked like a pavilion in a park. It had, however, never been completed. The unplastered brick walls had opened in spots and become nesting places for pigeons. The top floor stood waiting with its scaffolding, windowless and plasterless. On one side there was an abandoned limestone quarry, and a little to the other side stood an open shed remaining from when the workers had been there, with everything left just as it had been. The building had long since begun to fall apart.

A police sergeant with no hat or jacket asked Hüsmen what he wanted. The Hoca started to tell the story of the old man from the very beginning, relating how the children coming from the stream carrying water had brought the news that they had found him. Before Hüsmen had reached the halfway point in his story, the policeman casually walked away from him and began to throw bread to the ducks swimming in the river, then turned to a turbaned old man smoking a *nargile*† in the hut in the corner and asked:

"What's that, Hoca Efendi, your morning pick-me-up?"

---

*The section of the Arabian peninsula, containing the holy cities of Mecca and Medina, that is sacred to Muslims.

†Water pipe, hookah.

When Hüsmen learned that the judge had gone to Istanbul on leave, he wanted to at least tell his business to the *kaymakam*.* Leaving his shoes at the door and walking humbly in the ripped socks that exposed his toes, he folded his hands before him and began his story.

The *kaymakam* was a nasal, toothless kind of person, who wore a discolored, indigo blue jacket and dyed his mustache. Without showing the forbearance of even listening to the entire story, he said:

"Call the sergeant!"

For five days, Hüsmen Hoca wandered around the town, telling his tale to all he came across. The police sergeant would neither take the donkey nor let him go. At last, someone emerged who sympathized with Hüsmen and who persuaded the sergeant by saying: "Let him go and come back in two weeks. Let's leave the whole thing up to the judge."

The judge from this place was well known. The townspeople called him Judge Melonhead. He solved every problem and unraveled every knot. When coming from the market with his orange cape and red umbrella, he would place his hand to his chest and smile so benignly at all whom he met that the people were crazy about him.

Hüsmen returned to his village by the road by which he had come, with the donkey again tied to his saddle. He had gone through a great deal of money in the town, where bread and barley were expensive, both for himself and for the donkey, who had to be fed well. The villagers who constituted the council paid little attention to the matter of expenses, saying:

"The donkey is related to sacred things. Therefore, it's our duty to look after it!"

And Hüsmen never complained of his tiredness, since working for God made him forget the vicissitudes of travel.

In the week of the second trip to town, however, he was obliged to return home again with the donkey behind him. The judge had still not arrived. The police sergeant scolded the Hoca:

"You dumb lout, what's your hurry?"

The villagers doubted whether a donkey that had been donated to charity could be used in work or not, so they would have nothing to do with it.

Hüsmen's third journey home was like the previous ones, with the donkey trailing behind him. Someone with a sharp eye saw from the distance that the gray donkey had returned, and he spread the news to the village. Everyone was waiting with bewilderment and concern. Before Hüsmen even got down from his donkey, he said with a happy voice:

"Well, what the hell, we were supposed to bring a witness."

He explained the matter in one burst. Really, how had they not thought of this? But, there was no loss; the judge would accept the donkey. He'd write out the deed, three people would go in a week, and, if they had to, they'd swear an oath....

The gray donkey became fat from eating the fodder they spread before him as recompense for the occasional loadless journeys he had made. When they took him to be watered, he would run over to the female donkeys and, gradually, he became more and more ill-tempered. In this way, two and one-half months passed by.

Finally, preparations for the last trip were completed. As the travelers were saying goodbye in front of the mill, the newly dawned sun illuminated the particles of dust

*District chief in a province.

raised by the small caravan. The villagers trailing toward the rise looked to those who remained behind as if they were rising in a gilded cloud toward the heavens.

The gray donkey did not return again. The people of the village, looking at the deeds and the stamps affixed to them, finally decided that, according to the worth and honor of the donation of the donkey, it would go as far as the Hejaz without a load or any hardship, and that there it would carry water from the sacred well of Zemzem. In fact, on night in a dream Hüsmen saw the saddle of the donkey covered with green velvet, and completely believed it.

Anyway, they all spoke often about the donkey with the enthusiasm that is felt when one is doing something other than one's job. Forgetting how it had mounted the mares, they would fool one another and tell one another how, when left by itself, it would move its head from side to side and start to recite a litany.

In the same year as this event, however, Hüsmen Hoca went to town to sell rice and returned looking foolish. Just when the market was most crowded, he had heard someone shouting in the distance, "Get out of the way! Don't get hit!" The crowd divided in two, and Judge Melonhead, with the gray donkey beneath him and the familiar orange cape on his back, passed through the throng of well-wishers that surrounded him at a pace that shook his large body.

Feyyaz Kayacan

The Shelter

We were living at Forest Hill in those days. And on Dartmouth Road people walked with borrowed footsteps. Dartmouth Road flowed into the Channel, into war. I imagined that at the end of all the roads were wounds that dangled and fluttered, like sheep's wool, from barbed wires. I was out of work, with only a few withering coins to my name.

I did occasional translations to hold on to my skin—technical stuff mostly. I was paid at the rate of so many shillings per folio of seventy-two words. Oh how I used to lie, pretending to be a skillful translator. My life was measured in terms of switches, gearboxes, boreholes, axles, and component parts, which were all marshaled into groups of seventy-two to determine the translation fee. *Seventy-two* was the insignia of my guardian angels. And my wife was in York. As if people in York were the manipulators of the fountains of life in their minster-spired safety. As if the flying leeches could not just as easily doodle their way to those camouflaged aisles, and naves, and altared bastions. It seemed to me that every flying bomb was as greedy as a swarm of locusts, and there was no telling which way it would jump. But I was much too bored to be afraid. I was alone in London. Millions of people were ghosting the tricks of life in my eyes. In crowds of emptiness. Zombie-ing each other into stiff apparitions. My pockets were full of idling time; I had all the time in the world to kill. The library was bang opposite. It had become the slaughterhouse of my days, where, for want of better things, I developed an unerring gift for beheading one by one the shepherds of my daily breath. I thumbed my way through many books, but not a single page succeeded in papering my desultory mind. Books were entering me through one ear, only to fall into the abyss walking beside me at the other end.

Every so often the sirens would be heard waking, answering each other in sustained screams. And I counted the centipedes of fear on Dartmouth Road. But the voice of the sirens was worse than the strident fear of death. It was a screech that sent out hairs rising from the raised fathoms of de profundis. And on looking up, the sky was an experience in agony. When the sirens slowly fell silent, like old gramophones running down, there came the flying bombs. Sometimes one, sometimes two. Sometimes from the four corners of hell or the navels of the dark. All the buzzing blue above flew into the ears. Then in preordained suddenness the engines of the bombs would stop, and silence, like a sheet of lime, would settle upon streets, houses and people—till they fell nose diving purposively; till true, lived-in houses were scattered sky-high, as if they were so many castles built in the air; till lives went up like flying glass in the performed dominion of death and destruction. We had been forwarded into a focus of dead ends. Death was mailed to us registered. It knew its jobs by heart. There was no such thing as an enemy in sight. Who was the enemy? Death itself. The buzz bombs dispatched from the launching ramps on the other side of the Channel owed allegiance to no one but themselves. Somehow they were all alternatives rolled into one. They came from over dales and hills, whenever they caught sight of the smell of man with all their owls. Has anyone ever seen death going rusty? Let us say that it had been a fine day. Let us say that that day seemed to have nothing to do with the one before it, with all its spilt dark, and its siren-voiced, flesh-lessening sky face. Let us say that there are hundreds of barrage balloons, floating like bloated sentinels up there, huge silvery pebbles, there to bar the way in time of danger, to clash with death at its own chosen level. But more often than not, they miss each other. One is either a little below or a little above the other. It is as if the devil had something to do with it.

I was about to cross over to the other side of the road. Mr. Ellis suddenly dashed out of his flat with a shovel in one hand and a bucket in the other to collect some horse droppings in the middle of the street. Mr. Ellis loves his garden. He feeds it with sugar and spice and all things nice. As he was gathering up the droppings, blessing the horse like a happy beggar, he straightened himself a little and looked upward. He must have been counting the balloons, as if to make sure. If one had been missing,....

"The balloons are not as high today as they were yesterday," said Mr. Ellis.

"The balloons are not as high today as they were yesterday," I said.

"The balloons are not as high today as they were yesterday," said thousands of voices, echoing Mr. Ellis. The balloons hovered up there, like magic charms between Dartmouth Road and the Almighty. They were Mr. Ellis's amulets. The only thing Mr. Ellis feared was "What if the bomb should fall in my garden?" The rest he did not much care about really. Even if the house were to have gone west, he wouldn't have given much thought to it, provided, and on the sole condition that, death did not touch his plum trees, his delphiniums, his geraniums, and all his other Latin-speaking plants. Having filled half his bucket, Mr. Ellis went back into the house. One could see there was an understanding between Mr. Ellis and his God. Messages flashed back and forth. One could also sense that Mr. Ellis was getting, somehow through his fears, the best of God. Understandable enough.

And then I saw Vera, the postman's daughter, taking her baby out in its pram. Vera has jet-black hair. Full of long, warm glintings. My wife was in York. The balloons were not as high that day as they had been the day before.

"Good morning," she said

"Good morning," I said. I looked at her legs. They were long and shapely. Between Dartmouth Road and secret stars a woman was walking, undulating with all her inner cypresses.

In the reading-room of the library, two old men were going through the pages of the war. The last pages, maybe. In their hands were the first trembling greeneries of hope. Then the sirens suddenly began to sound. Not a cloud did they leave near another cloud. The old men picked up their gas masks and went to take refuge in the shelter next door. The sirens went on wailing, in endless shrouds. The seasons lost their breath all of a sudden. The barrage balloons looked now like breadless wheat grains scattered over the sky. Like the gypsy's fortune-telling stones and bones. Who was the gypsy woman who had left them there and gone? Mr. Ellis rushed to the shelter, carrying under his arms peat-covered boxes of seedlings, where summer kept all its sayings. As soon as the seedlings were old enough to speak, he was going to transplant them into his garden. Mr. Ellis was doing death out of a handful of earth, sorry only that his garden was not portable.

The shelter was glaucous, like the inside of a knotted womb. People stirred slowly like fetuses. A bleak light shed by a couple of electric bulbs was trying to pierce the dark that gathered in armpits. Rags of sweaty visibility were pinned on the faces of the fetuses. The slightest twitch caused the rags to fall. The womb had double-tiered bunks. Those who lived in double-tiered sleep slept with open ears under their eyelids. At the root of their eyes were puppets waiting for a pull on the strings of their fear. It was the gypsy woman who would turn the wheel of fortune, and doom would skid over our heads. In my mind hoops were about to race, whipped on by the stick of fate. Who was going to be the winner? When I was a child no one but I could get on my hoop. It was not a hoop to which others took the stick. It would turn only for me and in me, and only when I was free from the eyes and the fingers of the world would I bring it down from the garret of my garden. That I had such a hoop no one knew. It was my secret. I had declared it neither to mother nor to fate.

But now we are in the shelter. A garret of a different kind. A sunken one. I think we've been forgotten here. I say to myself we are old and frayed. I remember my mother. She has been dead a long time now. The walls that she had conjured up around me have collapsed. I have long ago left behind the games that she used to plot for me in the garden where I was a pawn crowing for loneliness. And would the world have lost anything if the world had been mine?

We are now waiting for the flying bombs, with a patience that verges on vertigo. They are coming. They will come; they will come. If only they could, if only they could come and come and come and fall and be done with it. Instead, they seem forever suspended over us and inside us, until the ever-coming end of the world. The end of the world comes differently to different people. For me, in spite of everything, it is like having my eyes pierced with the needles of an unwanted eternity speeding toward me. Eternity is not my way of life, and I become stiff with sadness.

Where are they? Which way is this death going to come? From under the ground or from above it? Or under the very nose of the sun? Or from the upturned *qibla* * of the sky, which now would not even fill a single fig pip? Or from the carrions of clouds or the sleights of hand, or in the name of stenciled gods who cared not to see? Where are they; where are they? This question was heard in places most adjacent to the dark. For example, on Darmouth Road, in Lewisham and Catford, at Beckenham and Crystal Palace, in Newcross and Ladywell, and at Kidbrook and Peckham, Gypsy Hill and Perry Rise, and a place called Lordship Lane, not far from Dulwich and as far as fear could reach....

"No need to rush, wait," said one of the old men playing dominoes. "You just carry on," he said. "The dark will come to a head in its own good and proper time. It will come roll calling our up-and-coming numbers. We may be among them, we may not be. No need to rush."

"No need to rush," said Mr. Ellis. "It'll do just as well if I plant my garden later. No need to rush. Flowers are like death too. They can't be rushed."

My wife was in York. This being so, I took my wife from York and put her in my mind. To her I fast added Vera, whose footsteps had not yet faded up and down Dartmouth Road. When she thus found herself, Vera the postman's daughter stretched, stretched, four-cornering me with her tides. An *innermosting* in my blood, cool and infinite hands were burning my ears.

---

*Direction of Mecca (to which a Muslim turns in worship).

Mr. Ellis's pockets were full of packets. The packets were full of seeds. In the shelter in Mr. Ellis's pockets, the seeds were thinking. "What is earth?" asked one of the seeds. "Earth," said Mr. Ellis, "is a place where you light the againness of the sun every morning, after the night has Christmased the trees and the rain has shown flowers what they can be." "But," said Mr. Ellis, "the earth has gone to the wars. It has gone to salute the dead." "What is war?" asked another seed. "You shall soon see," said Mr. Ellis. "No need to rush."

At the bottom corner of Dartmouth Road was the Capitol Cinema. By the bus stop in front of the Capitol, a woman and her child stood waiting. The child asked for one of the balloons. The mother stretched her arm, but could not reach it. She came back empty-eyed. The child did not mind. She said, "There's no need to rush. I shall reach it when I am older."

Inside the cinema there was only a handful of spectators. In the front row sat a man, only inches away from the screen. He must have been able to count all the dots that made up the pictures. He had ginger hair and rusty, wolfish teeth. Two long canines clamped upon his lower lip. But his eyes were blue, clear, and childish. He was harmless. The boys of the neighborhood—those who had not been evacuated—had nicknamed him "Carrot hair-carrot teeth." He used to enjoy being teased by them. After all, even this meant some kind of togetherness. The man was, maybe, seeing the film for the fourth time. He knew it backward and sideways. He was sitting almost on top of it. Then a warning was flashed across the screen. It said, "An air-raid alert has been sounded. Patrons who wish to leave are requested to do so quietly. The show will not be interrupted."

The man read the warning. For a moment he thought of his pigeons at home. He loved them very much. He had a finger in all their wings. It was his habit, together with his pigeons, to go on bird's-eye ventures. The time had not yet come for his birds to hang their wings up, he thought. They are clever, my pigeons; they'll know what to do—God is in them, in the strength of their instinct!

And thereupon, and for the fourth time that week, he jumped on one of the horses galloping on the screen and, donning his war paint, joined the Sioux, the Commanches, the Apaches, and the Cherokees, littering red-skinned hurrahs. But one day very soon his pigeons were to be blasted out of flight. And from then onwards (he, on his return one day from a posse ride through the canyons of the Capitol, having seen wrecked feathers madly jerking amid broken walls, his eyes having been sucked with them into the long-spitting jet of a burst gas pipe) we would find him, every hour of the turning time, beside a rusty stirrup pump spraying the week-sprouting ruins with the waters of his mind—until the moment he phoenixed into a final impregnable flight.

A flying bomb appeared over the other end of the Dartmouth Road, from the direction of Sydenham. Jerking its way forward in dark, continuous, stuttering jumps—as if it were counting the million points that formed the line of its trajectory. It looked like a gigantic grasshopper figmented by a desperate imagination. Uncoiling, as it flew, new shapes of fear. And questions scurried through the air. Who was going to learn in the jiffies of sundered breaths how much soul, how much body, goes into our making and perhaps be flung up on the right-hand side of God and perhaps have Him tattooed on his earthly remains as a shortcut to the mercy of the heavenly trilogy? Eyes huddled in their sockets, went in search of sacraments, of garrulous last words, which are never spoken by the dying, but by the interpreters of the amenned ghosts.

I myself was set on having a preview of houris. Otherwise, I was going to stay put, with a dandelion growing between my Muslim teeth. Mein Herr V.1 was getting nearer, trepanning the sky like a skillful surgeon. That which had been rehearsed and seen and heard a hundred times in anticipation, happened. The engine of the bomb dived into silence. And blank panics pursued the blood darting in the bodies' dead ends. And it came to pass that a huge black noise entered the ground and all those who tried to live on it. And it came to be known in most vocal places that not a single breath had been deducted from our midst. Our wall had withstood the writings of doom.

When the buzz bomb fell on the railway line, Mrs. Valley was frying chips in her kitchen. When the earth went into a fit, the frying pan fell on the floor. When it fell on the floor, the chips took to their heels. When they did that, Mrs. Valley closed her eyes and opened her mouth and let out a string of curses. And she had a voice like a chorus of stentors. Mrs. Valley was not a woman. She was a coalition of life. She was made of rivers and rocks and hills and chain-smoked cigarettes. No one knew when she had come to the neighborhood. According to rumors in the tongue of tales, it was she who brought up the sun and the stars. No one knew who had had a say in the coming about of Mrs. Valley. Children believed that she thundered into existence through her own most unheard hands, and through the apples of her eyes, which seeded the morning-starred Word, which, contrary to belief, never observed the Sunday motels of our landlord.

When the chips were down, Mrs. Valley raised the hackles of hell. North to south and round again. Not a swearword did she leave with which she didn't plaster death and its owling jet-propelled acolytes. Mrs. Valley hung fate by the ears. She dispatched a lasting kick to the sacrum of Azrael, whose cartilage went haywiring all over. "Do not try to measure up to me," she said. And thereupon Mrs. Valley put the lungs of the earth back where they belonged. And she rebirded the trees. She guffawed from her deep-seated fathoms. And her laughter topsied the turves of manhunting gargoyles. And, outvoicing the sirens, she, with her own fingers, prized the people out of their shelter and sent them all back to work and to living. And all roads were new and lovely in her name. We almost did not recognize Dartmouth Road. We had never known it like this.

Back in his garden Mr. Ellis saw the flowers, the fruit trees, the plants, and the birds in their best feathers dancing a *hora.* * And the apple tree and the plum tree held the clothesline. And everything in the garden started skipping.

AND THEN NIGHT CAME. LIGHTS WERE BLACKED OUT. THEY WERE TOLD TO STAY IN THEIR ROOMS.

It was now time for Mrs. Valley to take the road to the shelter. For this was the one night of the week when the shelter people feasted on her cheese and onion pies. She carried a basket in her arm. Darmouth Road smacked its lips. Mrs. Valley crowded in. The shelter rocked with her outsize hellos. The woman was 100 percent endless. It was she who had gathered in her thighs the semen of life and cast forth nine sons from her nine wombs. Like a satellite, Mr. Ellis edged toward Mrs. Valley.

"Any news from your sons?" he asked.

"My sons?" replied Mrs. Valley. "You want to know about my sons? What could you expect? They have all taken the powder. London was too much for them. They are all a lot

*A spirited folk dance.

of cowards. They've run away to this front or that, to fight. One is in Europe, another in the East somewhere; one is fighting in the skies, one on the seas, one under the ground, one in the sun and the moon and hell's bells and buckets of blood. They may be away from me, but I still have in my hands the clues to their navels. Those who are dead and those who are about to die shall most movingly arise in me again, until I myself decide to slow down and speak the end of my breath or until our world is caught in such ending worlds as were left by gods whom I, in my womb, never clapped eyes upon—but this much no one can know and is beyond the ken of canned deities, and if the errand boys of death should so much as dare level their homemade dooms against me, I shall let them have a spanking taste of my sun-spoken hands, and my anger shall drive them into thimble-size dustbins. And woe to those who do not see the meaning of such headlong words."

Four times these warnings orbited the earth, and those who heard them passed them on to those who had not. Trailing behind this long sentence, we grew hungry and fell upon the pies.

Orhan Kemal

Baby Born in the Field

Translated by Talat Sait Halman

In the cotton field, which stretched as far as the eye could see, farmhands, fifteen or twenty in a row, worked steadily at the weeds around the seedlings.

The temperature soared to a hundred and forty-nine in the sun. No bird flew in the shimmering, dust-gray sky. The sun seemed to sway. The peasants, soaked with sweat, pushed and pulled their hoes in a steady rhythm. The sharp edges of the hoes chopped the parched soil with a "thrush, thrush, thrush" sound. The song the farm-hands sang in unison to the measured beat of their hoes was swallowed up in the sun's scorching heat:

> Into what is left back they sow millet.
> They sow it, they reap it, and they wrap it.
> My darling sent me pear and pomegranate.

Ferho Üzeyir wiped the sweat off his swollen hands on his baggy, black trousers and turned his bloodshot eyes on his wife, swinging her hoe beside him. He spoke in Kurdish, "Wha? Whatsda matter?"

Gülizar was a broad-shouldered, husky woman. Her dried-up face, glittering with sweat, was contorted with deep lines and grimaces of intense pain.

She did not answer. Angered, Ferho Üzeyir jabbed his elbow into her side: "What's up wid yo', woman?"

Gülizar gave her husband a weary glance. Her eyes had sunk with fright into their sockets. Her hoe suddenly slipped from her hands to the ground. Pressing her huge belly with her hands, she bent over, then fell to her knees on the red earth everywhere cracked by the blistering sun.

The foreman, who stood under his big black umbrella, called out: "Gülizar! Is dat it? Quit workin'! G'on, quit!"

She was writhing with pain. She stuck her shriveled yet strong fingers deep into a crack of the soil, squeezing them tensely. With an almost superhuman effort, she struggled to control herself. Pitch-black blotches fluttered before her eyes. Suddenly she groaned, "Uggghhh!" It was a shame—a disgrace—for a woman in labor to be heard by strange men. Ferho Üzeyir cursed and swung a mighty kick into his wife's side.

The woman crouched meekly on the ground. She knew her husband would never forgive her for this. As she struggled to rise on hands pressed against the hot earth, the foreman repeated: "Gülizar! Quit, sister, quit! G'on now, quit!"

Her pains suddenly stopped, but she felt that they would come back—this time more sharply. She headed for the ditch, the farm's boundary, about a thousand feet away.

Ferho Üzeyir growled after his wife, then called to his nine-year-old daughter standing barefoot beside the foreman: "Take yo' mom's place!"

The girl knew this was coming. She picked up the hoe that was as tall as she and whose handle was still covered with the sweat of her mother's hands, and fell into line.

All this was a common affair. The hoeing continued to the beat of the song sung in unison.

The sun fell full on the ditch with its slabs of dung. Green lizards glided over the red earth. Gülizar stood erect in the ditch, looked all around her, listening intently through the scorching heat. There was no one in sight. The radiant void, echoing a shrike's shrieks, stretched endlessly.

She emptied the pockets of her black, baggy pants and put down a few items she had gathered when she knew her time was due: two long pieces of thread wrapped around a bit of pasteboard, a rusty razor blade, several pieces of cloth in different colors, rags, salt, and a dried-up lemon. She had found these in the farm's garbage can. She would squeeze the lemon into the baby's eyes and rub the baby with salt.

She stripped below the waist, folded the baggy pants under a big piece of rock, spread the rags on the ground, unraveled the thread and cut the lemon in two. About to kneel, she heard something move behind her. She covered herself below the waist and turned around. It was a huge dog! She picked up a stone and flung it. Frightened, the dog fled, but did not disappear. It waited, sniffing the air with its wet nose.

Gülizar was worried. What if she delivered the baby right now and fainted—the dog might tear her child to pieces. She remembered Ferice, the Kurdish girl. Ferice too had given birth in a ditch like this and, after placing the baby beside her, had fainted. When she came to, she had looked around—the baby was gone. She had searched high and low.... At last, far away beneath a shrub, she had found her baby being torn to pieces by a huge dog!

Gülizar took another look at the dog, studying it closely. The dog stared back at her—it had a strange look....

"Saffron," she said, "dat look o' yo's ain't no good, Saffron." She wondered how she might call her daughter who was about a thousand feet away. "G'on, beat it! Yo' goddam dirty dog!"

Reluctantly, the dog backed away about thirty feet, stopped, sat on its haunches and, with a blue gleam in its eyes, waited.

At that moment Gülizar felt another pang, the sharpest yet. Groaning, she fell to her naked knees, resting her body on her hands gripping the ground. Her jugular vein, thick as a finger, throbbed. Now came pain after pain, each sharper than the one before. Suddenly a gush of warm blood....Her face took on a terrified expression. The whole world collapsed before her eyes.

"Ferho, man," the foreman said, "go take a look at dat dame.... She may die or somethin'."

Ferho Üzeyir glanced in the direction of the ditch where his wife was in labor, shook his head, cursed, and went on working. Anger at his wife swelled inside. Cold sweat poured from his forehead, trickling through his thick bushy eyebrows.

"Look here, son," the foreman repeated. "Go see whatsa what wid dat dame. Yo' never can tell!"

Ferho Üzeyir threw his hoe aside and walked over. He would give her a kick and another kick.... He just couldn't get over the way that good-for-nothing woman had made a monkey of him.

He stopped by the ditch, stared down. Gülizar had fallen on the ground sideways. In the midst of blood-stained rags, the baby—purple all over—was twitching and a huge dog was pulling at it.

He jumped into the ditch. The dog leaped away, licking its blood-covered mouth. Ferho Üzeyir brushed away the green-winged flies gathered on his baby's face. The infant, its eyes closed, kept making motions. Ferho opened the pieces of cloth. The baby was a boy!

A boy!

Ferho changed instantly. He lifted his head to the sky. A smile filled his harsh face. He picked the baby and the bloody rags from the ground.

"Ma son!" he shouted.

He was nearly insane with joy. After four girls—a boy!

Gülizar, sensing the presence of her man beside her, opened her eyes and, in spite of her condition, tried to get up.

"Good fo' yo'," Ferho Üzeyir said. "Good fo' yo', woman!"

He dashed out of the ditch with his boy in his arms. The foreman saw him coming across the cracked, red soil. "Dere, dere, he said, "dat's Ferho comin' dis a-way!"

Hoeing stopped. The farmhands, leaning on their hoes, stared. Ferho came up panting, out of breath, shouting: "Ma son! Ah got me a son!"

He pressed his baby, still purple all over inside the blood-drenched rags, to his bosom.

"Hey, careful, man," the foreman said. "Take care, man! Quit pressin' like dat—yo gonna choke 'im.... Now get down to de farmhouse. Tel de cook Ah Sends yo'. Tell 'im he oughta give yo' some oil and molasses. Let's make 'er drink some. G'on!"

Ferho Üzeyir no longer felt tired; the heat no longer bothered him. Now he was as young as a twenty-year-old, as light as a bird.

He headed for the farm's mud-baked huts, whose thatched roofs loomed ahead.

Yashar Kemal

from *Ortadirek* *

Translated by Edouard Roditi

The first rays of the sun would soon be lighting up the slopes of the mountain opposite, which seemed to be drawing a deep breath and stretching itself as it awaited the warm, bright day. With its yellow, red, greenish-blue, mauve-circled, luminous-winged wild bees, its long-legged ants pressed closely against each other at the entrances to their nests, its eagles, one eye already open, nestling in their aeries, its cloud-white moutain doves huddling together in a single hollow, its savage hawks and falcons, its ladybirds crowding in thousands in the balls of thistle seeds that are called fairy's nests, its mountain goats and timorous jackals, its foxes, their long red tails tossing like flames, its soft purple bears lying full-length in their winter sleep over the withered yellow leaves, its springing, sad deer, their languid eyes like those of a lovelorn girl, its worms, its large and small birds—with all its creatures above the earth and beneath it, the mountain lay, with bared breast and open mouth, waiting for the day to strike its flanks.

Now, on the peaks, in the valleys, over the roads, there would be an awakening, a stirring, a tumult, a frightening activity, as the mountain, its stones, its earth and trees, all rose from their sleep.

The sun first lighted the space of a threshing floor on the mountain slope. Then the light crept down into the valley. Two ants at the entrance to their nest greeted each other lengthily with their antennae before going off in opposite directions. The sun then touched Ali's forehead, and woke him up. For a while, he could not gather his thoughts and remember where they had halted for the night. His eyes rested on the peak of the mountain, and a heavy pain settled within him like salt water as he rose. He laid out his bedding, wet from the night dew, to dry in the sun. A pungent odor of sweat rose from it and disappeared in the air.

His feet ached and could scarcely bear his weight as he limped through the fir trees. He rested his left shoulder on a rock and relieved himself. Still leaning, he tied up the cord of his baggy trousers, then sat down heavily on a stone. He was painfully sleepy.

Elif had risen before dawn to put the dried curds soup on the fire and now waited in vain for her husband to return. She went after him through the trees and roused him from his half-sleep when she found him seated on the stone.

"Your mother's still asleep. She's completely worn out, poor thing. You'll be shocked when you see her face all shriveled up. She seems to have shrunk to the size of a child. How are your feet?"

*The Mainstay: This book was published as *The Wind from the Plain* translated by Thilda Kemal.

"That saltwater did them no good at all. The pain's just the same, as if they'd been flayed, and it hurts right into my heart."

"If only you hadn't let your mother walk so long! If only you'd taken her on your back!"

"I couldn't do otherwise. She'll walk till she hasn't an ounce of strength left in her. Nothing can stop her. It's me you should be thinking of, woman. Our children will starve this year. Âdil Efendi will make me pass through the eye of a needle. Think of me, of my troubles! I'll never reach the cotton fields in time this year. Never!"

"I just said..." Elif began, then stopped.

Ali plucked the dried stalk of an autumn asphodel and broke off its end. A tiny bee buzzed out in a flash of blue. He then slit the stalk in two. It was filled with honey, which he started lapping up with his tongue. He broke another stalk, then another and another. The honey had a strange acrid taste that went to his head. It carried the smell of new fresh green herbs. Ali was drunk with sleep and honey. His feet were aching and all the scents of the mountain were flowing through his veins.

Elif was staring at him. "For heaven's sake, man! Why, you've become a veritable baby," she cried. "Come and drink your soup instead of picking at stalks like a child."

Ali paid no attention. Once, when his uncle was still alive, they had gone searching for honey together. His uncle knew every nook and cranny in these mountains and by noon had finally discovered in a valley a plane tree that was perhaps a thousand years old. Its trunk and even its long branches were hollow. Ali's uncle had lit a rag, placing it in a hole in the tree's trunk and had then kindled a fire that had filled the forest with suffocating smoke. About half an hour later a hive of bees had burst out of the tree, swarming into the forest in a vast cloud. "The whole village could eat of it for a year, and there'd still be more. Take out your bread, son," he had added and, cutting off a chunk of honeycomb, they had sat down to eat it. Ali had become drunk. A maddening wind had blown through his head like humming bees, and he had felt in his blood the scent of all the world's flowers, of cedars, firs, and pine trees, and the intoxicating smell of the earth fresh with rain.

Ali broke off another stem and slit it open eagerly. It was again full of honey, which he licked with his tongue. What a pity, he thought—a man should be able to eat a pound of this and forget the pain in his feet, forget everything.

"You're out of your mind, man," cried Elif, snatching the stem from his hands and throwing it down. She had begun to be afraid of Ali. She could vaguely discern on the edge of his lips a white line like that of a madman who tries to laugh but cannot and whose face is somehow frozen. "Come and drink your soup!"

Ali was smiling. Elif had never seen him like this. Only madmen laughed in this manner, all expression wiped away from their eyes. "What is it, Ali?" she murmured. "My darling, my brave one, what is the matter with you?"

Hearing Elif's pleading, Ali gathered his wits: "My children will starve this winter. I haven't been able to make it, and I never will at this rate. What can I do, tell me? What the hell can I do? Âdil Efendi will have me thrown into prison for my debts. And the villagers? And that rascal of a Mad Bekir, and the headman, that demon from hell?" He looked toward the spot where his mother was sleeping. "And it's all because of that old pig; may she die like a dog, the old whore, and leave me free. If it weren't for her, we two and the children would have reached the plains of the Çukurova long ago. As if all she's been doing to me wasn't enough, now she starts off back to the village and makes me run after her for two whole days. I've a good mind to leave her here and go. I don't care what happens to her."

Elif seized her husband's arm and shook him: "Hush," she whispered. "She's awake. If she hears you..."

"Let her hear," shouted Ali. "Let her hear and croak! Why should my children starve because of her?"

Elif clapped her hand tight over Ali's mouth. "For God's sake, Ali, she's your mother. Have you no fear of God? If she's heard you, she'll die. She'll kill herself."

"Let her kill herself," snarled Ali from under his wife's hand. "I'll be glad if she does it! I'll celebrate it, and in two days, not more, I'll be down in the cotton fields."

"We'll get there anyway. Don't be afraid. When one door closes, Allah always opens another."

"I don't care if He does," growled Ali.

Elif was horrified. "Say you're sorry," she cried. "Say it quickly! It's a sin."

"I won't," shouted Ali at the top of his voice. "Let Allah not open any door and let that house of His crumble in ruins over His head. Let it be wrecked! Wrecked! If He has eyes, He can see me, and if He has ears, He can hear me. I won't repent."

Elif sank to the ground weeping, her hands covering her face. Ummahan and Hasan had been standing at a slight distance, trembling at their father's anger. When Ummahan saw her mother crying, she ran up and, throwing herself down beside her, started weeping too.

Meryemce had been making her way toward the fire when she heard her son's words. Her ears buzzed, and her head swam as she dropped down where she stood. Gathering herself into a ball, she remained crouched here, still as the earth, not even stirring a finger.

At the sight of his wife and daughter sobbing their hearts out, Ali's anger subsided suddenly. He had released his pent-up feelings and was now hovering around his wife, not knowing what to do, how to console her. He laid his hand on her shoulder. "Get up, Elif," he murmured in a dead, weary voice. "I didn't mean anything really. Come, let's go and drink our soup. Get up, we must be on the road again. Look how high the sun is already."

Elif's and Ummahan's shoulders continued to heave.

"Shut up," shouted Ali to his daughter. "Shut up, you daughter of a dog!"

Ummahan's sobbing stopped as quickly as it had begun.

"Elif," pleaded Ali, "please don't cry. Please!" He smiled bitterly. "There, I'm sorry. You see? I'm saying I'm sorry to Allah." He took his wife's hand and pulled her to her feet.

"You've killed her," murmured Elif, wiping her eyes. "Even if she lives, she'll never recover from this. Poor Mother!" She walked to the fire and looked at Meryemce: "My good mother, my lovely one, you must excuse him, he's your son. He was so blind with anger he didn't know what he was saying. Would a man in his right senses speak of God like that? You must not worry at all. We'll get to the Çukurova anyway."

No longer angry, Ali was looking guiltily at his mother, as his wife helped her to her feet and led her to the fire.

Elif then laid the food before Meryemce and handed her a spoon. They all sat down to eat their soup. Throughout the meal, Ali could not bring himself to look his mother in the face, but Meryemce's eyes, wide open and bewildered, were fixed on her son, as if she could not recognize him. Was this Ali? Scenes of long ago rose before her eyes. She could not weep or speak, and something was choking within her. A baby as small as your hand...Ali...

You can't remember those days, can you, Long Ali? she murmured to herself. I've seen no good from you, Longish Ali and *Inşallah,** you too will see no good from your children! When you suffer this same bitterness, Longish Ali, you'll see how a bad word from your child is worse than a bullet, yes, worse than a bullet that pierces right through your heart!

She rose and said aloud: "I pray to God that your children will make you suffer as you've made me suffer, Longish Ali." To conceal her tears, she ran limping into the bushes.

"See what you've done, man," cried Elif angrily.

Ali drew a deep breath: "Shall I kill myself, kill myself right here?" His eyes fixed on Elif's, he was gnawing his forefinger, almost biting into it. Then he tore at a patch in his jacket and threw it down shouting, "Shall I kill myself? Kill myself?"

Elif was astounded at her husband's sudden fury: "For heaven's sake, Ali, don't! Not before the children," she whispered.

Ali went into the bushes after his mother and found her in tears, leaning against a sapling. He came up to her silently, took her hand and kissed it, then came back. "Go and get my mother, Elif," he ordered. "It's late, terribly late! What shall I do about these feet of mine? I can hardly walk a step."

Elif went and took Meryemce by the arm and led her out of the bushes.

"I'll never be able to walk in this state. See how swollen and red my feet are? I've thought of something, Elif...." His eyes were bloodshot, but there was no trace of anger left in him.

"What is it?"

"We have that sack, you know, and if we cut it in two, we could tie each piece around one of my feet."

"Suppose we use the horse's skin instead," whispered Elif into his ear.

Ali flared up again: "Are you mad? Why, the horse's skin would pinch my feet and make them worse than ever."

Elif hurriedly fetched the jute sack, which Ali cut into four pieces with his knife. He wrapped one piece around his right leg and tied it up with some hemp rope. It was just like a broken leg set in plaster. He carefully did the same to his left leg and then rose. It felt strange, but at least it was soft. Then he went to their load, tied it up, and heaved it onto his back.

"Get going, Elif," he ordered. "You too, children. Be quick about it. Mother, stay beside this warm fire, and I'll be back early in the afternoon to fetch you. For God's sake, don't attempt to go back to the village once more."

Meryemce pretended not to hear. She grasped her stick and made for the road, where she stopped. "God willing none of His creatures should have to be carried on other people's backs," she prayed, lifting her hands to the sky. Then she did the ritual rubbing of her face and added: "Amen, Amen!"

Ali hastened after her: "Don't be obstinate, my beautiful mother, stay here. You'll never be able to keep up with us. Sit here. See, you can't even stand on your feet."

"Who says I can't stand?" shrieked Meryemce. "My daughter, it's you I'm talking to, Elif! Look after yourselves. Just walk on and leave me. I'll go down to the Çukurova all by myself."

*God willing; I hope to God.

Ali took her arm. "Mother, please don't be obstinate," he pleaded. "Don't make things difficult for me. A little further off, I want to branch off the road in a shortcut which is hard to climb but will save us a great deal of time. You'll never find your way and we'll lose each other. Please wait here!"

Meryemce propped her stick against her waist and again lifted her hands to the sky: "Allah, my beautiful, black-eyed Allah, see to it that nobody should be reduced to being carried on another's back, not even a mother by her son! Amen!" She looked at Elif: "Walk ahead, my golden-hearted girl. I'll follow you slowly. Don't let your children go hungry this winter because of me...."

Realizing that his mother had heard his former outburst, Ali became angry again. "Stay," he shouted, "or go wherever you wish. I won't have my children starve because of you. Come on," he cried to his wife and children. "Get going. Let her stay or walk on by herself. She'll see."

from *Iron Earth, Copper Sky*

Translated by Thilda Kemal

Long before sunrise when the east begins to glow and cast its rosy lights upon the white snow, the village was awake, as though preparing to greet a day of festivities. Meryemce's appearance in her best clothes had set the style, and soon after sunrise the village square was alive with a colorful array of women decked in all the finery they could muster. The little mirrors that the young girls attached to their headdress on special occasions flashed in the early morning sun.

Arm in arm, a group of young men made their way to Long Ali's house.

"Take out your pipe and play us a tune or two, Uncle Ali," they begged. And Ali promptly followed them to the square, where the youths lined up for the *halay* dance. Further off, young girls were dancing and singing to the beat of a tambourine.

The village had shed all its cares. Âdil Efendi was coming at last. He would be there that very day, of this they were certain, and those bitter weeks of anguished waiting would be over and done with. Blithely, the morning wore on, and at noon a rumor set them rushing with sudden cries of joy for the town road. But not a living thing was to be seen. They straggled back somewhat chastened, still hoping. In the afternoon there was another false alarm, but when darkness began to fall, then.... Then they knew that there was not a shred of hope left. Utterly spent, all the blood drained from their veins, they crept back to their homes in a deathlike silence.

The *muhtar** was beside himself with worry. Hands on hips, he paced the house from one end to another. The younger of his two wives crouched in a corner hushing the baby she had borne him on their return from the Çukurova. Outside, a storm was brewing. The

* Village headman.

wind came howling ever more furiously from over the steppe, the frozen snow crackled, the world shook.

The *muhtar*'s discomfort increased. He must do something, he must think of a way out. Suppose he told the villagers that they need not pay back their debts after all? . . .

And let Âdil tackle me about it! By God, why not? I'll tell them their debts have been written off, that they never existed. What if Âdil comes along with twenty gendarmes? Can't Sefer, the king of *muhtars*, find a way out of that one? After all, he's only got that little yellow book of his to show. He could write anything he wished in there. Can you produce a promissory note, I'll ask him, certified by the notary? No? Well then, we don't owe you a jot, I'll say. Eh, just watch Âdil dance with rage then.

The *muhtar* was pleased with his idea, but his discomfort persisted. Suppose they did deny their debts, would any other merchant in the town ever give them credit after that?

He paced the room more quickly, almost hurling himself from one wall to the other.

"I'll do it whatever happens," he shouted. "I'll cancel the debts."

He was afraid. There was no knowing what the villagers might do now, after this long, frustrated wait. He would never be able to maintain his hold over them. They might even turn against him like angry waters breaking a dam, and join Taşbaş, his arch enemy. Everything was going wrong for him.

Look at what's blowing outside now! Why, this storm's going to uproot the whole village and sweep it right up to the top of Mount Tekeş! What a storm.... The very earth is shaking.

But then a sinister fancy gripped him, dragged him on against a dark wall of fear. The villagers waking up one morning to see Âdil Efendi there, in the middle of the village, motionless, his head and shoulders white with snow, the villagers quaking with fear, trembling, trembling, until slowly the trembling is no longer fear but rage, and closer, closer they creep to each other like sheep flocking together, pressing together, tighter, tighter, one solid compact mass gathering charge, a thunderbolt striking Âdil Efendi, and there they burst. When the mass breaks apart there is no Âdil at all! A spot of blood on the ground, a leg maybe, a bit of an arm, half a nose.... Where has that large man vanished to? The gendarmes are nowhere to be seen. Panic-stricken, they don't take long to decamp. The villagers are tired. There is no more Âdil. Arms dangling lifelessly, heads hanging, they stand about, irresolute, a ready prey to be led by the nose by anyone who chances to come along.

"Ah Âdil, you scoundrel, see what you've done to these people. Ah..."

The pacing became more frenzied. He felt himself choking, the world going black, and he hurled himself out into the night. The blizzard caught him with a slap and rooted him to the spot. The darkness, the gritty snow, the freezing cold.... Sefer retreated hastily and closed the door.

He felt better, but the nagging fear was there still. Suddenly, he remembered the girl. "Pale İsmail's daughter! It's ages since I've talked to her." At the thought his body tingled warmly.

"Quick," he said to his wife. "Put the baby in the cradle. Go straight to Pale İsmail's and bring back his daughter. That poor girl, we haven't been able to do anything for her. Be quick!"

By now the woman had got used to it. She knew what Sefer was up to and that if she delayed one minute things would go badly for her.

"Quick!" he shouted after her. "Bring her at once."

The passion in his voice shook her. She braced herself against the blizzard and ran.

Sefer could hardly wait. He was trembling all over, but he was afraid. What if his desire melted before the girl arrived? He opened and shut the door a dozen times, letting in blasts of snow. His elder wife and the children had come in at the shouting and were staring at him fearfully. Sefer was irritated.

"Get along, all of you!" he roared. "To your beds. Don't let my eyes see a single one of you."

"Don't shout like that, Sefer," said his wife. "What's wrong with you again? There, we're going! What's wrong with you?"

Sefer was silent. The pleasant tingling warmth was slowly draining out of him.

"Oh my God.... The girl.... Quick..."

The door opened. She came in, followed by his younger wife. Eagerly, he took her by the hand, and at her touch his body came alive once more, the tingling reaching deep into the very marrow of his bones.

"Come," he said, "come, my lovely girl, my unfortunate angel, whom I've left unavenged all this time. Come and let us find a remedy for your woes, let us bind your wound."

He led the girl to the fire and made her sit down. Then he squatted beside her. "You there," he said to his younger wife, "take the baby and go inside. I must receive the girl's deposition."

His wife picked up the cradle with the baby and retired into the back section of the house.

"Now tell me.... Quickly, quickly!"

The girl was used to it by now. She knew what she was expected to say, and she was no longer shamed to death, as in the first days of her misfortune.

"Speak, my girl, speak. Tell me, my gazelle, tell me all so that..."

She even felt pleasure now in telling her story and would let herself be drawn by Sefer's excitement.

"Well, you know İbrahim from the other village...."

"Skip the part about İbrahim. I know that."

"We were winnowing the grain close to each other that year...."

"Skip the winnowing. I know all about that."

"He set a trap for me. He said he would marry me...."

"No, no, skip all that and come to the part about the cave, when they brought you to the cave, he and his companion. You remember, the cave all filled with bats hanging heads down. Now, you went in, and then?..."

"We went in and İbrahim tried to strip me of my clothes. I wouldn't let him. We struggled and night fell. And then his friend came. He attacked me too, but I didn't surrender to them.

The *muhtar*'s face began to burn.

"Go on, go on. Quickly!"

The girl was taking her time. She smiled at him through half-lidded eyes, enjoying the sensuous warmth that quickened her limbs.

"Go on, go on!"

She knew what she was about and paid no heed to him. Unhurriedly, she began to speak again.

"His friend left us. 'I can't be bothered with this godforsaken girl any longer,' he said, 'You do what you like with her.' I was glad he was going. You see, I had my eye on İbrahim all the time. Then İbrahim threw himself on me, and what should I see, he held a knife, and with it he ripped through my clothes, and I was left naked. They had lit a fire at the mouth of the cave, and he threw all my clothes into the fire and held me pinioned until they were burnt to ashes. Then he attacked me again. I tried to hold him off. He was naked too, and his body was burning, burning my flesh. Oh how it scorched into me! I felt myself growing limp...."

Sefer quivered all over. "And then? Then? Quickly, what did you do then?"

She would not let herself be hurried. Slowly, drawing the utmost pleasure out of every word, she went on.

"I was going mad, mad. Ah, there is nothing in the world so pleasant as a man's naked flesh upon yours, burning into your body. I kept myself from fainting because I wanted to feel him taking my virginity. He held me tighter and tighter until my bones were cracking. He forced me to lie down in the dust of the cave and came upon me...."

She was trembling too now, like Sefer.

"He came upon you...." Sefer prompted her.

"His arms pressed me to the ground, his breath burnt into my flesh. I tried not to let myself go. It was his eyes, the fiery look in his eyes that broke me. I couldn't hold him off any longer. I let myself go...."

"Stop!" he cried, beside himself, crushing her hand in his. Then he snatched her up in his arms. She was as light as a bird.

Outside, the blizzard boomed over the steppe.

Samim Kocagöz

Dry Beans

Translated by Mina Urgan

The bailiff of the farm galloped furiously all around the bean field on his gray horse. He had mobilized three of his men and had sent them to the wood at the place where the estate was cut off by the river.

"If I could only catch the scoundrels..." he kept on saying, "if I could only get hold of them... I would break every single bone in their bodies."

The beans had been picked. The sheaves lay in rows like lambs ready for the sacrifice. The laborers, who had come in from the lower end of the field, carried the sheaves to the threshing floor. The bailiff stopped at the head of the sheaves, lined like soldiers in neat ranks. Like an officer who is yelling "Attention!" he inspected the ranks once more. It was clear that some of the sheaves were missing. At the sight of this, the bailiff got more and more angry; he was in such a rage that the blood rushed to his face. He got off his horse. He lit a cigarette. He shouted at the three farmhands, who were slowly shuffling toward him: "You rascals! Couldn't you find them?"

"We looked through the whole wood; we searched everywhere. There's nothing."

"The brutes! They must have buried the sheaves somewhere."

"Well," said one of the farmhands, "if they did bury them, we can never get them back."

When he heard that, the bailiff almost burst with rage. More than the burning heat of July, it was the thought of what the landlord would say to him that made him drip with sweat. With a murderous look, his eyes roved around. Then, all of a sudden, there was a gleam in them. A mean smile twitched his lips.

"You're not worth a damn without me," he said to his men.

"Come along now, we've got the thieves."

And he walked off.

One of the farmhands held the bailiff's horse and waited behind. The two others, like the bailiff, advanced cautiously, trying hard not to make any noise. But, in fact, the place where the bailiff meant to go was at least a kilometer away. Far off, right on the river's bank, rose a thin column of smoke. The smoke of this faintly smoldering fire formed circles in the still air. The bailiff, as he came nearer, was in an ecstasy of joy and excitement.

He kept on turning back in order to warn the two others: "Keep quiet, you rascals!"

At last they could see the river. The white foam that now and then appeared on its smooth yellow surface melted rapidly under the burning sun. Protected by the branches, they moved stealthily along the sandy banks toward the place where the fire was burning.

139

This was a little cave that the water in its rage had carved in the rock. Now that the water had ebbed, it could easily be used as a house. The fire burned in front of the cave. The lower half of a petroleum can, black with soot, stood on the fire. The bailiff 's nose caught the smell of dry beans boiling in water. In front of the fire, three children with wooden spoons in their hands were waiting. Two of the children looked like a pair of daisies spattered with mud after a rainstorm. The third one was a very dark little boy of four or five. His huge eyes were fixed on the boiling beans. Just then the mother came out of the cave and was petrified when she saw the men coming. Her hands dropped to her sides. Big tears rose in her eyes. The bailiff pushed her aside and walked into the cave. A young man, unshaved and with tousled hair, sat on the ground. The bean sheaves were piled next to him, and he was threshing them with a thick stick. When he saw those who stood in front of him, he left his work. He was neither startled, like his children, nor upset, like his wife. But a burning hate, strong enough to destroy everything around him, flashed in his eyes. For a while the young man and the bailiff stared at each other as if they meant to knock each other down. The young man began to grip the stick with which he had been threshing the beans. The bailiff was aware of that. For a moment he hesitated, trying to decide what to do. Now that he was faced by this man who sat on the ground like a piece of rock, ready to shoot up, all his rage died down. But he still wanted to behave like a bully. He pulled himself together and yelled: "So it was you!"

The man's voice was calm and clear: "So it was. What about it?"

"You just wait and see.... Don't get me into trouble now."

The bailiff, after saying that, thought again, trying to decide what to do. Then he gave an order to his men: "Come on, take these sheaves away...."

They took the sheaves. The man who was sitting next to them did not even stir. The bailiff turned away and walked out of the cave. The children still sat in front of the boiling beans, holding their wooden spoons in their hands. For a moment they could not help looking at the bailiff. The bailiff stalked toward them. The puzzled children did not move. The bailiff did not touch them. He vented all his fury, all his rage, on the can where the beans were boiling. With a single kick he knocked it down. He stamped on the fire.... Then he walked off with his men, who were carrying the sheaves.

After getting some distance away, he turned and looked back. The mother and the children were trying to pick up the beans scattered on the sand. The man stood motionless before the cave, gripping the stick and looking after them, his eyes burning with hatred.

Mahmut Makal

The Broom and the Dried Dung
from *Our Village 1975*

Translated by Niki Gamm

Daily life begins very early in the village. The sound of the ox and the donkey foal going out to pasture is heard before daylight. The donkey braying, the cow bellowing.... The dust these stir up begins to rise to the sky early.

While going to the cattle pasture, which remained in its location just as if it were eternal, and returning from the pasture, we saw the women gathering the hot steamy piles of dung which had fallen on the dusty road and sticking them on the wall...

The dung is now valued more for its convenience. Because the oven is lit once a day and a cover put on it, fewer people are needed to keep an eye on it the whole day. Since the stove burns in the room without a brazier, the people who warm themselves by it have increased. Because of this, dung consumption has grown.

When November came the weather got cold and Hasan Mountain was wrapped in snow up to the waist. The job of accumulating burning material was speeded up even more. The women swept up the tree leaves which had fallen in the garden and carried them into their houses in baskets. They worked to scatter these withered leaves in front of the house to dry before throwing them inside.

When the fuel problem of the school was taken up, everyone's heart suffered a pang. In forty years there hadn't been the slightest change in how the school was heated.

In the school we spoke with Abdullah Demir, the son of Kadir Usta. He mentioned how he had been the monitor while we studied together in elementary school forty years ago and that we had quarreled because I had forgotten to bring the dung one morning. When he mentioned it, I remembered the incident.

I asked teacher friends, "Have there been any changes in the situation after forty years?"

"There's never any change. On this subject, the appropriation and so on is provided in the budget, but even if it were shouldered with difficulty like before, it isn't being used for the school. Of course its needs can't be met. The matter still stands that the children bring dung every day. But in the village oxen are growing scarcer and because of it dung production is decreasing. The snow that falls on Hasan Mountain is essentially falling in our hearts..."

While we were talking about the dung, chalk came to my mind. To say it another way, the dung and the chalk were associated.

While I was in a bookstore in the district, two elementary school children came in and each one purchased some chalk.

"Which school are you from?" I asked the children.

"From Cumhuriyet."

"Doesn't the school buy chalk?"

"No, we use our savings."

Mentioning the purchase of the chalk which I had seen in the district, I asked friends whether or not the chalk business was still being continued forty years later, like the dung business.

"There is nothing new on the Anatolian frontier," Erol the teacher said. And he added afterwards. "Even after this I would not be surprised if we could never find chalk, because instead of directing the people to the solution of these problems we push them into partisan strife. While we struggle to educate the children we see that inspectors come one pair after another. And why? Erol the teacher is alleged to have engaged in partisanship, to have done propaganda for the People's Republican Party. After that, he is prevented from acting. Forget the dung and the chalk and think of the headache..."

And as if to reveal the situation more clearly, when the school's janitor Kumbulu Amca, brought out two old brooms made from grass, he stood in front of us and said, "The weather's cold, and the stove's ready. Don't look to see if there is any dung; if I burn these the room will be warm."

"Okay let's see you do it," they said.

The two old brooms ensured that the iron stove which catches fire and burns by itself warmed up and drove us from around it.

Aziz Nesin

The House on the Border

Translated by Gönül Suveren

We had moved into the house the day before. It was a nice place. That morning when I walked out, our next-door neighbor, an old man, was watching the street with avid curiosity and called us from his window.

"You shouldn't have rented that place," he cackled.

I stared at him coldly.

"Is this a new way of greeting neighbors?" I growled. "What do you mean we shouldn't have moved in there?"

He was not fazed.

"Thieves break into that house often," he announced with relish. "It's my neighborly duty to warn you."

As if the thieves couldn't break into his house too! Why should robbers favor only ours? Rather annoyed, I entered the grocery store at the corner to buy cigarettes.

"There are such characters around," I mumbled.

"What's the matter?" asked the grocer.

"Some old goat told me that thieves usually rob the house we just moved into," I complained.

The grocer nodded. "Well, the old goat was right. You shouldn't have rented that house. It's robbed frequently."

I was furious. Without answering him, I walked out of the store. The whole day was ruined, naturally. I fumed till evening. That night a couple from our block visited us. They were nice people. We talked about this and that till midnight. When they were about to leave, the husband turned and looked at us strangely.

"It's a beautiful house," he said, "but thieves never leave it alone."

Since they were already out of the house, I couldn't ask him: "Why is this house supposed to be irresistible to thieves? Why shouldn't they honor your home too?"

Seeing my ferocious scowl, my wife started to laugh.

"Dearest," she said, "don't you understand? God knows, they have thousands of tricks for scaring tenants away. This must be the newest one. They will drive us out, and, since the rent is low, they will either move in themselves or bring in one of their relatives."

It was possible. But I couldn't sleep a wink that night. It was as if I had a date with the thief. I waited for him breathlessly, whispering to myself: "He will be here any moment."

I must have dozed off. I jumped up at a slight noise and grabbed the gun I had hidden under my pillow.

"Don't move or I'll shoot," I yelled into the darkness.

As I already said, we had moved in the day before. Now, confronted with a nocturnal visitor, I forgot where the light switch was. Groping in the dark, I got entangled in every conceivable object and bumped into the walls in search of a switch. As if this was not enough, some darned thing coiled around my shapely ankles, and with a resounding crash, I found myself on the floor. "The dirty——," I muttered under my breath. "He tripped me." I decided to pump his stomach with lead, quite cold-bloodedly. Unfortunately, during my solo flight to the floor, the gun had fallen from my hand and bounced away.

The darkness was suddenly filled with a horrible laughter: "Heh! Heh! Heh!"

"Are we shooting a domestic horror movie?" I shouted. "If you are a man, show your face, you...you villain!"

"I suppose you were looking for the switch," a voice said in the darkness. "It's amazing how all the new tenants make the same mistake."

"Do you know what I'm going to do to you?"

"No," said the man in the darkness. "I don't know. Now, may I turn on the lights and help you?"

I heard the click of the switch, and the room was flooded with light. Apparently, when I had crashed down, I had rolled under the table. As for my wife, she was securely lodged under the bed.

There in the middle of the room stood a man larger than life—twice my size, I mean.

I knew that if I emerged from my hiding place, I couldn't scare him. I decided he wouldn't be able to size me up if I stayed there.

Imitating a basso profundo to the best of my ability, "Who are you?" I asked. It was a deep-chested growl.

"I'm the thief," he answered calmly.

"Oh, yeah?" I said. "If you think I'm a fool, you're mistaken. You're not a thief. You're trying to scare us away and move in here. Look at me, look closely. Do I look like an idiot?"

He didn't answer my question. "You'll see whether I'm a thief or not," he said instead.

You'd have thought it was his own father's house. He started to rummage through the drawers, picking out what items he fancied and talking to us all the while. I have to admit that he was quite friendly.

"So you turned this into a bedroom.... The family before you used it as a study. The ones before them too..."

"Now look," I said. "You're robbing me. I'll report you to the police."

Without stopping, "Please do," he replied. "Go to the precinct. And don't forget to give them my best regards."

"But you'll run away while I'm gone."

"I won't."

"You will! You will clean up the whole house and steal away." It was a dilemma. "I have an idea, I said. "First I'll tie you up, then I'll go to the police."

"Help!" shrieked my wife suddenly.

Were all the neighbors waiting on our doorstep, I wonder? As if on cue, they stampeded into the house, chattering excitedly. But did they look at us or offer sympathy? No. They were full of curiosity and in good spirits.

"Another robbery," they said.

"What, again?"

"Who is it this time?"

"Let's see."

Some of them were downright friendly with the thief. They even asked him how he was, while he calmly went on packing our things.

"Help!" I croaked. "Help! I must bind him up. I'll go to the precinct."

One of the neighbors shook his head.

"It won't do you any good," he said. "But I never stop people from doing what they want.... Go ahead."

What kind of a neighborhood was this anyway?

Suddenly emboldened, my wife brought me the clothesline. The thief didn't resist while I tied him up securely. We carried him into another room and locked the door.

We ran to the police. My wife considered herself the spokesperson of the family and told the story to the chief. He asked for our address.

"Aha," said the chief. "That house."

"Yes," I answered, "that house."

"We have nothing to do with that house," he informed us. "It's not in our jurisdiction."

"What are we going to do now? Did we tie that poor fellow up for nothing?"

"If you lived in the house next door, we could have done something," the chief said. Then, as if addressing a couple of morons, he added, "You would have been in our jurisdiction."

"That house was not vacant," my wife explained patiently. "So we moved into this one."

We learned that our house was right on the border between areas under the jurisdiction of two precincts.

"The other precinct should look into the matter," said the chief.

The other precinct was quite far away. By the time we reached it, the sun was already high in the sky. We told our story again, and again they asked our address.

"That house," said one of the cops.

"That house," I said.

"If you lived next door, we would have done something. Your house is not within our jurisdiction."

"Poor man," murmured my wife. "We tied him up."

"Tell me," I cried out impatiently. "Tell me one thing. Under whose jurisdiction are we? Who is supposed to look after us?"

"The state gendarmerie," said the cop. "You house is under their jurisdiction. The police have nothing to do with it."

We left the cops.

"Let's go home first," suggested my wife. "I'm worried about the thief. He might die, you know."

She was right, of course. What if the thief should die of hunger? Or heart failure? After all, he was trussed up like a chicken. What if the ropes would impede the circulation of his blood? What if...

We went home. The thief was where we had left him.

"How are you?" I asked anxiously.

"Fine, fine," he answered. "But I'm hungry."

My wife ran to the kitchen. Alas, we had spinach, but—would you believe it—it was the only dish the thief detested. My wife dashed to the butcher, bought some steaks, and fed the thief.

This time we went to the gendarmerie. After listening to our story, the commandant asked for our address.

"Aha," he said. "That house."

Apparently, we had rented a famous place.

The commandant shook his head. "This is not a case for the gendarmerie. You should call the police.

"Now look," I cried. "We went to the police. They sent us here. Now you say we must call the cops. Is this a runaround? Isn't there anybody to look into the case?"

The commandant pulled out a map.

"I hope you know how to read a map," he said. "Here, it gives the height. See? One hundred and forty feet. This is the water tower—116 feet—and here is the hill. Now, this area is under the jurisdiction of the gendarmerie. If your house were built further up, say about two yards toward the northwest, you would have been in our area."

"All this for two lousy yards," I said. "Do something, man! What would happen if you helped us now?"

The commandant pursed his lips. "What would happen?" he repeated. Then he nodded his head sagely. "Only we know what would happen.... Only we know." Again he put his finger on a spot on the map. "Look, this is your house. Right on the line that separates our area from the police's. See? Of course, a part of your garden is under our jurisdiction. But the robbery didn't take place there, did it?"

There was nothing we could do but go to the police again.

"Let's first see how the thief is doing," my wife suggested. "God help us if something should happen to him."

So we went home.

I almost clasped the thief to my bosom. "How are you?" I panted.

"Water! Quick!" he cried out. "I'm thirsty!"

After drinking the water, he looked at us sternly.

"Listen," he said. "Don't say that I didn't warn you. You have no right to hold me here. You are restricting the freedom of a citizen. I have a good mind to sue you."

"But what can we do?" I cried. "We don't know who is supposed to look after us. Apparently, we are in the middle of nowhere. Why they built this house right on the border line is beyond me."

"Didn't I tell you?... Now, let me go. Otherwise I'll drag you through the courts for restricting my freedom."

"Give me time," I begged. "Give me till tonight. I want to go to the police again."

"By all means," he replied affably. "Go and see anyone you wish. But it's futile. I've been aware of the situation for a long time now. They have to decide whether to include your house in one of the areas or change the borders. Till then..."

Again we went to the precinct. This time the chief brought out a map too.

"Look," he sighed, "this area is under the jurisdiction of the gendarmerie. Your garden and a small part of the house are within their area. Only a fraction of the house is under our jurisdiction."

"The bedroom is in your area," I pointed out. "And the robbery took place there."

He looked at me owlishly. "Quite. First this must be definitely established. Then there is another problem: the thief didn't fly in through the window, did he? He crossed the garden and then entered your house. Right? And the garden is under the jurisdiction of the gendarmerie. Yours is not a new problem. It is already under discussion. First they have to reach a decision; then they have to inform us of their decision concerning the area your house is supposed to be in. Then we can act accordingly."

We returned home. Our elderly next-door neighbor was at the window, as usual.

"So they broke into the house again," he cackled.

"Yes," I nodded.

"No one stays there long," he said cheerfully. "That's why the rent is low. Neither the owner nor the tenants could live there. The owner decided to pull down the house and rebuild it two yards further up. But then he found you fools—I mean he found you and rented the place."

His wife was looking at us sadly. "It's not your fault," she informed us. "It's the owner's. When they build a house they think of water, gas, electrcity, and the view. But do they think of the jurisdiction? No! What sort of a fool would build a house right on the border?"

I couldn't answer that question even if I wanted to.

Since we had paid the whole year's rent in advance, to move away was out of the question. So we went home and untied the thief. Then we settled down comfortably in the study and discussed the world situation for a while. The thief dined with us that evening.

"So long," he said after the meal. "I'll be back tonight."

Now we have five or six resident thieves. All our neighbors are familiar with them. We collaborate with the thieves too. That is to say, we help them to defend our home against other, unfriendly thieves, who are, after all, strangers to us.

I don't know what will happen eventually. Either all eight of us, my wife and I and the six thieves, will spend the remainder of the year here, or they will include the house in one of the areas, thus enabling me to complain to the authorities. But we are now used to our friends, the thieves. And to report them would be rather embarrassing—after all, they share the household expenses now.

Erdal Öz

from *You're Wounded*

Translated by Robert P. Finn

I

The cell was filled with Nuris.

You sat at a bench at a table that had just been wiped. The streaks on it were beginning to dry. You put your back to the wall, which was oily and shiny from being leaned on and rubbed against. The plaster had fallen down in places. You broke off some pieces from the solid lump of old, dry cheese they had carried in on a scrap of newspaper and left in front of you, and you tried to chew on them. You didn't even touch the stale bread they had pulled out of the bottom compartment of the wooden cabinet. From the door that opened to the area where the toilets were came a stale, sharp smell of urine, which struck your face and made the air bitter.

"Where's the trusty? asked the guard.

A fat, overfed man of middle height with a penetrating expression got up from where the beds were and came over.

"Yeah, boss."

"See, Nuri, I brought you somebody; he'll stay here for now."

"OK, boss."

The guard opened his jacket, which was too tight over his protruding belly, walked over and, throwing his arm over the trusty's shoulders, whispered something in his ear. The trusty, whose name, you knew now, was Nuri, looked at you out of the corner of his eye and shook his head as he listened to the whispering of the guard. When the guard had gone, he came over and stood by you. He looked at you for a long time, like someone examining with surprise a strange creature he has seen for the first time. You stood there motionlessly with a feeling of emptiness and expected a fist in your face.

"Welcome."

"Thanks."

"You hungry?"

"No, I'm not."

"Did you eat?"

"No, but I'm not hungry."

"Sit over there."

You moved over to the wooden bench he indicated.

Everyone was looking at you. You tried to seem at ease. Every once in a while, you unwittingly put your hand up to your head, within the tight group of gray skulls you saw around you; you were trying to get used to the fact that they had shaved your hair.

The door that led to the area where the toilets were was right across from you. Just to the right of the door was a bread cupboard. From the broken lower part of the door, you could see inside. On the left side of the door was an old water jug placed against the wall. The base was covered with green moss, above which white incrustations of saltpeter protruded. A long, jagged crack in its side was patched with raw cement; it was still leaking. The water that came out dripped slowly into an old cut-off plastic jug that had been placed directly underneath. On top of the water jug was a square wooden lid with a thick handle. Everyone who passed by would pick up the little water cup that rested on the lid, dip it full in the jug, then place it to his lips, drink, and finally put it back on the lid and go away.

The two or three pieces of salty cheese you had eaten burned your insides. You were thirsty. But it seemed very hard to you at that time to drink from that cup that had touched everyone's lips, to drink water from that jug that everyone had dipped into. Since you wouldn't find any other way of getting water to drink, you too, in the end, would dip into that unseen water, like everyone else, and put it to your lips. You realized this.

You saw the way the trusty treated everyone in the cell and you shivered every time he passed near you. He tried to appear heartless to those in the cell. As far as you could see, he had no friends. He talked very little, and whenever he did, he tried to leave a distance between himself and the person he was talking to. Everything there was new; everything was interesting. New ideas and observations were collecting, gathering. Everything seemed to be happening very quickly. You understood right away that Nuri spoke to everyone in a demeaning manner and that he made a great effort to act this way.

You still hadn't understood that the bald man who put the tables in the middle together and who lifted the wooden benches up and turned them over on top of the tables is the one on duty in the cell. The pale light that fell from the weak bulbs hanging from the roof seemed at first like a game to you as it occasionally gleamed on the man's bald head. He was standing in front of a table, and when he moved it over to the wall, you realized that the game had come to an end. You found yourself there like a stray insect exposed to daylight beneath a suddenly raised rock, searching for a crack to hide in. You went over to the shelter of the wall to avoid being underfoot, and you began to wait.

"Everybody in bed."

You felt the sound through your soles, and you were startled.

The trusty was standing up. He had no shirt on and stood in the middle of the room in his light purple T-shirt, which had obviously been dyed after he bought it. The cheap dye had faded from washing to washing. With his round, full, muscular shoulders he seemed more powerful than he was because the lousy light of the twenty-watt bulb fell on him from above.

You took one or two faltering steps in an attempt to seem like you wanted to go to bed like everyone else. But you had no bed. Going back to the base of the wall and sitting there quietly, you began to wait, in the belief that, as if erased, you would be forgotten or at least not be very noticeable.

Stripped to the skin in bed, the bodies decorated with tattoos moved like caterpillars across mulberry leaves.

"Hey, newcomer."

That's you. The trusty is staring at you.

Little pains in your soles, like needles.

"What are you standing there for?"

He comes over to you.

"Didn't we give you a bed?"

You swallow with difficulty.

He shakes his head.

"Well, just wait a little."

Leaning against the wall and waiting, you begin to wonder where the bed you're going to get will be and what kind of bed it is.

In the corridor people come and go, wearing worn-out slippers or scuffed shoes with the backs worn down. They can't help looking at you. You can no longer hide from anyone.

The door to the toilets crashes closed behind those who go in and out. When it is open or half-closed, the different sounds of water being used come from inside.

"I asked the administration for a bed. They'll bring it soon. I'm sorry you had to wait a little."

Nuri's talking to you this way calms you, even if just a little. He holds out a cigarette. The smoke filling your lungs makes your head spin.

"Don't you have any gear?"

"No."

"What're you in for?"

What were you in for? What'll you say now? Can you say, "I don't know"?

"You must be political."

Nuri saves you from your own hesitancy.

"I'm political."

You're political now. That's good. If somebody asks you can tell him what your offense is.

"Are you a student?"

"No, I'm not."

Nuri goes away without having understood anything very well. You try to lean against the wall like a political prisoner, but you give up immediately and pull yourself away from the wall. Nobody better say anything. Enough of being put down for now. It's been going on for weeks, months. You have no more strength to resist. On top of that you have no quarrel with the people here, no fight with any of them; you're seeing them for the first time, the people of a different world. They came here and settled before you; they were left alone, obliged to live together. They've made up some rules together. You have to learn them; you have to adjust to them.

It's tiring to wait standing up. How long had it been since you were even able to stand up after that torture? You still aren't used to standing up for long. Your soles are still hurt, really. You're hurt.

II

You understood everything when you opened the door.

You'd been waiting for days.

Your knees ached, and that gritty smell of soot filled your nostrils again.

There were five of them.

The one in front asked you for yourself.

"That's me," you said.

He was blond. Tall. Big. He gave a signal with his head to the four indistinct figures behind him, who were obviously his assistants. They pushed you aside and came in. The last one, the one with the mustache, closed the door.

You stood next to the wall.

"Is anybody else in the house?"

"I'm alone."

"Good. Go ahead of us."

They took you by the shoulder and pushed you in front of them. You stumbled forward a few steps in a daze, then stopped and looked around.

"Get in there," said the blond man, nodding toward the room.

He had a narrow forehead. His dark blond hair was divided in two by a thin, straight part exactly in the middle of his head. You could see how blond he was in his eyebrows. The helper of his who was dark and thin stayed with you. The other three went through the house. You heard the noise they made. Drawers were opened, things pulled out and thrown on the floor. You thought of the rustling that cockroaches make as they flee across newspaper spread out on the shelves when you turn on the kitchen light late at night.

The curly-haired, ugly little man with the thin mustache bent down and looked under the table and the chairs, tapped with his knuckles on the walls, picked up the rug, and looked underneath it and at the inside of the radio, which was covered with white balls of dust.

He worked with interest and confidence, as if he would find something. When he didn't find what he wanted, he looked around in disgust, seeking a new quarry.

He saw the picture hung on the wall. It was the only painting in the house. In the picture, one of those black, damp carriages of childhood with their smell of horses was dashing like a shadow through some washed-out greenery. The rider was waving a long whip, which seemed like an extension of his hand as he made a circle in the air with it. The two bay horses were falling on top of one another, as if they were startled by the whip cracking in the dense foliage and were reaching out, flying away at a gallop with the hide carriage on its rubber tires.

The man grabbed the painting with both hands, gave a good tug, and pulled both it and the nail its wire was attached to out of the wall. A fairly good-sized piece of plaster fell out of the middle of the unfaded square thus exposed. It fell on the tiling of the floor and broke into fragments, leaving a gash behind it on the wall.

"What kind of picture is this?"

"A picture of a carriage."

"You think I never saw a picture of a carriage? How is this a carriage?"

"That's the way they painted it."

"Who did this?"

"I don't know."

The blond man nodded as if to say, "We'll find out."

The dark, ugly little man tried to pull the frame apart. The nails prevented him from pulling out the cardboard on the back. He figured out the easy way. Making a fist out of one hand, he pressed with all his might on the corner where the two horses were tossing their manes and getting in each other's way. The horses' manes curled up terrifyingly and split apart. Beneath the solid fist, the childlike faces of the horses were stretched and twisted; a few nails fell on the floor. The fist came right through the picture. The man took the painting and hung it by the corner thus opened, then separated the picture from the frame with a cracking noise. He ripped open the brittle cardboard in back. He looked destroyed when he found nothing between the painting and the cardboard. Lifting what he had in his hand, he threw it in the middle of the room, next to the rug.

One of the men going through the house came in with an armload of books and dumped them on the floor.

Your nostrils filled again with that smell of soot, the smell of burned paper. The room suddenly filled with smoke, as if the ashes of the books you had burned three days before were coiling around the room. The words that had saved themselves from the fire were coming out of their hiding places and shouting out the great sin you had committed three days previously to the faces of those in the room. They were drawing nearer.

The man kept on leaving and coming back with armloads of books and then piled them all in the middle of the room. A bunch of journals, some books. They wouldn't find even one forbidden book among them. You'd burned them all. But you were afraid that they would see the storm of ashes raging within you. You mustn't let them find out what you had done. Even if you risk losing your life.

The blond one kneeled down and began to look through the books.

"Have you read all of these?"

"I've read most of them."

He looked over the book he had taken in his hand, read the title, and tried to look as if he knew a great deal. He sneered. Then he leafed through the book.

From the middle of the pile he pulled out a roll of journals. They were copies of the old journal *Forum*.

"What are these?"

"Old journals."

"What do you want with them?"

"They're old. I've had them since they came out."

"Good. Whenever there are forbidden journals, forbidden books, you always pick them out and buy them anyhow."

"Those journals aren't forbidden. Years ago..."

"Any kind of forum is forbidden."

"But sir, that 'forum' is a different kind. This is a journal...." you tried to say.

"You can tell them that when we get there," he interrupted.

You would be going, that meant. They were going to take you. You got tight inside.

The ugly, thin man examining the bottoms of the curtains turned.

"We'll take all of these books," he said.

You managed to say, "Sir, you won't find a single forbidden book, a single forbidden journal among these."

"Don't butt in," said the blond one. "Keep quiet." He looked into your eyes as if to establish that he knew a great deal, that he was hot on the trail, that he had caught you in the act. He began to look up and down the middle of the room, giving himself great importance.

"Sir, you have a list of forbidden books; if you'd like, take out the list and compare them. You'll see, you won't come across one of them. All of these are being sold freely at all the bookstores."

He came and stood right in front of you. A paleness spread across his olive face and disappeared. He might even have been clenching his teeth. He reached out his hand; his other hand was behind his back. You thought he was going to hit you; you tensed your face, but he didn't strike. He grabbed your chin and held his fist around it. A heavy smell of sweat, of the stable, came and settled in your nose. He was very close.

"Don't tire that chin of yours, pretty boy," he said. "I don't eat shit. Get me?"

He pushed your chin to one side, then walked away with his sharp smell of sweat. He stopped at the pile of books and took one in his hand.

"I don't understand." he said. "I don't understand what you read these dangerous books for. They're poison, and you don't even know it."

He threw the poisonous book in his hand back on the pile.

"I like to read too. In my free time I always read."

His voice was calmer. Puffing up his chest, he moved toward the middle of the room.

"Listen, if I told you, you'd be surprised. Do you know how many books I've read up till now? Exactly 2,784 books. I counted up the other day. I've read that many books, but I still don't think like you."

He had said this while standing in the doorway, waving one hand. He moved, came over, and stood in front of you again.

"It's easy to say," he said. "Exactly 2,784 books. What do you think, huh?"

He was in front of you. There was a wide oil stain on the left leg of his pants. The heavy smell of sweat exuding from his chest pressed into your nose. You couldn't lift up your head and look into the blond man's face, this blond man who surprised himself with how many books he had read. Something seemed to be aching inside you. Like some crevice had opened and stayed that way. Again that migraine.

"Man, we've studied too," he said in a loud voice. "We finished high school too, so, big deal."

You were angry. You were waiting for him to hit you.

"They made us read the same books they made you read. We read a whole bunch of books. We know how much books are worth, just like you."

As he said this, he drew closer to the pile of books in the center of the room. You were happy to get rid of the smell of sweat, but——

"You ruined your minds," he shouted, and suddenly, with all his strength, he punched a thick history book with a red cover that was right in front of him on the edge of the pile. The book flew from its place and crashed into the wall next to the door.

"Either change this head of yours or we'll break it for you, understand?"

In the corner, the open leaves broken from the binding of the red volume fluttered over one another and settled to the floor.

At that moment, in some corner of the world, in the hour of parting of the evening, a flower silently closed its crown of leaves and slipped into an endless sleep; a little flower born to one day's existence finished its unsatisfying life, bent its head, and died.

The hour of separation must have come; so they took you and sacks full of books from the ransacked rooms and brought you away.

That is how you were brought here.

O. Zeki Özturanlı

Then He Fell Asleep

Translated by Peter Jensen

He entered the room, undressed, and threw himself on the bed. He tossed and turned, but couldn't fall asleep. A voice in his ear kept singing the popular tune: "Those bewitching eyes turn away from my scream." He lit a cigarette, took a deep puff, and blew the rings from his mouth. The rings grew larger, then smaller–and vanished. But somehow his thoughts didn't go away. The song went on: "Come save me, lovely glances, come and redeem." He had come to this bachelor's room, which smelled of sweat, from a bright place where people laughed and enjoyed themselves.

Most days he would have dinner at Albanian Bekir's Diner. His daily meal consisted of kidney beans without eggs. After dinner he would return to his room and read books, underlining certain passages even if his hands turned purple from the cold.

Well, a man can't go through a rat race like this forever. A human being, after all, has other needs–and he was no different. Now and then, he would get the urge and say: "Aaah, who cares? I may be poor, but I refuse to be a damn slave!" And he would put up with the free meals of the Red Crescent for one week and paint the town red with his savings, which meant going out with friends with whom he would have drinks at Zafiris' Tavern at Sirkeci and then going up to the Beyoğlu entertainment district. Going up wasn't difficult, but he didn't care for going down from there. He wished he didn't have to.

He sat in bed and lit one more cigarette. The moon in the sky shone like daylight straight into his room. He counted the cigarettes remaining in the pack. Eleven. "Oooh," he said. "There's enough to last me until noon tomorrow. How about after that? Oh, well. What's the use of worrying about it? God is great. God is generous."

He thought of Kerim. Quite a guy, this Kerim. Last time they were at Zafiris' Tavern he had picked up the tab, saying to everybody: "Look here, guys. I don't want anybody to act like a smart ass. This one's on me." And what did he do when they were on their way up to Beyoğlu? He said: "Gentlemen, with your permission…"–and split.

He said to himself: "This Kerim lives it up every night. They say he gets three hundred from his father each month, and various amounts from his uncle, brother-in-law and God knows who else. So, the son-of-a-gun has five hundred a month. And here I am swimming upstream with a single arm. That night, when Kerim split, he made all sorts of excuses. He said he doesn't care for Turkish music. He talked against this and that. Then he went his way. I bet Kerim is still up. Heaven knows he must be at a fancy bar."

He took another puff, then another, and then one more. He put the cigarette out in the ashtray on the chair next to the bed. He slipped into bed, sticking his head inside the

155

quilt. He turned facing the wall, and shut his eyes. That voice sang in his ears again: "Come save me, lovely glances..." He tried to ignore it. But how come he couldn't get Kerim out of his mind? It wasn't Kerim so much. It was the bar Kerim went to. "I've never danced. Not once in my life. I just don't know how." His half-closed eyes opened. He turned on his back. Put his hands under his head. He began to stare at the ceiling. Then, from where he lay, he noticed his walking stick hanging on a nail behind the door.

That stick had been his lifelong friend. He just couldn't do without it. Do? Couldn't walk without it. "My faithful companion," he said. "I can't do without you. Oh, this goddamn fate of mine!" He cursed like hell, cursed everything in sight.

He kicked the quilt off, and looked down his waist—all the way to the tip of his toes. Took another look. "My right leg," he said. "You're a real tiger!" The left leg lay on the bed, shorter, thinner, weaker, weary and shrivelled up. "Goddamn leg! Year in year out, I have dragged you like a tail. You make me so ashamed. Because of you I feel miserable in the company of friend and foe alike." Then he sighed: "Oh, God. Goddamn. I wouldn't have minded, my God, if you only made me live to age thirty-five so long as you gave me good legs and feet." He prayed.

He pulled the quilt over him, and looked at the watch he had purchased at the flea market three years ago. The watch lit up in the dark: It was 1:13 A.M. "Ooh," he said. "Before long it's going to be morning. I have to go to sleep now." But 1:13 A.M. bothered him. He went through all the unlucky thirteens: At age thirteen he had become a cripple. When he was fifteen, his mother had died on October 13th. A year later, his father brought home a stepmother who heaped misery on the youngster. The stepmother was twenty-six years old. Two times thirteen. Double bad luck. But bad luck came tenfold. He was kicked out of his own father's house. He was forced to seek shelter at his grandmother's house. And then? She died—at age sixty-five, which is five times thirteen.

Stepmother, grandmother, getting kicked out and all that, one could forget. But this left foot. For ten years, everyone took pity on him. Some said: "Poor child, how sad. He's really a handsome hunk of a youngster, too." Some would ask: "Were you born like that?" If he did something naughty, they would put him down with a remark like: "Can you imagine what he'd be like if he weren't a cripple?"

He loved soccer. Actually, the injury to his foot had happened in a game of soccer. Whenever he had some money, he would go to a soccer match. He would plunge like a thunderbolt into the crowd. He knew what the sourpusses there thought about him even if he didn't hear what they said. "Shucks. Look at that guy. Weird bird, with a single wing. Man, who're you to come to a match," they probably said to themselves. Just to spite them, he would push and shove the guys in front of him and beside him and go up front. Then he would start hollering with that strong voice of his: "Attaboy, Naci, chew him up! Go on, get rid of the guy!"

During his early days in Istanbul, he happened to go on a streetcar that was jam-packed. He managed to get on by pushing and pulling the other passengers who were waiting. That way, he got hold of the handle of the rear platform of the streetcar. When he was about to step in, the ticket collector said: "Mister, you could use the front door, you know." He was baffled about this. He turned and leaning on his walking stick he moved to the front section. An old woman and he got in together. A middle-aged man got up and gave him his seat: "Go ahead, you sit, son." He took the seat thinking that the man was about to get off. He was mistaken: the man didn't get off. He rose to his feet, and at the next stop, he jumped down even before the streetcar came to a full stop. He walked, swaying right and left, dragging his bad foot, swearing like hell. He also cursed all the laws and regulations which discriminated against or gave special privileges to the handicapped.

"No use thinking about all this," he muttered. "Who are you to try to change the injustices in the system?" Then, he observed: "My, how this beer goes right down to the bladder!"

He rose and took a hold on the iron bedstead. He grabbed his stick and went to the john. After five minutes he came out, feeling lighter inside. "Oh, boy," he said to himself. "I really relieved myself. There's nothing in the world like good health. So long as my mind, stomach, and lungs are sound, nothing else matters. By God, I'm strong enough to squeeze water out of stone."

He lay face down on the bedstead. From the window near the bed, he stared out. He straightened out halfway on his elbows. He buried his face in his hands.

He looked at the night lamp that was burning red like the rising sun on the second floor of the house across the street. He thought of the people who must be sleeping peacefully under that light—the young handsome doctor and his lovely wife. A happy couple. "Healthy people without physical defects," he said to himself "means happy people." Then he thought of their love and affection. If the wife looked at the doctor's legs, she surely was not disgusted nor did she feel pity. She probably got pleasure out of it.

He straightened up on his left elbow. He pulled his hand away from his face. He looked at his own leg which was dangling from the bedstead. "Darn it," he said. "You can't face a beautiful woman like that with a dead leg like this." He lifted his right elbow. Then lay on his back. "Oh, man," he said. "What after all is a beautiful woman? I can always try to get a wife who's not good looking." He was reminded of the unattractive girls and women he had known. "Forget it," he said. "No use thinking of them. "Even his classmate Müzeyyen, who was also a cripple, had her eyes on the handsome youngsters. She used to come early into the classroom and save seats for them. Damn bitch, once she sat next to Hamza and told him she was not a cripple, but she had a special gait and rhythm when she walked, and all that.

"Oh, my goodness," he sighed. "Get off it. Better get some sleep, man." He wrapped himself in the quilt. Snuggling, he doubled up. He stuck his hands between his legs. He counted from one to ten. No good. Counted up to one hundred. Still no sleep. He recited prayers. But still couldn't fall asleep. "Is this any way to pray?" He withdrew his hands from between his legs. "Darn it, I have sinned." Thought of God again. "God Almighty! You have created everything and everyone. You separate right from wrong. You are omnipresent, omniscient, omnipotent. If you exist, my God, why didn't you see me, why didn't you take care of me, huh? That means you don't exist. You do not exist!"

With his right leg he kicked off the quilt. He straightened out and sat up in bed. "I repent, O Lord," he said. "I repent. I hope Murat will never find out about these thoughts of mine. If he does, he wouldn't speak to me ever again." Murat was a good fellow. They had been friends for only a year now, but they had a great deal of affection for each other. Murat was a devout Moslem. His friend Osman who also came from the same town was even more pious.

Osman came from a well-to-do-family. He was close to his father and mother. But poor fellow had a stroke of bad fortune recently. He contracted pneumonia about a month ago and left for his hometown.

Murat and Osman never patronized him with cheap pity. They accepted him and befriended him in an amiable and manly way. They didn't even once pay any attention to how he takes a step. They never treated him as though there was something unusual about him. They just accepted him casually, never causing him to feel uneasy about his handicap because of anything they said or with their glances or sentiments.

"Oh," he said. "It's shameful the way I've neglected Osman. I should have dropped him a line." He got up saying "Well, no use trying to get to sleep." He took his walking stick. Then, he turned on the light. From under the bedrest he pulled his wooden suitcase. Sitting on the edge of the bed he set it on his knees, and opened it. He took out the book that he had borrowed from Murat the day before. He placed a sheet of paper on it and began to write with his ballpoint: "Dear Osman." Then he put the date—March 7, 1948. He hesitated and put the pen down. He said: "How should I start? I guess I shouldn't mention the illness. That might depress him." He was flipping the pages of the book when he suddenly came upon a letter. He recognized the handwriting. It was a letter from Osman to Murat. "Son-of-a-gun Murat," he muttered. "He didn't tell me he got a letter from Osman." He wondered if he should read it. But then he thought: "What secrets could they possibly have from me?" and proceeeded to read. "Poor boy," he kept saying. "Osman, that poor kid is bedridden again."

The closing sentences read: "The cripple owes me five liras. He didn't pay me back. You get it for me. That lame crow gypped me. I feel like pissing on his foot."

He nearly choked. He almost had a fainting spell. The paper fell off. He threw the suitcase down and the pen. He rose. Counted the money in his pockets. He had one lira and a few pennies. He turned off the light and stretched out on the bed. "Tomorrow," he said. "I must find a way and make five liras. Should I borrow it from the butcher? Or should I sell sissy books in front of the University? Or should I write out envelopes and money orders for illiterates at the post office?" Then he fell asleep...

Fethi Savaşcı

Hamit the Drunk

Translated by James Lee Yarrison

The moment Hamit left the German café, it began snowing. He didn't feel like going to the factory lodgings so early. He wanted to have a couple of beers at another café. Night had begun to fall gently: he could tell from the fluorescent lights that went on in front of the main post office. The hands of the clock in front of the central station were no longer visible because of the snow. The clock, which was half the size of a car, could barely be seen from nearby. A German woman with long false eyelashes was waiting for someone in front of the post office. Hamit approached her hopefully, but she turned her head away when she noticed Hamit coming. Hamit was crushed, and walked on. Waving his hand indistinctly to the woman, he muttered: "Damn you, whore. I'm not going to devour you. I just thought we could have a little chat—not that I can speak that well. If I'm not German, it doesn't mean I'm not human. Goddamn bitch, you think I ain't human? Just look at that face—and reach for the bayonet. I swear to God, if that ain't the ugliest face."

He almost crossed the street against the red light. A car braked sharply. The driver, a fat middle-aged German, swore like hell. Hamit was pleased that he had angered the German. From the other side of the street, he yelled after the car: "Hey, damn you! Swear at my cross, at my idols. Thank God, I'm a Moslem. I got no cross, no idols. But, swear at my mosque, and I'll make you sorry you were born. God knows I'd make pulp out of you right in that car of yours or else they don't have to call me Hamit the Drunk. Get it?"

With the effect of the cold, Hamit seemed to come to a little bit. He looked about, and noticed that the speeding streetcars made a stop in front of the central station. He walked over to the park café that was not far. "I'll order a cognac," he thought to himself. "And get a chance again to pat waitress Monica's bottom." If you ordered two or three cognacs, Monica would even let you kiss her on the lips. He had seen her being kissed by others so many times. But whenever—and there had been many occasions—he talked of taking her to a hotel or rooming house, she had made excuses like: "I have my period" or "I got a date." Many nights, he had waited till 1:00 A.M.—the closing time the police set for the cafés in that part of the city. At exactly one minute past 1:00 A.M. a tall young blond German man would get into his car with Monica and drive away. Was it her husband? A lover? Hamit didn't know. This burned him more than anything else. He just couldn't bear the idea of a woman he liked going out with another guy. Night after night, he had prayed in bed, imploring God: "I wonder what to do about this tall German guy who takes Monica out every night? My God, you are mighty, you are all-powerful. Why don't you kill this second-story man in an auto crash so that Monica will be left to me. I've already taken the wedding ring off my finger anyway. So, she has no way of knowing I'm married. She'll go

159

out with me, I bet. Every so often she strokes my mustache, right? Please, God Almighty, please kill that German guy!" A little later, he would think it over and feel ashamed: "Dammit, Hamit, my boy," he would mumble to himself: "Sit on your ass. Enough of this shit. No one knows who will die when, where, how. Forgive me, God, for the things I said. I'll never do it again. Look here, sonny boy, this nation of heathens ain't gonna disappear no matter how many of them die, right?"

Hamit bumped into a linden tree in the middle of the sidewalk and laughed: "Hamit, you're drunk, buddy boy! You're a first-class lush; you gotta keep up your reputation."

When he entered the café where Monica worked, he saw a young German standing on a table delivering a speech to his friends. As he denigrated world politics and heaped abuse on statesmen, his friends around the table applauded now and then. Monica the waitress was leaning against the counter sipping the cognac someone had bought her. She smiled when she noticed Hamit coming in. Hamit cast a languid and seductive glance at her, and stroked his jetblack mustache. Monica smiled again. She came over and stood by the table at which Hamit wanted to sit. She went through the motions of cleaning the top of the table with a cardboard coaster she casually picked up. Hamit sat down wearily, and grabbing Monica's hand he kissed it. She quickly drew it back, and coquettishly hit the top of Hamit's hand with the coaster. With a choked voice, Hamit asked for a beer. Monica wasn't drunk yet. She would begin kissing the guys after a few drinks. The owner of the café was aware of this, but raised no objections because all this kissing meant an increase in drinks sold. Maybe he even gave Monica a percentage of the sales. The young German on the table kept getting an applause as he talked—and whenever he got a big hand, he took a big sip from his beer and became even more forceful. From all that haranguing, patches of white foam had begun to form on both sides of his mouth. They were visible even from afar.

"Friends, we will not cast our votes in the upcoming elections for those who are trying to cut off our beer or make it more expensive—right?" His audience expressed approval. Another young German, whose front teeth had been knocked off in a brawl, also jumped to his feet to speak: "Is it only beer? Have you forgotten the potato salad?" Those around the table laughed, holding their groins. Hamit began muttering: "Man alive, what other shit do you have besides beer and potatoes? I wish a friend of mine came through that door so that we could have a little chat. Damn these godless bastards. Honest, they're all godless. None of them gives a goddamn about a real godly man like me."

When Monica brought the second beer, she first took a sip herself and then she handed him the glass. Hamit was glad. Not disgusted at all. He liked her taking a sip from his glass. He ordered a cognac. Monica said "Şerefe!" (To your health.) She had learned to offer a toast in all languages. But Hamit had a different toast whenever he drank with friends: He liked to say, "May the spot it hits never know pain." But it would be hard to teach this to Monica. For one thing, his German wasn't good enough. Besides, he had already had too many drinks. And Monica, like most Germans, had difficulty pronouncing the "ş" sound, and made it into a "s". Anyhow, as far as Hamit was concerned, it was more than enough that Monica had offered him a toast in Turkish tonight.

After treating her to a second cognac, Hamit quickly pulled Monica into his lap. Without paying attention to her shouting, he kissed her twice on the neck. Monica heaved for a while. When she tore herself away, she slapped him on the left cheek, screeching: "Schweinhund!" The owner of the café, a short man with a constant fear in his eyes, who was now half-drunk, told Hamit to get out at once as he tapped his cigar ashes into Hamit's ashtray. If he didn't leave at once, he said he'd call the police. Hamit opened his eyes wide and then pushed the café owner on his chest. While the owner staggered backwards toward the bar, the cigar fell from his mouth. By then, Monica had already phoned the police. Hamit opened the switchblade knife he pulled out of his pocket and began shouting in Turkish: "Come on, goddamn bastards! What is it I've done? I didn't eat her up, didn't finish her off, did I? Dammit, you wouldn't do this to a dog! The whore hasn't been born yet who can slap me. Got that?"

He staggered once or twice. He stuck his knife furiously into the tabletop. His half-empty beer mug toppled. He pulled the chair he had been sitting in and held it in front of him. Two teardrops trickled down his swarthy cheeks. He wiped them off with the back of his hand, and cried out: "You, godless bastards! I can butcher you like sheep, you know. Let my blood flow like beer if I can't do it. You get that?"

Three cops appeared at the entrance. The other Germans fell silent when they saw the police. Hamit labored to pull himself together. He offered seats to the cops. The youngest of the three grasped the handle of the knife and pulled it out of the tabletop. The oldest asked for Hamit's passport. Hamit didn't have it with him. One of the cops asked the proprietor and Monica if they would or would not press charges. The third cop was minding the entrance. This is what they did during a search or interrogation lest the culprit escape. For a moment, Hamit seemed to sober up. He muttered to himself: "Hamit, you bastard! Now you're really fucked up!"

Zeyyat Selimoğlu

Green Gold

Translated by Nural Yasin

By the starboard lifeboat, their heads in the shadow the boat casts on the deck, their bodies out in the sun, they're lying on their backs. İdris's hands as thick as a pillow, under his head his pillow-hands, clasping each other, his eyes on the spotless sky, on a white cloud stuck in one part of the sky, he is thinking. Ali's right hand is on the thin rope hanging down from the front of the ship's rowing boat, playing with the rope. He twists the rope, twines it, and stretches it onto the deck; then he gathers it together and twists it again.

"Would this cloud over us walk on and on till it passed over our village too? This cloud that sees us now—would it see our village too?"

"I don't know myself. Wouldn't the clouds crumble and get scattered before they reached the village? What is it that you call a cloud—is it not just smoke? And smoke..."

"I won't put up with this sea any longer, this is my last voyage."

Ali turns his head from its rest and looks at İdris with amazement.

"You said your last voyage, did you? You won't put up with the sea; what is there for you then? What else are we good for? What was your father anyway, and his father, and his grandfather?"

"They were sailors. So we became sailors. They never did much else than turn the rudder before them. They bequeathed the rudder to us. From father to son, turning the wheel.... That is all you inherit if they stay with the rudder. If I can't have something else for my children, this is where they will end up too."

"The Black Sea has written such a fate on our foreheads."

"That fate must be wiped off and rewritten.... I will not go out to the sea any longer.... The sea gives naught. No end to this sea.... The earth of the harbors you arrive at does not belong to you, that I realize; you lose your way and end up far away from your land."

"Maybe your father thought your very thought, and so did your grandfather, but then he said, "This is my job, to turn the wheel; if one takes up a thing he doesn't know about, he gets lost in it. One does the work he's learned; he can manage no other. If he does some other, it gets tangled round his neck.

For a while the cloud darkens; the smoke thrust out of the chimney gets under the cloud and darkens it. From underneath the ship's beam, the rustling of the sea comes up; the sound of continuous tearing of paper rises up from the sea. Foam receding from the ship melts into the distance, each foam going out on the blue, leaving the calm blue to rule out there all by itself. The sun continuously polishes the blue; lightness takes over.

"The sea gives us naught.... The sea is a barren field for us....For we cannot sow this earth; neither can we mow it. The sea isn't ours; we are no more than a guest here...

temporary.... That rudder on the bridge—it is only the hands on it that change. Today it is my hands, tomorrow my son's, and the next day my grandson's.... Once your hands get old, the wheel thrusts them away, hurls them at the land, and by then it is too late—you cannot use your hands any longer, not even on your own land can you use them; you are broken with exhaustion. The wheel determines better than you the moment you are to leave work. Hundreds of people like you have worked at it; it's got cunning, cleverness.... The wheel determines hands well, knows your hands better than you; it's carried those hands on his back all its life.... I can't read or write, but I know what I'm talking about. You better realize that. You are not the master of your hands; it is the rudder at the bridge that is the master of your hands.... It is the rudder there that owns all the hands on this ship."

İdris rises a little from his place, points at the bridge with his huge finger, and lies back.

He shuts his eyes, and wheels in wheels come out in circles in his closed eyes; every wheel gives birth to a new wheel from its center, wheel from a wheel, wheel from a wheel.... Hundreds, thousands of hands wish to embrace the wheel, grasp the wheel firmly, and rest hanging on the wheel; then they loosen up, slip off, slide away from the edges of the wheel, and rapidly disappear one after the other in the swamping seas covered with dark waters. The swamp gulps down the hands; mouths all over the swampy sea—each gulps down a hand, swallows a hand. There comes an end to the hands in the swamps....

When he opens his eyes, he sees the white cloud above; would that white cloud go on without dispensing, go on till the village, finding the way for itself? Yes it would, leaving itself to the blowing wind, would slide away as if in full sail.

İdris sees himself up there on the cloud, sitting on one edge of the cloud, with his feet dangling down, going toward the village in just the opposite direction that the ship is now going. The cloud crosses a huge sea carrying İdris on its back. Below the straits, a coastline with bays and peninsulas, with ins and outs, rapidly passes by.

This is an unusual cloud—it makes one fly; swiftly crosses seas, lands, and coastlines; goes on, and how it goes on and on, like the melody that flows from the strings of a violin, goes as though flowing, hearty vibrating strings of the violin. . . . It goes high and low, far over hills goes İdris's cloud...no ship, no wheel, no bridge, no chimney, no boat at all.... Only the cloud and İdris and İdris's hands free of the wheel, rid of the wheel, saved from being drowned in the swamps—two hands still good for something. İdris's cloud has suddenly reached its destination, reached İdris's village, those upper parts of Rize—İdris's village, where stumpy hazelnut trees, icy waters that flow into dark black streambeds, weedy rocks with wet tops, wild pears, sour apples, scented grapes, hanging cucumbers with thorny backs, and black cabbages penetrate into each other, and alders elegant as poplars rise.

The cloud sees a roof among the trees, a chimney on the roof. A streak of smoke goes up from the chimney, singing "Elif Elif "; the smoke rises up to the cloud, rises up to İdris.

İdris recognizes this smoke; this is a cloud of old, one that carried some smell from the noses of fathers and sons and has now anchored before İdris's hooked nose. This smell, oh, this smell.... This smell that İdris has so long been deprived of breathing in is of his home fire, my child, of his father's hearth fire, of his mother's lap, of the corn flour rising from the corn-cheese pasty pan, of butter, of blackened pans, of those black cabbages, beans, peppers, beans, and black cabbages. İdris rests, sitting on the cloud, with nostrils as open as his eyes are closed, breathing in the smell of his home fire.

Fadime's hands are in this smell; her eyes, her hair, her sweet-smelling breasts are in this smell. His sons Hasan, Hızır, his daughter Elif–this smoke brings to İdris the smell of all that smoke that streaks gracefully out of the chimney. Has Fadime guessed that this is a different cloud and gone to cook a special corn-cheese pasty on her fire, to cook a black cabbage soup? "What is this cloud up to?" The cloud comes further and further and further down; this is a different cloud, descending to the earth from above İdris's home where it had stopped. The chimney smoke is left up there; the chimney is up there. The roof, the window all pass by the cloud upward.... This is a different cloud; it can't help delivering İdris to his door; İdris is at his threshold now....

How many years since he's gone out to the seas, since he's crossed his threshold? How many years since he's seen Fadime and his children? This is not the place to work that out now, standing at the threshold. One ought to dive in like the north wind blowing strong. The steps of the north wind cross the threshold and go in with a big bang.

Fadime has bent over the fire; she looks in the direction of the sound. Fadime has turned round looking at the door. "Who is it that's come in?" Oh dear.... How can I believe my black framed eyes, my eyes with tangled lashes; how can I believe them? Suddenly, I find İdris by me, İdris, whom I have not seen for years, whose hands have not touched mine, whose arms have not been round my waist for years....İdris, İdris, İdris.... İdr–an armful of his wife in his arms, his lips close his wife's mouth, half his name out, half in. His name breaks as their mouths unite. A shiver has taken hold of Fadime. Who says one can't dance without the violin? Fadime shivers inside out; once the north wind starts blowing, once İdris...oh, dear...what a warm north wind this is; what warmth is this that makes you shiver.... Were these hands of İdris's so large; did they grow so large with wheel-turning? How did these hands come all the way across the seas? These hands, these hands came, dragging İdris behind them. I feel İdris in his hands.... Heaven above, it is in his hands. İdris lives round my waist....His hands get larger and larger on my hips, grow larger, larger, larger, larger.... İdris is nothing but two hands. His hands drag me out from behind the years, my husband's hands...

"The children?"

"Sleeping."

İdris lets go of the thin waist, the hip. In front of a door, a thin mattress inside, the children's heads, the children on the bench, as yellow as quinces' heads.... These children mustn't get caught by this unfaithful wheel; they must own their hands, these two boys.... İdris will break the convention; he will break the wheel passed on to them from the forefathers. He'll get hold of the wheel, crash it down at the bridge, will save his boys' hands from the swamps; it's for this İdris has come back.

If the child that follows you lacks reading and writing too, he'll retreat, will go backward, even further back than you, a child less than you and more backward. If he curses over your grave one day, your soul cannot rest in sleep.... İdris feels himself shivering in his grave.

İdris wakes up from the dream with a shudder. Ali smiles and touches his shoulder.

"You've fallen asleep, you have, İdris; you are sleeping. You have no more voice and breath left; dead or alive–what are you?"

"I didn't sleep. I thought."

"What did you think of?"

"Of what I told you just now."

"What you told me just now."

"What I told you just now."

The sea is rustling below them; the white cloud is still up in the sky—it's gone nowhere. İdris's eyes get fixed on the cloud again. This is a different cloud; it deceives you, pretends it's gone somewhere else, whereas it never moves. Devil of a cloud, not even ashamed of its white beard is this cloud; what sort of a cloud is this?

"İdris."

"What?"

"What you've just told me is all in vain; forget it all.... We're born seamen, and we will die as seamen. This we shouldn't forget—don't let the devil get the better of us. Our fathers were seamen, and so will our sons be seamen. As soon as our turn comes, to the wheel.... The most you can be is a quartermaster. An uneducated man cannot be much else."

"He can."

"What?"

"He sows his soil and earns from his own soil's produce. If he earns well, his children won't have to think of how to get their bread. Those who don't have to do that can study more easily; they can retain what they read. They don't avoid the educated, but stand by them shoulder to shoulder. We have never been able to stand by the educated; neither can we now. For we...we are not educated. Our fathers have not been able to educate us.... I don't want to be remembered as such a father; I want to educate my child."

"I can read but cannot write."

"To read a newspaper is not to be educated. That's not what I'm talking about. To be an educated man is different. An educated man is one who's gone through all the schools there are. He is given a paper, a paper with his name and picture on it and the stamp of the state; it says this man in the picture is an educated man, it says, and then puts its signature down, the state does.

"Have you seen that paper?"

"I have. I saw it when I took Fadime down to town to see the doctor. That paper was on the wall in the doctor's room. Hung on the wall. It has a frame and glass; the paper under the glass cannot be touched. The doctor doesn't let anyone touch his paper; he's put it under the glass. I stood still before that wall, before that paper, forgot all about Fadime, forgot her illness, the doctor, and that we'd come to see the doctor. Then I realized why we can't stand by educated men. That paper.... We haven't got that paper.... That paper we haven't got.... What good is reading the newspaper in broken syllables? You don't have the paper. We are not educated."

"Did you see the state's signature on the paper too?"

"I did; I saw both the stamp and the signature.... The state has put down its stamp and signed it too."

Both are quiet now, listening to the tearing of the rustling paper below them. They have no paper. Their paper gets all torn before they get it. As long as they live, they'll listen to the tearing of that paper; they'll hear the rustling of the paper they never possessed. The seaman has no paper; he has only the sea, which rustles like paper.

"Am I not educated if I can read the newspaper?"

"You read the newspaper.... Once you can put the letters together, you can read the newspaper. But it is a different matter to be an educated man. An educated man is one who's read all knowledge, learned all knowledge, read about all knowledge we don't know of, read from books, read things that are hard to learn. He's learned such hard things that he's read and become a doctor, a lawyer, an engineer.... All you do is read the paper. The most you can be is a quartermaster who can read the paper. I want my son to be an educated man, one such as I've told you about. If I could not get an education, my son must; he must be an educated man, able to give a kick to the wheel.

Ali nervously plays with the end of the rope.

"Difficult.... What you want is difficult. Money.... The education you talk about requires money. Your son will need your money for his education; he'll expect you to pay." He points at the bridge. You can hardly give them enough food by turning the wheel there. Then there's the school, the book, the notebook. Once one gets an education, the others wish for the same; you cannot discriminate—the flesh and the bone are inseparable.

A deep fear has settled in Ali's eyes.

"You wish for things you cannot tackle. It's a hard job that you want to deal with."

İdris replies from his place, talking slowly.

"I know; sure it is hard.... It's hard, but possible. You sow your soil. I told you.... You sow your soil and get the produce."

He turns slightly sideways, digs his hands in his pocket, and takes out a rolled piece of paper from his pocket. A piece of paper as big as a small ball. He unwinds the paper slowly, with care so as not to drop it. Holds the paper in his large palm unwound. He stretches his hand, holding the paper, to Ali.

"Have a look and see."

Ali rises from where he's been lying and, turning toward İdris, rests on his elbow. He fixes his eyes on the paper in astonishment. There is a black-green powder in the paper, small dry leaves.

"Well what is this? What good is it?"

İdris lies back; he gathers the paper up in his hand and hides it there. He talks slowly, with his eyes on the snow-white cloud above.

"They sent it from home. They planted the seedling in one corner of the garden. When it had ripened they noticed the green shoots it had grown. Our soil does produce. That's what is in the paper, the tea that seedling gives: green gold..."

Sevgi Soysal

The Tank That Went Mad and the Child

Translated by Nilüfer Mizanoğlu Reddy

The row of tanks was lined up over there where the sun set, from the red line to the deep purple interior of the steppes. The pollen of the spring, the dust of the dry summers, the rain of the changing seasons, then the cold, snow and sleet, all these phenomena presented this motionless row with the changes of nature and with all their might were trying to digest and dissolve its sluggish metallic existence. The mice were proliferating in the gun barrels, the dead flies were getting stuck to the dusty metal bodies, a mad bee confused by the joy of pollen absorbed from flowers of the intermittent springs was getting scorched by settling on the hot metal.

Every now and then daisies, poppies, lavenders, or crocuses were sprouting in the secret hollows of the wheels with a mindless perseverance, trying to cover this metallic row with a blanket of vegetation. The ant and mole hills were getting ready for a future metallic feast in ever growing holes to swallow the tanks one by one. A wind that was blowing there from the gray clouds was getting wilder and pushing one end of the row of tanks to make them move from the purple of the steppes to the redness of the sunset to annihilate them in that redness. The heat, arriving suddenly, was longing for relief with a roar through the gun barrels heated up with frequent birth pains and then the never ending rains were rusting the tight gun barrels with a vengeful slowness.

On New Year's Eve:

Imitation gold wrapping paper. Packages tied with colored ribbons. Decorated store windows. Lottery men hawking. Indoor horse races and certificates for the henpecked husbands. Christmas trees, cotton balls, and tinsel. Colored bulbs. Presents arranged side by side and piled on top of each other. Silver that is shined, silver that is sold. Money and packages. Hands that stretch out to give money, arms full of packages.

Fingers that are reaching the goods, index fingers. Index fingers pointing in all directions in front of the store windows. Mouths that open, lips that pucker while counting the money. A slice of cake eaten between two packages. Cakes, turkeys, salads dressed with mayonnaise. Bingo. Raffle for prizes. A child about ten years old. Poor, he has no taste for acquisition yet: a child who has nothing to do with the stores and the ever increasing packages in the arms of the youths who are coming from the streets.

He wanted to taste the joy of owning something on this day of gifts.

He saw the little tank that could go both forward and backward with gun barrels that were spitting fire. Three other children were playing with it in front of the garden gate.

The child wanted to enjoy a gift. He chose the gift in his mind. His hand stretched out toward the tank. He wanted to touch this thing. First in his thoughts he separated his thing from the children who seemed to own it. Then he stretched out his hand. Many things came between his outstretched hand and his gift: first there were chasing children between himself and the toy tank; then there were mothers and fathers, then chasing traffic cops, then chasing functionaries, houses, apartment buildings, policemen, judges, and banks. The child was running and fleeing. Away from the gift, away from the objects. He was running away from the city that knew how to handle its possessions and did not want to give them away to a child. He came running to the outskirts of the city, to the steppes, alien to objects, where the row of tanks stood.

The hand of the child was added to the row of ants, moles, mice, flies, and all the living creatures. First the child touched the chained wheels. He felt the buttons on the inside of one of the tanks with his hands. All of a sudden the tank came to life. The child hopped into the steppes and took protection in the chain of living creatures of which he himself was a link. The tank came out of the row. It emerged from the stillness extending from the purple on the right to the redness on the left. It was left alone, all alone with the forces of nature that were being fought by this sluggish row. It stopped being a certain metallic coziness in a peaceful row. It advanced over the enemy, the living creatures.

Now the wind was wilder, the crust of the earth more fertile, the sun more forceful, the living more voracious and more consuming. All of nature, all living creatures, the purple of the steppes, the redness of the sunset were pitted against one tank: the tank that went mad after a century of sluggishness and sloth. First gun barrels became erect. Then the chained wheels shook. The mice came scurrying out. The wheels in motion crushed the poppies, daisies, lavenders, crocuses. The tank had gone mad. With the wind, cold, heat, and spring, and a superabundant madness, the tank rolled from the steppes. It left the redness of the sunset where the row of sluggish tanks was standing and arrived in the city.

Remembering its power the tank attacked the city with all its might. First it went over the traffic cops at intersections. It fired at the television antennas, telegraph and telephone poles. Then at the soldiers in front of the official buildings, government offices. All the employees lay down on the floor to escape from the death that was coming through the broken glass. Death found them in the most cowardly, most humiliated moment of their lives. Then the tank went over the apartment houses. They grew smaller and smaller. The tank passed over and crushed them one by one without respite, without skipping a single one. Then the houses, interiors, sideboards, trunks, refrigerators, washing machines, stores, and the cashiers; these were easier to crush and more fun. Then the banks, the money that was counted and the money that was being paid. Then the medals, stars, then all the seals, labels, and stamps. Then the official papers, "submitted for your approval," memos, promotions, records. Then the bosses, the bosses, the orders, the orders. Then me, then you, then us, those like ourselves. Then our children, our children's toys, toy tanks. Then the wheelings and dealings. My table, your table. Then all those little possessions that give pleasure. Then Madame Sitare's fur coat. Madam Betül's ring. Then all the jealousies, all the greed, all the gifts, savings, all the insurance policies, guaranteed tomorrows. Then success, fame, love letters, cheatings. My love, your lie, his bragging and boasting. Heroisms, treacheries. Parties, organizations, all those necks with swollen veins. Parties, organizations, all those necks with swollen veins. Newspapers, headlines, pedantries, vituperations. ME's in large print. It passed over all, all of them without getting tired, without skipping a single one. It destroyed as much as it could for a tank that went mad, if it were possible for a tank to go mad...

A child's hand that avoided all this destruction and wrecking, a hand that had nothing to do with these things in the first place, a child's hand with dirty fingernails, poor, with nothing to lose, tasting curiosity for the first time—touched his first toy and the madness of the tank stopped. The tank and the child looked at the burning city from the place where the madness was stopped all the way to the redness of the sunset: now where were the purple of the steppes and the forces of nature that made only one tank go mad? Where are you, where is he and where are we? Presently there was nothing left to go mad. There was only a fire that burned the infinite steppes and its infinite forces. There was the endlessness of the sunset. There was the burning of a big city, the burning of the vast steppes by a mad tank. All aflame from the place where the madness of the tank ended to the redness of the sunset. The madness of the tank was stopped by a poor, curious child's hand that was stretching out to his first gift. But when the steppes were in flames, the row of sluggish tanks there was confronted with a new disaster that was different from the disasters they were familiar with. They too went mad. If it were possible for a tank to go mad, now a row of tanks too would go mad when forced, and how? The row of tanks that went mad broke away from the redness coming from the city and arrived in other cities. They destroyed and they burned until the hands of thousands of poor children touched their first toys...

The child woke up with an aching forehead. His forehead that was resting against the cold glass was numb. How long has it been since he leaned his forehead on the cold glass plate of the store window and watched the row of toy tanks move? During that time the old year had ended and the New Year had begun.

Kemal Tahir

The Carter

Translated by Bedia Turgay-Ahmad

As soon as he left Çerkeş behind, the carter stopped the horses and jumped down.

The cart had no box. He pulled the rear axle up to the level of the water bolt. Thus, the cart was extended to the full length of the pole. Taking the feather out of the oilcan that was hanging under the prong, he oiled the wheels.

Delikır, the horse on the right, became restive.

Carefully, he fastened the sack of barley and the sack of hay to the rear prong. Then tying the bags of horse fodder, horses' rags and his eiderdown to the front prong, he climbed onto the cart. He took the reins and with his whip lightly touched the horses on the rump:

"*Döyyt!* Come on, my boy! My red lion!"

The sun was about to set. The tree tops were crimson. Through the smoky evening the road looked very straight. Along the ditches on the sides were poplar trees, at intervals, and field fences. The gray hills rose far off from the fields.

As Delikır's ambling pace quickened, Pamukkır, the horse on the left, trotted to keep up.

With pride and affection, the carter looked at his well-fed young horses. Like two trained soldiers, they were going in step.

He took his feet off the pole, folded his legs, and settled down to a cigarette. As the wheels hit the axle lids, they gave out a tinkling sound; this mingled with the bells on the horses' necks. The carter felt more cheerful hearing all these familiar, delightful sounds. He squinted as the smoke from his cigarette hit his face. Because of his prominent cheekbones and his drooping mustache, he appeared to be constantly smiling.

He was glad when he left behind the three villagers riding on their donkeys.

"*Döyyt!* Come on, my lion! Go on, son!" he shouted, patting the horses with the tip of his whip.

In a small puddle by the road, in the middle of the reeds, a stork rested, hiding one leg under its belly and its long beak in its chest.

Flicking his cigarette toward it with the tip of his fingers, he said:

"Here's a light, old man!"

Since his childhood he had always imagined a stork's beak to be a pipe.

The cart rattled across the wobbling boards of a bridge. As he came round the bend, he saw two women walking in the distance. Their skirts, the ends of their kerchiefs were flying about, as they hurried along. Despite the oncoming darkness, he could see that one was carrying a sack.

The carter thought of the fodder bags on top of the back wheels. I can let the poor things sit on them. The aunts will pray for me. He couldn't tell from that distance whether they were young or old, but, by way of preparation, he smoothed the brim of his black felt hat, which had sagged under the battering of many a rain. He stroked his mustache.

As the cart neared the women, they turned and stared.

He pulled up.

"Is this the way to Suhizar, aunts?"

The woman with the sack laughed in a husky voice:

"You won't get a free answer, son. If you let us ride on your cart, we'll show you the way and also pray for you."

"I'd gladly take you, aunt, but, as you can see for yourself, the box isn't there. We were carting logs, and so we took the box off and turned the cart into a raft. Can you sit on top of the bags behind?"

"God bless you. We can sit there; our feet will be off the road—that's enough."

"Come on then. Jump on."

In the dark he tried to guess the age of the silent woman, but he couldn't tell because she had covered her face up to her eyes. He whipped the horses, and, to start a conversation, he asked:

"How many hours is Suhizar from here?"

"Five or six on foot."

"Fine, the horses will get there in three then!"

"Of course, of course, God bless them!"

"Amen, aunt!"

All this time only the husky-voiced woman had talked.

They were silent for a while.

He was going to Suhizar to load smuggled logs. They had said it took three and one-half hours from Çerkeş. He was glad that this turned out to be right.

This time the husky-voiced woman asked:

"Hey, carter, are you from Suhizar?"

"No, I'm not, aunt."

"Have you been hired to go there?"

"Yes."

"After Taşpınar, you'll turn off at Köklü. We'll show you where to turn."

"Fine.... But I've to give water to the horses an hour before Suhizar."

"There's plenty of water on the way. You can let them drink at Taşpınar."

For the first time, the other woman said something. She stuttered. The carter tried to hide his laughter.

"Are you going to load logs?"

"Yes."

"Good.... Will you take them to Çerkeş?"

"Further than Çerkeş—to the Kurşunlu region. They're laying a railway line there."

"We've heard about that too; that's what they say. It will also come this far, they say."

"Not only this far—it will go right to Karabük and Zonguldak."

The husky-voiced woman joined in:

"My dead husband's brother lives over there. I wonder if you know him? He is a fair-haired sunburned man. He's slightly lame. His name is Abdurrahman."

"I don't know him, aunt!"

"His wife's village is near Ilgaz. He told me that the railway line brings famine. The daughters-in-law become bad. God save us!"

"Don't talk like that, aunt.... How can a railway line bring famine? My brother is a carter like me. But he's better off. Four pairs of horses, two carts. He doesn't like the railway. 'One day it'll snatch our food from our hands!' he says."

"God forbid, no one can snatch a carter's food."

"I say so too. For two years I have been working on hire along this line. We're getting along. Why should there be no work for the cart when the railway starts? They said the same thing about the trucks. But it turned out to be wrong. I'm going to Suhizar"—"to load smuggled logs," he was about to say, but decided not to—"the railway can't come to Suhizar to cart logs."

"Of course it can't, how dare it!"

The carter gave a friendly look toward his horses. He had had Delikır since he was a pony; while training him, he made him run on the ploughed fields to get him used to ambling.

The women were talking about the train. The husky-voiced one said:

"They've tied together rooms, one after another. By God, they say it's like a house. Huge! They say that after you put all the men and women of our village inside, there's room left for the people of Bulgurlu and Değirmenarkası. When it moves, it seems to be screaming like a herd of water buffalo."

The other one stuttered:

"What do you expect from an infidel's work.... Of course it screams like that...."

"Let it scream then."

When the carter struck a match to light his cigarette the husky-voiced woman asked:

"Do you have parents in your village?"

The carter knew well the words that would break the hearts of the old village women:

"I have no mother or father. I'm left alone in this world."

"Oh! You poor, poor thing! Don't you have any relatives at all?"

They hadn't noticed that he had mentioned his brother only a short while ago. He was glad about that.

"I don't have anybody at all, aunt."

"Where are you from originally?"

Instead of saying that he was from the Şabanözü region of Çankırı he pointed to a far-off place with his whip:

"It's very far from here.... I'm from Yozgat."

"Didn't you ever get married?"

The carter pretended to be very sad.

"How can a lonely man get married? I couldn't."

"What a pity!"

"Isn't it sad? It's a great pity, mother. It's very sad for me!"

"Have you done your military service?"

Since his birth certificate made him out to be younger than he was, he would go into the army in two years; but he lied again:

"I've done it. It's all finished. What do you say to this—I even became a sergeant in the army."

"God save you for the government, for the nation!"

"Amen, aunt!"

For a while they went on without saying a word. All this time the stuttering woman was getting ready to say something.

"Is the cart yours?" she asked.

"The horses and the cart are mine."

"Good, it's good that you have something of your own."

"I don't like to work for a monthly wage. Look at this Delikır. I got him when he was a pony and trained him myself. I looked for twenty days to find a match for him. But now I won't sell them even if somebody gives two hundred liras for the pair. I'm very particular.... Look at this cart; I had it specially made in Amasya. The spokes are not joined. They're made of one piece. You should see the harness in the daytime. I had it made by the most famous saddler in Çankırı and watched him fix the spangles, beads, roses, bells, and all the ornaments of the crupper."

"Maşallah, maşallah!* You're really particular. That's clear."

Night had fallen. It was hot, with not a breeze in the air.

When the carter sighed sadly, thinking that women would never understand about good horses, a good cart, or a good harness, the husky-voiced woman asked:

"What's the matter, Sergeant? Heart broken? Are you pining for someone?"

"No, nothing like that!"

"Come on. You're a young lad, nothing to be ashamed of. Just the right age for such a desire. Anyway, how old are you?"

"I'm past twenty-four. I'm twenty-five."

"You see, it's getting too late to get married.... You didn't have much luck, Sergeant."

The carter was chuckling to himself in the dark. He had been engaged for three months, and the wedding was going to be in the spring.

"A curse on loneliness, aunt.... To wander around with no home to go back to is wearing me out."

"That's sad!"

The women started whispering to each other. The carter was all ears, but he couldn't hear what they were saying. As he cracked his whip, the horses started trotting.

"Don't think I'm just a carter.... I know a lot about farming and farms. If you saw me making a furrow you'd be surprised. But I should have a heavy plough for that."

"Do you really know about farming?" asked the two women together in peculiar delight.

The carter turned round to look back:

"Know about it? What do you mean? You should see me ploughing."

"Farming is as hard as they say. It wears the man out. It's nothing like sitting in a cart and wandering about," said the husky-voiced woman, without letting the other stutter.

*"What (wonders) God hath willed!"

"Each work has its difficulties. It's hard to ride a cart at times. Suppose your wheel broke on the road, what would you do, eh? You're constantly wandering from place to place, no home of your own, not a relative. Your life passes away in rooms of some inns."

The women whispered to each other again.

The carter heard the stuttering woman say once or twice: "Is it possible? No, you can't be serious." He was used to eavesdropping on his customers when he drove his brother's cart. It was fun to do this. One could get carried away with words and not notice the distance. He was sorry that he had pushed the back wheels all the way. The noise made it impossible to hear what they were saying. He looked at his watch.

"Aunt! How far do we have to go? I have to give water to the horses an hour before we get there."

"Are you asking about Suhizar?"

"Yes."

"Hey, lass, what is this place? Is it Tahtaköprü?"

The stuttering woman confirmed this:

"It's Tahtaköprü; we're getting close to Suhizar."

"Take the turn when you come to the trough; did you hear me, son?"

"Take the turn! How long will it take after that?"

"Half an hour."

The carter had always been angry with those who saw no difference between half an hour and an hour. He stretched his legs, which had gone numb, onto the pole. What if the foresters catch me after I've loaded the cart with the logs?

Then they'll probably sell the cart and the horses at an auction. One day at Şabanözü they had caught his ağa's cart with its horses and the load. If it had been up to the ağa, he would have lost the horses too. But he had cut the ropes and let the horses get away. When they sold the cart at the auction, they started at ten lira, but the peasants, feeling sorry for him, didn't raise the price, and the ağa bought it back for ten. "Peasants don't bring harm to other people's goods," he said loudly, lighting a cigarette. Then he called out to the women:

"That's life, aunts....It's a miserable life we lead."

The husky-voiced woman smiled shyly:

"If only you could come to my village.... Did you hear that?"

"Is your village very far?"

"No, it isn't, it isn't...just a little bit further than Suhizar. Two hours further, or three at the most."

"It isn't far then. God willing, I might come by one day and be your guest. What is it called?"

"Oh! I only hope that you can come there. It's called Arslanlar."

"If I come to Arslanlar, will you offer me *ayran*?"*

"The best *ayran* for you, if you come.... I'll ask you something; tell me the real truth, Sergeant Ağa!"

"Ask it then."

"Have you any intention of getting married?"

"Who hasn't? If I found a faithful woman, I would marry her right away."

*Drink made with yogurt and water.

"That's good…If you come to our village, you'll definitely find the woman you are looking for."

"Is that so? A real good woman?"

He turned around halfway. The women were sitting there, and their heads were moving up and down as the cart shook. He couldn't see their faces.

"If you find a suitable one, I'll come, aunts. I give you my word; I'll push the horses and get to your village."

"Do what you want, son. But let me tell you, there's a suitable girl for you. She is pretty, works from morning till evening without stopping. If you ask about her virtue, all the villagers can confirm that."

"If she is good and a hard worker, that's enough for me. Beauty dies out, but honesty stays. A man is like smoke coming out of a chimney; when he leaves the house in the morning his mind should be at rest about her."

"Don't worry about that. Our daughter is very young, but her only fault is that she is divorced. Would you marry a divorcée, carter?"

"Of course. It's all God's will. I don't suppose her husband left her because of her immorality."

"Immorality? Don't you ever say that again. They just couldn't get along."

The carter sighed again to hide his amusement. They crossed another wooden bridge. The frogs were making a lot of noise on both sides of the road. At first he had talked just to pass time, but then he even forgot to water the horses when the women began talking about a young widow.

Having whispered something to the other, the husky-voiced woman asked:

"Have you anything urgent tonight, Sergeant Ağa?"

"Not too urgent, I can go there tomorrow."

"In that case, let's make a good job of it."

"Like what?"

"Look, I'll tell you everything openly, Sergeant; we are two sisters. The girl we want to marry off is my sister's daughter. If you want, let's go to the village. You'll see the girl, and she'll see you. If you like each other, everything will be fine. Many others from the village want the girl, but God has willed her for you, what can we say? That's God's will. Do you hear me? You'll have a home, a place of your own."

The carter was so amazed he couldn't answer right away. The woman went on:

"Come and have a look, son. If you don't like her, we'll even make good on your traveling expenses."

"Don't mention the expenses. Suppose that I leave my work aside and come with you to the village, where will I put this cart and the horses in the middle of the night?"

"Where will you put them? In the house of the girl you'll marry of course."

"Won't her father or brother say anything?"

"She has no father or brother. They are a mother and a daughter. I live in a separate house."

"That's settled then. Let's go, aunts."

Smiling sarcastically, the carter thought to himself that a brave man endures his destiny, and speeded up the horses. He had worn his new clothes and had had his boots polished at Çerkeş before he started the trip, as though he had known that he was going to see an eligible girl. He had been traveling back and forth on these roads ever since they started laying down railways in the area. He had had enough of this bachelor life. It wouldn't be bad to have a wife nearby. He could have an *imam* marriage;* then he could leave her when he felt like it.... Who'd find this lonely carter from Yozgat? It would be like looking for a shirt button in a barn full of hay. He felt like singing then, but he gave up the idea, thinking that he had to be serious in the presence of his mother-in-law. He started whistling as he used to when he watered the horses.

The husky-voiced woman started to talk again:

"They have no man in the house. You'll be head of the family. That is, if you like the girl."

"What's liking or disliking? She is faithful, isn't she?"

"The whole village will bear witness to that. It's good that you know something about farming. They have a vetch field at the end of the stream and a field for barley. If you are willing to work, there's plenty of land there."

"Never been afraid of work, aunts. If I get myself a strong wife, I'll double the pair of oxen in less than two years. We'll have our sheep and cows grazing about. God willing, I'll work day and night. Don't get me wrong because I'm a carter; I never drink or go to the coffeehouse. My father was a *hoca*.† That's how he brought me up."

"He must have been a good man—may he rest in light!"

"Amen!"

Seeing a dim light beyond the empty land to the left of the road, the carter got excited:

"Aunt, is that light from Suhizar?"

"No! That's Ilıca, a poor village with three houses."

The carter felt rather sad. He tried to hear the whispering women. These people were poor. Would a rich person look for a bridegroom on the road?

He whipped the horses unnecessarily. Talking to himself, he said, "Never mind, I'll say I've changed my mind when we get to Suhizar. If they cry and beg, I can tell them I've my folks and that my fiancée is waiting for the wedding." And, having decided what to do, he felt better.

The wheels were again rolling merrily.

He thought of the stutterer's daughter. He vividly imagined crazy Emine from Kurşunlu. He wondered if this one was milk-white and plump like her.... She must be hardworking, strong, tall, and broad. Just the right woman for the bed! That's good...but would her husband divorce such a woman? I wonder if the man passed away. He thought of asking about this, but changed his mind. What if she is a dark, rough thing? They say, See the mother before you take the daughter!

He was sorry that he couldn't see the stuttering woman in the dark properly. Just then the husky-voiced woman spoke:

"You go to Suhizar from here. Do you see the poplar trees down there? Turn right there and go straight to get to Suhizar. Remember this for your return so you won't get lost, son."

Waking up from his thoughts, the carter looked around. He had passed ten feet beyond the junction where he had to turn. It was more deserted and darker here. The word *son* affected him very much, and he couldn't understand why. He couldn't say,

*Marriage performed by an *iman,* a Muslim clergyman.
†Muslim teacher/preacher.

"I've changed my mind, you better get off here." The horses were running with such determination that despite his long years as a carter, he was puzzled each time he noticed it. Scratching his neck with the tip of his whip, he shouted:

"Come on! Go Tiger! Hurry up, boy!"

In order to get to Arslanlar village, they turned onto a dirt road that went through a pasture. The husky-voiced woman chuckled:

"Sergeant Ağa, don't let this flat land deceive you. Not every carter can make it into our village. Inexperienced ones even turn their ox carts over."

"The experienced ones can keep the wheels going, can't they, aunt?"

"Of course they can."

"Don't worry then. God willing, we'll get there safely."

"You know that better than I do, you're the carter—let's see you do it."

After half an hour, it was necessary to move the back axle from the water bolt a little to the front.

The road was covered with big stones, bumps, and holes. The cart was shaking and creaking; the wheels, which sank into holes, were moaning like human beings. Further on there was passage for neither a cart nor a shepherd. The carter had to tie the back wheel with a chain so as not to have an accident while driving down a steep hill.

The carter jumped down and held back the horses with his right hand. Hitting the horses' necks gently with his whip, he guided the cart down to the stream without turning it over or breaking the wheels.

Now he swore loudly at the road, the cart, the animals. Had he not said with such confidence, "We'll definitely drive over there," he would have turned back long before, leaving the women in the field.

Because he was sweating, he took his coat off. But, fearing that it might get caught on a bush, he put it on again. Just then his hand touched the gun tucked in his waist band.

He thought of the possibility of being tricked by these women. Perhaps they had been deceived by his clothes and looks. They may have thought that he had some money. How cunning these peasants are. He recalled, one by one, all the stories that he had heard about robbers. It wouldn't be bad, if they only robbed him. But they might throw his dead body into a stream. And sell the horses to the gypsies.... If somebody bought his real Amasya cart, better still.... If not they might burn it in the fire as wood.... And heat *ibriks** of water for ablutions!

Because of fatigue, the horse on the right was acting up, leaning onto the pole in order to make Pamukkır pull the cart. "Look at this wicked one!" he shouted at Demirkır and whipped him cruelly.

They came to another stream and climbed a hill. The moon rose like a red ball above the trees on a distant hill.

It was obvious from the slow breathing of the horses that they were exhausted.

The carter seated himself on a rock and lit a cigarette. The women had walked from the road to this spot. They said nothing and squatted down.

He was furious, but he would have laughed if he hadn't controlled himself when the old woman had said: "If you don't like the girl, we'll give you your expenses!"

*Ewer with a handle and spout.

Woman—may God punish you—would a sensible carter come to the end of the world to get his expenses?

They must have noticed that he looked at his watch, because the stuttering woman asked:

"What's the time Sergeant Ağa?"

"Two o'clock."

"*Alla turca* or *alla franca*?"

"*Alla franca*."

"What about our time?"

"Seven or eight o'clock."

"Don't worry anymore, Sergeant! We're close. Soon the road will be fine. It will take only long enough to smoke one cigarette from the stream to Arslanlar."

The carter knew that the way Turks indicate distance—with such phrases as "time to smoke one cigarette" or "beyond that hill; if you shout here, they'll hear it there"—could sometimes underestimate the time involved by an hour or two, sometimes even more.

When they got to the stream, he watered the horses. After this, the road was really not too bad. They were in Arslanlar in forty-five minutes.

The stuttering woman's house was at the entrance to the village, in a fairly big courtyard. As in all Circassian village houses, the lower story was of stone and the upper of wood.

While the carter was untying the horses, the stuttering woman lit a chip of wood in the house and brought it out.

"Come on, son, let's take the animals to the stable."

Pushing the pair of oxen, which were chewing the cud, along the fodder bin, he made some room. He carried in the sacks of hay and barley.

The stuttering woman asked:

"Why did you bring the sacks, son?"

"I'll feed the animals, mother."

"Why do you do that? Here's some fodder."

The woman pointed to a basketful of hay and half a bag of barley. The carter smiled, trying to catch a glimpse of the woman's face, which he hadn't been able to see all evening in the dim light of the burning chip.

"I had fodder. You shouldn't have bothered yourself in the middle of the night."

"It was no bother."

The animals were sweating. He covered them with their rags without taking off their collars and leather covers. He sieved the barley to remove the stones and shook the dust off the hay. Mixing them together, he filled the bags and hung them over their necks.

Holding the burning chip near her shoulder, the stuttering woman said:

"*Maşallah, maşallah!* You have brave horses, Sergeant."

Slapping Pamukkır's neck affectionately, the carter went out. He looked all around under the house.

"Let's find some water, mother.... I want to wash my hands and face."

"Come upstairs, son."

"I'm troubling you in the middle of the night."

He stopped in front of the stairs, not wanting to go up with his boots on. The stuttering woman said:

"Walk up. Come on, go up!"

On the upper floor, across from the stairs, sacks of grain were piled one on top of another; the smell of butter was coming from the half-open door on the left. From another door on the right; light was reflected into the hall. When she came to this door, the woman called out:

"Cemile, my girl! Come and serve the guest.... Run!"

The carter bent his head down.

Her mother said:

"Come on.... Pull off his boots.... Hurry up!"

He moved a step back to the wall:

"No, I can't let her; I can take them off myself.... Not her."

"Why not? Come on, girl!"

The girl squatted. The scarf covering her cap was white. The red flowers on her bloomers looked redder under this whiteness. The carter put his foot forward.

When he went into the room and lay down, he wanted first to sleep, in spite of his hunger and the sharp smell of butter coming from outside. Just as he was spreading his feet, which had been freed now that his boots were off, to lean back, he saw Cemile coming in with a basin and an *ibrik*, and he sat up. He took his jacket off quickly and rolled his sleeves up.

The basin and the *ibrik* were shining as if they had been polished an hour before, and the hand towel was clean as if it had just been washed.

Without lifting his eyes from the small hand on the bright handle of the *ibrik*, the carter mumbled:

"I'm giving you so much trouble in the middle of the night!" When he was alone, he looked around with a smile on his face. The floors and the divans were covered with rugs. But they were all old and patched.

The three of us will ruin the poor woman's home—what a situation! thought the carter. He smiled when he realized that he had counted the horses too. The oil in the green jar of the lamp hanging on the wall was only a finger deep.

Hearing some whispering outside, he pricked up his ears. He thought of the anxiety he had felt when they were on the road, of the possibility of being robbed and killed. He walked slowly to the door to see if there was a man's voice among the whispers. "It won't be nice if the stuttering woman comes in now!" he said to himself.

The cold water woke him up. He felt his gun as he looked out of the window. The ox cart stood in one corner of the courtyard, and to the left of the door was the lavatory, which resembled the huts of the railway pointsmen. His cart was just left there in the middle. There were trees beyond the stone wall of the courtyard. Everything looked quiet and harmless under the moonlight.

When the stuttering woman was placing the black and white tablecloth, a handicraft from Kastamonu, on the hard divan, he said in the manner he had been repeating ever since he had entered the house:

"I'm giving you so much trouble, aunt!"

The woman didn't bother to answer. She had changed as soon as she had entered the house—like all widows who never married again and who had no sons. She was no longer shy.

The carter found it strange that the husky-voiced woman who had talked incessantly and got him into this situation was not around. He thought he missed her and that he would be able to relax if she came in again.

They placed fried eggs with cheese in brightly tinned copper dishes and stewed *pestil**
in a zinc bowl, on a low wooden table in front of him.

The husky-voiced woman and the stutterer came in together and sat on the divan on the
other side.

"Won't you eat too?" he asked.

"We've already eaten; you help yourself."

It is nice to be the man of the house, he thought.

The girl was standing near the door. He had a glimpse of her face when she put the low
table before him. She had full and fleshy lips.

He couldn't lift his head to look at her while he was eating even though he was burning
with desire. He had traveled for years and had fun with women. He reproached himself for
being such a coward now. He asked for some water so that he could see her eyes. But when he
was taking the mug, all he saw were a pair of feet clad in flowery woolen socks under her wide
bloomers and a hand with a silver ring on the middle finger, resting calmly on her sash.

He only lifted his head when he felt that the girl had turned away. The back of her three
layered skirt fluttering, she looked fine from the back. Her hair is jet-black.... The
woman with such black hair must certainly be as white as milk.

When he was drinking his coffee after the meal, the husky-voiced woman suddenly
asked:

"Well, son, did you like our girl?"

The carter blushed. He wasn't expecting such a question. He looked down; the coffee
cup was shaking in his hand.

He just couldn't make himself answer her.

The woman asked again:

"If you don't like her, you won't offend us. Everything is open in Islam. Tell us the
truth...."

The carter put the coffee cup slowly on the floor.

"All right, aunt!"

"Then you liked her?"

"I liked her, God bless her!"

He saw that this short answer wasn't sufficient, it sounded silly. So he said:

"If she liked me, I liked her."

"Why shouldn't she like you? You are such a fine, strong man. An honest man who is
not lazy is good enough for us."

The husky-voiced woman spoke solemnly:

"We have one condition, son. My sister has no man in her house. You can't take the
girl to a far-off place. Look, you don't have anyone in the world. Take this woman as your
mother. The fields have been left in the hands of a tenant."

"Certainly, of course..."

Saying this, the carter stood up!

"Let me groom the horses. It's getting late. You'd better rest."

Taking the night-light lit by the stuttering woman, he left for the stable.

The animals weren't sweaty anymore. When he took the rags and the harness off of
them, they rolled on the dung, shaking their manes.

---

*Fruit pulp pressed into thin layers and dried.

The carter, feeling sleepy, groomed both without much care. Then he brushed them down with a broom. Having refilled their bags, he hung them around their necks.

When he went back to the room, he saw a bed laid out for him. He quickly undressed, put his purse and his gun under his pillow, blew the lamp out, and got into bed. He was just about to pull the eiderdown over his head when he saw that the door had been left ajar. Somebody was walking on tiptoe outside. He was about to call out and have the door closed, but he changed his mind, thinking that they might send the girl to him.

In spite of his fatigue, he couldn't fall asleep. "If they don't have such intentions, surely they'd close the door," he said to himself.

"The girl stayed a divorcée for so long. She will probably wait till the women fall asleep and come here with an excuse...."

He watched the empty walls for a while. Those cupboards—one is for eiderdowns, the other one for towels. The moonlight sped into the room through the window; it was all quiet outside. He was angry with himself. He just couldn't visualize the girl's face, eyes, arms, legs.

Two small feet and a hand... Black braids.... He just thought that she had never spoken. What sort of voice did the bitch have?

He breathed in the odor of dry grain, which had penetrated the house gradually ever since it was built.

It was hot under the eiderdown.

He fell asleep after a while.

He got up when it was getting light without paying any attention to his tired body and buzzing head. He went to the stable, trying to be very quiet.

After grooming the animals, he watered them with a bucket he found there.

While he was filling their fodder bags, he noticed that the oxen, which had looked thin in the night light, were fairly fat and strong. Yet the stable was falling apart, and the troughs were in ruins.

They had put hot milk in the room before he went up.

He drank the milk from the bowl, but didn't touch the bread. When he went to the bed again, he looked to see if his purse was where he had put it.

"They don't have a man, poor things.... The stable needs to be taken care of," he said, smiling.

When he was having his lunch, the stuttering woman was sitting on the opposite divan—alone now, since the husky-voiced woman had gone home.

The girl was again standing by the door. She had black eyes. She was almost as tall as the door. She had a silver bracelet on her wrist. Her face was tanned. Her cheeks shone as she stood there perspiring. From time to time she stole a look at him.

After the meal, the carter stayed in the room alone for a long time.

They had taken the eiderdown away but had left the bed, thinking that he might lie down again.

Fiddling with his silver watch chain, he was wondering what to do. As he looked out of the window, he felt sad and lonely. They had just harvested the crop, and the whole village was nothing but a bare yellow surface. Beyond the window everything lay still and irritatingly cloudy and sad, like a faded picture in a newspaper. Even though he could never envisage it, he shuddered at the idea that he might have to spend the rest of his life here. In winter he would sit in front of the stove, cut wood, gossip in the village room, and then, starting from the beginning of the summer, he would work incessantly, killing himself up to this period. All these things were worse than being in prison or lying ill in bed.

A few yellow leaves dropped from the young plum tree standing in the middle of the courtyard. The dog, yawning and stretching its legs, looked filthy, as if it were a part of the dirt it lay on. One of the horses, obviously Delikır, neighed happily.

The carter stood up immediately. While he was walking toward the stairs, he could hear the clattering of pots and pans from the opposite room.

He stopped again at the threshold, wishing to speak, but since it was rather dark in the room, he couldn't tell whether the person who was doing something in front of the cupboard or the one who was taking flour from a chest by the side and putting it into a basin was the stuttering woman.

"Look here, mother.... I have my belongings in Kurşunlu. I must go and get them."

The stuttering woman shut the cupboard door and turned round.

"You have belongings?"

"Of course. A chest of drawers, a bed, some other things."

"Go and get them, then."

"That's what I was saying, mother."

"Don't go now, though. You can't start in this heat. Let's wait till the evening. Your horses will have rested by then. What do you say to that?"

"All right!"

As he went to the stable, he was feeling happy that he had overcome the difficult part so easily. The horses were well rested. Delikır had lifted his head, pawing the ground. While the carter was inspecting the troughs, he saw a hammer and some rusty, bent nails in an old basket. He took off his jacket, hung it on a pillar, and started repairing the troughs. He sang a song from Çankırı

> Don't fly high thinking you're pretty;
> Strangers are strong, they'll bring you down.
> Don't let your black hair loose on your neck;
> The strong morning wind will blow it away.

He sang well and in a rich, full voice.

He hit his finger with the hammer. Swearing, he lifted his finger to his mouth. The evening had come; the small window of the stable was dark.

He stepped back and looked at what he had accomplished.

Then he slapped Delikır on his broad rump:

"What do you say, son! I was absorbed in work. The troughs look like new, don't you think?"

Now all he wanted was to get the cart ready to go, nothing else.

He would be ashamed to eat another dinner at the widow's house. He even tried to find a way of paying her for what he had already eaten. When he couldn't do this, he muttered: "Let them think that was their fare."

While he was brushing his jacket with his hand in the room, the girl lit the lamp. The carter sat on the divan, feeling rather uneasy.

When they brought the table, he was sulking.

"It's been too much trouble, mother."

"It's no trouble, son.... Today you have brought joy to this house—ever since this morning." Her voice was trembling. It's bad to have no man around, son.... When you were singing in the stable, I cried over here. Very sad with no man around.... I saw the troughs.... God bless you. It has been twenty years since her father went to the army. When he went Cemile was tiny. That was the last we saw of him....I had put forty liras in his chest. Some said: 'They killed him on the road for his money.' Others said: 'He was blown to bits when a cannon exploded when he was in a mosque.' Death comes from Allah.... If only I had received a note and had it read by the *imam* then I wouldn't suffer so much. We didn't hear that he was martyred either, what do you say?"

"Which war did he go to, mother, the Great War or the National War?"

"He went to a war, but I don't know which one."

As the carter harnessed the horses, the late-night call for prayer was heard. The stuttering woman, holding a candle, its flame flickering, ran and opened the gate of the courtyard. Cemile, beside the plum tree, looked at the carter, her hands joined on her sash.

The carter inspected the side belts and the axle lids and saw that the sacks and the fodder bags were securely tied; then he stepped onto the pole and jumped into the cart. When the horses started to go, he waved to Cemile.

"Good-by for now...."

By the gate, the stuttering woman lifted the candle.

"What day will you come back, Sergeant?"

The carter was ready for this question. Without turning his head he said: "Tomorrow. If not then, I'll be here, the evening of the following day."

"Have a good ride, my son!"

Even though he focused his attention on the cart and the horses on the bumpy road, his sadness grew deeper and deeper. The troughs will be ruined again in six months or more. How the old woman had stuttered that "it's bad to have no man around." If he were to come back next evening and enter the courtyard with his stuff, how happy the poor things would be.

As he kept thinking the same thoughts over and over, feeling ashamed and guilty, he didn't notice how long the ride was. When he bounced over the hills and reached the pasture on the plain, the moon was shining in the sky. He looked around, lost in thought.

In the meadow here and there were some willow trunks, which, with their short and bent branches, resembled human beings standing still. Suddenly, he saw the highway. It was above the pasture; both ends were lost among the trees.

As soon as the carter saw the highway, he felt relieved—as if he had come home from a strange place. Pushing his wide rimmed black hat above his forehead, he chuckled: "Don't be such an idiot, son!"

When he reached the highway, the horses trotted, pricking up their ears. The road ran straight into the hot and quiet night.

Haldun Taner

It's Raining in Şişhane

Translated by Tatiana Moran and Adair Mill

An American photographer ,is reported to have taken some photographs using a horse's eye instead of an ordinary lens. From these pictures it appears that in a horse's retina, things and people are reflected half as big again as they really are. I say "as they really are," but perhaps it would be better to say "as they appear to us." Whether they are actually the size they seem to us to be is quite another problem.

Following up the American photographer's discovery, a German scholar came up with the claim that the fact that animals see everything as larger than it really is has given them an inferiority complex, which from the very earliest times has reduced them to the slaves and servants of the human race.

No one knows how the American photographer carried out his experiments with the horse's eye, but it certainly seems to me that the German's hypothesis only applies to proletarian horses like the milkman's or the water seller's or the dustman's. Can you really believe that the aristocratic horses of the Agha Khan, bred with every care in special stables and having pedigrees kept as carefully as a lord's family tree, are likely to see men larger than they really are? On the contrary, they are unlikely to see them even as their true size! They've mixed so long in high society that they've become used to seeing men as tiny—as if they were looking at them through the wrong end of a pair of binoculars.

However, the hero of this tale is an ordinary dustman's horse—the kind that sees everything half as big again as it really is. He was just over twenty, and, for horses, twenty is the equivalent of sixty or sixty-five in human beings. As a matter of fact, he had joined the staff of the Municipal Sanitation Department in the days when Muhittin Bey was governor of Istanbul, so he had very nearly reached retirement. What's more, his name was Kalender.* Thus, taking all of this into consideration, it would have been quite natural for him to see things not just half as big again but at least twice as big as they really are.

It all happened around three o'clock at Şişhane, where Kalender always did his daily rounds.

A porter was walking along carrying a large mirror on his back, and it was just at that very moment that Kalender happened to see his own reflection. Naturally, he saw this reflection as larger than it really was, or, should I say, as larger than we would see it.

*lit. meaning: carefree, maverick.

And HE NEIGHED!

Two possible explanations suggest themselves: Kalender realized that the reflection in the mirror was his own, in which case he neighed because, used to seeing everything else as large and himself as small, he suddenly realized his true size and worth. But to reach such a conclusion it must be assumed that Kalender had never before seen his own reflection anywhere. But it is absolutely impossible that throughout the whole of his twenty-one years, and particularly in a big city like Istanbul, he should never have seen his own reflection. If not actually in a mirror, he must have seen it in a drinking trough, at the edge of the water, or in a puddle. At least he must have whiled the time away sometimes, while the dustman was piling the rubbish into the cart, by watching through languid eyes the image ruffled by a light breeze on the surface of a puddle, or by admiring the perfect harmony of composition formed by the reflection of his head in the water against a background of blue sky and scudding white clouds. But, on the other hand, there's a great difference between seeing one's image in the muddy water of a puddle and seeing one's reflection in an actual mirror. Since the surface of a puddle cannot be anything but horizontal, it always reflects one from below, like newspaper photographs of speakers standing on a high platform, and you can't deny that photographs taken from that angle show people, and also horses, rather more impressive than they are in real life. Whereas mirrors, being vertical, never give rise to such flattering optical illusions, and reflect people quite ruthlessly as they really are.

So it would obviously be a terrible shock for a horse that had always been used to seeing himself from an artistic, romantic, flattering angle, suddenly to be faced with the naked truth as revealed by the mirror. So when he neighed it was the perfectly natural result of a shock of disillusionment.

Horse or human being—it's never an easy thing to accept getting old. "I'm just the same," you say. "I'm still the same nimble steed I was when I first joined the cleansing department." Days pass, years pass. The Şişhane garbage never ends, but the bloom of youth fades away like smoke. And finally, one day, fate holds a mirror up to your face, and you're scared to death. "Can that really be me?" you say in horror. "Is that old, shriveled up, asthmatic hack really Kalender?"

Yes, if Kalender had really recognized his reflection in the mirror, then that's the way he probably thought, and that's why he neighed.

Or, on the other hand—and the police, the passengers, the shopkeepers, and others tend to defend the second alternative—Kalender may have thought that the reflection in the mirror was another horse, a real, hostile, alien horse pulling a dust cart just as he himself was and making straight for him as if to trample over him, and in that case his neighing could be considered the perfectly legitimate exercise of his instinct of self-preservation.

Besides it shouldn't be forgotten that the enemy horse, because of the enlarging effect just explained, must have appeared half as big again. Yet, on the other hand, if it is recalled that all horses have been accustomed from birth to seeing everything on this large scale, then it is obvious that this factor couldn't have played a very important role.

Nevertheless, whether the first or the second alternative is the true explanation isn't so very important. Even the optical illusion I have described in such detail is of no great importance either. It's what happened afterward that's really important.

Kalender NEIGHED!

Whether from fear, surprise, disillusionment, some confused, unconscious sense of inferiority, or for this reason or that, or for any reason at all, whatever the cause might be, he neighed. A bitter, angry neigh. And, like any other terrified horse, he took the bit between his teeth and began to rear. In any case, the street was on a slope, and slippery after the rain.... The cart skidded off at high speed, mounted the pavement, and went smashing through the electrician's shop window.

As no other brainy American has so far thought of making a recording using a horse's ear as a microphone, no one has any idea how sounds may be amplified in a horse's brain. But in the case of Kalender, they must have been amplified quite considerably because he was utterly terrified by the sound of the breaking glass and, above all, by the explosion of a hundred-watt bulb that fell out of the shop window, and galloped off with the cart behind him.

And it was then that the real accident took place.

When he got the urgent cable from the Sao Paulo firm, Artin Magusyan went right out of his mind. At the very last moment the firm was reducing the price he had proposed by 20 percent. Artin Magusyan immediately rushed out into the street without hat or coat and leaped into the driver's seat without even bothering to look for the chauffeur. Now he was driving along and thinking at the same time. Actually, you couldn't really call it thinking. A number of unrelated ideas were coursing through his mind at high speed. *"Asvas barkevede Antranige acebarelov mevanasi cimitsine."** he grumbled. Antranik was both his partner and his brother-in-law. Although he himself was a Catholic and Antranik Gregorian, they got on very well together. As a matter of fact, he had sent him off to the bidding that day instead of going himself....

He glanced again at his gold-plated watch. Nothing was lost as yet. There were still fifteen minutes till the bidding. For heaven's sake, Antranik, don't lose your head. (The policeman chose that very moment to stop the traffic. To Artin Magusyan the seconds passed like years. As soon as the policeman waved the cars on, he stepped on the accelerator and took the corner better than he had hoped.) Is he a crook or what, this Lorenzo? Can you cut the price by 20 percent at the last minute? Goodness knows what dirty business is going on here! (It was drizzling down continuously on the windshield.) "That's the last straw," Artin Magusyan grumbled, and pressed a switch. But it made no difference to the windshield. He'd pressed the switch for the rear lights.

Of course, an amateur who still has some weeks to go before getting his licence couldn't be expected to know all the ins and outs of a car so well as a professional driver. Artin Magusyan pressed another switch. This, unfortunately, turned out to be the right-hand indicator. But Artin Magusyan was a patient man. As a matter of fact, he owed his position in business very largely to this particular virtue. Consquently, he calmly pressed a third button. And finally, thank God, he achieved his aim. The wipers that had refused to obey him up to now began to move right and left, wiping the windscreen with the rhythm of a metronome. While rejoicing at this small triumph, Magusyan took the Tepebaşı corner with his rear lights—even though it was full daylight.

It's all very well, but it's you who's the loser on this percentage business, my boy.... What was the commission we were going to get on the first price? Trois fois quatre makes douze milles, sept fois douze, huit cent quarante. Si le prix d'achat est abaissé de vingt

---

*"Let's hope Antranik doesn't lose his head and make a mess of it."

pour cent, le bénéfice en diminuera d'autant. Whenever Artin Magusyan got excited he thought in Turkish, Armenian, and French at the same time. He knew a smattering of English, but he only became fluent in that language when he was smoking a cigar.

He smiled. You're counting your chickens! How do you know you could have won the bidding on the first price? Now it's guaranteed. Antranik's going to get a real surprise when he sees me! And not only him! Ali Tomar, Kamil's men,...Anesti,... Kevork Kavafyan,...Naili.""Gentlemen," I'll say, as a plaisanterie, "Gentlemen," I'll say, waving the telegram like a flag, "Don't waste your time. Coffee has never been offered at this price anywhere before."

While these thoughts were running through his mind, there suddenly loomed up, in the clearest, cleanest part of the windshield that the two wipers had been busily wiping away, the number 515 in huge white figures on a green background that grew bigger and bigger and bigger—like the camera lens at the end of a Fox newsreel. Then suddenly there was a tremendous crash that plunged everything into complete darkness.

"It suddenly shot out into the middle of the road," said the tram driver. "I immediately seized the hand brake and prevented an accident. How could I see what was coming behind me? What was the stupid brute doing right in front of the tram?"

The passengers were of the same opinion. The dustman's horse had rushed out like mad into the road. All the passengers had collapsed onto one another like a pack of cards, but they all approved of what the driver had done. It was the driver behind who was in the wrong. Even if he'd been an experienced driver, he shouldn't have stuck so close to the tram, and even though he had, he should have seen that the driver had put on his brakes and not crashed straight into the tram like a fool!

The traffic policeman ought to have let the tram go on and settled accounts with the inexperienced driver.

By now there was a long line of trams waiting behind them, and the seventeenth tram in the line happened to be standing right outside the Beyoğlu Town Hall. Now it was raining even more heavily. A flock of crows that had risen up from over Kasımpasha flew screaming over the Finance Department and disappeared.

The crows, the rain, the belching sound trams make in wet weather, the drops running down the steamed-up windows, and, above all, the sickly smell of damp overcoats saturating the whole of the inside of the tram—all got on Süheyl Erbil's nerves. He went out onto the platform and stood there. Then he lit his pipe and threw the match into the street.

In front of the Town Hall six taxis were waiting with their flags down. Just at that moment a wedding party appeared at the top of the steps. The bridegroom was a middle-aged man wearing a dark-blue overcoat with velvet lapels. As for the bride, she was a dainty young thing with a thin veil over her face. (Why do most girls wear veils on their hats when they're going to get married?) The girl was holding a lovely bunch of flowers in her hand. She kept on raising her head and looking up at the sky. It probably occurred to her that rain was supposed to be lucky at a wedding, but she just couldn't summon the courage to tell her velvet-lapelled husband. The woman holding a hand-kerchief to her face and weeping tears of joy must have been the bride's mother. The bride and the bridegroom got into the first taxi. Baskets of flowers were piled into the same car, and friends and relatives got into the others. The very last taxi was right in front of the platform Süheyl Erbil was standing on. Three women and a gray-haired man got into this one. The gray-haired man must have just made a witty remark.

"Really, uncle," said one of the women, still laughing, "you're a real joker!"

How is it that at every single wedding there's always the jocular old uncle!

Süheyl Erbil sighed sadly as the taxis moved off. It was in weather like this that he really felt the loneliness of a bachelor's life.

Now, he was thinking, one should have a nice, cozy little house...and a sweet little woman—the kind that blushes easily—like that young bride.... The rest doesn't matter so much. I would have pulled all the curtains down so as not to see the rain....not too big, just three rooms and a kitchen...a little birdcage just for us. My wife hums a tune while she's making coffee in the kitchen. And I and the air and everything around is filled with a love of life.

Süheyl Erbil gave another sigh.... Then he looked at his watch.... The tram still gave no sign of moving. If they waited for another five minutes, he would certainly miss the ferry. He got off the tram, turned up his collar, thrust his hands into his pockets, and began to walk briskly.

Süheyl Erbil was an extremely sensitive young man, in spite of his eighty-three kilos. But because he thought that too much sensitivity wasn't manly, he concealed this side of himself behind a mask of severity. He was thirty-two and still single. He'd had a few girl friends, but he'd never had the courage to make up his mind and set up a home with any of them. Now he sometimes got a bit depressed to see that he was getting a bit thin on top. "We're going to seed," he'd say sadly. He was a lawyer at the Ankara Bar, and earned, on an average, three or four hundred liras a month.

That's the sort of young man Süheyl Erbil was, and now he was making his way down Şişhane with the collar of his camel's hair overcoat turned up.

If I can still smell, it means I'm alive, thought Artin Magusyan. Of course, he thought it in Armenian, as the pungent smell of the ether penetrated his nostrils. Perhaps he was injured, but at least he was alive—that was the main thing. The rest could always be taken care of. Even if it was quite a serious injury.... And was it a serious injury? He didn't dare move. Cautiously, he opened his eyes. Everything around him was even mistier than it had been through the steamed-up windshield. There was a funny buzzing in his ears.... Someone was bending over him bandaging his arm.

"He's come round," a woman was shouting.

The phrase seemed quite familiar to Artin Magusyan. He's—come—round. Surely Artin Magusyan knew what it meant. He must know what it meant. He's—come—round. Of course—he's come round, he's come round—of course he knew what it meant; how could he fail to know? But he couldn't really gather his thoughts together and get a meaning out of it. "I wonder if I'm still unconscious," he asked himself. This time another head emerged from the mists and mumbled something. Magusyan couldn't understand anything of what was being said. The man who was bandaging his arm repeated the words slowly, one by one. Again he couldn't understand anything. But among these words there was a short, two-syllable word that kept on recurring. Li-cense, yes, license. The word seemed not unfamiliar to Magusyan, but what the devil...

"I'll give him an adrenalin shot," the man bandaging his arm said to the people around him.

No, I'm not unconscious, he thought as he felt the jab of the needle in his bare arm. No, I'm not unconscious, but I'm not really conscious either.

A crowd had gathered around the car. Everyone had something to say.
"Look at the mudguard, just look at it! . . . That was a real bump!"
"He had a lucky escape, that chap!"
"He'd turned on the rear lights, the poor fool!"
A sergeant and two constables had come running to the scene and were now taking a statement from the tram driver, Kalender's dustman, and the other witnesses.
The electrician whose shop window had been broken came dashing out and immediately presented the sergeant with an estimate of the damage.
A girl in a white raincoat who had been choosing a lampshade when the window was smashed was now standing at the shop door waiting for the electrician to come back.... It was at this very moment that she noticed Süheyl Erbil. Süheyl Erbil had as much distaste for anything to do with the police or any kind of ordinary traffic accident as he had for rain, and for the stench of damp overcoats in closed places in rainy weather. Neither the crowd, nor the police, nor the smashed-up car, nor the injured, half-conscious driver could hold him back. He pushed his way through the crowd blocking the pavement and made straight for Bank Street. The girl in the white raincoat would have preferred Süheyl Erbil to have seen her first, but since he was obviously going to pass by without even noticing her, she had no alternative.
"Süheyl Bey," she called out, then bit her lip as if ashamed of what she'd done and looked straight in front of her.
"Why, Serap, is that you?"
The girl went on biting her lip, blushing, with a sweet, rather shamefaced smile.
"Yes, it's me," she said, raising her head and looking straight into his eyes.
Süheyl Erbil felt a warm sensation in his throat. My God, but she's become really beautiful. Why on earth had his heart suddenly begun beating as if to burst?
"Aren't you in Ankara?"
"I've just come here for a case. I'm going back Monday."
"Er...," said Serap, "Er...good!"
The neck springing out of the collar of the white raincoat like a tender shoot and the cheeks brightly flushed with the cold were still the Serap of five years ago. She hadn't changed at all. She was even prettier.
"How do you like Ankara? Do you like living there?"
While she spoke, she kept fiddling with her hood, taking good care to show off her hands. There was no ring on her finger. So she wasn't engaged.
"Ankara, Istanbul, Izmir," he murmured, drawing his lips down to the left in an American smile. "And even New York, Paris, Barcelona.... When you're alone.... And especially when it's raining..."
"You never used to talk like that," said the girl, smiling. And when she smiled, two lovely dimples appeared on each side of her mouth. And because she knew this she would often seek an opportunity to smile when she was talking to a man, or to women who had sons of a marriageable age. That's why people thought that she was always making fun of them, although she wasn't like that at all.

It's true, thought Süheyl Erbil, I never used to talk that way. I was inexperienced then. Really, what a fool I was! When one is young, one is so stupid and foolish; you become a rightist, a leftist, a racialist, a Pan-Turanist, an anarchist, an idealist. That's the age when even if you're burning with desire you torture yourself to show the girl at your side that you don't really care for her! What stupidity! And at the same time how ambitious one was! In those days it seemed just as easy to become a cabinet minister as to be elected to the committee of the students' union. And look what happened! All I managed to do was to become a back-street lawyer in the Ankara Bar!

"Come in under the roof," said the girl. "You're getting wet out there."

The tone of her voice showed a female concern to protect the man. And not only the tone of her voice, but her whole manner and attitude. You know, the self-sacrificing spouse one often sees in films.

Serap prided herself most of all on her kindness of heart, the female compassion that permeated every fiber of her being. And, in addition, she'd just seen a film like that at the Melek two days before. It was about a woman whose love and compassion softened the heart of a tough gangster and won him over both to herself and to society. How she would have loved to be that kind of woman. It's true that Süheyl was no gangster, but he was a pretty tough young man all the same. He continually talked about not being understood. At the university he was standoffish with the girls and spent his time on endless discussions of society and social problems with his male friends.

"That's how I am," he had said once. "I can't feel any affection for those self-centered people who think of nothing but their own interests. Even if you try to force me, I can't."

They were standing at the Faculty gate that opens on to Mercan Street. They were alone.

"All of them?" said Serap, very meaningfully, raising one eyebrow. "Without any distinction?"

Süheyl didn't answer her question. He couldn't answer it. But Serap understood everything from the momentary sparkle in his eyes and the flush that spread over his cheeks. If there, on that day, he had been able to free himself from his ridiculous pride and had uttered the three little words Serap was waiting for, everything would have been different, everything. Serap would have been ready to follow his tough young man with his hair falling over his forehead to the remotest corner of Anatolia, to the farthest corner of the world. But Süheyl didn't utter those three little words.

"What are you thinking about?" said the young man.

"Nothing!" answered the girl.

"I was wondering what you were thinking about."

"I was just thinking. I wouldn't think my thoughts would be of any interest to you, would they?"

"Of course they would! Do tell me!"

"No, I won't."

"Don't you remember? In those days we always ended up in a quarrel!"

"What days?"

"Those days of course!"

Artin Magusyan was now fully conscious. And not only conscious; the adrenalin had put him in a terrific state of excitement.

"Let me go," he shouted, trying to tear himself free. "Let me go and telephone my partner! After that I'll go anywhere you like!"

"Come along to the station," said the policeman. "You can phone from there!"

"I implore you, for God's sake, constable, let me go!" Artin was moaning, pointing to his watch with the broken glass and bloodstained strap. "The bidding's going to begin in five minutes. If I can't let them know, I'm ruined."

The policeman thought for a moment. He himself would probably have agreed. But the sergeant and the other policeman were busily taking down statements a little further on. A crowd of people had gathered round.

This is no time to be soft, he thought to himself. It's not up to me to look after his interests!

One of the tram passengers took Artin's side.

"Why don't you let him go? He may lose money; he may go bankrupt. He's not a murderer, after all!"

Just at that moment the sergeant was coming toward them, so the policeman frowned and looked severe.

"Don't interfere!" he said, in a voice as official as his uniform. "This is my business! Come on, chum, let's get along to the station."

But by now, Artin was clinging desperately to the sergeant.

For Süheyl and Serap it was as though Şişhane didn't exist, as if it wasn't raining, as if there were no people crowding around a few yards away. It was as if they couldn't hear Magusyan pleading with the police, the continual clanging of the tram bell, and all the various street noises that made it practically impossible to hear what the other was saying.

"You may be right," said Serap. "You may be right, but you've got to take other people's feelings into consideration. Or perhaps I'm wrong; I don't know."

Magusyan was shouting at the top of his voice.

"Yes, I know; I ran into it. I'll pay for it. I haven't a license. I know I'm going to be punished. I accept that. Put me in prison. Do whatever you like to me. But for God's sake let me get to a telephone!"

"I know it was negligent of me," answered Süheyl Erbil, "but tell me, how could I possibly write? Especially after hearing about that boy from the Army Medical School!"

"Nedim?" she said laughing. "That's really funny! Whoever told you that was telling a lie! He's my cousin! He's like a brother! Besides..."

"Take that car back a bit, a bit more, more, go on, go on, a bit more! That's fine! Come on, fellows, let's get together and push this car into the side street."

"You can't blame me if I don't understand that kind of attachment!"

"So you don't believe me?"

"No, I don't. Even if it was true, that's no reason!"

"I'm responsible for enforcing the law. The rest is none of my business."

"What are you sounding your horn for? The road's blocked! Do you want to go over the top?"

"When they're taking people to be hanged, they ask for one last request! Have human feelings gone on the black market too?"

"Black market yourself! Do you realize you're insulting an officer of the law?"

"One eighty-two! Wake up! They're waving you on!"

"It never even occurred to me! I only..."

"You only what? Why don't you finish? You're no good at telling lies, Süheyl Bey!"

"Cemal! Cemal!"

"Which Aykut? The one from the English department?"

"Get out of my way, grandad! Move over, folks! Let me through!"

"Sweetshop? What are you saying? I can't hear!"

"It's..."

"Cemal! Cemal!"

"It's too noisy here!"

"What's the matter, Kâzım! Get a move on!"

"I was saying, it's too noisy here. Let's go to a sweetshop!"

"I've only got three minutes left, officer! I'll be ruined!"

"Let's go to a sweetshop and go on with our discussion there, or to the movies."

"The movies?"

Serap had a sudden inspiration. Yes. She must take Süheyl to the film about the reformed gangster. After that it would be easy to come to an understanding.

"I don't know! I don't know if I could!"

"Of course you can!"

"Mother would worry!"

"You could telephone from here and let her know. After the movie I'll see you home."

This last remark gave Serap quite a bit of hope.

And the two of them dived into the shop with the telephone sign above the door as if they were walking on air.

The crowd was slowly dispersing.

The road had cleared, and the jammed vehicles were at last beginning to flow again. Kalender was in the side street where he had been dragged, happily pissing against the wall.

For some reason or other the constable was beginning to relent a little.

"You're making a real fuss, aren't you, nob!" he said to Artin, who was still clinging to his arm. All right, go on and phone and get it over! But be quick about it!"

"It won't take half a minute!"

With Artin in front and the sergeant and the two policemen behind, they all marched into the shop with the big white telephone sign. But Serap was already holding the receiver to her ear, standing on tiptoe to be able to reach the mouthpiece, talking to her mother.

Meg ays bogas ers, * Artin was cursing under his breath. If he'd been left to himself, he would have snatched the telephone out of the girl's hand and dialed the office where the bidding was going on. But Süheyl was standing there glaring like an angry bull at the unwanted guests who had pushed their way in without so much as saying, "Excuse me."

Artin rushed out. He intended to head for the nearest shop with a telephone, but, although the sergeant had recently softened, he must have felt that to go trailing around from one shop to another after Artin was a bit below his dignity.

"Come on," he shouted irritably. "We haven't got time to waste on you!"

They had quite an argument in front of the door, but, in the end, the sergeant relented once more. Serap was still talking to her mother; so the police were forced to go along

*"Oh, darn it!"

with Artin into another shop a couple of hundred yards away. But the only reply Magusyan could get was the sound of the bell ringing desperately away at the other end. It was exactly three minutes past three.

He opened his mouth to say, "It's finished." but all that came out was a whistling sound like steam coming out of a valve.

And, for the second time in half an hour, he fainted.

At Şişhane, where all this was taking place, it was November, but at Sao Paulo, in the same month on the same day—because of the difference in latitude—it was spring. Moreover, although it was 6:30 P.M. according to the clock on the Central Bank at Şişhane, it was—for the same reason—1:30 P.M. by the electric clock in the office so of the firm Lorenzo and Filho.

But, by a strange coincidence, there was a south wind blowing in Sao Paulo, just as in Istanbul, and old Lorenzo never felt well when the south wind was blowing. As a matter of fact, he had got up that day with a terrible pain in his shoulder. The pain shot up from the right shoulder blade, then divided into two paths, one going into his neck, the other right down behind the biceps as far as his right elbow.

He poured some mineral water into his glass, took a box of pills out of his pocket, and swallowed two at once.... The doctor had recommended vitamin B complex together with salicylic pills. They certainly relieved the pain, but they made one sweat like hell.

From the next room came the sound of a typewriter rattling away like a machine gun.

Sevira Marono Lorenzo took out his handkerchief and wiped away the large beads of sweat on his forehead.

"Hey, Pedro, Ha novadades de Istanbul?" he called out to the glass partition at his side.

His son, Pedro, was sitting with his head in his hands thinking of the dark calves of the Argentine dancer Conchita Montanegro in the bar he'd come back from in the early hours. It was as if behind the rattle of the typewriter he could still hear the blare of the trombone playing that rumba all by itself: "Kumpan kumpan kumpan kumpancero...cero..."

"I'm talking to you, Pedro! Are you asleep?"

"Que mande?..."

"Is there still no telegram from Magusyan?"

"Not yet, father!"

"Probably, he didn't win the bidding."

"And yet we went down 20 percent at the last moment. They must be sleeping! Where the hell can I sell the stuff now?"

He was perfectly justified in talking like that. The trucks from Fazienda were continually arriving with coffee and dumping it in the storeroom below.

The typewriter outside had stopped. There was complete silence for a moment. You could even hear the fizzing of the mineral water in the glass. Lorenzo finished what was left of it in one gulp. Now he was thinking, and at the same time holding the bottom of the glass and turning it round in his fingers, as he always did when he was thinking deeply.

Pedro stood up and came over to his father.

"You remember, we had a telegram from Hamburg from an Alois Morgenrot. You didn't agree to do business on credit, although he had good guarantees. If you like, let's send him the goods we were going to send to Magusyan."

Old Lorenzo looked at his son.

"Bravo!" he said. "That's not a bad idea!"

"Noch eins Papa, bitte noch eins!" pleaded little Helga.

Alois Morgenrot had made four sailing boats out of a three-month-old copy of the *Frankfurter Zeitung*. When his daughter begged him for another, he tore the business page out of an old newspaper and just managed to get two more boats out of the yellowed page with its out-of-date import lists.

Helga had let her yellow hair fall over her face and was sailing her boats on an old torn rug that she pretended was the sea.

It's just as well Helga doesn't want dolls like other girls, Alois Morgenrot was thinking.

Inside, a tinny Volksempfraenger (radio) was playing the overture to Smetana's *The Bartered Bride*.

Alois Morgenrot put the boat he'd just made on the rug and went over to the window.

The squalor of Hamburg had been partly hidden under the previous night's snow. Morgenrot gazed at the new blocks of flats rising up from amid the ruins. Whenever these new buildings caught his eye, he was filled with a warm feeling not too unlike hope and courage. His own life was like these ruins. But sooner or later, new buildings would rise up from their midst; new shoots would grow. In due time his troubles would end, must end. What does the Old Testament say? "To everything there is a season, and a time to every purpose under the heaven. A time to be born, and a time to die; a time to plant, and a time to pluck up that which is planted; a time to kill, and a time to heal; a time to break down, and a time to build up; a time to weep, and a time to laugh; a time to dance and…

"Isn't Mutti coming back?" Helga was whimpering.

"She'll be back in a minute or two," said Morgenrot.

Frau Morgenrot had gone out shopping a little while before. Alois Morgenrot's wife was of pure Hamburg stock, but Alois himself was descended from a Czechoslovakian Jew who had migrated to Hamburg half a century before. Alois still hadn't been able to atone for the crime of his birth. First of all, there was the monster Hitler. Then the Second World War. Fleeing here and there, from one country to another. He was so penniless that he was reduced to selling his gold teeth. Illness, hunger, poverty. And when the war ended and he was able to return to Hamburg, what did he find? True, he hadn't rotted away in concentration camps as some of his friends had done—he was alive and well—but this wretched unemployment was breaking his back. If he'd had some capital—not very much, only about 20,000 D.M.,* yes, about 20,000 D.M. capital—it would be enough to change his whole life. But he had no capital. And without capital he'd had no alternative but to work as a commission agent. And now every day he was combing through the commercial advertisements in all the languages he knew and then typing out on a hired typewriter detailed applications to all the foreign firms he hoped he might be able to do business with.

Just then the doorbell rang.

"Mother's come, mother's come!" cried little Helga, clapping her hands.

But Frau Morgenrot had a key; she never rang the bell.

Alois Morgenrot opened the door and found himself face to face with the postman.

"Grüss Gott, Herr Morgenrot!"

"Grüss Gott!"

---

*Deutsche Mark (German marks).

"A cable from Brazil!"

"What do you mean?"

First Morgenrot went as white as a sheet. Then he suddenly went red. He read the cable once; then he read it again and again.

"Endlich!" he shouted.

He was so overjoyed he thrust half a mark into the postman's hand. The postman, who had never got so much as a single pfennig tip from Alois before, was afraid the good man had gone out of his mind. But now Alois was hugging his daughter, with tears running down his cheeks.

"Now I can buy you dolls, Helga!" he was saying. "The most expensive ones. Tell me, darling, would you like one of these? You know, the ones that close their eyes when you lie them down and cry when you press their tummies."

A fine November rain was falling silently over Şişhane. The air was filled with the smell of a mixture of soot and damp. The roads were still as slippery as they'd been two days before. The only difference was that the wind had changed from south to southeast.

Kalender had been tired since morning. His cart was full to the brim with garbage, and he was pulling it slowly and cautiously down Şişhane Hill. Just at that moment he saw himself in a mirror. But this time it wasn't in a full-length mirror on a porter's back; it was just in an ordinary traffic mirror the municipality had recently erected. But once again he saw his own reflection in this mirror half as big again as it was in reality, or rather, half as big again as we see it.

But in spite of that, HE DIDN'T NEIGH.

No, HE DIDN'T NEIGH.

One can think of two possible reasons.

I looked in a mirror once in my life, Kalender may have thought, and there was an infernal commotion. Thank God, that's over. I shan't look in one again ever! In any case, as far as my face is concerned there's nothing much left to look at!

Of course, for him to be able to reason like that, one must assume that horses, just like men and some more intelligent monkeys, are capable of learning from experience and making a logical connection between past and future.

Or, yes, or—and the second alternative is more plausible—he was simply tired that day; he was feeling depressed. Perhaps he hadn't got any sleep for squabbling all night for a place with the other horses in the municipal stables. He was out of sorts; that's why he couldn't be bothered neighing or shying, or causing a commotion around him, as he had done two days before. In short, there are several plausible physiological reasons for his not neighing, as well as psychological ones.

In any case, whether one accepts the first or the second alternative, the important thing is not that, but what came after that.

KALENDER DIDN'T NEIGH.

He cast an ugly look at his reflection in the mirror and turned his head away. With a dignity in harmony with his mature years, he continued on his way cautiously and sedately.

İlhan Tarus

The Thirty Liras

Translated by Bedia Turgay-Ahmad

I told the judge in the town once.... Why do you keep asking? They say this is a higher
court or whatever for crimes. So what? I know that you won't give a light sentence to a
woman like me who's killed somebody. But I suppose I'll have to repeat it all over again.
All right then, I better. Since there are so many people here, I won't be wasting time; they
can listen and learn a lesson from it.

This is how it happened, sir.... I had barely finished the four-year village school than
my father wanted to marry me off. I was such a young girl; I used to play fathers and
mothers with the neighboring kids, in front of the house. When it was prayer time, I used
to cover my head with my scarf, go to the water pipe in the yard for a wash; I never missed
a prayer. Not only me, my little brother Mehmet and our elder sister Ayşe also never
missed their prayers. Before dawn my father used to stand by poor Mehmet's bed with a
stick, when he was only four, and get him up for prayers. At one time the boy was ill,
coughing blood, couldn't stand on his feet, the poor thing. But he went on with his
prayers. We all started to fast at the age of five. Not like the way you fast, though; we
would start fasting three months before the holy month of *Ramazan*. Like this we fasted
almost half the year. That is why Mehmet is always ill and weak. He coughs blood, he's
sick and puny all the time. Yet, the unfortunate thing still holds onto life. What about
Ayşe? Only she and God know the number of beatings she had on the prayer rug. Well,
never mind; I am not complaining. We may have paid our debts to God or we may still be
paying them, but the beating of this brute that we call a father has done away with
religion or faith. I don't want to offend God, but he rid us of such beliefs.

At one time a *hafiz,* * came to the village. My father brought him home to stay with us.
On the third day the man came to my bed and tried to put his hand through my panties. I
gave him such a slap that he couldn't get up for two hours. There was such havoc in the
dark. Do you know what happened in the end? My father blamed me for it. "Unless a
bitch wags her tail, a dog doesn't go after her," he said. He gave me such a thrashing. The
next evening at the table the man grinned at me. The devil tempted me even then to kill,
but I controlled myself; kismet had it for today.

The *hoca* †, who came during the following *Ramazan* was a more ferocious womanizer.
After he touched me and Ayşe, he tried to molest my mother, and right in front of my
father too. But my mother got thrashed, "You are all prostitutes, you even seduce these

---

*Reciter of the Koran.

†Religious teacher.

religious men," my father said and left it at that. We endured this, waited with patience, cried and suffered together. The neighbors tried to talk to him. "Be sensible," they said. "Don't let strangers into your home. We can find a place for the *Ramazan hocas* to stay." Would he ever listen to them? Whenever a man with a turban on his head came to the village, he was at our table that evening. And on condition that we would eat with him too....

One day he brought home a green-turbaned man, with a black beard down to his belly. He sat me in a corner and insisted that I open my belly so that he could write my fortune on it. I protested, cried, and begged. My mother tore her hair out in distress, but it was no use, sir. Even my mother was forced to help undress me. They spread my naked body in front of the *hoca* and let him write on my belly; such a young girl, already out of luck, and this scoundrel was supposed to bring her luck!

If only he could be a little human to others, one could forget. When I was eight I couldn't go out with a bare head; neither could I pass in front of shops. Because I spoke to the watchman once through the crack in the door, my father branded my thighs with hot iron, broke my bones. "If I hear you show your fingertip to a man, I will kill you even if it is a lie," he screamed.

Luckily, my kismet wasn't far away. When I was thirteen, this unbelieving idiot came for me. He was a government forest watchman at Keçibelen. When I saw his walrus teeth and his scabby neck, I covered my face with horror and ran out screaming. Oh, my mother, my stupid mother, said:

"Girl, what will you do if you stay here? Instead of being crushed under your father's stick, go, set up your own home, tuck your skirt in your belt and be comfortable. Let the marriage be blessed; he that seems a demon to you today will seem a gazelle tomorrow. Listen to me—don't miss your chance; don't kick it away with your own foot."

The man had a hut in the mountains, in the middle of three villages, each half an hour away on foot. He wasn't getting anything from the government; he ate by begging from the villagers. Crying secretly, I called him a husband and submitted. As if he had never seen a woman before, he pounced upon me like a hungry wolf; dribbling and spreading out on the floor like a corpse.... Such a shameless sight!

Keeping quiet with great effort, I said to myself, "Stick it out girl, forget it, you can't cheat God's kismet." Always with a smile, always with a nice word, but who to? He comes dead drunk in the middle of the night, beats me harder and harder. Before three months had passed, he had had enough of me; he didn't come near me anymore. He went to prostitutes in the town. Damn him, I said, and didn't go after him, didn't even care what he did. But it was hard to live in that scrap of a hut in the middle of the howling forest.

I'd embrace the little Koran my mother had given me, crawl on the floor, and pray, the trees creaking, the bats flapping. I'll go mad; there's no other way. I'll crack up.

Gathering my bits and pieces one morning, I left for my father's place. My father was in the coffeehouse. Upon hearing of my arrival he came with a stick he had picked up from the shed on the way. Such a beating he gave me.... Look at this arm of mine—I couldn't move it from that day on. I fainted then. He got the cart and sent me home with the shepherd. When I woke up on the shepherd's lap, I couldn't even move my finger. Wasn't that dirty dog grinning at me then? Didn't he pounce upon me then? What the hell, I said, and let myself go.... After half an hour, the shepherd left wiping his mouth.

After two or three days, my husband came home with a huge fellow. They sat there; I made them coffee. Bringing out a bottle of raki they drank till midnight. My husband even made me sit and poured it into my mouth. The man beside me was pinching my arm or leg now and then. At first he seemed to be doing this secretly; then he did it openly. I nearly went mad; even though my husband saw it, he didn't say a thing. Gradually, the whole business got out of hand. The man hurled himself upon me. While I struggled with him, I screamed for help. What did he say: "Go on, he is not a stranger; it doesn't matter!" I felt dizzy, my head was bursting. Whatever I did, I couldn't get out of it. Then my husband left, closing the door behind him. The man immediately blew the candle out. I couldn't stop him, sir; I just couldn't.

When I woke up the next morning, there was no one around. Leaning on my elbows, I tried to get up, but I couldn't. What a rotten drink that raki was; I vomited like anything and lay there like a corpse till evening.

With great difficulty I got up; even my feet were burning. I dragged myself to the village and told everyone what had happened. My mother and sister started to cry. My father thought for a moment and said: "You go back; he is still your husband. I'll see what I can do. And we have to enquire and see if he took any money for it."

I got back home at midnight, scared, in agony. Till morning I begged God to let me die and be saved. But God Almighty didn't take my life. There I lay for three days and nights. Then again one night—I don't know which—the door crashed open. Lying there half-alive, I jumped up with a scream. A blue-eyed man wearing a tie stood by him, grinning at me. My head throbbed, and I felt a bit sick. "Take these things and prepare us something to eat," ordered my husband. They had brought some cheese, olives, and meat. I felt helpless. After two bites, I spread out by the fire, half-conscious. They dragged me up. My husband went out; the blue-eyed man put his arm around my waist. "This is my chance," I said to myself, and kicked him in the stomach. He got up, swearing, "You bitch, I gave him thirty liras for a night."

"If you touch me, I'll kill you," I said. He called in my husband, who came and got hold of me; beating and kicking me they forced me on the floor. Then my husband disappeared again.

This made us prosperous—bread, onions, and all in every parcel. But when the third customer came through the door, I stood up. Opening his eyes with anger, my husband came for me. Grabbing the bread knife, I swung it at him. It got into his throat, opening a huge slit; his head fell back, he wriggled a little more, then lay there. The other one had already run off. I went after him with the knife, chasing him for half an hour in the dark forest; but the beast got away.

Unable to run any more, I collapsed in the bushes. When I came to, I got up and went to the village with the knife still in my hand. The blood on it had dried. I don't know what I was thinking, but I washed it in the stream and dried it up with my skirt. Perhaps I hoped to get away with it; perhaps I was only scared of my father. My mother was terrified when she saw my face. "God, you've gone and done something." She screamed for the neighbors. My father came. Squatting on my knees, I touched his feet with my head and told him everything. The knife was in my bloomers. He gave me a kick and shouted, "Get away, you whore; you are a real prostitute, telling lies all the time and then doing whatever you want. Go and rot in prison. Get out of here!" I rose to my knees. He didn't know what was happening. I knifed him in the middle of his belly. The devil fell down like a rotten tree. His prostitute daughter gave him what he deserved.

My mother ran to the watchman, crying, "My daughter has gone mad. Help!" They gathered around me, and someone tied up my hands. They brought me here, to the government. This is my whole story. Please don't make me say it all over again. I am finished; you can do whatever you want to me.

Bekir Yıldız

Şahan the Smuggler

Translated by Louis Mitler

"Let the ears of those smugglers whose permits bear the government seal ring."

He stopped. When he stopped it seemed as if all the sound and life in the world had dried up. He wanted to hear the noise of his own footfalls again. So he walked. He was afraid of silence because that night the silence of the steppes was bigger than a giant.

Şahan had changed the money he had earned at Aleppo to gold. Now he had two pieces of gold. If things went well, he would come and go a couple of times more; then he would get out of this business because he didn't love smuggling.

He heard a dog howl in the distance. Şahan shortened his steps and looked around. Then he looked up. There was a half-moon up there.

He stopped for awhile. It seemed as if the moon were running. Şahan was surprised.

He wobbled his head from side to side. "God bless!" he said and heard the words he had said. It seemed to him as if someone had crept up beside him He bristled. He wanted nothing to do with anybody or anything now. All that he wanted was to get over the border just ahead and into his village. He knelt down. Rolling a cigarette, he lit it, hiding the flame between his palms. He took a few deep breaths. In an instant his thoughts carried him home. His wife and the children would be asleep now. For some reason his heart yearned for his littlest son. He loved him a lot. Was it his curly hair or his black eyes or his way of running about naked? Şahan didn't know very well why he preferred him above the others. But his love for him was big and warm.

Şahan let his head fall forward. I won't let this kid grow up a smuggler, I won't taint his life with fear like this! he thought to himself. Then he got to his feet, burying the fire of his cigarette in the ground. He started walking toward the border. The dog's howling, now coming from nearby, was like a bullet exploded into the stomach of night. Şahan headed west from the howling.

Five or ten minutes later he reached a narrow creek to the accompaniment of the croaking of frogs. He took his slippers off and held them in his hand. Then, as if he didn't want to waken the water, he slowly waded through to the opposite bank. When he reached a flat place after having gotten through the creek bed, first he sat down and then he lay down on his belly. He advanced, dragging himself along for about a few hundred feet. He thought he might have to drag himself along further. But he understood that he had been mistaken. He had come to a tree with dead branches that he had marked with a sign. As soon as he saw the tree, all of a sudden his lungs felt too tight to breathe, about to explode. He was suddenly worried. Without caring, he let his head fall forward, and his lips touched the ground.

Fear had control of Şahan. Whatever else he might do, he couldn't bury this fear in the ground. He raised his head. "My God," he said in an audible voice, "either take the fear away or take my life." For the second time he thought of his curly-haired, dark-eyed son. It made him ashamed of himself. "One shouldn't, he said to himself, "one shouldn't be afraid! Smuggling is a business for brave men. With God's help..."

And, as he invoked the name of God, he got to his feet and slowly entered the field planted with mines.

Now Şahan wavered between life and death. There was life in the foot he pressed on the soil, while in the other foot, quivering with fear and raised in the air, was death–preparation for destruction. Three or four seconds he waited; then he put his foot, raised in the air, on the dark face of the land. He waited. Now death was not under either foot. He was almost happy. But it seemed that his rejoicing was borne away immediately by a faintly blowing breeze.

For whatever reason, Şahan, while passing through such a field, where death was concealed here and there, felt a fear this time that he had never before felt in his other passages.

He didn't dare move his feet, which assured him—even if for only a short while—his life and his survival, didn't dare challenge death by trampling its crown of glory. Yet to go back to the Syrian territory would earn him nothing. This he knew quite well. What was now important was to bring those two pieces of gold into his fatherland. The hope of survival of his wife and children hung on those gold pieces, even if they were tainted with blood, dishonesty, and death.

Gently shifting his weight to the right, he raised his left foot. Then expertly, patiently, yet fearfully, he tested the ground. The ground yielded like a woman caressed by her lover. Taking courage, Şahan carried his intimacy further. Setting his foot down with its full weight, he leaned his body forward. But before he could put down his right foot, he was blown into the air.

He couldn't feel how much of his body was missing when he hit the ground on his back. So he remained there for a while in fear and amazement, without being able to move. Only the dust and soil that had spurted into the sky with himself slowly, gently rained on his face. When he thought of closing his eyes, he realized that one of them was missing because as he squeezed his eyes shut one of their lids wouldn't move. He carried his right hand to his face. A soft, warm, round, and mutilated thing smeared on his fingers. "One of my eyes has spurted out," he said to himself. Then it seemed that he was pinwheeling into the abyss of an obscure terror. His body became light. The ground on which his back rested wasn't hard now. In a voice choked by death, he said, "Woe is me—I'm going! Oh Lord, Just one more little breath."

The thought of his curly-haired, dark-eyed son passed again through his ever-shrinking consciousness.

He opened his remaining eye, on which the earth had rained down. A light streamed directly on him through the unbroken darkness of the plains. The light wasn't brilliant; it was flickering and dim. It revived his consciousness. Then the light disappeared. I'm rising to heaven, he thought to himself. He twisted his mouth wryly at this heavenly ascension. Both worlds are closed and dark for the likes of smugglers, he thought. But the flickering, dull light struck his eyes again. He turned his head gently from side to side. It was a jeep, sent out from the police post a little way away. It was coming straight toward him. The exploding mine had aroused the gendarmes.

He suddenly remembered the two gold pieces that he had knotted in his cloth purse, in the pocket of his *şalvar*. * He tried to raise himself from the ground, ,but he couldn't. The dim lights that he had seen a little before now connected themselves to the lights of the jeep; growing stronger little by little with each breath, he made one last effort. "God help me," he said, "for the sake of my wife and children." He sat up. But he couldn't rise. Then he felt an unbearable pain in his right leg. He put out a hand and searched for his leg but couldn't find it. His hand smeared over another warm sticky mess. Half his leg was gone, and the ceaselessly flowing blood each instant decreased his life a little more. Like a hog smashed on the head with a mallet, he was thrashing about. The blood oozing from his leg was dragging him slowly toward his death.

Just then a ray of light came from the jeep parked nearby. The surroundings were illuminated here and there. And now in a section of this light Şahan saw his torn-off leg. It was as if he wanted to take the leg lying on the ground and reattach it to his body. He was totally confused. He turned his head back with difficulty. The jeep wasn't far away. There were gendarmes round about it. He collapsed onto the ground without being able to resist.

One of the gendarmes saw Şahan: "Look over there," he said, nudging his companion. Then he shouted, "Who's there?"

No sound came from Şahan.

The other gendarme said in a rage, "It's a dog of a smuggler."

"Hey, speak up!"

"Maybe he's kicked the bucket."

"He ruined our sleep, the bastard."

"He's got his. Let's go."

"Suppose he *didn't* croak?"

"Oh, he'll shove off by morning, anyhow. We'll come and get him by daylight."

"Let's make dead sure, like last time."

Şahan heard this conversation in bits and snatches. He no longer had any unfinished business with the gendarmes. His life was going, almost gone. With a final hope, he put his right hand in his *şalvar* pocket. With death only a notch away there remained only the duties of praying and swallowing the gold pieces. He must save them from dishonest hands. He took hold of the coin purse with difficulty. His life quivered now on his fingertips. He untied the purse with his teeth. He emptied the two gold coins into his mouth and tried to swallow them.

Just then one of the gendarmes discharged his German-made mauser rifle haphazardly in the direction of the writhing, human stain under the jeep's headlights.

Şahan's life offered no resistance to the bullets that entered his body. It ended instantly.

One of the gold coins slid into his throat while the other was still in his throat. None the less, his mouth didn't fall open, and a little while later the gold pieces were sealed in his mouth as if in a steel safe.

In Ancekent village, the roosters' call had been forgotten. The sun was about to rise to its zenith over the village. Only very small children with dirty, fly-blown faces wandered here and there, indifferent to the events in the village square.

*Baggy pants.

Şahan had been thrown haphazardly on the ground. Alongside him stood his detached leg. The sun that baked his corpse had dried the blood flowing from his dripping eye socket onto his face and hair. Pasted here and there to his hair, a thin path of blood from between his joined lips rested like a seal stamped on his mouth, and the flies played to their hearts' content on this bloody playground.

The villagers' heads were bent forward. Every eye was fixed on Şahan, whose body was caked with dirt and blood. But the thoughts of very few were there in the square. Most of them were speaking with their own departed in their hearts and were telling them their troubles. Some of their hearts burned with grief for father, some for a brother or a son. The tender hearts of the women, fluttered like a newly slaughtered chicken.

The lieutenant bellowed.

"Let the women go!"

The women began to slowly disperse. God had denied even weeping to these women, because it was one of their laws not to betray the identity of the dead man in order than the house of the dead smuggler might not be searched and that his whole clan, fallen under suspicion, might not be dragged to an interrogation every now and again.

Şahan's wife looked at her husband one last time with a wry face. She would gladly have given her life just to be able to throw herself on top of him and flail herself, crying "Oh, God!" But thoughts of her children entered her mind, and her courage failed her. She dared not endanger their sustenance and that of her relatives with a moment of grief. She shuffled away to her one-room hovel, doubled up as if possessed by some violent cramp. It was impossible for her to cry straightaway. Before she went into the house, she found a curly-haired, dark-eyed boy. His tattered shirt left him almost naked. With his thin hands, he was messing the ground, which he had just wet with his urine. He laughed when he saw his mother. The woman bent down and seized him, but the child started to cry, because he had been torn from his game. Then the woman hurried into the room and threw herself on the child. Mother and child wept together. Outside, the lieutenant shouted in a nervous and exasperated voice at one of the gendarmes standing behind him. As soon as the gendarmes received the order, they pushed, and shoved those around Şahan, muttering, "Further off, further off, one behind another, that's the way!"

The men of Ancekent got into a line. They were used to what had to be done in such situations, and then too, they were used to saying that they did not know the dead man at all. One by one they began to come up beside the lieutenant, their heads downcast and their eyes narrowed, with hard lines round them. The lieutenant kept asking the same question, "You know him?" Whoever heard the question behaved as if he were seeing Şahan for the first time. He thought. Then, shaking his head from side to side, he said, "I never saw him, lieutenant." Again the same question, this time to another one, "I swear I never saw him."

The lieutenant was angry when no one appeared to know the man, but he couldn't keep from asking yet another.

"Do you know him? Come on, tell the truth. See, there's no one here but the two of us."

The man bent down and peered at Şahan for a while as though he were trying to identify him. As he did, the flies that had nestled in the socket of the torn eye took flight, buzzing about. And the man who tried to identify Şahan was perhaps his next-door neighbor or perhaps his nearest friend, who danced the *halay* with him at weddings. But he shook his head from side to side, repeating the same answer, "I swear, I never saw him."

The lieutenant was stupefied by the heat. It seemed to him that the sun radiating over the plains had come down and settled on his head. Now he wanted to bring this business to an end. He yelled at the few people who had remained behind.

"Come on, come on. You people who haven't had your turn, quit stalling!"

It was the turn of an old man. Paying no attention to the lietuenant's orders, he started walking very slowly, straight toward Şahan.

The lieutenant went wild with rage: "Hurry it up, granddad!"

Still the old man did not lose his poise. It seemed as if a millstone were attached to his feet. The lieutenant walked up to him; seizing him by the arm, he jerked him.

"Didn't you hear what I said?"

The old man said in a moaning voice, "I'm old; I'm too sick to mind you."

"Don't stall!"

Then they went up to Şahan. The old man's withered hands trembled. The white hairs of his face, not shaved in days, bristled; his shrunken eyes receded even more. The only life in that aged face that hadn't lost its vitality and majesty were the eyebrows, which were thick as a finger.

The old man squatted down. He wanted to see Şahan close up, but this wish was not from a desire to betray him. In Ancekent village anyone might have told who Şahan was, but this one old man was the only human who would never tell that Şahan was Şahan.

For he was Şahan's own father.

The lieutenant nudged his shoulder. "Come on, man; you've squatted long enough!" he said. "If you know him, speak!"

The old man slowly rose. He reached for Şahan's leg, lying near by. Taking it in his hands, he corrected his son's defect, and, as he moved off, his aged voice could scarcely be heard.

"Don't know him. Never saw him."

That day in Ancekent, little was spoken, little eaten, little drunk.

The old man squatted at a corner of the gendarmerie. He had been there since sunset, seeking the opportunity to slip to his son's side. He rose. At any moment now, light and darkness would blend. Hunching himself up small, he started to walk. He slipped up close to the police station. When he was four or five paces from his son, he squatted down. He looked carefully about him and listened. There was no movement or sound. Without raising his body he moved over to Şahan, shuffling his feet. Şahan lay under an old, half-disintegrated straw mat, because the government doctor had not come from the township with the burial permission. His burial had been put off to the next day.

The old man bent all the way down. He raised a corner of the mat. He realized that he was at Şahan's feet. In order not to waste time, which was now shredded into narrow slices, he instantly passed to Şahan's head. With one hand he raised the mat, and with the other hand he sought and found his son's face in the disintegrating darkness. With a heavy heart he now obeyed the instruction his son had given him before he went on his smuggling expedition. He had to take the gold. He found his son's mouth with his fingers, but suddenly he felt his heart contract with paternal love. Taking his hand from Şahan's mouth, he felt over his whole face. His love spread from his heart to his son's bloody face, and, without his being aware of it, his eyes watered. Taking his hand back, he sat down again in the same place. As a man unable to claim even his own dead, he felt torn in a thousand pieces by shame. He wanted to hurry away from the spot, but to go empty-handed to his daughter-in-law, not to be able to take the gold pieces to his dark-eyed, curly-haired grandson, the gold won at the cost of his father's life, shamed him in another way. "Cursed be poverty," he said to himself. Then, shaking his head, "Just suppose you had been a little more careful, my Şahan. What a difference it would have made." But in the same breath he felt that he had committed an injustice having recriminated his son even this much. "Black destiny," he said. "Mines are the invention of infidels." He was unable to conclude his thoughts, because a few roosters crowed in the village a little way off, impatient for the break of day.

He was not able to accomplish this thing. He did not want to further torture the dead body that had already suffered so much indignity.

He could not bear to give it any more pain. He waited for a while. His hands were trembling. He got up. If his son had not said, "Father, if I should get killed, the gold is your responsibility; you have to look for it first in my mouth and then in my belly," perhaps he would have walked away. Yet he couldn't go. Pushing everything from his mind, he squatted down, and he forced open his son's jaws.

Tahsin Yücel

Haney Must Live

Translated by Özcan Başkan

Haney is dead. But I say with all my might, "She will live! She must live!" But what I have in mind when I say this is not the resurrection, the other world, the things like heaven and hell. Ever since I came to know myself, I have never cared about this kind of thing. I have had enough of it in this world; the problems in this world have been more than enough for me. It would have been stupidity to try to solve the problems I knew I would never solve. What I have in mind is something different. When I say, "Haney must live!" I mean something else. I mean she should live in people's talk, in their minds, as songs, as books do. Everybody should talk about her, should praise her. She is that kind of woman; she deserves it. We should make up to her for what we have done. We just have not been able to appreciate her truly.

A few years before she died, Ali Rıza said something. Don't you remember? Many of you were over there. None of us had anything to say in particular. We were watching people passing by. They were playing backgammon and dominoes at the other tables, and Uluk Osman was sipping his drink way back at the end of the shack. He was drinking, and he kept cussing by himself. Right then Haney was passing in front of the coffeehouse. I remember it as if it were yesterday. Her feet were all black with dirt, were cracked all over as usual, and they were all calloused, the skin like a hide. As usual, she was wearing her wide, blue trousers. She was in rags, and her clothes were covered with patches in various colors. She had a dirty rag wrapped around her head—when she died she must have had these dirty rags on. Ali Rıza was moved by Haney's condition. Ali Rıza did not think of her so much as I did, but he was a kind-hearted fellow all the same; he was humane. "Shame on you, fellows!" he said. "Just take a look at Haney. You should be ashamed of yourselves! Should she walk about like this? She's done something for all of us! In a way, she has brought us up. And what we do now is forget about it all and smile while she passes by. Is this fair?"

Yes, that is exactly what he said. "We've all grown up," he continued, "and we've all got an occupation. We can all afford to lose a couple of bucks in a single game, and not give a damn about it. Suppose each of us gives five bucks, Haney will have a better life; she'll have some comfort during her last days. Come on, boys, let's get something done. I'll put up the first five bucks." You had all laughed as if it were something stupid. I do not want to make a point of it, but I was the only one who did not laugh. There was also Ali Rıza. There was nothing to laugh about; the boy was dead right.

She was a good woman; may her soul rest in peace! Do not laugh at me as you did at Ali Rıza. Do not say, "She wouldn't be a whore if she were good!" Forget that nonsense!

Remember that many whores have got themselves apartment houses through their occupation. Do not forget that some of them earn in a single night more than we can in a whole year. And remember that they are sometimes liked and respected more than we are. Is Haney's case more startling than all these? Well, let me tell you something. Whores get better the cheaper they are. Haney was just as nice as she was cheap. Do not say, "She would earn nothing if she weren't cheap enough." Do not say that, because you know damn well that she would. She could have easily increased the fee from a dime to a quarter, and even to a good buck. But she just did not do it. When the prices went up, she was the only one who remained reasonably cheap. She just did not want to deny the boys the right to visit. So she just increased the fee from a dime to fifteen cents. She became obliged to get some odd jobs to make ends meet. She carried water to houses, and that kind of thing. She did all this for our sake. But we just have not been able to repay all this; we just have not been able to reward all she did for us....

Some of us did not even take her death seriously, and some of us even laughed at her death. But it is no joking matter. Yesterday death found her, but tomorrow it might reach you. It might get you some day, you might find yourself in its grip. Death is no laughing matter, you cannot make fun of death. Especially not of this kind of death, not of the death of such a person. Do not forget the bygone days. Just try to remember when you were ten, twelve, or fifteen. In those days, none of you would call her, "That hillbilly hussy!" You were not disgusted with her age, her dirtiness, and ugliness, nor with her pockmarked face. When her name came up, all the eyes would open wide; all the bodies would quiver. You would all give up the game, go to a corner, and talk about Haney. Once the talk started about Haney, it would go on and on. Haney was what you most wanted to get in those days.

Just remember those nights! Or have you forgotten them? I bet many of you suddenly woke up in the middle of the night, and lay wide awake until dawn, thinking of Haney all the while. I hope you will excuse me for saying this, but in our town, mother, father, boys, and girls all sleep in twos or threes in beds spread on the floor. Everything happens in this same room. In our town even a five-year-old kid knows all about it. Older ones surely know a lot better. I am sure all of you suddenly woke up in the middle of the night when your future brothers and sisters were conceived in your mothers' wombs. How could you have thought of someone else but Haney at such a time? Are you sure you did not stretch yourselves in the beds, thinking of Haney?

And the feast days! How about the feast days? Have you forgotten all about those feast days? Everybody would wake up even before the cocks started crowing. Everybody would wait impatiently for dawn. One would say, "I wish it were dawn already." Another would say, "I hope the morning is near at hand." Then the horizon would get brighter, and soon afterward the call to prayer would be heard. Blankets would then be thrown aside, and the mothers would make the kids perform their ablutions. Children would then go to the mosque with their fathers for the holiday service. Kids would grow restless if the *hoca* * kept on preaching. It would look as if the sermon would never come to an end. But the sermon would be finished soon; so would the service. Then the kids would rush back home. Eating rice with chopped meat, they would dash out. They would call on houses and kiss the hands of the elders. When they were given money in return, they would be

---

*Muslim teacher/preacher.

delighted. It would not matter if the sum was big or not. What was important was that it should come to fifteen cents. The money would be counted for this purpose again and again. What was all this about? Don't you remember? How is it that you cannot remember? Is it possible to think of the feast days of our childhood and not remember kissing hands and Haney? Well, Haney would actually add something to those feast days.

Don't you remember how you would walk up and down in front of her house, or, rather, her hen house? You would give anything just to be able to go in there. Feast days were of course different. Anybody making fifteen cents would rush to Haney's door. One would think there was an amusement park in front of the house. The whole crowd would look like a beehive. You could not walk about easily for the crowd. It really was a problem to be able to get in. Bigger boys would scare the little kids away. Lots of brawls would occur. Haney did not like brawls; she never liked them. She would then get angry, and she would say, "That's enough for today. I'm tired, you'd better come tomorrow." Then people would start begging; they just could not leave her door. A mere day would look as though it were a lifetime. Finally, they would somehow manage to convince her. When she saw people begging, she would suddenly yield. Not because she cared much about money, but because she was softhearted, because she liked everybody so much. You know it, she would not accept anybody else except children. The grown-ups would never be able to get into that dark room, however hard they might have tried....

This dark room gave some color to many of your dreams. It was in this same dark room that you saw what you were most anxious to see. She would treat you nicely in her room, but one would still feel dizzy when he got in. Haney would try to make you as little self-conscious as possible. All the same, you would still feel giddy when you went out. When you breathed the fresh air, you would feel as if you had been born again. That was exactly what Haney wanted; I have no doubt about it. The village boys had fancy ideas about the thing. They thought it was something fantastic. Haney wanted to show them that it was not something strange after all. To show this to the boys was her only aim. In spite of feeling happy once they were out of the darkroom, and in spite of feeling nauseous in the darkroom, there were many who visited her again. But there were also many others who felt that it was useless, and that it was stupid to try it again.

That is why Haney is so great, why she should be exalted. That is the reason why I keep saying, "Haney must live!" Really, she must live! In a stinking and disgusting room, with her repulsive smell, with her rags, with her pockmarked face, her calloused hands, and her leathery feet, with all her ugliness, dirtiness, and, finally, her shamelessness, she actually tried to show men what a woman really is. She cried, "Open your eyes, you fools!" And this she did, not in words but in actions. She spent all her lifetime on showing this. So, this woman must live! She did not lower herself as many "great men" or politicians did. She did not boast about what she did. She did not try to show that what she did was important. Whatever she did, she did without self-importance, as if it were all as easy as eating a sandwich.

So this woman must live! We should be ashamed of it. Because when she died on a cold winter night, her body had to stay in that dark room, because she had to be buried without a shroud. We should be ashamed, because we did not provide a shroud for her. So we should do something in return. We should try to keep Haney living, keep her living as long and as much as we can. We should never stop calling her name. To those passionate lovers who make use of knives, to those who cannot afford a woman, and to the growing adolescents, we should try to teach what this woman with a philosophical bent tried to prove during all her lifetime.

PART 2

Poems

Nahit Ulvi Akgün

Someone

Translated by Murat Nemet-Nejat

Something between us
Obvious from the way you look
My burning face.
We nod off occasionally
Perhaps thinking the same thing.
Start the conversation laughing.

Something between us.
Finding it, we let it go
Willingly.
But no use hiding it
Something between us,
Shining in your eyes
At the tip of my tongue.

Nazmi Akıman

Gaff

Translated by Murat Nemet-Nejat

whatever there was walked with the rain
the glass in the windows kept silent
on our back there was always that sun

our foreheads were stuck to the water
a scream at every crossroad
if we take one step it is the sea

boats have come and have gone
as though they are fire in a lion's mouth
a gaff pushes us to the blue

Gülten Akın

Ellas and the Statues

Translated by Nermin Menemencioğlu

Feeling a pain in his breast, when he speaks
Feeling guilty. As though forced to swallow
Unpalatable things. Nauseated
He casts taut threads into the world with his voice
Facing him one...two...three statues of mud
Upright, shout at every movement
With every movement crumble a little
Yet
Somewhere there have always been warm rooms
And old men in the warm rooms
Silent men, whose forefathers
Made miracles, always sacred tombs, saints
And candles burning on the gravestones
And birds circling at shoulder height
White birds.
Men have said their morning prayers in open country
Then returned with the birds to the ancient rooms
These two hundred years, the road has been traveled
Captain Dursun's ship has been boarded
Sails have been unfurled. In the middle of the Black Sea
A storm. The passengers pray.
Suddenly someone with a hoary beard—
Hey, captain, who is it, who, who?
She is gone as he has come
The storm has fallen asleep
The sails are full, the ship on course
Someone tells the tale back in Ünye
And as he tells it

The birds disappear, the candles go out
The ancestors are dead in their cupboards
But the ordeal goes on, and on
By every hearth
Everyone will die someday, will die
God will remain, the fire will be lighted
There will be people in the rooms

Smiling, bowing their heads, sighing
The wicked as they hide
The good as they grumble
Tall and thin, and wearing soft white garments.
His hand is an ungainly stone upon the table
To hide, but why? One of the statues laughs:
"You have been crushed."
"Look again...me or you?"

Taking breath from the people, breathing incantations on them
O dirty mud of the city, me or you?
The hand on the table has grown more shapely
It will be lifted slowly
The table will shake. This much is clear
The table will be upturned in the end
The hand will grow soft, more delicate
A cluster of yellow narcissus

A gust of wind across the corn
Sudden festivity upon the earth
Girls and machines hand in hand.
Some education from Paris, says one of the statues
To enlighten the towns. The villages...how coarse!
Thou knowest, God! Where are you, grandfather, saint
Who with birds upon your shoulders
Gathered the scattered soldiers together
Steered the ship safe upon its course
Destroyed the statues grown too smug

The tangled skein is unwound
Potatoes are buried in ashes, the coffeepot boils
On the path facing the window
The sick on their stretchers, the dead on theirs
Anger is not the broken shoulder, the motionless leg
Anger is the corpse rolling off the stretcher
The secret in the books. The crossways are abandoned
Untangled the skein of wool
The end of the tangled skein in sight

Living with people, as they live
Inhaling the air they breathe
Breathing knowledge into them

Sabahattin Kudret Aksal

In the Night

Translated by Murat Nemet-Nejat

A foal is neighing, wet
In the dark

The dead sleep, naked,
In their loneliness

The wells of my night
Are lengthening

And of the light, outside,
One single dot.

Embellishments

Translated by Murat Nemet-Nejat

I planted in a flowerpot
The free trees of the sea;
I dyed them red,
No use,
So I dyed them, from the top
To the deepest roots, deep blue;
I embellished my pot with lights,
Fancies and thoughts blossomed,
Encircled by glittering rituals;
I let the trees dance, they sang my song,
And I washed them
With the sunbeams of love.

Fantasy

Translated by Murat Nemet-Nejat

I am going to tell you a story, listen now!
It is longer than children's dreams; it won't end.
Daughters of kings, sons of kings, colorful
midgets, tame ogres, shepherds with inner glow,
and lit flowers not in bloom yet.
Cats smaller than mice, smiling
Green squirrels will be its heroes;
I do not know where the event will take place either.
I am dead, a skein is wound, a very cold
winter night, you in your bed, warm;
you will put yourself in their places
and the flocks of starlings longing in flight.

Feriha Aktan

Pendulum

Translated by Talat Sait Halman

Good-hearted timid aunts
Are gone from their dingy homes
Shy girls who have never known love
Sold their hair to the wind
And their lips to the sun
Widowed mothers have salt
All over their faces and eyes

Boys sing glittering
Songs of war
And to the deathlessness of eternity
Scorching to heal their hearts
They go far, far away

In the sacred gardens of God
Through those frozen nights
Stretching into winter mornings
Grannies dream of their grandchildren

It is so hard to get to know
Without being roughed up blind and deaf
If only the buds could see their flowers
If only the downpour of memories
Wouldn't put the grandfathers to a slow death

Melih Cevdet Anday

On the Nomad Sea

Translated by Talat Sait Halman

I

You and I, and our flowerpot on the balcony:
Busybee Elizabeth. The building's first triangle.

Neither old nor new. As if the most lucid
Moment of our destiny is trembling

On the nomad sea. We're not aware of it.
The sound of the rock resembles the human voice.

At a glimpse you find out: The flowerpot
On the balcony has replaced the cloud. The clouds

Turn themselves into horses in all that foam.
You and I keep running, ahead of us

A red bird shakes the ancient elder tree
A blind child was looking at a moment ago.

Then the cloud turns into the flowerpot again,
Horses begin to heave, we rest, in our ears

A murmur lingers like indecipherable words
Spoken by the walls. Out of this day, this morning.

II

Not to remember, not to forget. Where the ends meet,
Along the crimson smells of the shores,

Growing like the trills of a crippled nightingale,
In the heavy and slow symbols of our gaze

And I emigrate to you moment by moment
I return, in an exodus, like a vibration,

Seeking the rocks of your lips,
Seeking your name which I wrote in rain.

Now you vanish in the crevices of your own valley,
Now you gush out

All over your vanished valley.
Time and again I am lost to myself.

This is all there is to it. Neither old nor new
Like the most lucid moment of our destiny.

Countless blue transforming into a thought
Unused as those words which cannot exist alone,

Which emerge out of nowhere;
The soul is a coal crystal, rises out of darkness

Like a scarlet moon, and watches over the night.
And pioneering the numerical shapes,

It closes in on all things that scatter
And come together, like a carnivorous plant.

Scattering is none other than coming together.
The sexual fluid that breaks out of its shell,

The sun's taut, then loosened, bow, first images
Of the starry oysters twinkling.

The sky's wing turning red and growing pale;
All sorts of fruit on branches, feet sealed,

Sprouting frantically to a new infinity, then falling;
The soil whose panting like a sea lion

Moves us deep down, full of bleached bones.
Neither old nor new. That's all there is to it.

That is all. You and I and our flowerpot on the balcony.
Alone in the fluttering of heavy symbols.

III

There. I sprinkle all the words by the handfuls
To the birds, to the roots of roses,

To the lip of the sun, to the skirt
Of the prancing morning, to the red velvet of rocks,

To the moon's horns, and to the honeysuckle
Hanging out of the railing of your hair...

All by myself I cast my image over all shapes
And over the cross-eyed bottoms of the seas.

IV

Henry Moore is busy picking up pebbles on the beach,
Little fertile, some with holes in the middle,

Just like women's teats, like figs,
Dreams on their shoulders.

The heart is meant for the wisdom that no form
Is doomed to suffering.

Rocks that ennoble the world, with lodes, slab by slab,
Wave like flags that have wiped

The bloodstains of being alive.
Bones, all those human bones and animal bones,

The daintiest and the mightiest wreaths
Of the passage from one shape to another.

And the sea shells, grooved inside out,
Smell of shadows like the forehead of a billy goat.

Delight was meant to cross
Animals and grass.

All those trunks of trees covered
With graffiti like the walls of the mad...

The locked gem of the birds
Transforming the dead into the stars.

Man craved more, so much more.
All the more. Neither old nor new.

Perhaps it is a giant that dies and is resurrected
Time and again or a goddess frightened to death

These mute monuments which bloom like flowers
With their helter-skelter lines to the eye.

The eye is the god of its own harmony,
Segment by segment, against and opposite the whole.

Shape turning into shape, the resounding water
Of the present, life's alarm clock;

The enigmatic masts of change, the shriek,
The diamond of action, woman, noun, and verb.

Like a bull that dashes through a village
I shooed away whatever you had in you.

Now I know how hard it is to divest oneself
Of a two-dimensional raid and to live in a blue moment.

If the eye that sees is the eye that is seen
Then I am someone else.

This framework belongs neither to yesterday nor to tomorrow.
Tomorrow is an image, so is yesterday.

The sea, the bird, the wind, the rain
Belong to this day, this morning.

V

Freud is seated in the subconscious of a tree,
He keeps poking the dreams of the earth.

There are poppies that brighten these dreams.
Sea, bird, wind, rain.

The dream, a star distilled late
From action's bed of milky figs,

Late or early, the fish that leaps suddenly
Out of yesterday's waters;

A scarlet turmoil that has turned daylight inside out,
The face of a cramped well asleep and awake.

Epochs seem hidden in seeds,
Swings creaking in the soil.

Sea, bird, rain, wind.
And I found myself crucified

Between the past and the future, like a dream.
Neither old nor new. As if the most lucid

Moment of our destiny is trembling
In the waters of the sea laid waste.

Explanations of the Moon

Translated by Talat Sait Halman
and Brian Swann

I

The moon had been standing on the earth-line.
It left its weight behind like a heavy rose.
It suddenly gained speed when it touched the clouds
With Nazım Hikmet's tiny footsteps. Speed
Is always a black and white picture.
When the moon moved ahead of the clouds
Ahead of the clouds ahead of the clouds
It got faster as it passed the clouds
Now in the flowerpot.

II

In the old days the moon was a goddess. Later
It became the umbrella of Anaxagoras
The first to discover the sun is reflected on the moon.
Reflection is a scientific myth.
The common people used to say "old-new light,"
Which means they saw the reflection on the goddess.

III

Endymion the shepherd took sleeping pills
And waited for the goddess:
"The moon was a big mussel
At the lake bottom. Its inside
Billowed with the waters. I used to sleep
Embracing a girl covered with hair
Who covered me with watery dreams."

IV

The moon is our shepherd of the mountains
Our goddess left without a man
The courtyard of our family home
The first to make us look up to the sky devouring it
To free us from earth
Our first ordeal which made us hold our head erect
The skull of our ancestors.

Pigeon

Translated by Talat Sait Halman

The pigeon
The applause that breaks out at the window

Like Our Hands

Translated by Talat Sait Halman

Animals can't talk, so
Who knows how lovely their thoughts are—
Like our hands.
Before starting to read
One should water the flowers.

Horses before Troy

Translated by Talat Sait Halman
and Brian Swann

I   THE RACE

The story's told by a blind poet—
Before Troy even horses had souls.
Their neighings could be heard way down in Hades,
Horseless neighs making the dead shudder
And the dog frantic with fury.
At times hoofs drummed Trojan skies:
The restless soul of an unburied horse.

If the Achaeans had held the race for someone else that day
Achilles would have carried first prize to his hut,
For he owned immortal horses,
Poseidon's gift to his father Peleus
Who in turn passed them on to his son.
Now the horses mourn Patrocles,
Spirits broken, manes brushing earth.

Diomedes harnessed horses from Tros to his chariot,
Spoils from Aeneas
Whom a god had rescued.
Then fair-haired Menelaus, son of Atreus,
Godlike hero, rose and yoked two horses to his chariot:
Agamemnon's mare Aethe and his own horse Podargus.
Antilochus harnessed his horses from Pylos.
Then Ruşen Ali the folk-hero mounted his Gray Horse
With wings on his flanks.
Distance had no meaning for him.
Then they brought out the haughty Wooden Horse.
Burning cedar spread all through the air;
Its magic scent disturbed the other horses.
Then Düldül appeared, Mohammed's gift to his son-in-law Ali;
Düldül the even-tempered mule, its genitals covered,
Walked slowly among the polytheistic horses.
Alexander's Bucephalus came next,
His head tilted, casting deep glances like Hindu girls.
From time to time he looked south,
As if he knew how near the Granicos flowed.
Then El Cid's Babieca appeared, and soon Rossinante showed up
Weeping.
                    Don't talk to me of horses!

I know they come from a mother's womb, at night, in the dark
Stable. Someone holds a lamp whose light flickers
On the straw. The mare coughs and pants,
Turns her head and looks: "Is he like me?
Are his fetlocks white?"
                    Don't talk to me of horses!
Like fields of morning severed from the earth,
Like its screaming cataracts, Pegasus leaps
The sky's chasm. My youth, my son!
It was a time of madness and mourning, vengeance of the dead,
Bodiless bird, shattered star, wound of forgotten rose,
Seedless little lakes rising like a monument of death,
And naked void, cowed space, that unending race....
Horses, horses! I have never seen one grow old.
Some try toppling castles with their manes,
Some still scratch at the soil.
                    Don't talk to me of horses,
I can't bear the thought of them struck, struck down,
Defeated, lying on the ground, don't tell me,
Don't. I didn't see the Trojan War.

II THE VENOM

                    Have you heard
What Mehmet the garage mechanic from Bursa has heard?
Because of his premonition that the city smelling
Of tar, fish, and pinewood, of an unsatisfied meadowlike woman,
Was to go up in flames,
Laocoön was bitten by the poisonous snake.
Women and children stood there writhing
On the shores of windy Ilion.
Remnants of death, scraps
Of life and love, heap on the shores,
The word lost and found in thought,
Infinity, like a searched-for broken statue.
Fame, greatness, and the enemy heap on the shores.
For the sea has not yet reached its fullness; it is sleepless
And half complete. It settles in its pierced barrel,
With its dregs of the ancient dead.

            "On the bus coming back from the Izmir fair,
                I saw Troy enveloped by a cloud."

They dumped all the books into gas chambers
In Dresden, Cologne, Munich.
Über allen Gipfeln ist Ruh . . .

"They say planes and birds are clashing in the sky,
    Wings feathers beaks are raining on the city."

                    Have you heard?
All the girls in our brothels are foreign.
Their names are La, Li, Lu...

                    "All right.
What happened to the child left on the mountain?
Everyone's talking about this now.
Did animal or bird get him?
Couldn't we at least find his remains?
Couldn't we collect them and make up a person?
But then, what if he were left bodiless?
Could, couldn't, what if?"

III   THE DREAM

                    "Before dawn,
At the hour which, like an always hungry pigeon,
Picks up night's crumbs quickly,
When unborn children bend the bow of dreams,
The woman dreamed of child and fire."

"So they left the child on the mountain, where dream and fire
Lingered. If only they had left the dream behind."

"Yes, the dream frightened us, it had to be so,
We had no power not to interpret the dream
And do what we had to do.
The fire will wait until the child grows.
Let the crippled inscription of future days wait too,
And the mirror bloodied by bird beaks,

Wine is always aged and sipped,
Since blood gouts are red,
Day's color in ebb and flow, persisting song.
Haven't we split day into seven and night into five?
Haven't we sealed the waters of this sleepless resistance?
Haven't we flung the moon so far from birth,
Lengthened sleep's heavy funnel?
Let the reed wait in mysterious waters
And the eye-bird that peeps from the moon's skirt,
The blunt knife blinding the stone before the city's built,
Let them wait, the forehead destined to wait must wait.
I say hold on to the tide; it holds and waits.

Water, earth, the mind's wild weeds,
Merry-go-round, veils, temple and stairway endure,
Immortal happiness and boredom endure,
We wait, living what has been given us."

"The Sage has suffered so much.

Do you suppose that together we can bear this anxiety
Which will last for unknown years?
We had no idea what our tomorrow would bring.
We still don't know, but this child is a hope,
The hope of our hopelessness.
Go and find him in the forest."

IV   THE TURNING

The forest's a magic net cast by naked natives,
And the mountain, like a hunted bewildered horse,
Struggles to cling onto life,
Climbs on and on toward the sky's hollow waters.
Down below,
Between walls and sea left desolate seven times,
Between the two wings of dream and fire,
Between day's front tooth and the shadow's rock,
Between the river's enduring dance, stretching time,
The single bullet of nothingness, which makes
Hasty willows speak death's tongue,
And the lake, the end's neighboring wall,
The horses kept turning.... I saw none that was aging.
Some try to topple towers with their manes,
Others still scratch the ground with their hoofs
To one side the prize waited: a woman,
A tripod with handles, a six-year-old mare,
A cauldron untouched by fire, a two-handled kettle.
Shouts, sound of hoofbeats, clouds of dust....
Über allen Gipfeln ist Ruh.

"All right, then,
What happened to the child left on the mountain?"

V   TELLING THE FUTURE

"See that blue bead? The other day
A camel driver held it. He was really strange.
He wanted his fortune told, but fearlessly
Fought against it. I don't understand. They say

He drowned crossing the Euphrates. Fortune's
A hungry dog—you chase it away, and back it comes
To find you. I pour lead to tell fortunes,
But whose fortune is this?
I told Macbeth he would be king: it didn't happen.
But I never told him he would kill the king.
It's not in my power to lengthen time either,
Nor shorten it. '*Yat sat tat ksanikam.*'
Look, I blinked: all things were past and gone.
Tomorrow is yesterday, and yesterday has yet to come.
Let this bean be the child you hold: I push it.
It tumbles down the mountain. How long did it take?
I can't tell. I still can't tell if it's him or not.
Light a lamp. It gives one light in the evening,
A different one at midnight, still another before dawn,
But it's still the same lamp.
Santana ksana dharmas. Believe. Do not believe."

VI   LOVE

The forest would start when you held my hand,
Split in two like a fig.
We would run up, bent double, breathless,
Tumbling with trout, pine-needles
Hindered our speed. Do not let go my hand. Do not let
Go my hand....
              Then we'd slide all the way down,
And silence stooped like a tree,
Growing roots in us both, look for
The soil's streams, one after the other.
Your sunflower breasts turned their faces to the light.
Like the hours of noon, I walked all over your breasts;
I walked on both sides of you like an arch of triumph.
              Then we'd start running again,
Up, higher up, to the sky's hollow waters.
I'd kill you and you'd tremble. Love
That unites broken moments sees no dream. Forest,
Fate of hunted horse, hungry pigeon of new beginnings!
We have no fortune to be told.
We burned it like a speck in the eyes of migrant birds
Or the single grain held in their beaks
At daybreak.
We have no fortune to be told.

Talip Apaydın

Old Building

To Yashar Kemal with affection

Translated by Talat Sait Halman

We strike our pickax into its depth
Shallow sounds echo down below
This building decayed for countless years
We'll rebuild it from the base up

Go ahead try a bit more go on
Already it's trembling all over
The bugs and the lice in its burrows
Are in a hue and cry as in doomsday

We'll raze it there's no other choice
We'll raze it and from foundation to roof
We'll build a new and decent house
In which we shall live like human beings

Orhon Murat Arıburnu

As the World Turns

Translated by Talat Sait Halman

Hope is the poor man's meat.
Eat, my man, eat
Eat, my man, eat

Eat, my man, eat...

Freedom

Translated by Talat Sait Halman

All things grow toward the sky
Except the weeping willow's branches

Dearly beloved
Freedom
Why don't you grow
Toward us?

Ahmet Arif

Thirty-three Bullets

Translated by Murat Nemet-Nejat

I

This is the Mengene mountain
When dawn creeps up at the Lake Van
This is the child of the Nimrod
When dawn creeps up against the Nimrod
One side of you is avalanches, the Caucasian sky
The other side a rug, Persia
At mountain tops glaciers, in bunches
Fugitive pigeons at water-pools
And herds of deer
And partridge flocks...

Their courage cannot be denied
In one-to-one fights they are unbeaten
These thousand years, the servants of this area
Come, how shall we give the news?
This is not a flock of cranes
Nor a constellation in the sky
But a heart with thirty-three bullets
Thirty-three rivers of blood
Not flowing
All calmed to a lake on this mountain

II

A rabbit came up from the foot of the hill
Its back is motley
Its belly milk-white
A mountain rabbit, pregnant, lost up here
Its heart heaved to its mouth, poor thing
It can draw repentance from man.
The hour solitary, a solitary time
It was a faultless, naked dawn
One of the thirty-three looked
In his body the heavy void of hunger
Hair and beard all tangled
Lice on his collar
He looked, and his arms were wounded
This lad with hellion heart
Looked once at the rabbit
Then looked behind
His delicate carbine came to his mind
Sulking under his pillow
Then came the young mare he brought from the plain of Harran
Her mane blue-beaded
A blaze on her forehead
Three fetlocks white
Her cantering easy and generous
His chestnut mare
How they had flown in front of Hozat!
If he were not now
Helpless and tied like this
The cold barrel of his gun behind him
He could have hidden on these heights
These mountains, the friendly mountains, know your worth
Thank God, my hands will not put me to shame
These hands that can flick off at the first shot
The burning tobacco ash
Or the tongue of the viper
Sparkling in the sun
These eyes were not duped even once
By the ravines waiting for avalanches
By the soft, snowy betrayals of cliffs
These knowing eyes
No use
He was going to be shot
The word was final

Now the blind reptiles will devour his eyes
The vultures his heart.

III

In a solitary corner of the mountains
At the hour of morning prayer
I lie
Stretched
Long, bloody...

I have been shot
My dreams are darker than night
No one can find a good omen in them
My life gone before its time
I cannot put it into words
A pasha sends a coded message
And I am shot, without inquest, without judgment

Kinsman, write my story as it is
Or they might think it a fable
These are not rosy nipples
But a dumdum bullet
Shattered in my mouth.

IV

They applied the decree of death
They stained
The half-awakened wind of dawn
And the blue mist of the Nimrod
In blood
They stacked their guns there
Searched us
Feeling our corpses
They took away
My red sash of Kermanshah weave
My prayer beads and tobacco pouch
And left
Those were all gifts to me from friends
All from the Persian lands

We are guardians, relatives, tied by blood
We exchange with families
Across the river
Our daughters, these many centuries
We are neighbours
Shoulder to shoulder

Our chickens mingle together
Not out of ignorance
But poverty
We never got used to passports

This is the guilt that kills us
We end up
Being called
Bandits
Killers
Traitors

Kinsman, write my story as it is
Or, they might think it a fable
These are not rosy nipples
But a dumdum bullet
Shattered in my mouth.

V

Shoot, bastards
Shoot me
I do not die easily
I am live under the ashes
I have words buried in my belly
For those who understand
My father gave his eyes on the Urfa front
And gave his three brothers
Three young cypresses
Three chunks of mountain without their share of life
And when friends, guardians, kin
Met the French bullets
Out of towers, hills, minarets
My young uncle Nazif
His moustache still new
Handsome
Light
Good horseman
Shoot, brothers, he said
Shoot
This is the day of honour
And reared his horse...

Kinsman, write my story as it is
Or they might think it a fable
These are not rosy nipples
But a dumdum bullet
Shattered in my mouth.

Özdemir Asaf

Selected Aphorisms

Translated by Yıldız Moran

The most important death in history is the death of man.

If you stare into the sun, you spoil your eyes.... If you put on glasses to look, you spoil the sun.

He was born, they shed tears of joy. He died, they shed tears of sorrow.
He lived in between, this they never thought of.

It is wrong to look for honesty in great deeds....As wrong as to look for great deeds in honesty.

Stairs, while ascending...love, while descending, strain the heart.

The wind even without the sail is still the wind. Yet the sail without the wind is merely a piece of cloth.

All that is destined to grow old is called "new."

Translated by Talat Sait Halman

Those who live as the dead begrudge the dead who are still alive.

Someone views someone else as something—that is life.
Someone views someone else as many things—that is affection.

Someone views someone else as all things—that is love.
Someone views someone else as nothing—that is the Orient.
Someone not even views someone else—that is death.

The biggest lie can be told to a crowd.

I stagger when my loved one deals a blow—and when my
enemy commits an act of love.

Even a burglar would not steal from the person who guards
his feelings.

Point

I'd have taken it if she told me lies,
Instead she told me a lie.

Jury

All colors gathered dirt at the same speed:
They gave the first prize to white.

Bound

Make me believe in such a lie
That its truth may last all my life.

Arif Nihat Asya

Amnesty

Translated by Talat Sait Halman

Accident, affliction, death knell,
Cain and Abel,
And Azrael
Whom I find hard to take as an angel,
I pardon them all.

The tongue with its curses of hell,
With tales that have no end,
The head, the foot, the hand,
I pardon them all.

As leaves burst open and roses bloom,
Land by land, town by town, hill by hill,
Shadow of my shadow news of gloom,
You too,
Decree by fate, destiny, doom,
I pardon you too.

O eternal journey;
Your voice tarries on the pathways,
Your word is what the tongue says,
O my heart's progeny,
You too,
I pardon you too.

The flowers that find my garden humdrum,
The food that disdains my table as glum,
Those who have come and have yet to come,
I pardon all.

M. Sami Aşar

Weekly Agenda of Love

Translated by Talat Sait Halman

Monday I expect a letter from you
Tuesday I pour my distress to papers
Wednesday your voice resounds in the void
I shall sigh my heart out on Thursday
Friday I am in the theater of memories
Saturday is pregnant to so much
How about Sunday my love
Just wait for Sunday

Oğuz Kâzım Atok

We Turned the Mill with the Water We Carried

Translated by Talat Sait Halman

Our toil grew by leaps and bounds with all that sweat
With our hands we scattered the sleepless mornings
Passing over the peaks and meadows where winter pulsated
On our chests we melted down all that black snow

From our specter it descended wingless in a blind flight
Its dark rays came all over us eye by eye
Under the raw night no one could make out
Our faces which heaved with pain and sorrow

We hung the poison-filled serpents on their dreams
We have routed our fate in the hardest combat
And now we live towards springtime and flowers
Towards the warmest of essences and shapes

Ece Ayhan

The Phaeton

Translated by Güngör Dilmen

Those tunes played on his master's voice gramophones
were the exquisite melancholy of her loneliness
as my sister in a suicide-black phaeton
rode through the streets of the love-of-deaths pera.*

My sister must have been tipsy who owned gardens and gardens of flowers
she stopped in front of a flower shop with no flowers
yet in the window were a purple montenegro pistol wrapped in gauze
and photographs of oleanders and african violets

I have not committed suicide for the last three nights so I can't tell
a suicide-black phantom ascending to the skies with horses and all
could it be because of my sister's buying the african violets?

*Europeanized section of Istanbul.

To Draw in Hebrew

Translated by Murat Nemet-Nejat

My legs are long
They are long wherever I go
Wherever I go they come and find me
My sister in a blind alley

To draw a dove in a town
To draw the eyes of the dove
One dove
In the Middle Ages one dove with chalk

Along the whole wall trees cool
I draw a sound
In everything in everywhere I want a voice
In the dove a voice in the Middle Ages in my sister a voice

Wherever I go they are long
They find me from my legs always
As I draw a different voice
And a holiday full of flags in a city
In Hebrew

from *Orthodoxies*

Translated by Murat Nemet-Nejat

It is his only child that can be talked about, the space between his legs. And now he has grown mustaches and a beard. An inveterate pervert. Such talk about him. He does not approach women as he should. He whets suspicion. On his head a plume, a barber's masterpeice. He is buried alive into the ground, head downward. A few barges, startled, shine at a distance. Why didn't I understand?

A shame is held in his hand delicately. A girl, lemon burn. Walks under the Vees of her man. The door locks have given in by themselves. A shroud moves. She has grown pregnant by leaning over the corpse. Which does not rot in a church. She has reared the baby in the marshes. I was burning a letter by pouring petrol on it. On the bird envelope. Wax.

It is the crookedness in a child's heart. His craft, elegant wrist. And how he holds a hawk, stuffed whole. He tries to gather its feathers. He has writings etched over his breast in saffron. He repeats one word from the lexicon endlessly: hermaphrodite. He makes love biting his own mouth. He plays the lute of the coward, secondhand. I was reading the Maltese Jew. I took shelter in a coffin.

Davut has a mane. A dark-skinned child like my hand. Facing the ground, he is dissolving in the bird-plain of Tirnova.

This ogre is recent. Lift your skirt–scramble. And he has written his name on the exercise slate. Dexterously, he plays the obstacle game.

Davut with tortoise-shell mane. The sharp, Latinate bullets of truth know first the schools of the land.

The eerie sea of Maydos. The porpoise has become Jonah. It's swimming. Bedecked with holsters, stirrups, harness.

He is combing his hair with gonorrhea water. Inverted. From time to time blinking his eyes, with huge, hanging earrings.

What is an orthodox lad doing at Maydos? He is after the instinct of knives in his agitation.

The encounter between a church elder and a saint of the sea. Novotni. Bread and fish have put their faces on each other's shoulders. Good. During the Equinox dreadnoughts are beating the flour factories at Gallipoli.

M. Başaran

I've Registered for Germany

Translated by Nermin Menemencioğlu

Before the tractors I was a laborer
That is why my arid face
The nights knew my loneliness
Someday do you think I shall find
In the coolness of some morning
My poor bruised hands
After the tractors I was without a job

On the roads since that day
Bent in two since that day
I have gone far for my bread
Down in the mines with my eyes
This soul weighs heavy
A pair of oxen cannot lift my tiredness
I have registered for Germany

Its people, its God may be different
I've registered for new roads
Someday do you think I shall find them
My dirty quilt can stay behind
My heart beats in a strange way
I cannot bear to look at our mountains
I beg of you, German master
Send me tidings soon

The Soil Is Burning

Translated by Talat Sait Halman

Take a deep breath and smell the air
Then take a look at the grass
Listen to the farmhand whistling
A blade licks your face doesn't it
The soil is burning

You cannot reach out and touch
Its borders with your hands
Like eyes one cannot look into
Its lips are parched and scorched
The steppes stretch far and wide
The soil is burning

Its heart weighs down
Under the yearning of a thousand years
Blood and tears
And an unceasing ache
As sunset clutches the mountains
The soil is burning

Destitute distressed villages
Smolder in the bitter smoke
An ashen light covers the barren fields
Though you see it you don't speak out
Though you hear it you keep quiet
The soil is burning

Seyfettin Başcıllar

And a Child at the Bell Tower's Crying

Translated by Murat Nemet-Nejat

In Dallas, at the Church district,
A woman, half-Chinese and quite loving,
Sleeps with the church chorister every night
After praying for the health of the Pope.

In the morning at the end of a fishing tackle
Stripping her heart, she confesses
Sin'n Christ side by side in her
And love, a long memory

Her black eyes, flowers on a bench,
Are being shaved, being shaved like a cedar tree;
Poor Mr. Chorister, how could he possibly know
About benches, about love, about rice.

He has other things on his mind
On the sky's floor a mansion, and a white swan,
And a child at the bell tower's crying
The childhood of that sensuous woman

In Dallas, at the church district,
A woman, half-Chinese and quite loving,
Sleeps with the church chorister every night
After praying for the health of the Pope.

Ataol Behramoğlu

How Bad It Is That a Poem Gets Old As One Reads It

Translated by Murat Nemet-Nejat

Three dots and behind the blue curtains the city
Which Saturday, how many packs, bodies run from the markets
I thought of a sailboat in the street, poppies with white hats
Someone dropped his cigarette into the water
Seagulls dropped to waters, women with pride to markets
I was going to write poems, bored, tired of old things
Eat, my mother was saying, behind daily habits; finally,
Camus or whatever, my mind will crack,
Everything will grow out of your hair after it loosens

Is the essence of a tablecloth to be spread? How bad it is to hide
in familiar words
One should forget oneself—but in what kind of color—
From the core of winds evenings enter as thoughts
Quinces soft and sweet

Overeating, I will exaggerate my bellyache, will cry wolf, scared.
After the boy sick in his lungs if jilted many times, they will come—
All flows to an abyss,
Colorless; perhaps writing poetry is the sweetest lie—
And they will sketch his face, and go, drink some wine

I'd make myself into a brand new sailor if I were god.
More things perhaps on the other side
I hurt to write as though rabid, hungry, can't you see?
Whatever doctors may call it
Who knows best anything
Which religion does not stale—
What is knowing best anyhow!—
My hands, wrists, eyes are tickled with lust
I have no wish at all to see your tired faces
There's such a dynamite of boredom in me that if it doesn't explode
I'll die
I should write; I am bored, disgusted with my old habits
Without thinking, if I let loose my hands, they may say a lot.
Like a solitary cockroach, I run to the nook of the ceiling.
I must kiss you on your nose before you turn into an ugly hag
My dear.

Cengiz Bektaş

Violet Flowers

Translated by Murat Nemet-Nejat

I can't look at the walnut tree
Right there, two steps from me one of them
Its face is bloody,
Bloody
Face,
Violet.
I am getting old.

Look

Translated by Murat Nemet-Nejat

A bridge is watching its feet in the water
I am going and making myself a dome to an old building
The sun is setting on the one side
The other, angling for your eyes,
Lift your head, look.

My Sound

Translated by Murat Nemet-Nejat

I am calling your name to the room
The ceiling,
The walls,
The floor
Are becoming my sound
Suddenly.
I am living in my sound.

Şemsi Belli

Nights in the Shanties

Translated by Talat Sait Halman

You cannot silence the howling wolf packs
Or muffle the struggle for life.
This puppy is born, so he'll live his life through,
He'll eat whether you feed him or not.
You cannot stifle the laws of nature, the hormones.
Horses will neigh no matter what you do.

The shantytown woman will read cheap novels
And slip into bed with the doormen at midnight.
You cannot gag the nights or the shantytown people
Or the cats on the roofs.

Bitter songs linger in exhausted hearts
Like cinnamon candy that melts no matter what you do.
You cannot silence. Don't even try, it's all in vain.
Each web has its own sovereign spider.

You cannot silence the howling wolf packs
Or muzzle the struggle for life.

Süreyya Berfe

The Wall

Translated by Murat Nemet-Nejat

My youth is surrounded
If I cross it over...

No stone, no plows
Paper, ink, star
If I take a step

A wedding in the house across
A wall between
At night watch me
If I leave and come
For a drink of raki

On the other side of the wall
Gathering bones
Two flowers newly in bloom
They fell into the garbage can
Before the sun came down,
If I smell them...

One day I collapse one day I laugh
Papers grow yellow
Words give no sound
Stars drop
A wind starts up
I blow away

İlhan Berk

Istanbul

Translated by Nermin Menemencioğlu

A small, flat rectangle. And a heading: Istanbul, 1574; Braun-Hogenberger. An inscription in Gothic characters: *Byzantium, Lunc Constantinopolis* (or so I read it). Clearly, in Hogenberger's own hand. Gradually, he begins to weave in the picture: downward lines, triangles, rectangles, perpendicular lines. Attractive. Autonomous. Hogenberger's own alphabet, transforming itself into the great vocabulary of ISTANBUL. On wood. An engraving, therefore to be scratched in with a steel pen. Looking carefully at a lithograph. Given by a Galata Jew who sensed the soul of a Bohemian engraver in Hogenberger, a longtime vendor of mulberries and figs. A bit of a mapmaker, too, as a man who has traveled should be. He lives in the guild hostel. Nowadays he works on wood. At night, spreading before him pictures of Istanbul. City of seven hills. Of plains. Of valleys. Walled and turreted. As in this engraving. *(This engraving: is it not the point I want to come to? What other meaning is there to this prelude? Like all preludes it is an addendum, and unnecessary. But then one cannot do without them. Think of all those masters! Which one has freed himself from them? And entered straight into his subject? Like those beautiful textbooks, simple and direct. With merely a table of contents on the first page, listed in large letters one below the other, geometrically. But why is it, then, that one does not come to the point at once? Without unnecessary delays. And with a rough outline of the subject. And without delving into history? Simply saying, it's a peninsula, for instance.)*

A peninsula. Resembling a triangle. Three-dimensional. Horizontal and bulging. Rising to peaks at one point. And drawing a line at the Golden Horn. And breaking into bays, islands. Abutting onto a continent. Seen on three sides, and from the top. For this is a bird's eye view. *And so it shall remain.* Completing itself with a level of some eighteen miles. With its ins and outs. It will close itself in, straightening its peaks. From seven points, silent and upright. Down its roads, its avenues. Crossing long, narrow straits. To die at a sea spelled out in Greek letters. With a marginal note: TÜRKELİ. * There are three seas, for this is always the bird's-eye view of a mapmaker. And the city rests in every bay, curving into S's and U's. Then returns to itself. Leaving islands behind, like extended feet. Stretching out arms like an octopus. Reproducing there, beyond its body. And old men: in mosque yards, holding children by the hand. Taking children to bed, their beautiful mouths. Imperial and in stamboulines. And dark—that is the way Hogenberger has caught it too, dark and plunged in sorrow. That is why he makes engravings, using black dyes, black ink. On wood. Veinless. Smooth. Drying them in the sun. The grease still trickles through. And now it slips under my hand. Walnut. Separate from itself. For that is the way it has always lived. Those migrations, those fires, have served no purpose other than to increase its loneliness. That is why it is the Land of the Turks. Straight and still. And to this

*Turkish lands.

day. Those towers were not built in vain; tall, two stories high. Because of all this, alone and lonely. Turned toward the right, with crenellations. Reproduced as far as they could be on this engraving. That is, indistinctly. Reproduced on paper; therefore the city will leave to history its name and that of Hogenberger. Even if Pera and Galata should grow transparent with time. With its twelve gates. Its tower of Christ. And its Latin inscriptions. Since he is making a picture, he must use shadows. Dark, light, lighter still. Making notes all the way. Measuring the scale, like any mapmaker. What he is making is a picture map. Is it not clear from the way his roads are traced? With all their curves, and black. The seas are white. And the Bosporus. Well, a peninsula.

That is why he engraves: he has a picture in mind. For a monograph. Contemporary. For he has thought of our times. He drops portraits of the sultans into place: Orhan, Murat I, Beyazıt I, Mehmet I, Murat II, Selim the Grim, Beyazıt II. With Mehmet the Conqueror in the middle. Long-faced and bearded. Greater than all the others. Only Süleyman the Magnificent on horseback. Dark, and with big eyes. Three horsemen clear a way for him. (You know the Magnificent: broad-browed and short-whiskered. Unsmiling. He has never dallied with odalisques. He wore powder and mascara.) Three horsemen clear the way. Armed. They look straight ahead. He has placed his portraits by Tophane, in circles. Full-face and in profile. In crested turbans. Past galleys of Venetian make. (Is he not Venetian himself? Of German origin. Wellborn. He never leaves Galata. For that is where he is looking from, back to the sea and pencil in hand.) Now we see the imperial mosques one by one. All on one promontory. In motion, widening toward the top. Like a final quatrain. The houses should rise, the seashore residences descend. And so they do. With a steel pen, adding his signature. Now he returns to the guild hostel. He is yearning for the sea. But he stops first at Karaköy. Now he engraves the voices of children. Curves around a bird, lifts up a fish, etc. Now it is the turn of the grasses of Istanbul. He works in a leaf, shapes a love, as an old inhabitant of Scutari. Raises a tombstone. Draws in Balkapan Han with a thick line, so that it will remain within his framework. But it does not. He wanders over the seven hills. Brushes against the Tower of Almenas, leaving the Theodosian walls to the right. He rests at last beside a cross. In the hands of a yellow Jesus. He kisses these hands. And again he engraves walls, towers. He stops beside a seaside house. With two entrances. Dark. So as to have a better look at Seraglio Point and at Topkapı. Topkapı, a city. 699,000m^2. A ceiling: domed, and encrusted with mother of pearl. A commemorative poem. Long. White eunuchs. Thick walls, made of stone. Four rectangles, one within the other. A rising Tower of Babel. Wooded. With tasseled palace guards. Colliding with a galley. At last out on the Hippodrome. A quinquangular shape. Hand in hand with John the Evengelist. To see the palace birds? Or the Egyptian Obelisk? With a copper globe, as in the day's cosmography. Now he will look out of the window of a coffeehouse. Letting his cross hang down. His eyes fixed on the Mosque of Süleymaniye. Its great, square courtyard. He remains there for a while, drinking tea. In his hand Melling's engravings. (Or so it pleases me to fancy: my beloved Melling, and Selim III, who spent so much time in bird shops and spice shops. And wandered along the shores of the Bosphorus. An umbrella in his hand. Wearing a stambouline.) Where is he now? On the steps of Step Street? St. Nicholas? The Thousand and One Columns? (Perhaps.) His face turned toward Hagia Sophia. Bolt upright. Erect. Broken up at the Gate of Petrios. Into the shape of a *tughra,* an imperial seal. After a long while he will walk down to the shore, studying the map of Piri Reis, stopping frequently.

An island, according to the historian Asagik and to Lazarus. Full of ins and outs. And full of Armenians. With an inner belt of fortifications twenty feet in depth, outer walls of ten feet. With its 225 turrets. Its light cavalry. Andreas, first bishop. John, a saint. Satkis, who sent him greetings. Macedonius, first consul. Plotius, last patriarch. Hagia Irene, a church (not visible). John the Baptist. Rosario, a virgin. Michael, imperator (like the Conqueror). Hydraulis, an aqueduct. *Khrisi Pili,* a building. Hovannesian, a money lender. *Of Pera. He sleeps in his shop. An intimate friend of Lazarus. And, like Ahmet I, he hates the number fourteen.* Ayvansaray's suburbs. Seventeen Jewish quarters. Gothic columns. Obelisks. Horses and donkeys. And hans. So it is an island. And also an engraving. On wood. It winds about houses, walls, books, tries metals, iron, zinc, goes out to women, but remains on wood in the end. Dying there. So as to be always Istanbul. Toward 1574. Toward a morning? And toward today. This hour. Unaffected by any law of preservation. Then it will turn to a wall. In origin an engraving. Its ditches Theodosian. As it is: Berk-like. And

he stops. Because he is at Galata. An administrative district. With two steep slopes. With ditches, and curves. Down there they are filling in the area. An Arab blocks his view. Night is announced in Latin. Chains are drawn. Its twelve gates. Its bitter water. Its 246 steps. Its sleepless monasteries. And voyvods. Its square. Its Latin church. Its icon of the Virgin Mary, made by Lucas the Evangelist, embossed with silver. Which Eudoxia, wife of Theodosius the Younger, sent ot Pulcheria, and which Pulcheria always carried with her. At the spot where the Virgin appeared to two blind men, and they regained their sight but never saw her again, at Hagia Dichola. Surrounded by fortifications. Venetian and Pisan. Where the archers were installed. They lived in the turrets. Forty-seven years, three days and five hours.

But let us return to the engraving. And to Hogenberger. And describe exactly what we see. In the first person singular. The present attracts us. The nearest and shortest road to reality. (Since I began with what I saw.) Therefore: O eye of mine! You must begin by seeing a road in the distance. Curving over there by Psamathia, in front of a city wall. Too many walls, you say? How else could it have been? Since a highway begins here, then the entrance must be blocked. With the wind. In medieval fashion. Well, what else do you see? Hills? Ending in sky? That is right; we had forgotten the sky. Like a corsair's map. It never leaves Istanbul. Yes, that sky you are looking at is the face of Byzantium. Was looked at by Constantine the Great. *They say he was fair. And very frightened. Because he lived so long. And he wore red garments, and feared the Goths, and loved the Visigoths. Bronze. Wood and stone.* Now stop. Taking this engraving into your hand. Torn from a book and spread on the poet's table. That he keeps looking at, lighting his pipe. Every morning. In Atacity (an ugly word, but I won't scratch it out.) As he gets dressed. A kind of life, a place to wander, with the Crusaders. A kind of life, then. So let us stop. And end this. With a dash. It is better thus. Did we not begin thus? We must continue the same way. Parallel to the prelude. Without a summary. Without marginal notes. Without O's. Wring the neck of poeticism. Thus.

This Caesar weighed the land.

Sofia

Translated by Nermin Menemencioğlu

A woman strolls with her children in Alexander Nevski Cathedral
As though in a garden. Two men are saying their prayers.

A priest like a tall black candle stands looking at me
His face is lemon-colored, his slender hands yellow

I walk, hands in pockets. Sounds from the Ruski Boulevard
Is it a woman shouting from window to window?

Or a rose dropping into the morning. I time
My watch by that of a Bulgarian peasant

His name begins with *G,* which he cannot pronounce
Then I ask a street vendor the way to a street

Because a woman is arranging flowers
I understand why her hands are delicate, her face white

One afternoon I look for Dobruja Street
With Hüseyin. He constantly strokes his whiskers.

Pablo Picasso

Translated by Feyyaz Kayacan

L'Homme au Mouton
A lonely cloud, a lonely branch, a light,
Sky, a flower, the water's feeling of nothing to follow, of love, yearning, and joy,
A little hope, a little ray, the morning a little further on,
Different one by one, differently beautiful, differently lonely and near,
All these worldly things drifted by uselessly.

Picasso picked up his brush.

Nature morte
Picasso woke up
Into his sunburned hands.

Sonnet

Translated by Talat Sait Halman

The suns, she is all in all, I stood on a sea,
In a bright dawn, like Menelaus, I arose
And now I reign supreme over a new country.
Catching sight of your face, I turn white like a rose.
Perhaps we were in the skies of earliest days
Where a cloud and an old galleon collided,
One morning I absorbed the word with a deep gaze:
Into the breath of the colts my dark face glided.
In that age in Troy your beauty stood alone
When they wafted the ocean to your side,
Once again, like the dawn, your beauty shone;
Now my sunbeams will fall to carry you astride.
My carnation breath, you passed but couldn't see,
Yet at one glance you would have made me lovely.

The City

Translated by Nermin Menemencioğlu

I arose early this morning. I woke up the sea
A man had caught a squid, he was holding it up
I bent down to look at his eyes, they were blue and round.
He heaved when breathing like a heavy laborer.
Three men sat drinking tea and reading the sky.
One was describing the south wind, acting out
The part. "In B.C. Bodrum there were only the quarters
Of Salmachis and Zephyria," said another.
I thought of the Dorians and of the great Alexander
Of the castle of Saint Peter, the chevalier de Naillac.
At six the sun came up, we all dispersed.

Egemen Berköz

Utrillo's House

Translated by Murat Nemet-Nejat

a bony hand, walk on
epileptic keys, happy days
are too far away,
far away.
only late afternoons I am a poet.
the city
expands
bricks. bricks.

these papers, nor this table,
am I a poet,
your delicate face darkening your voice,
the slide rule, scissors, ashtray,
head-typesetter. I strike
the keys. A. C. I.
there is no sky above the houses,
nor gun makers, glass makers,
bricks, bricks, where is
the city? the teacher
now only eats candies.
nor raising the flag, wearing a hat,
this foppish teacher, on Saturdays, to town,
to town. newspapers, letters,
rubber balls, children,
children.
the teacher now only eats candies.
the world oppressing my sound,
a bony hand moves
on epileptic keys.
again, sidewalks,
look, my poet, on your window
leaves fall yellow and drunken.
Beyazıt Square had a pool, and the pool
had a fountain,
did they play ball, children?
a bony hand

249

is directing the band
playing an epileptic leftover march
from the eighteen ninety-three war.
it must be holiday. firecrackers,
and, again, children, children.

I strike the keys.
A. C. I.
from Pangaltı* straight to Yıldız Palace,
without raising the flag,
or my hat, unlike
a foppish teacher. in silence. like a child
looking at the sea for the first time,
it is raining, gun makers, glass makers,
raining. I am an afternoon
poet,
in the cornices of the city. delicate faced.
the fall is dividing my sound into two.
delicate faced.

the fall. the parquet sidewalks become
poems on yellow papers.
the fall. a shapeless poem. introvert.
hooked on loneliness.
the fall watches the gun makers,
the bricks,
children.
it strikes the keys. we strike them.
it is late afternoon. I did not see it.
I heard it is late afternoon. they told me.
A. C... no.
bricks,
city, more and more.

the fall is dividing the city into two, happy days
are too far away. perhaps,
a saturday,
in Utrillo's house am I a poet
to Pangaltı. then to Yıldız Palace.

*A section of Istanbul.

Salâh Birsel

Güzin's Youthful Years

Translated by Murat Nemet-Nejat

As I thought of Güzin
Güzin had her own thoughts.
Her fingers were so thin
Her tiny face minute

On Güzin's mind
There were carriages
Horses
Other men, other men,
Other lives.

Güzin had cats
Like me wanting to be caressed
But mention love
She frowned.

Güzin also belongs to tales
Her princes are real princes,
A large book filled
With her dreams.

When I sit in a room
Güzin had also rooms where she sat.
She had a bed belonging to her
She had her sleep.

Geography Lesson

Translated by Talat Sait Halman

The subject of today's lesson is geography
Don't be wary at all to go near the guys
There Bolu forests are straight ahead
Take a love stroll early in the morning
Don't be bashful our subject is geography

Look this is the place they call Asia
Here's Beyoğlu Avenue this is in Hong Kong
Watch your step don't crush the Chinese
Stuff the yellowest of them into your bag
Don't forget our subject is geography

I could tell this was going to happen
See you smashed the Calcutta elephants
Hold it now climb the Himalayas at least
Take off your clothes on the Tibet plateau
Don't be shy our subject is geography

Miss you aren't listening to our lecture
Look these are the sultans of Africa
Who tirelessly eat pineapple four seasons
Well love your Ethiopian lads if you like
Don't be ashamed our subject is geography

And these here are the Alps
Don't say you can't see for all those men
Going down you have the Venetian counts
Go to sleep in the streets of Rome at noon
Don't forget our subject is geography

Now look this is the sea of Paris
Held in the hands of Queen Brigitte Bardot
And higher up you have the Bank of England
High time you made off with the sterlings
Don't be scared our subject is geography

That's all for today some other time
We'll see the United States with Texas Rangers
But go ahead hug your husbands right away
I guess your husbands won't mind it either
Don't forget our subject is geography

Edip Cansever

The Bedouin

Translated by Nermin Menemencioğlu

Through the deserted dim brown city of my eyes
The white-necked camels pass, their tired drivers,
Day after day, as though to renew their grasp
Ceaselessly look at something very far.
Ask, do they see what they look at, even as a fairy tale,
In the deserted dim brown city of my eyes

Toward the unknown, not day, not death,
They merely look.
A Bedouin stands among the white thorns
The gods the suns the mirages
Not even a fire, not even a seedling, a prayer
In the deserted dim brown city of my eyes

Looking, perhaps, for water to slake a thirst.
No halting place for him, no rest
He will not hear the white-necked camels
Though their tired drivers should sink in front of him
Like the coldest desert bird dying once more
Into the world's monotonous color

The Quarrel

Translated by Doğan Türker

Pointed are his feet as he steps on hard stones
The women have breasts—Let's drink either whisky or beer
And there are tables, you know, that are not living
Just like that, a table in them
Tell Mike and Jim—tonight to the women.

Mike does not like women, so we'll drop him at the coffeehouse
He will play cards a while, then sail to the oceans
And there are islands, you know, that are not living
Just like that, an island in them
You know us—he winks—to the women.

Pointed are his feet as the sky reflects on the roofs
This quarrel, a quarrel from its hundredth exponent
And there are people, you know, that are not living
Is it you Mike, or is it you Jim
Let's not care about it—he sighs—tonight to the women.

The Rooster and the Stairs

Translated by Talat Sait Halman and Brian Swann

Upstairs is upstairs and downstairs is downstairs a bit
The rooster and stairs are right in the middle
Dazzling rooster! He gathers colors on the stairs
A kid is more a kid for the red of a whistle

A ten-fathom thread calls out my mother
I stick my head right into the bucket
As much fish as I think fish

Eyes

Translated by Talat Sait Halman

It seems nothing can provoke
Our inner silence
No sound no word nothing
The eyes bring out the eyes!

Nothing else but this unites us
A leaf touching another leaf
So close and so docile
The hands bring out the hands!

In our age love is an opposition
Let us unite to cast two single shadows...

from *Tragedies*

Translated by Murat Nemet-Nejat

CHORUS

Since they are crumbling, turn on the radio,
The streets, dogs, god's all assets

EPISODE

Loosens out of our hands, spills out everything
We stop, like blood, frozen in a hymn
With sounds and broken nails
Freezes our madness, captains are at no ship,
None, since seas are enormous, dead ones large
A chilly moon is heard, cold
In solitude. Loneliness is the season,
Where "flowers themselves bunch up."
And times are at each other's throats, each thicker
Than the other
Running
Tea times crack, memories relic,
Seep up dead bodies over white tables
And billiard tables, pale, disappear
And sunglasses are worn again
The pen squeaks stop, telephones are silent, the last stamps
Are glued,
Some things are missing, gentle, copper rust.

CHORUS

We who are remnants of a fall, we are men, women,
Stuffed deer, frightened, flow out.

EPISODE

And our half warmed fright remains; the sky is creatured
Of neglect,
Sips its drink, stretches back
In its own glass,
A corpse, both deathless and dead; for it
A mere novelty, irresolute in its freedom, alone
An embalmed tale,
This corpse.

And there is another not dead,
Because if something like this is needed among us,
It wakens our exile.

From one to another what can move in these times?

CHORUS

When the fright moves for a loss: something
Darkening its waters slowly into a stone among us,
A lexicon of silence.

EPISODE

It is that thing, a bit of hate and
Petrified hair, both petrified in those flower shaped
Of rocks—dark-painted,
Hate
Painless, endless, all of love in one.
That day of sudden diappearance without good, without suitcases,
Shadowy, but in that completely labyrinthine stop
With chilly hormones
One beauty topping one more beautiful than a third, but all understanding
Flying,
Daily newspapers bulging with street screams,
All fished out of the same heart, tired,
Disnatured, lazy, after long
Comings and goings, and cracked nails,
An image we built suddenly, a myth
That binds us whole in its laws.

CHORUS

We are dead. Dead ones gather themselves here.
Age thickens, tenses up, systems get prepared.
The bloody hours fall, the markets remain.

EPISODE

Blood. Generated of pain, blood of the obstinate what,
And cold
At those hours when our throats change tunes,
Those hours when things remain, things inside us
Remain the same, and insects, worriless,
Change spots; at those hours to become a little
Something

Some blood!
And numberless gestures meet with their muds,
In succession, carings and defeats
And everything, suddenly everything,
Years, cold wishes, hell without fires
In those days of death in those undecorated rituals
Blood rises in piazzas,
Victorious.

CHORUS

This blood,
The most elementary lesson of birth and decay.

EPISODE

Whereas appearing, one day, palmless and without suitcases,
Shadowy, but in that completely labyrinthine stop,
All days, uneventful, tickets going to numberless spots:
Counters, cold
Waters and sunglasses,
Slipping in tremor,
Slipping, unknowingly, and without finally caring,
Rid of dimensions, thinning, helpless like a deer,
A stuffed deer, stumbling and shy, in drinks
In drinks,
Building, among leaves opening newly,
Building its love of nest and indifference.

CHORUS

We are unmade, and our lot is unmade. We just wear
Now, the unmourning clothing of you.

HEAD OF CHORUS

We all have remained gods. No one should pretend
Gladness.

Arif Coşkun

Hollow

Translated by Talat Sait Halman

hollow beyond the snow-capped hills
aching starving
roads on the march with village and town
with mountains and meadows
at each other's throats for a terrible death
over bridges all roads lead to hunger

its cells are dead
so give it water or food
our huge crime
wakes between death and sleep
resounding as it thumps and flogs

the bone must march beyond the flesh
hunger beyond the bone
bone beyond rock and soil
our huge crime
resounds as it thumps and flogs
arriving in terror on crusty hills

the bone must pierce the flesh
hunger must crack the bone
and the bone ram through rock and soil
our huge crime
resounds as it thumps and flogs

Necati Cumalı

At the Inquest

Translated by Talat Sait Halman

At Urla's Özbek Village, Orphan Ali shot his neighbor Slim Ömer for trespassing half an acre into his land. Let us now hear what the Özbek villagers and the wives of Ali and Ömer had to say about the incident and what testimonies they gave at the gendarme station.

I

**Ballad of a Villager who Saw Ömer at Dawn
on the Day of the Shooting**

At those daybreak hours
I saw Ömer on his auburn horse
Galloping from over there
He had his hunter's jacket on
And leather boots on his feet

Dewdrops twinkled on the grass
Flanked by poplars green and white
A bird dashed ahead of him
And the brook beckoned from behind
While Özbek lay in dense shadows

Fresh blues bloomed into the sky
At those daybreak hours
Ömer rode his auburn horse
Greeting the bird and the newborn day
At full gallop from over there

II

The Elegy of the Old Woman of Özbek

This morning at Özbek
We ran out at gunfire
This morning at Özbek
Windows opened to gunfire
And a tearful daylight
Flooded our desolate homes
And the downcast skies
Dangled before our very eyes

Go take a good look
Where gunfire can't be heard
Are white-plastered roofs
And white-flowing waters
And white poplars over there
As black and grim as ours?

Go take a good look
Where hearts harbor love
See the sun there

See the sky
See the soil
Joyful and happy

Then come take a look at us
See the stampede of the skies
Our children shudder when we pat them
Fear reigns in our hearts
Our brides are pale as withering saplings

III

The First Elegy of Killer Ali's Wife

For three days, three long days
Since Ömer's plough cut into our land
Tuesday Wednesday and Thursday
For three days, three long days
My Ali grew dark and grim with fury
Not a trace of a smile on his face

Tuesday Wednesday and Thursday
Morning noon and night
I set a useless table for him
His head sagging
My Ali didn't even touch the bread

Three nights three long nights went by
His eyes fixed on the ceiling beams
He smoked one cigarette after another,
Deep in thought and with deeper sighs
These three nights of my life
My Ali didn't embrace me or caress me

Three days and three nights went by
Tuesday Wednesday and Thursday
His heart was scorched
When his eyes caught a glimpse
Of our son or daughter or me
He was lost in deep thought
My Ali my brave Ali

IV

The Second Elegy of Ali's Wife

Ominous evil darkness
Hovered over our house
My heart in anguish
Tortured by fear and worry
I clutched his hands:
"Don't, Ali dear, don't!"

Ominous evil silence
Roamed about our house
Then I saw Ali get up
His revolver on his hip
I stood before him:
"Don't go, Ali dear, dont!"

I looked him straight in the eye
I'd never seen him like that
He'd never hurt a bird or ant
My arms dropped my strength ebbed
Then I felt the chill through the door
And I heard the three shots

V

The Elegy of the Dead Man's Wife

A brook flows past our house
Flanked by white poplars
All planted by my Ömer
It was Ömer who broke ground
For the footpath down to the brook
In our front yard my Ömer raised
Geranium and mint and dandelion

Year in year out
If our hearth was on and we had gas
My Ömer was cheerful and happy
So the poplars rejoiced too
But if my Ömer was downhearted
When the crop was poor and our flour scarce
Then the poplars turned dark too

Year in year out
When I got home his breath fondled my face
At night we went out into the front yard
Geranium and mint and dandelion smelled so nice

I can no longer look at the path to our brook
Nor at the white poplars
Out of the windows or through the doorway
I can no longer look at the sun or at the moon
Whenever I come home now my heart aches
The smell of geranium and mint and dandelion
Out in the front yard
Is like a curse on me

VI

The Elegy of the Old Men of Özbek Village

At Özbek's Akkum site
Flanked by mountains
Sea to the left, brook to the south
A stony cragged chalky field
Runs between the mountain and the sea
A stunted wild pear tree in the middle
Cuts the field into two or does it
Ali tills the northern part
Ömer tills the south from the tree to the brook

Hey there, poor Ali, for shame
Hey there, poor Ömer, for shame

One day we saw Ömer's plough
Half an acre past the tree
For as long as we can recall
South was Ömer's up to the tree
And the northern part was Ali's

Hey there, poor Ali, for shame
Hey there, poor Ömer, for shame

At Özbek's Akkum site
Between the mountain and the tree
A stony cragged chalky field
A couple of skimpy olive trees
A couple of stunted wild pear trees
Scorched under the sun
Green under the rain
Couch grass jsckal weed and thistle

Hey there, poor Ömer, for shame
Hey there, poor Ali, for shame

We saw the sun on the pear tree and the olive
While a cool breeze blew from the mountain
The sea stirred with mad blue foam
We saw the couch grass turn green
While others wilted
We saw
Ant hills standing still
And locusts
And solomon's seals stood still
We looked
No more does Ali show up
Nor is there any sight of Ömer

Hey there, poor Ömer, for shame
Hey there, poor Ali, for shame

A Mother

Translated by Nermin Menemencioğlu

The woman must have been out washing
A bundle on her arm, her rough hands chapped with soda
Like all Jewish women of her age
She wore a faded black velvet coat
In her looks an expression of complaint, of tiredness

The freckled boy with straight red hair
Unsold newspapers under his arm
Like all small children who are cold
Sniffled, blowing on his hands
Shuffled along in his old shoes
Keeping step with his mother

They went ahead, I behind
One night in March, after eleven
So we walked from Taksim to Tünel
They talked in soft voices to each other
As though a windmill were turning, turning
As though life, very slowly, were flowing
Like turbid, dirty waters
Between the great dark buildings

A Small Place in the Provinces

Translated by Talat Sait Halman

A strange fear hovers
Over the faces I recall
Whenever I think of them
At the marketplace or at the café
Those faces darken like a well

The men there always look haggard
They toil but earn little they seldom talk
Their hearts bulge with anger
At the slightest doubt they smack their wives
And lying in ambush they shoot a man

The people I used to know there
Gazed at the sky with fear
Gazed at the sea with fear
And trembled at the sight of the landlord
Scared of God scared of death
Scared of the gendarmerie
Scared of all government officials

Asaf Halet Çelebi

Ancient Egypt

Translated by Tunç Yalman

did I perhaps like a horse spring from earth
perchance was I lost in the stars
and am I forgetting time
when time's forgotten it's ancient egypt time
when I myself forget you I live
to live
          is to live this moment
ammon ra hotep
          or *tafnit*
I do not want to know who you are

only to breathe around you I must
dut bu a'ru unnek pahper
  kama pet kama ta
sentences read in egyptian sources
the ones we read together were different it seems
I feel you and I are in a garden
but I am there and not there
in truth I become the entire garden
and cease being what I am
  kama pet
    kama ta

The Guest

Translated by A Turan Oflazoğlu

looking at you
            to forget all faces
tired
of myself
            and of too many
                        entangled stories
I come to be your guest
amid the voice of the seas
and midday suns
            perplexed

I come to be your guest
a little nearer to sleep
  a little more absent
      a little farther from other things

Mara

Translated by Nazmi Akıman

better to be unaware than aware
let's live without thinking
            mara
what's the use of days and hours
even the years do not count

I remember neither the days with you
                              nor the years
I remember you only
                    a human being like me
better not to know than to know
once I knew you
I got to know the pain of life
let's taste this pain together
                              mara

don't mind my talking in sleep
                while my head is on your shoulder
take me wherever you like
we're both neither asleep
                              nor awake

Mehmet Çınarlı

They

Translated by Talat Sait Halman

Patiently, we stood still, but they forced us to prate.
The deeper was our love the more they taught us hate.

In one fell swoop, they became the prophets of the land,
And heaped sins upon us as we bowed to our fate.

With a thousand deceits they killed respect and faith,
Coerced us to doubt, to bear malice, to negate.

While hell's crucibles were raging in the open,
They told us stories about peace and Heaven's gate.

Without us they lacked the strength to stand on their feet,
Usurping our power, they crushed us with their weight.

Fazıl Hüsnü Dağlarca

Beacon

Translated by Talat Sait Halman

Jutting far into the high seas, the promontory,
Cherished as the lazulite and silver night, smolders.
A terrestrial love starts in the dark
While the beacon shines
Despite destiny on the boulders.

Clouds fuse in crepuscule dimensions,
From distant harbors fogs descend,
And sadness stirs in the darkness of fate;
Blazing and blinking, the beacon inquires:
Where in life do you stand, where in love do you stand?

If the heart cringes in the starlight,
Memories might recede and recoil.
Time may tread on without the soul's cargo
As the beacon has stood for ages
With patience on this same soil.

It witnessed sea battles and ancient pirates,
Caught the wind asleep and the waves in flight,
As blue and black as a single eye,
And vacant as the vast seas;
Ill-fated fishermen struggled in its sight.

In your hair a cool air smells of salt and death,
On your face a cyclone's flavors linger.
You stand weary and forlorn,
Suddenly flickering, quivering with joy:
Something, perhaps life, is now longer.

Dolorous as the widows' indomitable desire,
Upon its prowess the gargantuan night lies.
Insane, taciturn, and awake,
It craves from disaster the charity of end-all;
It is wise.

Our drunken vessels roll and sway,
The sleep of buried hurricanes is stirred,
Rocks stretch far like pelagic graves,
From the sea to heaven
The sailor's curse is heard.

Time vanishes and life abandons time;
From the galaxies descend no bulletins.
Heavy and tired with an ill omen,
When all men are thought to have ceased,
The beacon grins.

Gleam in Time

Translated by Talat Sait Halman

I am in the dark, beyond all light;
End of World War II, ominous and heroic,
Far away slave nations chant a song,
I am aware of being a Turk.

A breath descends from the worlds across,
And shadows pour from time.
Upon the earth and over the atmosphere
I am aware of my chilly night.

Forms cuddle the houses and furniture,
What never was now comes into being
And shapes border on eternity,
I am aware of my mind.

Neither the trees grow with my seasons
Nor are the stars as real as my own light.
Atoms astir by love fly in my heart every which way:
I am aware of life.

Warning

Translated by Feyyaz Kayacan

I want my heart to shine
Before it is driven into blankness,
I want the water to open the green
I want the green to open the light,
Earth, let me walk in your warning.

What is, after all, Time's archeologies?
Walking life after life after life
I walked generations adding up
To less than the feeble height of an oat.

Jobless

Translated by Talat Sait Halman

He called fate
His foundering in the street.
For three years he had no job no fear no respect,
In dreams a multitude of mouths craved bread.
So hungry were his hands and feet
He ate his fist.

The wind was good, it fondled him at least
As it fondles bird and beast.
Its cool air which sets no one apart
Brought no food, but a little solace.
So hungry was he as he grew in the quiet
He ate his lips.

Now darkness shivered with blood.
—When passersby could not see
Nor the stars
Nor even God—
So hungry was he for life
He ate his breath.

The Marketplace

Translated by Feyyaz Kayacan

This marketplace frightens me
There are people in it
Some ugly, some fair.
I pulse the sum of their breaths
As if I had risen from their beds.

They shape stones into man,
Man into earth;
They pretend not to know,
Self is pretense's monolith.

Cabs, trams, street vendors pass by
I fall asleep a little,
People scatter toward the squares
My sorrow stays put.

Hungry Plain

Translated by Richard McKane

Here the steppe tree sleeps,
here in going it's taken away taken away.
Under the black earth?
It's not clear, even the grasses don't sway.
On the blue lakes?
It's not clear, even the sparrows have flown there.
Here the steppe tree sleeps,
here in going away it's taken away taken away.

Long ago the ox ran out of breath,
one heart opens and closes in dreams about the bitter pasture.
The cart's empty with couch grass, gigantically empty,
from the strength of thousand-year-old oxen to our day,
carrying carrying unfinished, carried carried unreduced,
but remaining more difficult for the oxen of today.
Long ago the ox has run out of breath,
one heart opens and closes in dreams about the bitter pasture.

Ah, all the birds have fallen in the darkness,
ah, if anything senses the mountain senses the night.
Neither did they communicate one to the other in the East and the West,
nor did they understand the tongue of the winds and floods.
Nor did they hear the distant day's call had happened,
they grew so small, became so little, became lost in the blue,
ah, all the birds have fallen in the darkness,
ah, if anything senses the mountain senses the night.

To Be You

Translated by Murat Nemet-Nejat

Do you know,
The birches
Your beauty is with water and grass,
How the earth loves the long.

Do you know,
The night,
Darkness lacks eyes,
Find you with the dexterity of its breath.

Do you know,
Death,
Regardless of all obstinate numbers,
Your essence continues.

Do you know,
The lonely one,
Exiled from God,
A hairy coat is on your back.

Do you know,
Heat,
At Mount Ararat I was ice,
You were guest to me.

Do you know,
Knowledge, water at my toes,
I have counted you,
One to five.

Do you know,
Woman,
I was the child knowing of your breasts,
Not knowing.

Do you know,
Child,
Your mother is not the one kissing you first,
Your child of last year was.

Do you know,
The star,
I see you first,
Before shepherds, before the ship prows.

Reflection

Translated by Murat Nemet-Nejat

Knowing me
Is knowing the dead,
Their faces blank,
The darkest.

On the road of broad daylight,
The wise one arrives,
And possesses
Three beyonds in his two hands.

As long as, as far as the universe strips
Naked,
Its arms, its chest
All hair,
Our emptiness grows even cooler.

The water is beauty,
Despite itself, slow in its moving;
When life is flowing,
Bares broken rocks.

As though night
Could touch us,
Our hands could grip planets,
While heats disappear in heat.

Knowing me
Is knowing the dead,
Their faces long
Of loving.

A Corpse Turns Cold

Translated by Talat Sait Halman

In the distance, the hearses came to a halt.
In a far-off temple, the candle went dead.
At midnight all the crops turned pale,
And faith left the body as in a deathbed.

Kites were soaring dawn after dawn:
The wind snatched a kite from a kid.
Climates at their loveliest, all blue:
The tallies, like a flask, were emptied.

And songs in villages, from light and toil,
Stars swimming like fish in the northern skies,
The seas whose waves give life its form
But beyond which no ocean lies.

Far away, the pounding of a brave heart,
In infidel factories, trains full of spring.
Twinkles return to its distance
As dreams that the ultimate images bring.

Crucifixes are affirmations of eternity;
Horizons are their own lack.
It stretches into the sky as a line,
Turn the lamp off, smoke is raging black.

A mad crowd beckons and rejoices,
Thrusting in my way their hands like bony threats.
"Someone else has arrived, someone else"
O sky teeming with minarets.

Those I left behind are with me now,
The mercy, silence, and fear of hearts.
The world's wooden stairway.
In the huge barracks the guard duty starts.

Caught between the two crowds, all alone,
Homeless circles in the sky's arch.
Leaving life and death behind,
Over the fallen martyrs they march.

Memories and nights are torn asunder,
Golden streams seek to have their fate revealed.
On the children swarming like ants
Doors, huge as mountains, are sealed.

All over my face, by someone's bony fingers,
Soft soil is hurled,
Then my eyes are covered by someone else
Who is jealous of his blessed world.

To Wake Up opposite Forty Thousand Villages

Translated by Richard McKane

Is there no one who has woken in your village,
one crying crying crying?
Like this hundred of years emptily flowing,
with stones with rocks we were left barefoot,
just as sheep did not change,
just as poplars did not change in their waiting,
just as ploughs did not change,
so we did not change, barefoot.
> One more one more night grows,
> with one more one more voice I call.

Is there no one who has woken in your village,
just one like a lake, like a mountain, like a forest?
Like this it sparkled with blue power when the sky fell upon it,
be like a lake.
Be like a mountain,
like this it stood up to it when the wind struck it.
From the earth's darkness it kept turning green,
be like a forest.
> One more one more night grows
> with one more one more voice I call.

Is there no one who has woken in your village,
who has woken, asking questions?
What is this? Why this utter nakedness?
Don't I work? Let's work.
What's this, who took and carried off all this tax,
who didn't bring that breath of civilization from there?
What's this? Each to each, only each to his stomach, only
each to his heart, pitch-dark,
is it a snake, is it a polecat, is it a hyena?
    One more one more night grows,
with one more one more voice I call.

Is there no one who has woken in your village,
who has woken lighting the dark?
In his hand the new light of day before day,
he who rubbed out all that's old, all that's backward, all sleep,
in the plains without boundary without end of the new war,
lake on foot, mountain on foot, forest on foot,
he who has stood up anew on new beliefs,
he has taken his bread from the wolf's, the bird's from the
      ruler's, from the ağa's from God's mouth.
    One more one more night grows,
with one more one more voice I call.

How Can I

Translated by Talat Sait Halman

How can I die
When a mad bird
On a mad branch
Twitters

Beyond

Translated by Talat Sait Halman

Whenever I love a woman
I feel deep in my heart
That before me
God loved her

Our First Bondage

Translated by Talat Sait Halman

The mind has no freedom
Its thoughts
Are nurtured
By old ideas

Different Warmth

Translated by Talat Sait Halman

Homes
By multiplying forever
Arrive
At our loneliness

Hope

Translated by Talat Sait Halman

Here
I believe
There
The bird flies

Echo

Translated by Talat Sait Halman

When a poet
Dies
God
Feels it first

Fellow Citizen

Translated by Talat Sait Halman

Before day breaks, any morning,
Before the mountains swing open the world,
If any of you wake up,
I too wake up.

Wind in the fields, hub in the markets,
Living always throbs anew;
If any of you get hungry
I too get hungry.

No man, if human, can be ugly in love,
And no warmth could ever shiver.
If any of you love,
I too love.

Audience

Translated by Talat Sait Halman

I am Halim the Third, majestic and sacred,
King of Kings.
When my white hands move,
My subjects come upon their mornings.

The moments I conquer carry my lust
To unknown virgins time and again;
I discovered time in the golden pleasure
Of my enduring reign.

Along my wisdom they stretch,
All the world's dimensions;
Comfort flows from my body
Into my palaces and stately mansions.

In legion with the mighty eagles,
I set science, poetry, and victory free
So that generations to come
May rejoice on land and sea.

Dark-ridden and blue, heavens lie
At the beck and call of my head;
Poised as two infinities,
My love equals my blood.

Noble and hale, glorious and supreme,
Farther than the mind's eye can see through,
I am Halim the Third.
Mountains and rocks, who are you?

Poems of the Mediterranean

Translated by Talat Sait Halman

The globe was calm
With only the Mediterranean on it.
On the Mediterranean
Just the two of us.

I said: "Do you love me?"
She closed her eyes to the horizons.
"Just the moment to ask," she smiled,
"Just the place to ask."

*   *   *

A mass of green, a mass of gray
Over the winds,
They collide, and both crash into the horizon.

A rim of the stars on the crest of the waves—
Each foam is a tempest,
Each tempest, a world.

The sea and the sky may be concealed.
My love for you
Cannot be hidden.

*   *   *

It's like air and flame and tree
But most of all like water,
This love of ours.

Purple has anguish but no end.
It blends into our life
By itself.

They say man turns to dust at death.
No, not us...
Clearly, we shall turn to water.

Foetus

Translated by Osman Türkay

Birds come and go,
Heralding the spaciousness of the sky.
They apprehend
The rapacity of the legs of blue water
In your birth.

One is alive, one dead
in birth.
Before swinging, before even oscillating just for a while
There issues in slow motion
The still warm love of universes.

Snakes, elephants, tigers, gazelles, wolves, and rhinoceroses
Create shelter, greatness, and food
in birth,
Before our bodies comprehend—for wine leaves are naked with gray
Before our teeth set on edge.

In your birth,
There is the colic of pregnant stars,
From the night
Which the barefooted dead
Dug with their nails

One is you,
The other I,
God is one, but
You are divided Earth and Heaven
in birth.

Question

Translated by Feyyaz Kayacan

Who will take me to his garden
Cool with willows and coy water?
When my body, painless, shines from the dark,
I shall ask: whose is the garden?

A thick sleep will be cast in my eyes,
I'll gather good marks for good behavior;
Floating aslant within a strange sea,
I shall ask: who sleeps this sleep?

They'll take away my face, my arms, my neck;
In a place where life runs deep,
On the last rung of my straining ghost,
I shall ask: who dies this death?

Awakening

Translated by Nazmi Akıman

What have we shared from thousands of lights
For thousands of nights
My eyelashes are wet hear me
Come on turn

Beyond evil thoughts
Our being has long lost all memories
This is it whether we like it or not
Come on turn

There is more to mountains and woods and stars
More to death
I shall not awaken you again
Come on turn

Bird Temple

Translated by Talat Sait Halman

Birds
Are the new arrival
Of the oldest Gods
And their new departure

Shadow

Translated by Talat Sait Halman

The person we love
Is the shadow
Of our face
In the future

Unawakened

Translated by Talat Sait Halman

Our eyes
Awake only once
In that last light
Just before we die

Banks of the Red River

Translated by Talat Sait Halman

Brother, what you say isn't so.
This is not the land where people dance and cheer.
Come out to Anatolia,
Come by trucks or by ox carts, but come.
You aren't far from here.

Their pine trees are gone, their poplars scarce.
Hillsides are not naked, but covered with grief.
After seven months of winter,
Your life turns green,
But not the leaf.

For three hundred years you fed on this land's food;
Might is not right though your power holds sway.
A world squandered by neglect,
All its seasons chilly, its waters dwindling,
Its wheat not the wheat of the Seljuk heyday.

Trail the ox whose skin is in shreds.
His toes are torn, his nails black with mud.
Your hands and feet flinch with shame.
Take a close look, you would shudder.
His hands are not hands, his feet a thud.

The sun rises, the larks take wing,
A heavy light, not your familiar daybreak.
She has sunk so deep in her sleep of centuries,
Unless you wake her up,
She will not wake.

Darkened and muddled by black corpses,
Grief and misery are her lot.
Whatever cascades are,
Or an easy flow,
The Red River is not.

Brother, I can't see, but I can still feel.
Neither the bygone ages nor the days to come glitter.
Rising like the affirmation of faith over time,
In the gleam of the night, upon all victories,
Not the flag, but the mountains flutter.

Arif Damar

Don't Go, Stay

Translated by Edouard Roditi

Remember the lot of sorrows
Remember the lot of poverty
These tears we shed, remember them
Don't go, stay, is the wish of a child
Who refuses to believe what can be, what can't,
So don't go, remember

Over barren fields
The sun shines when the rain stops
The fig tree grows green above the bare rocks
In the wilderness of mountains
A quiet flower
Spreads its blue in solitude

Don't go, remember how joyful we were
In unity and friendship
Remember everything, everything
Remember the midnights
Remember your own words
Stealthy rains were pouring
It was cold
Remember the fire we made

Remember the things you are forsaking
Don't go, remember joy
Everywhere on our planet
When those tired hands gather the roses
Remember the joy of the hands
Remember the joy of the roses

Remember how we loved you

Zeki Ömer Defne

Forbidden Fruit

Translated by Nazmi Akıman

would anyone see me each evening
in the very eyes of my children
who think looking at my empty hands
I'm off each morning to summer gardens
                            of yellow and red

they wouldn't know I dwell
in a garden of giants each day
in I go and I flee and quinces laugh
and pomegranates cry at me each evening
                            as the roads go by

I too am a tantalus I reach
the branches for my children not for myself
and they go higher and higher
knowing not who eats the fruits each evening
                            up there

with the seeds of change at heart
wish I could dash out each morning
and come back home a busted tree
with one or two branches bearing fruit
                            each evening.

Hasan İzzettin Dinamo

The Will

Translated by Talat Sait Halman

I don't hold it against Nature
That she made me a poet
With the diadem of the rainbow on my head
Or that a lion with ferocious paws
Sits in my heart's iron country
With its eyes fixed on the evening sun.

If my poems have
                    no rustling of silk
                    no purring of cats
                    or anything like that
It is because I have left all this
To those teeming poets
Gulliver ran into on the island of Lilliput.

I want to build my own dreams
Sitting bedraggled
Among the marble pillars of moonlight
While in Europe's huge prisons
The beloved people whose photographs we kiss
And whose books bring tears to our eyes
Are made to clean the latrines of dope addicts.

I tell you, my fellow poets,
If all I have left to me is my poetry,
I should be happy to fling all that at your feet.
I don't care if they say I am not a poet
Just because I talk about these rags I wear
And the onion soup I eat.

No matter what,
I shall give my poems
To the generations that will sing
                    the songs of freedom.
I shall always uphold
                    the vision of happiness in my Turkey.

Let her planes and boats, her trains and buses
Transport my people who have the spring in their hearts.
Let everyone in the neighborhood
Come close to eternity.

I spit on the conscience of those
Who are Laval and Quisling in disguise.
Even if I am the last person to do it,
I shall forge my poems with my fists.
I shall sing the songs of struggle.
My feet naked, my head defiant,
I shall carry freedom in my arms all the way.

For the last time I shall look at the blue sky
Now possessed by flowers
                    by light
                    by birds
Where lovely sounds saunter like carefree rains.

And when I fall dead at the battlefront
They will find my gun,
And in my pockets
The songs which proclaim that the world
                    is destined to be happy.

Ahmet Muhip Dranas

Have and Have Not

Translated by Talat Sait Halman

Two trees by an odd creek that flows alone
            Stand young strong full-grown;
They have something to say, they do, and yet,
        Dead or alive, they always keep quiet.

After sunset, under the stars, see the way
            The trees sway,
Whatever they have to hold back or declare,
        Dead or alive, it is all laid bare.

By the creek two desolate trees stand
Pegged onto the ground;
They have something to say, they do, and yet,
Dead or alive, they have said it or not.

Oblivion

Translated by Talat Sait Halman

Twilight hours are always gruff and gory;
When the day departs beyond its glory,
Loneliness attacks and souls surrender
As colors stir and shriek in the garden;
Then a hand unloads our heavy burden
Of dark despair that smells of lavender.
Twilight hours are always gruff and gory.

Remorse assaults like waves that beat the shore
To force and fell oblivion's brass door;
An arrow-riddled soul, without hope, dies.
You're home where you first saw the light of day
Whose lamps and stairs now watch and ward your stay
As cradles creak with muffled lullabies:
Loved ones are lost or dead and hearts are sore.

So lovely is mute love in his true heart
That the poet cuts his flaming lines short;
With shutters now swung open on the breeze,
The smell of rain along the rising sun,
The cloud at rest, the bird in flight or gone,
The rock you pick to eat your bread and cheese
All come alive, for love invades your heart.

At summer's end young lovers drift away
Like girls in clusters in a dance of joy;
Dragged along with the fugitive moonlight
From lonely gardens of dead foliage,
The merry skirts of some mad bygone age
Condemn the weary men to dreary night,
Then again they flutter, woo, and play coy.

Deceived by false promises, the flower
Waits in vain for her eternal lover
Where spring will never dote upon the steppes.
Now delusion sings life's loveliest song.
Give in! Forget that winter has come along
Or that snow covers the lonely footsteps—
Flowers dropped by lovers gone forever.

Through twigs that sway or stir or twitter
You appear and vanish like a glitter.
What is it you want of me at twilight?
A woman dark and grim, without a smile,
Looms deathless in love's mirror all the while.
Fierce memories pray on my mind tonight
As you stalk the trees that cringe and flutter.

Come oblivion, come shut your window.
The ocean drags me into its depths now
Drowning my world in its dark destiny.
Where old loves and wild adventures languish
Hearts are sore again aflame with anguish.
Oblivion, unfurl your might on me,
Redeem me from all this pain and sorrow.

Fahriye Abla *

Translated by Osman Türkay

The air filled with a pungent charcoal smell
And the doors closed before sunset;
From that neighborhood as languid as a laudanum
You are the only surviving trace in my memory, you
Who smiled at the vast light of her own dreams.
With your eyes, your teeth, and your white neck
What a sweet neighbor you were, Fahriye abla!

Your house was as small as a neat box;
Its balcony thickly intertwined and the shades
Of ivies at the tiny hours of the sunset
Washed over in a nearby hidden brook.
A green flowerpot stood in your window all year round
And in spring acacias blossomed in your garden
What a charming neighbor you were, Fahriye abla!

*Literally, "elder sister"; often used as a term of affection or respect for a somewhat older girl or woman.

Earlier you had long hair, then short and styled;
Light-complexioned, you were as tall as an ear of corn,
Your wrists laden with ample golden bracelets
Tickled the heart of all men
And occasionally your short skirt swayed in the wind.
You sang mostly obscene love songs
What a sexy neighbor you were, Fahriye abla!

Rumors had it that you were in love with that lad
And finally you were married to a man from Erzincan
I don't know whether you still live with your first husband
Or whether you are in Erzincan of snowy mountaintops.
Let my heart recollect the long-forgotten days
Things that live in memory do not change by time
What a nice neighbor you were, Fahriye abla!

Refik Durbaş

Its Grief

Translated by Talat Sait Halman

with this furious face in the old days
I used to transport wooden birds
to my mouth's country which grew feathers
each night the dead with the dead
I carried this diminishing face of mine

those birds used to be my knife
because I went hunting with them
if I had to water my dead ones with blood
if dusk whirled around my neck
I swear to god that's how I hunted

in truth it is the way a wooden bird
takes wing on our forehead
before death lays siege with knives
on our grief-stricken sky
death is the way love takes wing

Metin Eloğlu

The Address of Turkey

Translated by Murat Nemet-Nejat

I

The energy in a dying wind,
The water's resistance to vapor
The night descends
As the grass gropes for morning.

There is still a year for the night,
                    what is the thief's ladder doing here?
What is more, you hesitate on the way out
—His mourning eyes are heavy!—
This place is crawling with poison
                    ivy, come, squat a little...

Toward the fall a bird sings in Istanbul's summers;
What bird, why summer, where is Istanbul? You fool!
This place is first Turkey, then Pompeii's last hours.

II

A glittering sea,
A haggard sky,
How will babies furnish homes
Beyond their cradles...

Out of the havocs of if's and because's,
Out of perhaps's, maybe's, not yet's...
And so his eyes roll as first casualties, and, yet,
                    You are his child!
Then he loses one leg, then they hold both his arms;
His teeth are all gone, or, if not all...
He still yokes his plough to his liver, drags it
                    Across the land;
And sows some wild oats, half of them his own guts;
They spread, fall on frothy dung. We discover
Balding hair, finally, at the crossroads of the city. No heart,
No veins, no eyelashes.

Yes, turn to him;
You are his child.

III

This mixture is of meat
And fish bones, and the garfish can grow no thinner;
The water is quiet, but scum is yellow, and the grace,
Slender, is self-made
Of this flower rudely thumbed.
His poodle is white—pure, like steaming milk,
And its fluffy hair softly combed...

As watch chains, patent leathers glitter,
Discarded by the lord,
The dog's fawning shadow plays on the breeches,
Walking behind it he airs his dog, but why are
The doves scared off?
This young man has a boy in the cradle back at the village
—I think his third—is eaten by cats, even the press
mentioned it,
And here the man walks his dog.

IV

The leech wrenched from the raw earth and
Let loose on blood
First nurses its own worm;
A feathery vine feeds
On a bare trunk;
Dung feeds the rose.

In his cycle of freedom
He stands, fixed, not a hair stirring;
We keep on screwing what fat, small fingers loose;
A stealthy greed chisels the white, delicate shirts
An arrogant enmity and hesitant love.

An intimate bird flies a straight, wide path
In the eternal agitations of the sky,
Fluttering, naked.
After the traveler has traveled so many roads,
There is no room to stretch the body;
Yet the poet-saint found a tomb in every mountain.

V

A lichen-crusted nomad rock
Is chipped to sand
By rich downpours of nature;
Yet owns a grit of essence;
Bakes in the yellow frost of July,
And, then, the next petrification is slow.

Turning the corner, you will ask for a red watermelon
              by showing the seed on the map.
They will laugh at you from the rotting assholes of melons
              with castrated stems,
"How many eggs do you want for the load on your
              shoulder?" they will ask,
And will grab the old-new dotted shirt from your
              shoulder, and go away,
Fitting a badge of guffaws on your lapel.
              —Add the trefoil yourself-

This is a harlot child;
Not sweet melons,
Nor red watermelons,
Nor superduper Electras.

VI

The fish that slowly grow human in the water
Possess the lidless sleep of first shudders;
The curing progress of the hourglass narrows,
Flies grow fat and die in the fall.

"Only if this wick burns will the bottom of the pool
              light up," they said,
But neither the sparkle, nor the wick, nor the bottom;
They likened the lights of a deathly banquet to the
              stained glass of a Sultan's villa;
Cross the threshold, now, sweet basil leaves
              grazing your face,
Move round the burning smells of the pot, stray cats
              at your feet,
And don't hurt yourself for blowing too hard
              on the wet sticks for fire...

And, then, turning round, press hard on the closed gate
        to withhold the vast terror of a sea,
Take shelter, in pretense, in the innocence of streets;
Ask for the drunken villa, peddlers of safety pins
        will tell you;
At Yemen they would put out one's tongue for it, God knows—
False soldiers trim a handful of grass...

To find Turkey is easy, Turkey is the palm of your hand;
But you should tell its true place to no one;
Believe me, they will laugh at you.

Sidewalk Superintendent

Translated by Talat Sait Halman

Days chase one another, and then the months;
At dusk, at noon, at sunset,
Years of love
And years of learning;
The bright years that we wear like a crown
—Don't let Mom find out about my grim years—
In pursuit of tall dreams and fleeting hopes,
In love with every girl around.
For love I was stabbed in the groin
And gambled away my coat and pants.
I frittered away my youth overnight.
"Was that for love, too, sucker?"
Can I find a parallel for this phase of my life?
Let me see, for example, let's see now:
The reign of İbrahim the Mad in Ottoman history?

At the beginning of my sidewalk career
I used to go steady with a girl from the shantytown
Who prayed no less than five times a day,
Patched up my suit, fluffed up my mattress.

What came of it?
Well, you know what.

In those lonesome bachelor days
I used to drive a jalopy
All over the lovely city of Istanbul
Where I saw so many heartrending sights:
Honest people on a par with swindlers,
And man nothing but a beast.

Some autumn evening, ambling toward home
A little tipsy with a couple of drinks
I ran into my folks at the corner
My sister was looking for customers
And grandma was begging.
Honest, I wouldn't lie at my age.

Tears flooded my eyes,
I rushed to the post office.
Dear brother İlyas, I wrote,
Rush me thirty bucks:
I'm in dire straits and got no one else to run to.
Believe it or not, good old İlyas,
Son of a gun, never even bothered to write back.

The rest is almost too painful to tell.
Take a look and watch me in pursuit
Of work and bread, of friendship and freedom.
Take another look, I'm in and out of courts.
"Your Honor," I say at the closing session,
"My far-out ideas were simply meant to kill time.
"You interpret them much too seriously, Your Honor.
"I certainly want no part of jail, Sir.
"From now on, wherever I go, whatever I do,
"I shall heed the voice of reason."

Müştak Erenus

Migrant Mustafa

Translated by Talat Sait Halman

See the huge mountain
With a black bird perched on it.
That lovely flower crestfallen from its dirty green
Will bury its head in the wind
And just stand there waiting for the rain.
Having swaddled her baby in rags
The nomad woman thin as a rose sapling
Will stand and sing a burning elegy
To her husband who is on the path of blind hope.

He will not hear that sad song
He'll walk on, his hope growing like an avalanche,
and arrive at the city bent double.
The place they call the city is a son of a bitch too.
Its streets and alleys are drenched in dust,
From its chimneys smoke comes out crooked.
Its people only seem to be living.
Migrant Mustafa is at first wonderstruck with the hubbub
Then ties a knot on fear and feels strong.
He is well-trained for hunger.
In the city's gutters he marches toward bread
And on one of those very long days
In a public square of no return where he's sick at heart
They bring hope on four wheels into the market for workers
And pick up Mustafa and the likes of him
at a pittance for daily wages.
And thus Mustafa's story too founders into the tumult.

Abdullah Rıza Ergüven

The Lonely Ones

Translated by Talat Sait Halman

My eyes twitch, Julie,
Like a black mulberry tree, I am steeped in blood
And I listen to the songs
Of the elms, labdanums, and hoopoes.
Didn't my wild pigeons visit you
To tell you of my wan solitude,
Didn't they tell you
My eyes twitch, Julie...

Poplars frighten me when they sway,
Take your hands off me, Nymph,
I must make you a bed
A tender bed
Out of celeries and asphodels
And write fiery songs in your name out of wild flowers;
Yes, songs, but
My eyes twitch, Julie...

Didn't you see the dewdrops dripping
In midafternoon down the white poplar,
Dewdrops I had sent you?
Empty out yourself, my cup, down to the last dregs,
Our 29-letter alphabet has just been adopted
From soft straws and fragrant pines,
Early roosters ushered in the dawn too soon;
My eyes twitch, Julie...

They say the cranes chase the plough
And I chase you, Julie.
I got new shoes on my feet,
Summer flowers in my hat;
Don't bother me, Nymph,
On those nights when I carve your name on logs and trunks
I must sing the songs of yearning, but
My eyes twitch, Julie...

Like a black mulberry tree I am steeped in blood
And I listen to the songs
Of the elms, labdanums, and hoopoes...
Didn't my wild pigeons visit you
To tell you of my wan solitude,
Didn't they tell you
My eyes twitch, Julie...

Nüzhet Erman

from *"The Turkish Alphabet"*

Translated by Talat Sait Halman

A: ANATOLIA

"The peasant," Atatürk declared, "is our master."
He's master in name; we're the chosen few, we hold sway.

"Should the call to prayer be chanted in Arabic or in Turkish?"
We pray for rain while others go to the moon, all the way.

"Per capita national income, so on and so forth"
But it's with pounded wheat soup that we start each day.

"In villages, filthy waters flow and cesspools are wide open."
We seek no solutions, we just try to hide it all away.

"We lag centuries behind the Common Market countries."
We still forge ahead on an ox cart, that is to say.

This is what I know, this is what I must tell:
All we know about Anatolia is just the initial A.

The Big Tale

Translated by Talat Sait Halman

Two Sultans—Murat I and II—
Fell at Kosovo and, as martyrs, became glorified.
Carbuncles shoved Selim the Grim to the other side.
It was a blood clot to which Süleyman the Magnificent succumbed.
As for Beyazıt the Thunderbolt and Sultan Aziz, suicide.

Afflictions like cirrhosis and TB
Had Selim the Sallow, Murat IV, and Mahmut II mortified.
Mehmet the Conqueror, Young Osman, and Selim the Poet
Were victims of regicide.

Ahmet III, Mehmet III, and Osman III,
Mustafa II, Mahmut I, and Abdülhamit I
Suffered apoplexy, that's how they went by the wayside.
As for Abdülhamit II and Sultan Reşat,
They had weak hearts.

And so on with all those majestic rulers—
The glorious Ottoman Empire,
On whose realm the sun never set for 624 years,
Kept the whole world petrified:

It was a legend, it died.

Bedri Rahmi Eyuboğlu

The Saga of Istanbul

Translated by Talat Sait Halman

Say *Istanbul* and a seagull comes to mind
Half-silver and half-foam, half-fish and half-bird.
Say Istanbul and a fable comes to mind,
The old wives' tale that we have all heard.

Say *Istanbul* and a mighty steamship comes to mind
Whose songs are sung in the mud-baked huts of Anatolia;
Milk flows out of her taps, roses bloom on her masts;
My childhood in Anatolia's mud-baked huts
Sail to Istanbul and back on that mighty steamship.

Say *Istanbul* and mottled grapes come to mind
With three candles burning bright on the basket—
Suddenly along comes a girl so ruthlessly female,
With a figure so lovely that I'd give up my life for it,
Her lips ripe with grape honey,
A girl luscious and lustful from top to toe—
Southern wind and willow branch and the dance of joy—
Hailing from a wine cellar, she makes you tipsy;
As the song goes, "Like a ship at sea
My heart is tossed and wrecked again."

Say *Istanbul* and the Grand Bazaar comes to mind:
Beethoven's Ninth hand in hand with the Algerian March;
And an immaculate bridal bedroom set
Is auctioned off without the bride and the groom.
A chubby lute inlaid with mother-of-pearl
Recalls the famous lutanist on old records.
Brandishing candlesticks and hookahs and rusty Persian swords.
American cowboys prop up:
"Hands up!"

American sailors wear lily-white uniforms
Plucked from a huge daisy, clear as milk, clean as a cloud;
Death looks ugly on so pure a white,
But when they fight

They put their combat uniforms on
—Color of blood and gunpowder and smoke—
Which gather hate but no dirt.

Say *Istanbul* and a huge fishery comes to mind
Like a rusty cobweb over the Bosporus,
Or sprawling off the Marmara coast.
Forty tunnies toss in the fishery like forty millstones.
The tunny, after all, is the king of the sea:
You must shoot it in the eye with a rifle and fell it like a tree,
Then suddenly the face of the fishery gets bloodshot
And the emerald waters become muddled in the turmoil.
With forty tunnies at a clip, the skipper is spellbound for joy.
A seagull perched on the mast catches a mackerel in midair and gobbles it,
Then it flies away without waiting for one more;
The fisherman smiles, sweet and kind:
"That gull's Maria," he says,
"That's the way she comes and goes, always."

Say *Istanbul* and the Prince Islands come to mind
Where the French language is murdered
By sixtyish matrons who sit around puffed up as hell;
If only the lonely pine trees there could tell
All about the hanky panky of the boy with the gal.

Say *Istanbul* and towers come to mind:
If I do a painting of one, the other one grumbles.
The Tower of Leander ought to know that's the way the cookie crumbles:
She should marry the Galata Tower and have lots of kids.

Say *Istanbul* and a waterfront street comes to mind:
Anatolia's poor godforsaken huddled masses land
In its coffeehouses day after day,
Some must go begging to survive, but shame keeps them away;
A few manage to find a broom and become street cleaners - no less,
Their faces smeared with a filthy fusty grin;
Others shoulder a pannier or an ornate backsaddle,
And they all get lost in the city's hubbub and fiddlefaddle.
Tied to a greasy girth, some carry a piano on their backs
Their legs wobbly under the weight, melting like wax,
They pant and heave, drenched in sweat.
A gentle porter is a must for a fragile item.
Do the tender hands value a piano the way the porter does?
Suddenly a mushy voice blares on the radio across the street:
The most popular crooner of them all,
Yelping and yawning, smudged with the greasy perfumes of Arabia:
"Life is full of joy and sorrow,
"Some stay and some go."

Say *Istanbul* and a stadium comes to mind
Where twenty-five thousand voices under the sun
Sing our national anthem in unison
And the clouds are fired like cannonballs.
Dazzled by the sight of twenty-five thousand strong
I rejoice in their joyful song
And offer to pluck my heart for them like a red poppy.

Say *Istanbul* and a stadium comes to mind
Where my blood flows into the veins of my fellow men.
Rubbing shoulders, we holler together
Till our throats are sore:
Lefter's kick is a sure score.

Say *Istanbul* and a stadium comes to mind
Where multitudes share the grandeur of the joy
Born at the same moment:
Myriads and millions
Band together in my head.
Then a line out of a poem fearfully fluttters in the air:
"Blessed are those who embrace their loved ones."

Say *Istanbul* and Yahya Kemal* used to come to mind;
Nowadays it's Orhan Veli† whose name is on the tip of my tongue;
His flair and flamboyance, his poems and his face
Hover overhead like a wounded pigeon
Which descends quietly to perch on this poem.
Where?
Just look, you'll find it there.

This city just drives you out of your mind;
Good thing Orhan Veli's drinking glasses remain behind.

Say *Istanbul* and Sait Faik‡ comes to mind:
Pebbles twitter on the shore of Burgaz Island,
While a blue-eyed boy grows up in circles of joy
A blue-eyed old fisherman grows younger and tinier,
When they reach the same height they turn into Sait
And they roam the city hand in hand,
Cursing beast and bird, friend and foe alike!

---

*Yahya Kemal (Beyatlı) was a famous neo-classical poet (1884-1958) who wrote many poems in praise of Istanbul (see Inroduction).

†Orhan Veli (Kanık), who died in 1950 at the age of thirty-six was famous for numerous poems about Istanbul (see the Kanık section of the Anthology).

‡Sait Faik (Abasıyanık), who lived from 1906 to 1954, was one of the leading short story writers of recent decades (see the Abasıyanık section of the Anthology).

On Sharp Island they gather gulls' eggs,
By midnight they're in the red-light district,
In the morning they go through Galata:
At the café they kid around with a harmless lunatic,
"Whaddya know," they say. "You're holding the paper upside down."
Then they set the poor guy's newspaper on fire,
Then they sit and weep quietly.

Say *Istanbul* and Sait Faik comes to mind
All over this town's rock and soil and water,
A friend of the poor and the sick,
Whose pencil is as sharp as his heart is wounded,
Bleeding for the lonely and yearning for the pure and the good.

Say *Istanbul* and Sait's last years come to mind:
At his best age he's told he has just a few years to live;
How could Sait bear the thought of it?
The blue-eyed boy doesn't give a damn,
But the old fisherman broods like hell;
And a green venom bursts out of the sea
Piercing the heart that feels, ravaging the mind that knows.

The little blue-eyed boy
And the old fisherman
And that green venom smeared all over our lips...
So long as Istanbul throbs alive in the sea,
So long as language lives, so will Sait's poetry.

Say *Istanbul* and a gypsy woman comes to mind
With a bunch of flowers taller than herself,
Wherever the spring comes from, so does she.
No crackpot that woman, but every inch a gypsy,
She is the sun and the soil from top to toe,
And a mother matchless among mothers:
One kid on her back, one at her breast, one in her tummy.
A gypsy woman always bulges with a baby.
Devil may care, her life has flair:
She roams the city from one end to the other
Humbly selling tongs or doing the bellydance.
"How about a quarter, dear?" she says,
"You want me to tell your fortune, love?"
Till the day she dies, she tells nothing but lies.
Then comes the dream she had the night before:
"I see a yellow snake. Son-of-a-bitch keeps bugging me.
"I wake up and what do I see?
"My little ones are on the edge of the bed sucking my toes."

Say *Istanbul* and a textile factory comes to mind:
High walls, long counters, tall stoves...
Tender slender girls toil all day long on their feet,
In blood and sweat, weary and sad,
Their faces long their hands long their days long
In the factory where the windows are near the ceiling.
Red-heeled fair-skinned girls– "No loitering, girls!"

Rows and rows of trees stretch out there,
But the endless walls cut the girls off from them,
From the amber fields and the purple streets
Where the fair season rumbles and tumbles.
A nineteen-year-old working mother,
Is dazzled by the white foamy flow of silk
Which whets her appetite no end, she gets ideas;
But printed silk is no good to make pants for her sons.
Now if she could get a roll of ivory-white calico:
She can do so much with it: drapes and sheets and underwear;
The very thought of ivory-white calico dazzles her.
When she dies giving birth to a third son,
She still longs for a roll of calico.
Young mothers like her are dime a dozen:
At the factory somebody else takes the place of this one.
That's the way it is: If one goes, another comes.
Damn you death.

Say *Istanbul* and a barge comes to mind
Brimful of onion, green as poison on coral red,
Sailing in from the Black Sea ports winter and summer
With one more patch on its filthy sail each time
And the rust of its iron rods on our tongues
And its motors speeding along our pulsebeats right into our hearts.
A mermaid with huge scale-covered buttocks.

Say *Istanbul* and a barge comes to mind
Demure and heedless
Called the Sea Tiger or the Triumphant Sword.

Say *Istanbul* and Sinan the Great Architect comes to mind
His ten fingers soaring like ten mighty planetrees.
Then the monster of the shacks and shanties rears its head
Where smoke and filth and blight ruthlessly spread.
Our city suckles dwarfs at her giant's breasts.

İlhan Geçer

End of September

Translated by Talat Sait Halman

A pale September recedes
With weary steps
Away from routed memories

Sparrows, their wings skittish,
Break loose from shrinking joys
As the face of waves darkens

The warmth melts in our blood
Giant-mouthed clouds vie to snatch
The green encounters
In the gardens birds hold no flowers in their beaks
Snows of Mt. Torment lie on caved-in shoulders

Each gossamer wing founders
Lost long ago unable to fly to blush-pink horizons
On the tips of our eyelashes a speckled bird
Twitters a dark tune
It refuses to smile at our suns
Fate that buffoon

The scissors of night cut up despair
Autumn's cups are filled with mawkish dregs
The tired doughboys of joy have piled their rifles
Our hands cling to the tattered ropes

Enver Gökçe

On My Eyes and Head

Translated by Talat Sait Halman

In
This
World

There's
Death
There's
Cruelty
There's
Oppression
On
My
Eyes
And
Head
Brother
Where's
It
Written
That
I
Must
Work
So
Others
May
Seize
It
All?

Sıtkı Salih Gör

Beyond the Time of the Birds

Translated by Talat Sait Halman

Like solitudes in their supreme quintessence
The deep anguish of a sense of eternity is born
On the rising hatred the thirsty feel for the night
Tumultuously chiming death out of the dusk
Behind the rays of light the serpents in a scurry
Arouse and warn the sea with their teeming eyes

Flowing waters carry us back to our lands
In its density the child's wing of our scattered song
The sky takes hold of the burden of the lonely
And ties it to its sunken shoulders before losing its balance
Sated we arrive somewhere with those flowing waters
The harmony of love drives the sun to its royal tent

The palms of the wind's hands stretch into the roads
Bathing in the shadow of a sphere that has diminished
Whoever dedicates himself to the heart that has no cure
With their weary violins a multitude of sorrows those dwarfs
Make music in the evening of whoever has been abandoned

The tiny birds asleep in love's outer space die

Nedret Gürcan

Execution

Translated by Talat Sait Halman

Love hastens you through the longest road.
If his chest is inflamed,
A man might drink muddy water.
For the last time, a moldy wind crosses the face.

The hill breaks open, the moon flees. A giant dawn,
The hands of a clock, the creak of a door,
A pale warden—they all
Prepare Recep for death's bridal chamber.

Wakefulness is numb.
Roosters weave the hour of damnation
The echo of the funeral prayer
From the minarets.

Awaiting the night's vanishing breath,
Last words writhe, hands tied,
A carbine hangs on the wall.
Sadness, the splinter in the mouth—
Recep glares as never before.

A cloud breaks away,
Descends from the bluest of skies:
With the first sun
Grass floods the barren soil—
Delicate tinder blossoms
On Recep's forehead.

Blood flits from hand to hand—
Growing huge,
It turns into Recep.

Feyzi Halıcı

In the Mirrors

Translated by Talat Sait Halman

Your sunset eyes with a hue and cry
Resist a fire in the mirrors.

You vanish in a song far away,
You grow with the first rays in the mirrors.

Why this flutter in a pigeon's wings—
Your hands secretly scuttling in the mirrors?

Over and over you put a knot on the ages
Time and again you are suspicion in the mirrors.

What road is this that gnarls your steps,
What summer is this sip by sip in the mirrors?

Ceaseless rains pour down your hair
You live so many longings in the mirrors.

I banish loneliness from our no-man's-land,
Is that you so calm and clear in the mirrors?

Nazım Hikmet

from *The Epic of Sheikh Bedreddin*

Translated by Ali Yunus

THE IMPERIAL LAND

It was hot
very hot.
The heat was a knife with a bloody handle
      and a dull blade.

It was hot.
The clouds were loaded,
ready to burst
  to burst right away.

Without moving, he looked down
  from the rocks
   his eyes, like two eagles, descended on the plain.
There
the softest and the hardest
the stingiest and the most generous
the most loving
the greatest and loveliest woman
    the EARTH
      was about to give birth
      to give birth right away.

It was hot.
From the Karaburun mountains he looked down
  with a frown
   toward the horizon at the end of the land.
A five-crested fire came gushing from the horizon
plucking children's heads
like poppies in the fields,
dragging stark-naked shrieks in its wake.
The gushing fire
  was Murat the Royal Heir.
An imperial command had been issued to him
  to storm the province of Aydın
   and crush Mustafa, the disciple of Bedreddin.

It was hot.
Mustafa the disciple of Bedreddin looked
Mustafa the peasant looked
He looked without fear
            without anger
            without a smile
Standing erect
            he looked
            he looked straight ahead.
The softest and the hardest
the stingiest and the most generous
the most loving
the greatest and loveliest woman
            the EARTH
                 was about to give birth
                 to give birth right away.

He looked
and Bedreddin's braves looked at the horizon from the rocks
The end of this land drew closer and closer
on the wings of a bird of death bearing the imperial command.

And yet these men looking down from the rocks
had opened up this land
with its grapes and figs and pomegranates
and its cattle whose hair is fairer
            and whose milk is thicker than honey
and its horses with tight rumps and lion's manes
with no barriers or boundaries
they had opened up this land like a brother's meal.

It was hot
He looked
and Bedreddin's braves looked at the horizon
The softest and the hardest
the stingiest and the most generous
the most loving
the greatest and loveliest woman
            the EARTH
                 was about to give birth
                 the give birth right away.

It was hot
the clouds were loaded
the first raindrop was about to fall on the ground
like a sweet word.

Suddenly
       as if flowing from the rocks
       pouring from the skies
       growing out of the ground
like the latest bounty of the soil
Bedreddin's braves jumped on the royal heir's army
They were clad in seamless white shirts
            bareheaded
            barefooted, their swords naked.

In mortal combat they fought fiercely
Turkish peasants from Aydın
               Greek sailors from Chios
                        Jewish merchants
the ten thousand comrades of Mustafa
plunged like ten thousand axes
            into the enemy forest.
The ranks with red and green banners,
ornate shields and bronze helmets
were torn into pieces
but when the rain-drenched day passed into night
the ten thousand were but two thousand.

For the sake of singing in unison
           and pulling the nets together from the sea
           forging the iron together like a lace
for the sake of ploughing the soil
           and eating the honey-filled figs together
for the sake of saying
           all together
              everywhere
              in everything
           but on the cheek of the beloved
the ten thousand braves gave their eight thousand.
They were defeated

The victors
           wiped their bloody swords
              on the seamless white shirts of the vanquished.
The earth they had tilled together
           with their brotherly hands
like a song sung together
           was trodden under the hooves
           of horses bred in the Palace of Edirne.

THE IMPERIAL VERDICT

It is drizzling,
frightened,
in a low voice
like a talk of treason.

It is drizzling,
like a renegade's pale naked feet
running on the damp dark ground.

It is drizzling:
in the market of Serez
in front of a coppersmith's shop
my Bedreddin is hanging on a tree.

It is drizzling
Late on a starless night.
It's getting drenched in the rain
the stark-naked flesh of my sheikh
                swinging from a leafless branch.

It is drizzling.
The market of Serez is mute,
the market of Serez is blind.
The air is filled with the cursed sorrow of the mute and the
                                      blind.
The market of Serez has covered its face with its hands.

It is drizzling.

Letter from Prison

Translated by Ali Yunus

To My Wife

My only one
in your last letter
                  you say:
"My head is aching
      my heart is bewildered."
You say:
        "If they hang you
            if I lose you
                I cannot live."

You will live, my darling wife,
My memory will fade like black smoke in the wind.
You will live, my heart's red-haired woman.
In the twentieth century
      mourning the dead
           lasts but one year.

Death...
A corpse swinging at the end of a rope,
I cannot resign my heart
        to such a death

But you can be sure, my beloved,
that if the hairy hand
          of a poor gypsy
              like a black spider
                  puts the noose around my neck,
They will look in vain
        into the blue eyes of Nazım
           to see fear.

In the dim light of my last dawn
I will see my friends and you
and I will only
      take to my grave
the sorrow of an unfinished song.

My wife, my very own,
My tender-hearted bee
with eyes sweeter than honey.
Why did I ever write you
      they asked for a death sentence?
The trial is only just starting
and they don't pluck a man's head
          like a turnip.

Don't give it another thought.
All this is a distant prospect.
If you have some money
      buy me flannel underpants:
I got sciatica pains in my legs again.
And don't forget
the wife of a prisoner
      must always have cheerful thoughts.

Poems of Twenty-one and Twenty-two O'Clock

Translated by Murat Nemet-Nejat

How lovely to remember you: among the tidings
Of death and victory,
In my cell,
And my life beyond its fortieth year...

How lovely to remember you:
Your hand lying forgotten on a blue sheen of cloth,
And in your hair the posed softness
Of the dear earth of Istanbul...
Like a second person
                    Throbs within me
The joy of loving you...

The smell staying at the tips of fingers
Is from geraniums,
A sunful ease,
The invitation of the flesh: a darkness,
                              deep
Warm, divided by red, bright rays of light...

How lovely to remember you,
Write about you,
Lying on my back in jail,
Think of you:
The words you uttered at one place,
One day,
        not the words,
                but the universe in their tones...

How lovely to remember you.
I must carve something again out of wood
For you: a drawer,
A ring.
I must weave three or four yards of silk cloth,
Then, again, hurtling from my place,
Clutching the bars of my window,
I must shout to the milk-white
Azure of freedom the lines
I wrote for you...

How lovely to remember you: among the tidings
Of death and victory,
In my cell,
And my life beyond its fortieth year...

Provocateur

Translated by Bernard Lewis

This man
         sold his comrade
sold on a tray of gold
              the bloody, severed head
                  of his comrade.

Fear stalks this man
         like his shadow
This man lives
         like a dark stream
every evening at sunset
it is he who draws near you
         creeping on tiptoe
              dragging his wife's culotte along the pavements.

Know him
         by the tinkling leper's bell swinging from his heart
and know
         that slowly his leprosy rots the flesh of his soul...
Today this man is hungry
He is hungry, but in him
         even great and mighty hunger
              has lost its holiness.

Friends, this man
one evening at sunset
              sold his comrade
sold on a tray of gold
              the bloody, severed head
                  of his comrade.

Today Is Sunday

Translated by Talat Sait Halman

Today is Sunday.
For the first time they took me out into the sun today
And for the first time in my life I was aghast
that the sky is so far away
        and so blue
        and so vast
                I stood there without a motion.
Then I sat on the ground in respectful devotion
leaning against the white wall.
Who cares about the waves with which I yearn to roll
Or about strife or freedom or my wife right now.
The soil, the sun and me...
I feel joyful and how.

Poems from Prison

Translated by Talat Sait Halman

October 5, 1945

We both know, my darling,
they taught us
        how to brave hunger and cold,
        weariness unto death,
        living apart from each other.
So far we have not been forced to kill
nor faced the prospect of getting killed.

We both know, my darling,
we can teach
        how to fight for our people's sake
        how to love a little better each day
           a little more
                from the depth of the soul.

November 8, 1945

Over the roofs of my distant city,
from the depths of the Sea of Marmara,
above the earth of autumn,
                    mature and moist,
                            your voice came through.
This was a three-minute call.
The phone was cut off, darkness, that's all.

November 13, 1945

It defies description—they say—the misery of Istanbul,
famine—they say—has mowed down the people,
tuberculosis—they say—is rampant.
Tiny girls are taken—they say—
    in buildings ravaged by fire, in loges of movie houses.
. . . . .
. . . .

Dark tidings from my city far away:
the city of honest, hardworking, poor people—
                          my real Istanbul,
the city where you live, my darling,
wherever I am exiled, wherever I am in jail,
    I carry it on my back or in my sack,
    bearing it in my heart like the grief of a dead child
    the city I take along like your image in my eyes.

On Victory

Translated by Talat Sait Halman

Your frightful hands will clutch your wound,
        biting your lips till they bleed
        you shall endure the pain.
Now hope is a shriek
        naked and pitiless
And victory
    will be snatched away tooth and nail
        so it will forgive nothing.

The days weigh down,
days bearing tidings of death.
The enemy is grim
        cruel
            sly.
Our men are dying in combat
—yet they were so worthy of life—
our men are dying
            —so many of them—
as if they were up in arms
        with songs and banners on a holiday
            so young
                and daring.

The days weigh down,
days bearing tidings of death.
With bare hands
        we set the loveliest worlds on fire,
our eyes can no longer weep:
we are left a little sad and stiff
        our tears have abandoned us,
that is why
        we no longer know how to forgive.

We can only reach our goal
        amid bloodletting
and victory
        will be snatched away tooth and nail
        so it will forgive nothing.

Since I Was Thrown into This Hole

Translated by Taner Baybars

Since I was thrown into this hole
the Earth has gone round the sun ten times.
If you ask the Earth, it will say,
    "Don't deserve mention
    such a microscopic amount of time."
If you ask me, I'll say,
    "Ten years off my life."

The day I was imprisoned
        I had a small pencil
which I used up within a week.
If you ask the pencil, it will say,
        "My whole lifetime."
If you ask me, I'll say,
        "So what? Only a week."

Osman, serving a sentence for murder
            when I first came into this hole,
            left after seven years and a half;
            enjoyed life outside for a time
            then came back for smuggling
            and left at the end of six months.
            Someone heard yesterday, he's married;
            he'll have a child come spring.

The children conceived
            the day I was thrown into this hole
are now celebrating their tenth year.
The foals born on that very day
            trembling on their thin, long legs
must by now have become
            lazy mares shaking their wide rumps.
But the young olive shoots are still young,
        still growing.

They tell me new squares have been built
            in my own town since I came here.
And my family of that little house
        are now living
            in a street I do not know
                in another house I cannot see.

The bread was white as virgin cotton
the year I was thrown into this hole
and then it was rationed.
Here, in the cells,
            people killed one another
                    for a handful of black crumbs.
Now things are a little better
but the bread we have, has no taste.

The year I was thrown into this hole
          the Second World War had not started;
in the concentration camps of Dachau
the gas ovens had not been built;
the atom bomb had not exploded in Hiroshima.
Oh, the time has just flowed
          like the blood of a massacred baby.
Now that's all over
          but the American dollar
              is already talking
                  of a Third World War...

All the same, the day is brighter now
          than it was
              When I was thrown into this hole.
Since that day
          my people have raised themselves
              halfway up on their elbows;
the Earth has gone round the sun
                              ten times...
But I repeat with the same fervent yearning
          what I wrote for my people
              ten years ago today:
"You are as plenty
          as the ants in the Earth
              as the fish in the sea
                  as the birds in the sky;
you may be coward or brave
          illiterate or literate.
And since *you* are the makers
          or the destroyers
              of all deeds,
only *your* adventures
          will be recorded in songs."
And the rest,
          such as my ten years' suffering,
              is simply idle talk.

Sad Freedom

Translated by Talat Sait Halman

You squander the gleam of your eyes
and the sparkling toil of your hands
to knead dough for countless loaves of bread
          which they won't even let you taste.

All this great freedom is yours to slave for others,
to turn into Croesus those who suck your blood:
                    You are free.

The minute you are born, they swarm around you
and build mills of lies which grind till the day you die.
All this great freedom is yours to bury your head in your hands
            and rack your brains about freedom of conscience:
                    You are free.

Your head is bent as if they cut it at the nape,
your arms weigh down at your sides.
All this great freedom is yours to drift here and there,
            out of work, jobless,
                    You are free.

You love your country with all your heart,
but some day they might sell it, maybe to America,
All this great freedom is yours so you may be sold
            or become an air base:
                    You are free.

Wall Street grabs you by the neck with its cursed hands:
You might be shipped out to Korea some day.
All this great freedom is yours to fill a grave
            or to take the name of the unknown soldier:
                    You are free.

You say man must live not as a tool or number or cog,
but like a human being.
All this great freedom is yours for them to handcuff you,
            yours to be jostled, jailed, or even hanged:
                    You are free.

No iron curtain, no bamboo curtain, no lace curtain in your life
No need for you to choose freedom;
                    You are free.
This freedom is a sad thing under the stars.

That's How It Goes

Translated by Taner Baybars

Am in the middle of a spreading light,
my hands inspired, the world beautiful.
      Cannot stop looking at trees:
      they're so hopeful and so green.
A sunny pathway stretches beyond the mulberries,
I stand before the window in the prison hospital,
      cannot smell the smell of medicine:
      somewhere carnations must be in bloom.
That's how it goes, my friend.
The problem is not falling a captive,
it's how to avoid surrender.

The Armies of China Saved Me Too

Translated by Taner Baybars

I'm serving the twelfth year of my sentence;
for three months past I've been
            just like a corpse.
I was the corpse
      stretched on a narrow bed,
the living I was looking at him
      warned by his deadness;
and the living I could do nothing, nothing else.
That corpse had consumed himself for nothing,
he was alone like every other corpse...

An old woman came and stood in the doorway,
she was my mother, she and the living I together
lifted the corpse, mother and son together.
I held him by the feet, she held him by the head,
slowly and slowly we brought him down
and threw him into the river Yangtse

And from the North bright armies will come down.

The Darkness of Daybreak

Translated by Nermin Menemencioğlu

In the darkness of the daybreak the telegraph poles
                                    the road
In the darkness of daybreak the shining mirror above the chest
                                    the table
                                        the slippers
The objects in the room recognize each other
In our room the darkness of daybreak turns bright
        as an unfurling sail
The blue coolness is like a diamond ring
The stars turn pale in our room
Very far
        the stones in the riverbed of the sky turn pale
My rose's head lies on the pillow
A swansdown pillow as wide as wide can be
Her hands are two white tulips on the quilt
The birds begin to twitter in her hair.

In the darkness of daybreak the city's wet trees
                            its warm smokestacks
In the darkness of daybreak the first steps traced on the asphalt
                    go through out room
    the first rumble of a motor
        the first peal of laughter
            the first curse
The steaming glass case of the traveling pastry vendor
The booted driver going into the milkman's shop
The cries of the neighbor's child
The dove on the blue poster
The manikin in the showcase
        with yellow shoes on her feet
and the Chinese fans made of sandalwood
and the full red mouth of my only one
and the most hopeful and the freshest of all awakenings
        go through our room in the darkness of daybreak.

I turn on the wireless
Metals with giant names mingle with giant numbers
The oil wells are racing the cornfields
The shepherd awarded his picture in the front pages

(I have seen his picture in the front pages
          his whiskers hanging thick and black)
Sounds like a bashful girl
Then comes the news from the Polar regions

Then, at six o'clock of this morning
          as the third Sputnik
                    goes round the earth for the 8879th time
my rose opens her huge eyes on the pillow
as yet like misty mountain lakes
blue fish curve sparkling in them
green firs rest in their depths
the end of her dreams breaks shining against
          the darkness of daybreak
I am filled with a new recognition
I am ruthlessly happy
          a little ashamed
                    but only a little
In our room the darkness of daybreak
          is like a bright sail unfurled for a journey
My rose arises naked as an apricot
White like the dove in the blue poster is the bed
          in the darkness of daybreak.

Translated by Nermin Menemencioğlu

My woman came with me as far as Brest,
she got off the train and stood on the platform,
smaller, smaller, smaller she grew
a grain of wheat in the immense blue
then all I could see were the rails.

Then she called out to me from Polish soil,
I did not ask, "Where are you, my rose?"
"Come to me!" she said. I did not go.
The train hurtled by as though it would never stop,
I was drowning in sadness.

Then the snow lay rotting in patches on the sandy earth,
then I knew of a sudden that my woman could see me.
"Have you forgotten me, forgotten me?" she asked,
Spring's naked, muddy feet trailed across the sky.

Then the stars came down to roost on the telegraph wires,
the darkness beat against the train like rain,
under the telegraph poles my woman stood,
my heart was beating as when she is in my arms,
the poles flashed past, she stood there motionless,
the train hurtled by as though it would never stop,
I was drowning in sadness.

Then I knew I had lived on this train for endless years—
though how or why I knew this surprises me still—
forever singing the same confident song
as I travel away from cities I love, women I love,
carrying my longing for them like a festering wound in my flesh,
closer and closer to some unknown destination.

My Funeral

Translated by Nermin Menemencioğlu

Will my funeral begin down in the courtyard?
How shall you take me there from the third floor?
The elevator will not take a coffin
The stairs are narrow

Perhaps the courtyard will be knee-deep with sunlight and
          pigeons
Perhaps the air will be full of snowflakes and children's cries
Or the asphalt wet with rain
The rubbish bins will be in their usual place

If my face is to be open, as is the local custom
A pigeon may drop something of it, for luck
Whether there is a band or no, the children will come
Children love a funeral.

Our kitchen window will stare at me as I go
Our balcony will see me off, waving the laundry
I have been happier than you can think in this courtyard
Dear neighbors, I wish you a long and merry life.

Plea

Translated by Ali Yunus

This country shaped like the head of a mare
Coming full gallop from far off Asia
To stretch into the Mediterranean
          This country is ours.

Bloody wrists, clenched teeth
         bare feet,
Land like a precious silk carpet
This hell, this paradise, is ours.

Let the doors be shut that belong to others,
Let them never open again
Do away with the enslaving of man by man
         This plea is ours.
To live! Like a tree alone and free
Like a forest in brotherhood
         This yearning is ours!

Ayhan Hünalp

Before Christ

Translated by Talat Sait Halman

At the curve of a road on the ropes of a ship
In a playground where three roads intersect
We find living remnants from ravaged times
They bore us we turn our backs and go away
I hurl autumns on the ground crushing them
All those drinks I finish when I see your picture
In a playground where three roads intersect

If you hold me by the hand I shall fall
I'm helpless as soon as I find what I seek
Couched in helter-skelter knotty memories

Am I the only one who doesn't know what he wants
Bugs race toward the sun we oppress and ruin life
One day I shall give up all this fretting
I shall fall if you hold me by the hand

As the scorpion fish leap to the sky
Can you hear how the flowers crackle
I say I'm here so long as they read my name
Although I have been absent for ages
At bus stops and landing stations on masts
Nicotine scorches us at information booths
As the scorpion fish leap to the sky

Then we both get lost
A smoke engulfs us on all five sides
On the roads red over green
And green yellow rays on red
We are baffled should we walk or come to a halt
Our hands stay helpless so we break them
Then we both get lost

My solitude had started before Christ
Turn off the switches pull down the shades
If I had fire alive in all hours of the night
I would have embraced the seas in adoration
Folded the oceans into four if they let me
Come back if you didn't wait for me this way
My solitude had started before Christ

Rifat Ilgaz

Neighbors

Translated by Talat Sait Halman

As if our own troubles weren't enough,
On top of it, we got the neighbors on our neck:
All hell breaks loose at the clerk's apartment
On account of his wife's stockings;
Our family gets all involved.
The director of requisitions suffers a stroke

At the tail end of an investigation,
Our family worries all over the place
And our measly little fun goes down the drain.

There's no such thing as a household without yak-yak
Especially in times like these.
Well, we too have
Our share of yakety-yak.
Little people have petty problems:
There are times we quarrel
Over meat or bread,
And suddenly we find out
We're what all the neighbors are talking about.

At any rate, the drapes we thumbtacked
Never quite managed to veil our privacy
And everyone got to know our secrets:
They saw that little did we need
Pots and pans;
On our washdays they found out
Everything down to my shirts and shorts;
There was endless talk
About my reading novels in bed on cold days.
As for our humble background,
Well, nobody even bothered about that.
What did they expect, anyway?
The tenants in the basement
Couldn't be seventh-generation aristocrats, after all.

Cahit Irgat

Songs for One Who Has Gone Away

Translated by Mina Urgan

I

A wind that smelt of melons blew that morning,
Blowing from the fruits in the fruit-piled barges;
Clouds fell over the city,
Evil songs were whispered from ear to ear.
But still, life tasted like the flesh of a melon that morning.

II

Lads throwing the dice of their own fates,
Their bones cracking under the cringing lights,
Cross-legged, kneeling, lying flat on their bellies,
Raped the pavements of the city.

They shared between them the heritage
Of the proud-eyed condemned
For whose last sleep the gallows is a cradle.

III

In your proud eyes,
We have seen good days, and we have seen bad days.
How shall we forget the alleys?
The whores of the city mothered us.
With them, on the naked terraces of sweaty streets
We have possessed the earth and the air and the sea.

IV

The laughter of children under the bridges,
The laughter of children over the asphalt,
Shot a defiant gun at the skies.
And a wind that smelled of melons blew that morning,
Everything was just where it ought to be,
Not a leaf had fallen from the branch.
And we prepared songs for the victory that comes with the morning,
With the melon wind we sent greetings
To the friendly palms of the hands that hold the guns.

V

They have swept away your shadow from the streets,
They have flung the evening after you like mud,
And the city is dizzy with longing.

Bursting with rage we wave good-bye to the ships that set sail,
With the sea-eyed children whose hands smell of the sea
We throw stones at the waves.

VI

You went with the melon wind,
With the melon wind come back.
We cannot live without you in this city.

Melodrama

Translated by Feyyaz Kayacan

One had a knife in his hand
The other a white rose,
Both were tired
Like street urchins.

One plunged his knife,
The other gave the smell of his flower
And into taverns they both disappeared.
The knife and the rose like siblings
Lay together on the pavement.

Türkân İldeniz

No Solution

Translated by Talat Sait Halman

Wherever rain falls on the desert
My hair gets drenched all alone
Like those nights of utter quiet
Modern vehicles halt
And the tumult ends
Foreign violets bloom there
Water.

Mutable
In its monotony
Constant down the ages
Night transforms itself into morning
And beyond
Takes on a season's spectrum.

It perpetuates its secret with such ease
From chaos to eternity
Evolving—that is to say,
Well—it's a bit obscure:
What sage could solve it for certain?

Yes which sage can solve it with precision
Sometimes a polyphonic melody
Sometimes a dot or a dash
"To be or not to be..."

Attilâ İlhan

Poems from *Suite in the Ottoman Mode*

Translated by Nermin Menemencioğlu

[The poems from *Suite in the Ottoman Mode* are part of a long sequence in which İlhan ranges over the period 1908-14, evoking the Young Turk Revolution, the Balkan wars, and World War I. He uses intricate rhythms derived partly from classical Ottoman poetry and partly from various modes of *alla turca* music.

Note: Kuzguncuk, Kuleli, and Beykoz are villages on the Bosporus. The military academy at Kuleli traditionally harbored many young conspirators against absolutism. Yıldız Palace, on the European side, was the home of Abdül Hamid and of his successor, Mehmed Reşad. *İkdam* was an Istanbul daily newspaper. Bekirağa was a military prison, much used during the Young Turk Revolution. Yakup Cemil was a notorious adventurer, tried by a military court and shot for planning to overthrow the government and assassinate Enver Pasha. Rumeli is a general name for the Ottoman Empire's European provinces. Üsküb (Skopje) and Salonica were part of the empire.]

istanbul gate of felicity

world war years with the beauty of a frightened woman

when the *good cheer* kept vigil at the kuzguncuk landing
turned like the pessimistic cadets of kuleli toward sultan reşad
and no one was there for the last autumnal ferry
no halvah vendors from beykoz or phonographs with odeon* horns
pouring out songs in an ancient mode only the captain's cymbals
alla turca made in yıldız and lifted from the bazaars

istanbul straits with the sulkiness of a wounded vulture

*Brand name for musical instruments.

when monocled german officers argued at kramer's beerhouse
von moltke versus bismarck in their fissured tongue
downing three bitter dark green doubles of pilsen beer
torpedonet heroes rich in numbers as the imperial band
return to the galician front under the cold russian rain
swept night and day by long-range battery fire
red crescent tents blossoming like wet flowers
enormous flowers of extremely bloodstained white
back to the galician front the operetta remedy

in *ikdam* false news of victory on the syrian front

at the ministry of war the commander in chief enver pasha
with colonel süleyman of military secret intelligence
knows nothing of how time passes until morning worship
in the unfiltered glass-shattering darkness of a cellar
before an execution the nervous motions of prayer
of cowardly shadows in bekirağa prison
the sticky sweat crawling on yakub cemil's temples
the torn *union and progress* membership card on the floor
the rattle of a mauser being loaded the order to shoot
the lilacs fade like lightning in the water jug there is no cure

those world war years with the beauty of a frightened woman

old rumeli

I   bridal reception song

stolen from balkan slumbers
an old honeysuckle melody
the unforgettable duet of ahs
of müjgân the chanteuse
and a gold-embroidered lieutenant
out of an üsküb spring

mustafa kemal's revolver
bitterly silent in salonica
young turk trains morning and night
colonel enver's finger on the trigger
monastir* taut as a tambourine
every mosque resounding with chants

*The Balkan town of Monastir.

the lute settles on a lyrical theme
the oleaster sighs bloom by bloom
the stars are errors in a sky gone mad
müjgân changes her tempo now
in yanya tower in the arsenal
a bulgar is caught a comitadji*

lightning flashes are tacked above the yıldız palace
the rumeli officers clamor for constitution
a little jug of raki melon and white cheese
niyazi's riding whip is inlaid with silver
a spark is nourished in the mountains of macedonia
to light a fire in istanbul gate of felicity

II last days of müjgân the chanteuse

it rains on the wisteria her sleep dissolves
into the loneliness of widowhood
a thread of ink oozes from her torpor
a faded pink
  against her face every quarter of an hour
  crushing her sharps and flats as fine as flour
  the heavy iron gates of the balkan war
  clang shut
she reaches every so many seconds to touch
the pale hands of her lieutenant in a caress
he was wounded
  not far from çatalca
in the feathered darkness of that morning of defeat
nightingales from the hills of çamlıca fall into her lap
in twos and threes they fall
  electric flowers grow on the tram lines now
  part bitter oleander of hell
   part hemlock
"...under the damsons I sit
beside our house at turnova
my deceased mother is combing my hair
an ivory comb in her hand
  hairpins between her lips
   a bitter smell of gunpowder in our nostrils
    the reserves are holding maneuvers
whatever piano I happen to touch answers
with tatyos efendi's three-beat rhythms
in the gardens the apricot branches are breaking

*Member of secret Balkan revolutionary societies.

it is evening in turnova
the rebels have all withdrawn to distant mountains
    in my heart a tired clock strikes the hour

death on the electric garden of the tram lines
when the moon-dark nights are full of dogs
regrets and tears that come too late
    the secret glimmer of hydrangeas in a flowerpot"

"...lieutenant ihsan's song
the one I sang that friday in the *selamlık* *
trembling like a palm tree
with sunshine in its very sap—
    beloved light of my eyes my master
    istanbul officer from kalamiş†
    chestnut-haired a trifle stern of look
embroidered upon my heart with finest gold—

lieutenant ihsan's song
in actual fact the song of my lost youth
in another sense the song of lost rumeli
    pomegranate sherbet clouding the glass
    pastries bursting in the oven
    the green light of rain across the mosque courtyards
    stone thresholds washed till they creak with cleanliness"

III   last days of lieutenant ihsan

graceful and inward-turned behind the lattices
fuchsias the red of wine
a black and white cat in her lap
müjgân is singing in the *selamlık*
her eyes gilt insects of imagination
her long yellow hair spilling across her shoulders

where immense water lilies come to life
in distant gardens soft with string music
reflected in the loneliness of pools
her clouded beauty alone slender mauve
heavy with premonitions of evil
the ashen tuesday when I left her
the whirligig of death keeps turning

*Men's parlor in ottoman mansions.
†Section of Istanbul.

so it has been since I left turnova
my shutters tightly closed my hearth extinguished
one ray of light filtering through my clouds
a tiny light delicate humble
my love for müjgân intense and deferent
lone immortality within the balkan rout

Ancient Sea Folk

Translated by Talat Sait Halman

pebbles chant an odd song there and the sea shepherds
drive their herds into the high seas
while on the mussels' iris harlot blues crouch
in the boundless western time's green galleons
unforgettable and emerald and sighted
blood-drenched slab by slab
you hear the ancient sea folk in harbor taverns
those kinky sea people if you listen
spanish songs and italian wine
and godlike you create curses
from fifteen meridian to twenty you create universal curses
atop the mainmast
you god of blasphemy and tumult and of my enigma
you god of lost treasures
you shall not look behind nor spit at the wind
unless black flags are hoisted on the admiral's mast
no honest breeze shall spark your corsair's eyes
unless you chew on the rain or on tobacco

I never forgot the mediterranean
I plunged into flames and wept voraciously
the joy of creating
and being created flared tremulously in the sky
and prayers burst open like titanic sails
then lo and behold three crescents arose at once
barbarossa songs released like hawks from their arms
cyclone-sized barefoot mariners of the algerian skipper
who arrested the caravans of ships
and held the straits of messina and septe and all others
there is no god but God
arrested and set all the vessels on fire
fire's joyous and memorable dominion

stirs in constellations and beacons isthmus by isthmus
then bound for rome in legion with hannibal
the phoenicians carried the alphabet and the glass long ago
dragons breathed fire and the avatars of the sea monsters
and the ghost of a genoese galley slave haunted a rhodes castle
his feet shackled
a dagger stuck in his back
while latin songs poured forth
from the vessels of antonius

you unexpected unforgettable unbearable and deep
and magnified
as roguish as a cabin boy or a sailor's mustache
the wind uncontained in its rose and in its own dimensions
the centuries-old buccaneer fate of yours
tattooed on your arms and infinitely on your chest
green and speckled
angel-face mermaids and unctuous dolphins
you sense from the world what the children sense
while time keeps aging you remain a child
you are the ancient sea cemetery of pirates and sailors
the graveyard of barbarossa songs
with your mighty waves you are the ocean
the starry multitudes of the plankton and the skate
you are god and bear gods in your kingdom
the master skippers who tyrannize the currents and eddies
cruise north-northeast and some cruise westward
there once was captain joy whom we buried in the iceberg sea
an andersen and a kidd
a salih a burak and a memi
together exploding our laughter as cannons in salvo
at a giants' carnival
winnowed and scattered we had died
then the fish garths near the shores and archipelagos
being so ancient and stately as to defy memory
forsaking all the stars to recognize the north star at one glance
italian fishermen with beards dripping with salt
then as in purgatory raveled and fibrous
to disembark sahara-parched at a port where foxes spit copper
and to come aboard truculent in a deluge of wine
blessed be thy name
whenever we cruise toward the south pole
from tierra del fuego
from the flameland

hannelise

Translated by Nazmi Akıman

you'll come out of the rain hannelise
the rain will come out of your eyes
one afternoon in paris hannelise
they'll play the song of grand boulevards in a café

paris and yellow leaves around me
a wind passes flapping its wing on the seine
now the clock in gare d'orléans will chime three
you'll come out of the rain hannelise

I'll look into your eyes and say almost blue
I'll say almost a child
they'll get brighter
an old man fishing on the quay
will throw his cigarette
into the water to drown
one afternoon in paris hannelise
they'll play the song of grand boulevards in a café

one cannot live in spite of himself
we cannot say black when the heart says white
we cannot hannelise
you speak of the dukedom of lichtenstein
lime trees in front of the cathedral shed their leaves
I dress a fanciful garden of fire inside of me
as white as snow
as white as hannelise

trees like children clap their hands
from far away bells of the saint augustine chapel
the clock in gare d'orléans will chime three now
you'll come out of the rain hannelise

The Dead Have Grown Old

Translated by Talat Sait Halman and Brian Swann

the torrent of stars is just like an obsequious salute
lilies are white and whites are just like lilies
over swamps mosquitoes breed by the million
insects and bugs are linked forever in embrace
the torrent of stars is just like an obsequious salute

all the old horsemen drive the wayworn horses up the hill
sweltering in galaxies horses will burst
on gray battlefields the wounded and martyred lie
willows and pines are linked forever in embrace
if a girl comes alive or a mortal dies or a star falls
all the old horsemen drive the wayworn horses up the hill

hyenas refuse to remember festivities
life's flight from the body and man's flight from humanity
a hundred killed a hundred orphaned a hundred lost
mothers raise sons for combat overseas
hyenas refuse to remember festivities
if a girl comes alive or a mortal dies or a star falls
whoever is dead is dead and the dead have grown old

Birds of Imagination

Translated by Nilüfer Mizanoğlu Reddy

the most frightening crimson ones hit the windows of my sleep
with pointed beaks shiny like the scales of fish

their loneliness is untamed their eyes are heavy maharajah eyes
their magnetic crests like a handful of sparks

their slender necks reach out to all kinds of daydreams you think
they're the red velvet holders of purple hubble-bubbles

when they open their wings the clouds change their colors
in their complicated feet they wear cloven slippers of lightning

the echo of their horrible green screech narrows the horizons
their shrieks pierce the bloody palms of the tyrants

they're the birds of imagination elusive turn into dust when touched
to exist in freedom only is their most unforgivable crime

Özdemir İnce

Poet

Translated by Larry V. Clark

I

it snowed all winter a heavy dream
it snowed all winter on our forlorn country
the forest breath merged with the wet earth
the northwest wind raced by, stripping the hillsides
white shrouds relentlessly yellowed and rotted
children lost their flesh, the best of them lost
roses of measles blooming on their shoulders
      it snowed all winter
      and I thought of you
our country   our home   our love   our brotherhood
our country   our home   our light   our childhood
at seven   at thirty   at seventy
we are united in the salty bones of time
our country   our home   I mean our unbeatable hope
our country   our home   I mean our evergreen bride
our writing pens   our angry joy
our destiny   our unending trial

your country and your home
wet cells   narrow rooms   heavy keys
so that you would vanish in the forest of stones
so that your ears would burst from the silence
so that your voice would age on the iron bars
so that your bones would turn to chalk and rust
they founded countries and homes for you
made of black keys and cold rooms
      it snowed all winter

and I dreamed of you
but you didn't perish, recalling you to yourself
the *lodos* rattled on the shutters of your windows
the northwest wind slew the oranges and the strawberries
but your silence became your resistance
from the iron bars you forged telegraph wires of blue steel
from the rattling of the key you composed a folksong
of the keeper of the cell you made a friend
you milked verses from sweat and blood
you wove poems from hope and love
your heart tempered in the high oven of your fight
your exhausted heart bloomed like a poppy field in May
through the years this became your bread and your milk
     it snowed every winter
       on the forlorn plains
from your way of standing up you seemed a miner
from your feel for village ways you conceived endurance
even though friends were not always friends
even though breadth was measured in meters
you passed the days and nights like a villager, a worker
you were the villager of endurance, the worker of hope
through the years you shared your heart
as glorious as a festival place

II

you are far from your country
your heart is pierced with a thousand longings
tired   indifferent   alone in a hotel room
in love with your whole being
in love with your whole being with every woman that is loved
in love with the blue dawn, the bubbling waters, the
     sprouting grass
the friend of red fish and black-eyed ants
eternal passenger of trains, planes, and boats
young at nineteen
young at sixty
in love headlong and tirelessly
perhaps you are in Paris on the quay of St. Michele
an orange streetlight behind you
you are far from your country
your heart is pierced with a thousand longings
Istanbul passes like a pigeon
within your blue eyes

Sarayburnu, Kadiköy Gülhane* Park
pass with a bitter sadness
within your sad blue eyes
you may be flying over the snowy plain of the Ukraine
but the plain of Konya and the Salt Lake is in your mind
eight thousand meters high your country is in your mind
perhaps you are in Prague on the Legionnaire Bridge
with your eyes on the waters of the Viltava River
but your mind is in Beyazıt Square in Istanbul
in Bursa, in Çankırı, in Diyarbakı†
you lived the hardest of arts
old tired far from your country
dipping your bread into your own blood
increasing like a sad river
far from your own warm friendly deep blue seas
you lived the bloodiest of arts

you, worker in exile far from your country
you, poet wounded by a thousand longings
I learned from you how to put together words out of hope
I learned from you the sweet language of belief
you were young at nineteen and in love
you were young at sixty and in love
you, worker in exile far from your country
you, poet wounded by a thousand longings

I mean, you
I mean, you who will never be forgotten.

*Sections of Istanbul.
†Provincial cities of Turkey.

A. Kadir

from *My Life*

Translated by Nilüfer Mizanoğlu Reddy

My father was the one to hear my voice first
On a sunny morning in July 1917
Then the folks in our neighborhood
came one by one crowding the room.
And then one late afternoon
        they named me Kadir.

III

Our teacher in the neighborhood school
was called Mr. Sait.
I remember him well.
I think I was four and a half.
I met my first friends there.
I loved my elder brother there;
As he was crying,
there was something touching in his voice,
when the teacher gave him a beating
        in the evening class once.

VI

In my big wide world
people were always well-fed and happy.
Large wheat fields were
always laughing in the wind.
The workers weaved a cloth of many colors
only for themselves
And freedom,
roamed the streets fearlessly
        singing a folk song.

VIII

I watched the night sky through the bars
                of a small window.
In the morning I wrote poems under the poplar tree
I chatted with the prisoners by the pond.
I had a wonderful life,
I felt light like a well-lit room.
While things were in such a state inside.
According to the rumors outside
I was executed quietly and without much fuss,
in the middle of the night.

Orhan Veli Kanık

There Must Be Something

Translated by Bernard Lewis

Is the sea as beautiful as this every day?
Does the sky look like this all the time?
Is this furniture, this window
always as lovely as this?

No
by God no,
There must be something behind this somewhere.

As Death Approaches

Translated by David Garwood

Toward the coming on of evening, in winter time,
At the window of a sick man's bedroom—
I'm not the only one to be so alone;
It's dark on the sea, the sky is dark, too.
Funny, how the birds are behaving tonight!
Don't mind that I'm poor, that I'm alone in the world;
—Toward the coming on of evening in winter time—
I too in my time have had my love affairs.
To be famous, to have women, to make money—
In time one gets to know the world as it is.

Is it because we're to die that we have these regrets?
What were we, what happened to us in this world,
In this mortal old world, except evil?
We shall be rid of our dirt at our death,
With death we'll get to be good men at last.
Being famous, having women, making money, and all—
We'll forget all that when we die.

Free

Translated by Bernard Lewis

We live free
Air is free, clouds are free
Valleys and hills are free
Rain and mud are free
The outside of cars
The entrances of cinemas
And the shop windows are free
Bread and cheese cost money
But stale water is free
Freedom can cost your head
But prison is free
We live free

All of a Sudden

Translated by Anıl Meriçelli

Everything happened all of a sudden.
All of a sudden daylight beat down on the earth;
There was the sky all of a sudden;
All of a sudden steam began to rise from the soil.
There were tendrils all of a sudden, buds all of a sudden.
And there were fruits all of a sudden.
All of a sudden,
All of a sudden,
Girls all of a sudden, boys all of a sudden.
Roads, moors, cats, people...
And there was love all of a sudden,
Happiness all of a sudden.

Fine Days

Translated by Bernard Lewis

These fine days have been my ruin.
On this kind of day I resigned
My job in "Pious Foundations."
On this kind of day I started to smoke
On this kind of day I fell in love
On this kind of day I forgot
To bring home bread and salt
On this kind of day I had a relapse
In my versifying disease.
These fine days have been my ruin.

Sadness

Translated by Anıl Meriçelli

I might have got angry
With those I love
If love
Hadn't taught me
To be sad.

Tail Song

Translated by Bernard Lewis

We can't come together, our ways are different
You're a butcher's cat, I'm an alley cat
Your food comes in a tin bowl
Mine is in the lion's mouth
You dream of love, I of a bone

But your way isn't easy either, brother
It's no easy job
To lick the man's hand every damn day

Reply

Translated by Bernard Lewis

From the butcher's cat to the alley cat

You speak of hunger
That means you are a communist
That means you burned down all those buildings
The ones in Istanbul
The ones in Ankara.

What a swine you are!

Tamerlane's Price

Translated by Talat Sait Halman

One day, Tamerlane and Hodja* together take a trip
To a bath where they start washing as soon as they strip.
While bathing, out of the clear blue, demands His Highness:
"If I were a serf for sale, how much would you bid?"
Of course, Hodja knows no cowardice nor shyness:
First he pretends to ponder, then, with customary slyness:
"If you ask me" he says, "I would bid a hundred quid."
Tamerlane is furious: "You must be insane!"
"Our towel here alone is worth at least a hundred."
Hodja shakes with guffaws that he cannot restrain;
Then he bows and blandly says to Tamerlane:
"In fact, it was the towel for which I made my bid."

*Nasreddin Hoca, a preacher, wit, and raconteur who lived sometime between the 13th and 15th centuries.

If Only I Could Set Sail

Translated by Özcan Yalım, William Fielder and Dionis Coffin Riggs

How pleasant, oh dear God, how pleasant
To journey on the blue sea
To cast off from shore
Aimless as thought.

I would set my sail to the wind
And wander from sea to sea
To find myself one morning
In some deserted bay.

In a harbor large and clean
A harbor in coral isles
Where in the wake of clouds
A golden summer trails.

The languid scent of oleasters
Would fill me there
And the taste of sorrow
Never find that place.

Sparrows would nest in the flowered
Eaves of my dream castle
The evenings would unravel with colors
The days pass in pomegranate gardens.

This World

Translated by Talat Sait Halman

This world drives you out of your mind,
This night, these stars, this fragrance,
This tree bursting with flowers from top to toe.

I am Listening to Istanbul

Translated by Talat Sait Halman

I am listening to Istanbul, intent, my eyes closed:
At first there blows a gentle breeze
And the leaves on the trees
Softly flutter or sway;
Out there, far away,
The bells of water carriers incessantly ring;
I am listening to Istanbul, intent, my eyes closed.

I am listening to Istanbul, intent, my eyes closed;
Then suddenly birds fly by,
Flocks of birds, high up, in a hue and cry
While nets are drawn in the fishing grounds
And a woman's feet begin to dabble in the water.
I am listening to Istanbul, intent, my eyes closed.

I am listening to Istanbul, intent, my eyes closed.
The Grand Bazaar is serene and cool,
A hubbub at the hub of the market,
Mosque yards are brimful of pigeons,
At the docks while hammers bang and clang
Spring winds bear the smell of sweat;
I am listening to Istanbul, intent, my eyes closed.

I am listening to Istanbul, intent, my eyes closed;
Still giddy since bygone bacchanals,
A seaside mansion with dingy boathouses is fast asleep,
Amid the din and drone of southern winds, reposed,
I am listening to Istanbul, intent, my eyes closed.

I am listening to Istanbul, intent, my eyes closed.
Now a dainty girl walks by on the sidewalk:
Cusswords, tunes and songs, malapert remarks;
Something falls on the ground out of her hand,
It's a rose, I guess.
I am listening to Istanbul, intent, my eyes closed.

I am listening to Istanbul, intent, my eyes closed.
A bird flutters round your skirt;
I know your brow is moist with sweat
And your lips are wet.
A silver moon rises beyond the pine trees:
I can sense it all in your heart's throbbing.
I am listening to Istanbul, intent, my eyes closed.

Ceyhun Atuf Kansu

The Critics

Translated by Talat Sait Halman

They know their English:
The Victorian Age,
Eliot schmeliot
Are complete on their shelves.

They know their French:
From its origins to the present
The grasshopper and the ant
From La Fontaine to our day

I am not even mentioning
Those who know Italian or German
The erudite scholars
Those who do it the American way.

Bookworms!
When I open the windows,
In the bazaar, at the café, in the sun's garden
Turkish is a lively rose.

They smell poetry as fruit vendors
Smell the rear end of melons
To find out
If they are ripe or not

They forbid you
The heart's most natural right
Which is to sing sincere songs
In the mother tongue

They set strict rules and laws
The bugs of taste in chests
Eating away at life's fabric,
Worms nibbling away at the core of poetry.

They are bigwigs,
Like cabinet members
Or congressmen who live it up
And dupe poetry at every election.

The Daily Rose

Translated by Talat Sait Halman

Unless they carry the news of spring days
All the newspapers had better be closed
And unless the type metal smells of rose
All the pages ought to come out blank.

He who knows not the rose should not govern;
No one should talk of social order and whatnot
If the people forsake the time of the rose
And abandon the sagging acacia to rot.

They are the only true friends of the seasons:
From heavenly gardens a grade-school girl descends
Holding the loveliest of orders in her hands
A red rose and a white rose.

Living is the oldest of all constitutions:
Blood is a rose, joy is a rose, love is a rose
And bread is a rose awakened at daybreak;
So the headlines of daily papers should read:
Beam like a rose, laugh like a rose, be a rose.

Mustafa Necati Karaer

Hourglass

Translated by Talat Sait Halman

On these tables I forgot my hands
Side by side with cigarette packs,
Bosom friends of shattered glasses,
Unaware of human warmth...
I have no hands, as you can see.
On these tables I forgot my hands.

I left my eyes in the distant Aprils
At the age of acacias gone mad;
Clouds drifted through, boorishly.
Now I meditate the Great Wall of China...
I have no eyes, as you well know,
I left my eyes in the distant Aprils.

In these streets I lost my songs,
Perhaps a gust of wind swept them away,
Maybe some wild youngsters found them
Or some women where nights take a turn...
I have no songs, as it must be clear to you,
In these streets I lost my songs.

Our blue stretches and goes
With repentances still smoldering
Through the springs to dead points.
Where beams keep coming and hush
Let life's hunger keep growing,
Our love resembles an hourglass.

Sezai Karakoç

First

Translated by Murat Nemet-Nejat

You got off at the wrong stop, they filtered you through the mirror of the city
I watched you for years out of the window of yearning
The fleeting, naked and childish window of yearning...
The houses that diminish narrowing toward the sea
You greeted with grace, naturally
In this joyful world, this joyful world you were a fistful of joy.

Knowledge of spring, color of sunlight, snorting horses and you
I call you, come out of the crowd of weeping virgins
Stone-like women, all white, stroll among the yellow rocks
From each of them you move, you whisper to me
I say it is blindness enough to search for the queen among concubines
It is blindness descending over the sun and me...

Are you the new moon brightened by
A hand's gesture?
Your every corner is etched, embossed with pictures of deer
On a deer's skin flows
The first river wrought by a hand's gesture
If, at the turn of the first street, you disappear, I shall weep
Since lilacs and scorpions are turned human by your look
Suna, you must be committing the first sin in a young Paradise
The glittering seas, noiseless poems and closing doors
Toss you the meteors of the sky
And the first arrow sent to the wrong target
Raves of you

Mehmed Kemal

The Gazelle

Translated by Talat Sait Halman

A gazelle goes down to the lake
Weeps.
One lake blends into another.

A gazelle goes down to the lake
Its feet shackled
Its neck in an iron ring
Looks around,
Looks to see, at what
It should be crying or laughing.

There are sounds out there,
Footsteps of the rain
Drop by drop.
The sounds of the rain's footsteps,
Footsteps of the rain,
Drop by drop

Proud, arrogant, crushing,
Cruelty, tyranny, bloody terror,
The monument of an emperor,
Like a myth or epic or legend

Its fate is a rose in full bloom,
Round red rose, alive forever,
Rosebud, corolla, petal by petal,
The chopped off head in the public square,
The prize lying there.

Say everything in my language,
Clear, lucid, simple.
Can one say footsteps of the rain?
Or the patter of the night?
Know this: All things have a sound
A voice rings undiminished in our ears
The voice of life, of those who live it or grant it,
The voice of pain, of those who feel it or inflict it,
The voice of death, of those who die or kill.

A gazelle goes down to the lake
Weeps.
One lake blends into another.
A gazelle goes down to the lake
Its feet shackled
Its neck in an iron ring.
Looks around
Looks, crying and laughing.

Ayhan Kırdar

A Camp in Hell

Translated by Ahmet Ö. Evin

A dagger in each hand
I must have woven red sins

These hands are my hands expelled from heaven
Into the bloody night gushing in streams
Drowned in spit crushed damned
How many times have I fled from those foul looks
How many times have I clawed my heart with my nails
But I died not
Why not

I kissed the mouth of death reeking of boiled glue
With its damp hair where no light touches
And where black crabs make their home I hanged myself
And perhaps I hanged there for a thousand years
But I died not
Why not

I am sick of carrying the giant burden of my loneliness
In this country of friendly midgets
From my exhausted forehead
Drops of sweat streamed into dank wells
And those seas which quenched the thirst of
Snakes scorpions and biting insects
They were all kerosene and
All I did was to build fires on shores called the sea
But I died not
Why not

Puny desires open their hungry mouths
Their teeth gnaw at my flesh like nettles
I go and break the doors of temples open
I look for God
They say he is not why not
I become a fist and squeeze myself

My fingers fall and
I break a few glasses of the frozen heaven
I know I am more than half-guilty
More than half-dark is this place these people this ocean

—And after how long the calendar shed its
Leaves like a boat departing from the docks—
All songs had stopped the god of death was quiet
Quiet were the bells within me I was quiet
It was hard to find space in hell

I hung my most embarrassing sins on the bridge to Heaven and hell
The sun was blonde like a prostitute. I was cold
From the marble thresholds of iron-grilled hot doors
Slimy flames were flowing
We were bathing in a sea of flames—yo ho ho—
In a sea of flames
Flames
Sea
Flames

From the skeleton of God blood was trickling

Necip Fazıl Kısakürek

Eyes

Translated by Bernard Lewis

Lingering from the past
Nothing remains but eyes
All our being dies
Why then do they last?

Starlike in the skies
Flickering in space
In a dry death's head
Open staring eyes.

Rage

Translated by Murat Nemet-Nejat

As you are a nymph escaping to the mountain,
So am I a monster chasing after you;
Call your world, if you will, to ease your burden,
In my world, we shift alone.

The chill paths you follow will frighten you,
And my steps will echo in your ears;
Nightmarish arms in delight will engirdle you,
Hearing my heavy breath bite your neck.

Alone in your room a wintry night,
When you tremble, remember me!
Think that it is I who push against the window,
That I roar outside, not the wind.

The poison that my panting spits
Will press dry, like a rose, your life;
Run wandering, whereso you will, town after town,
For in the end, I take you.

If, like my dark purpose, you are eternal,
Wait, I shall take death for a friend;
If my rage must contend with being dust,
I myself will carve your stone; wait.

The Pavements

Translated by Aptullah Kuran and Talat Sait Halman

You belong to these streets flesh and bone
Like a hero who sold his head to some cause.
Couched regally on your littered throne,
You must fly as far as your fancy goes.

Your souls melt in the same pot of sorrows
Since your fate and the pavements merged:
The sidewalk's eyes amassed your shadows
And with your skull its stones converged.

As free as a shriek and like silence lonely,
Neither of you has kin or friend or wife;
You drag around your own barren bodies only
With just yourselves to care for in life.

Even a rock would get tired from this walk,
When the road ends, death will strike you.
No one could know you better than the sidewalk
Nor anyone understand the pavements like you.

Cahit Külebi

To Guillaume Apollinaire

Translated by Nermin Menemencioğlu

Are there two planes, Guillaume, in the skies of Paris?
Do the past days battle against the days to come?
Are you on board the somber one, the black?
And is it me driving the white ahead?

Days go by, and weeks, does time not go by, Guillaume?
Do the loves of the loved of old never return?
Can the Seine flow slowly under Mirabeau Bridge
And men not fall in love?
Where is Lou's auburn hair, where her fine feathers?
She is my grandmother's age now, I know!

In Strasbourg, once, on a Sunday,
You sat down to a meal in a restaurant.
The waitress was enchanting, her little white apron,
Her tiny haunches, her hat, her airs and graces,
You longed to kiss her, fondle her, so you have said!

I was a child when you were in the trenches!
There was no bookshop in my village, Guillaume,
No novels by Dumas, Féval, Eugène Sue to send you
In trunkloads of greetings from one who would like to have sent them.
Guillaume, are the streets of London barred by fog?
How many minaret lengths is La Tour Eiffel?
And the girls of Holland with their budding mouths,
Is that the country where kisses are blown by hand?
I do not know those countries at all.

I too love the whirling smell of manure,
Mares replete with their foals, I too love them.
I think of the auburn witch from Bokhara
And wish to die.
When I hold a woman's picture in my hand,
In the evening, I hear distant voices, distant voices,
then I drink, and drink again, and I sigh.

Paris

Translated by Nermin Menemencioğlu

When they talk of Paris I hear
A woman with a husky voice
She sings songs to sleeplessness
Her breasts heaving

The customers are filled with gloom
Yet they continue to pay heed
A song about unfaithfulness
How could they think of leaving

The lights shine in their glasses
Dark with a waiting drink
A fog like raki clouded with water
Settles on the streets outside

Ceaselessly till break of day
This woman sings her songs of love
I have never been to Paris
But so say those who have

The First Half

Translated by Nermin Menemencioğlu

The first half of the twentieth century
Is the age of death
The age of tyranny
The age of lies
The people of the twentieth century
Have hanged and slain
Have maimed and cut down
Have piled the dead in mountains
And drunk their blood in rivers
They have made children cry
They have raped women
Who should weep
If not the people of the twentieth century

Cebeci Bridge

Translated by Talat Sait Halman

Cebeci Bridge is like an anthill
Teeming with men, swarming
With porters, blind beggars, cripples
Who sit and wait for what fate may bring.

Cebeci Bridge rises high,
Under it trains come and go.
What goes through my mind
No one can know.

This world, this lovely world,
Ticks like a machine on the go;
But why do all men but all of them
Bicker and quarrel all the time,
I shall never know.

The parapets on Cebeci Bridge
Were painted black as jet.
And you, Cahit Külebi,
You have so many bridges to cross yet.

Song

Translated by Bernard Lewis

Your lips are red
Your hands are white
Take my hands, child,
Hold them a while.

In the village where I was born
There were no walnut trees
That's why I yearn for coolness
Fondle me a while.

In the village where I was born
There were no cornfields
So scatter your hair, child,
Flaunt it a while.

In the village where I was born
The north winds blew
That's why my lips are cracked
Kiss them a while

In the village where I was born
Bandits struck by night
That's why I hate to be alone
Speak with me a while.

In the village where I was born
Men did not know how to laugh
That's why I'm still so unhappy
Make me laugh a while.

You are light and beauty, like my country,
The village where I was born was beautiful too
Now tell me of the place where you were born
Tell me a while.

A Small Spring

Translated by Özcan Yalım, William Fielder and Dionis Coffin Riggs

I am a small spring
On a forgotten mountain
My waters are never dry
Under the starlight I flow
Without ceasing.

Far from my voice
The traveller, by night or day
Passes by without hearing.
I cannot bring an end to the drought
on this parched land
Nor relieve the dryness
Of burdened hearts.
We all suffer endless longing.

But at times the animals approach
And drink their fill of me
And though they are mere beasts
With little understanding
Still their eyes sparkle
As they drink.
My days pass in this way.

If a seed should fall in my waters
Embrace it, my neighboring earth.
Oh seed, strong seed, sprout quickly
Let your roots reach into the earth,
Thrive. Though I am but a small spring
I shall never be entirely useless.

Ercüment Behzat Lâv

If I Had a Magic Wand

Translated Bernard Lewis

If I had a magic wand
If where I struck
Roses bloomed
Flying roses.

If I had a magic wand
If I could strike a pomegranate tree
And make the pomegranate burst with laughter

And baby-faced girls
Stick out their hands
One by one from the boughs

If I could stuff them into my pockets
And take them to my crystal palace
To live happily ever after
In a fairy tale.

To a Poet of the Sea *

Translated by Talat Sait Halman

Green eyes blink and twitch
on the tips of the shrubs.

Alligator and rhinoceros off the grass.
As in a dream, the fish
with a kiss-filled splash
drift while the sea's nipples bulge.

Their inmost sounds pierce the silence:
Roes are blue lanterns in the limpid dark of green,
cuddling the sea's bosom,
serpentine, gliding, bright, and brittle.

They jostled the sea turtle, upside down
turned it into a cradle for their newborn;
in moonlight they slept,
they woke in moonlight.

The mussel hermaphrodite Pina
inside the same shell;
in its love dream, it gave birth to little ones
pink and green, blue and yellow.

Are the fish on the brink of a dream?

The dark velvet of sponges moves in ripples
and the sea beads from a necklace
around the bride seal's neck.

The sea has its own streets
where the fish live
wide
narrow.

When the moon
writhes in the night's pan,
the fish
shiver...

---

*The original title of the poem is *"Halikarnas Balıkçısına"* (To the Fisherman of Halicarnassus). "The Fisherman of Halicarnassus" is the pen name of Cevat Şakir Kabaagaçh) 1886-1973, a leading figure of modern Turkish fiction, one of whose main themes has been the life and the love of the sea. (See his biography among "Writers of Fiction".)

Yusuf Mardin

Lullaby

How strange this lullaby
In a misty evening, after the rain,
More melodious than pain,
More glittering than happiness.
It has been stripped of its music and words
Like a twitter of a bird
So warm...

Is it because it trickles through the branches,
Through the leaves,
Which keep twinkling like stars?
Is it because it is unaware of its being heard,
Why is it so unique?

How strange this lullaby,
How unspeakably beautiful:
Is it because it cares
For all the mothers, young and old,
With endless pity,
Looking over starry domes of mosques
To the city....

Muazzez Menemencioğlu

Forbidden Feelings Grow in Awareness

Translated by Murat Nemet-Nejat

Three-quarters of my brain
is sex
the rest courses.
I used to be sick of Freud
now his book is near my bed.
At ten to nine the alarm will ring

I know
how Japan has developed,
the Alps are in Europe,
in the mountains Che Guevera was killed,
in the South warm,
sunny men...
Men keep us from sleep...
Is there no drink, none?
Some drink, the crown
of your bar?

I am placing the scale between the pit and the mountain
that arm of the clock between what I want to reach
and my reach
not enough....I need growing
within a world built of you.
I cast the dice to win.
With her modern Marx and huge earrings to show off—a woman strolls
round the chairs at the sidewalk café....
Horses ride in me.
One part of me is mankind, the other
You, my machine.

İbrahim Minnetoğlu

Blood

Translated by Talat Sait Halman

This
Field
Is mine all mine
Go plough your own field

I
Came
For a good life
And for love into this world

What
Good is justice
If for a mere handful
Of soil our blood is spilled

You
Reach
For knife or pistol
Axe or sickle is what I wield

A
Blow to you
And a blow to me
Our hands are smeared with blood

You
Will reap
Death or jail
Hanging or hard labor will be my yield

Come
Let's both
Forget our ancient grudge
Let's put an end to this blood feud

Behçet Necatigil

The Venus Line

Translated by Talat Sait Halman and Brian Swann

Summer or winter, they hold us by the hand
On moonlit nights under a tree.
Endless galaxies
run away as we stalk them.

The Venus line grows longer
with their hands open,
soft veins around the wrist.
A lovely curve begins at their half-naked arms.

If they're hungry or thirsty, you need give nothing.
They just stare all the time, summer or winter.

Fly

Translated by Talat Sait Halman and Brian Swann

Sinews dangling, morning shave before mirrors.
If we're late, kids wait at the table again.
Without water a flower fades and dies.

Crack and crash. The tails of strong horses swish.
Sheath-wings broken, feet maimed,
A fly squirms and writhes.

The Voice

Translated by Talat Sait Halman and Brian Swann

Those trapped under the avalanche
could still be seen.

A woman
sobbing and a man
calling out to someone
invisible
could still be seen.

But the Voice could not be heard.
Without the Voice not one of them seemed to exist.

Secret Love

Translated by Talat Sait Halman

It was seven or eight years ago.
Remember the girl you had?
Yesterday I ran into her,
She seemed very glad.

We stood on the sidewalk
And made small talk and so on:
She's married and has kids,
A daughter and a son.

She asked how you were.
I said he hasn't changed a bit,
Same as ever.
She knew it.

She's happy and loves her husband;
The house is their own property.
She sent you her greetings
Looking crushed as if she felt guilty.

Harbor

Translated by Nermin Menemencioğlu

Ships whose masts are torn in violent storms
Come for refuge—we think we have found them.

They do not see us—only the distance
We mend, repair. They go, we stay.

Then at night—let it be the last, last
Send no others! we beg of the sea.

And our loneliness grows
More monstrous still.

Building a Bridge

Translated by Nermin Menemencioğlu

He has something to say
There are whispered sounds
As he wanders nearer
His eyes alert

He holds out something
Toward a hole in the barbed wire
Someone approaches to forbid
Before his hands can touch

And that is our only encounter
And only late in the evening

Eternal House

Translated by Feyyaz Kayacan

When they are this age
Their mind spills into the world outside,
They do not look at me,
Day and night their eyes roam the streets.

Even a strand of hair would weigh
Heavier than me in their sight.
Let it be so, I can wait
Whether the waiting be short or long

Sons have left me, daughters too
But only for a short time.
Let them, I say, they're young,
Let them enjoy the endless streets.

I too have tried that very often. But I know
They can't do without me, they'll come back,
And I am big, I am the House,
I forgive.

Bone

Translated by Talat Sait Halman and Brian Swann

And the tallow smell of the candles quietly extinguished
Spreads and settles over all the ceilings
And men, glancing left and right, bury something
In great haste, unnoticed by anyone,
And then run off down endless avenues.

And a sheep strays from the flock into night
And men, glancing left and right, pass by something
In great haste once again before they scuttle off.

Then they dig an old bone from the walls
And crouch among solitudes to lick it.

Dead

Translated by Talat Sait Halman and Brian Swann

Wax boats sail fiery seas.
Are the vessels sturdy enough to cross love?

Someone's at the window.
Outside, nets are spread.
Over there, fish being dried.
He could come alive if he bathed vigorously in eternal fountains.

The road leads back to two great dead poets.
The dead are so many, the nets so strong.

At night, someone weaves from her hair dappled nets.
Back there a candle burns and things scuttle off.
Moths die so fast, one after another.

A sturdy ship would come alive on the seas.
But the dead are so many, the nets so strong.

Four-Leaf Clover

Translated by Talat Sait Halman and Brian Swann

Angle A of the equilateral triangle gets broken
That's the door
The kid in the street

Angle B gets broken
That's the window
Cold air floods in
Flu, sick, beat

Angle C gets broken
That's hunger
He had nothing to eat

Three angles joined like three clamps
Joined hand to hand, welded
Each craves to break off
Wait till he grows up, that kid

Leather Sole

Translated by Feyyaz Kayacan

I have got a wooden leg
The noises it makes
Ahead of me empty my surroundings
Like leaving a child in a forest.

There were many things,
If nothing stays where we put it
It means it is near.

If we want to live we must, for instance,
Hasten to go deep down into our future
—Almost toward loneliness—and then lift it too,
A leather sole over a hole in the eye.

The Horses

Translated by Nermin Menemencioğlu

Hoop after hoop the juggler tosses
Into the air, then catches again
You too have two hands, however
Someone, something waits in vain
Where no seats are left, in the crowded rows.

Confused, you wonder which to tackle first,
A new task calls while the other is half done,
In Texas three horses are off at a gallop,
A cowboy jumps on all three at once.

There's soot in the chimneys, everything is old,
Do not take it amiss, but you are late, a little—
The swifter horses have long since crossed the sea.

Treadmill

Translated by A. Turan Oflazoğlu and Güngör Dilmen

Where did it come from, and why?
I can't tell unless I find out, can you?
It doesn't matter, really:
I came, they made room for me, so I sat
There were people who went in and out
When I came in, anyway.

There were other things, too, like bread and water,
Laughter and kisses and all, what do I know?
Couldn't figure out if it was a wedding or what
Then some people were deep in thought and silent
I never found out why some of them went away
When I came in, anyway.

Was it a fair or a concert or a show
Couldn't figure out because of the crowd ahead of me
Time drifted swiftly where I was hemmed in
Look, they said, I did, but didn't see much
It was dark all around
When I came in, anyway.

My only concern at the corner where I was crowded in
Was how to leave when told to get up and go
Quite a thing to get through the huddled rows
After all, they'll get up and stare after me
All the fuss they made about my elbowing my way in here
When I came in, anyway.

The War of the Houses

Translated by Nermin Menemencioğlu

Puniness is a defect
Houses abhor.
Our houses wage against us
A deadly war.

Each day they send us abroad:
Go, get!
The commanded bread is won
With sweat.

The little houses crush
As mountains might,
They pull the rope about our necks,
A leaden weight.

Inexplicable fury
That nothing sates:
With the inanimate, against
The animate.

Kitchen pot and dining table
Conspire together;
One keeps boiling what melts away
At the other.

Every object enters the fray
On the houses' side;
Pipes burst, windowpanes break,
Open your purse wide!

Cloth and leather juxtapose
Their treacherous share:
Scarce bought, they begin to show
Signs of wear.

The larder's enmity
Is not less men—
Gone the butter, soap, sugar,
The gasoline.

A snake stretches out in the sun:
Light a fire! The room wails.
Refuse to obey if you can,
Cold winter prevails.

Puniness is a defect
Houses abhor.
Our houses wage against us
A deadly war.

At My Touch It Turns into a Faded Rose

Translated by A. Turan Oflazoğlu and Güngör Dilmen

It falls off a lot of people, Heaven knows,
Yet no passerby catches sight of it,
I bend and pick it up
At my touch it turns into a faded rose.

In one of those big cities
He wanders at this or that crowded spot
In the country at a far-off place he is
In a hotel room or a coffeehouse;
Wherever he goes at this late hour
He sticks his hands into his pockets
And through cigarettes and pieces of paper
It gently slips out and goes,
I bend and pick it up, no one materializes
At my touch it turns into a faded rose.

Or it lingers on the lipstick
That a lonely girl takes off
On the threshold of another weary night
When she rests her head on the pillows.

Sometimes at midday it cuddles up to me
You know it's on that same cloud of sorrows
That descends mostly in autumn or at rainfall.
I reach out and clutch it, no one materializes
At my touch it turns into a faded rose.

On hands and lips and desolate inscriptions
It gets caught in nets drawn across the night
Panting like a wounded animal,
In anguish, he yearns to escape the net's throes
To run along the roads and mementos.

Time and again I take it along, it stays awake all night
Stirring in darkness, whenever I touch it
At my touch it turns into a faded rose.

Ümit Yaşar Oğuzcan

Ballad for Undies

Translated by Tunç Yalman

Don't dismiss the undies just like that
Nice or shabby we all wear them
Woolen or cotton
Silk or nylon

Miss Ayşe's are pistachio green
They cover her skin like a leaf
Miss Fatma's are coarse linen
Rose-colored underneath

The engineer's wife
Prefers hers in nylon
Sits cross-legged showing off
Her dainty panties

The engineer himself
Wears two in the winter
So thick that you might say
Surely they are bulletproof

Miss Fitnat who has sciatica pains
Wears them long and woolen
Miss Zehra being poor has hers
Covered with patches in many colors

Madam Leman prefers them
Light blue or soft pink
And so small they'd fit your palms
But then the lace might stick out

As for Pakize with the gold teeth
I'd rather have her than the rest
If you'll forgive my saying so
She wears just nothing at all

Quatrain

Translated by Talat Sait Halman

To Yashar Kemal

It should all end, I say, all this darkness should end,
Poor people's gnawing hunger and distress should end.
We came as equals, so we should go as equals,
Cruelty and injustice that oppress should end.

The Left Ear of the Grand Vizier

Translated by Talat Sait Halman

It itches: the left ear of His Lordship the Grand Vizier
Like nobody's business itches that ear
The Grand Vizier is a most eminent peer
He thinks about the nation sitting here

Now itching is a function of the ear
And thinking behooves the Grand Vizier
Yet it so happens that in our land
What itches is the Grand Vizier
And who thinks is the left ear

Ahmet Oktay

All Men Die

Translated by Talat Sait Halman

Because the skies grow white with boredom
    the wind wrinkles and the leaf falls
    and in the midst of a withered blue
    the gulls escape and the crimson deer.
There, see the gold and black currents
    mothers, lost souvenir picture
    poverty, that frightful woman.
Quiet, it's the day for all remembrance,
    black rain and the rainbow
    Slowly gently all men die.

    Human voices would stand still
For trucks may fall off the mountain road.
A silver watch in hock at the pawnbroker
and the suitcase forgotten at the checkroom
    are meteors that come to pass
through the air and the blue celluloid.
Loneliness with its defective marble
    is a sacred prey offered to God,
    then it turns into the luster of ruby.

Because the skies grow white with blood
    a vein throbbing and out of breath
    in the heart of the petulant sea
    and in the pulse of the soil,
    bloodstream is like being forgotten.
The gallows and the cross and the flower
    shiver in the same wind,
    the whisper of the bed should cease,
    the amber glittering in the hand:
with bread, shackled and heads bowed,
    the men of those women pass by.
    And the sad delta of brief lives
    an album, a song, a child.

The ruby of some frozen sorrow
as pale as the scratch pads of kids
sparkles over the battlefields
all the groves are the moonlight,
loves are the fulcrum you cannot reach,
the dirge that slashes and makes the hands bleed.
Oblivion is what lingers in the mind,
Leaping, defeated, dying deer
pen and pencil from which agony never strays.
Men are a brief word,
Non pasaran in Spain,
church bells turning red
a long shadow over the cathedrals
Mamma mia in Italy
the rocks where the palms feel the whole world,
In Mexico a drooping mustache *Viva*.
Rivers dry up, love keeps quiet
and men are the harshest word
in barren squalid Anatolia.

Men are big and defeated,
an adventurous boy will heed no one
a sick man who mumbles in the splash of water
and a mad lover until daybreak
inventive, terrible, and ashamed.
Useless are all the lilac trees,
men can never understand
the sadness of children born and dead,
for they die beforehand.

Because the skies grow white with blood,
there are always vanquished stars,
the diary, the sundial and the battlefield,
a face
are all that blood.

Crystal spreads its sparkle,
deathlessness, that intractable tomb,
moonlight makes the sea endure and itself,
while all things pass on and go forth,
slowly gently all men die.

İsmet Özel

A Shroud for My Darling

Translated by Talat Sait Halman

The shrine of a woman whose hair blazes in henna
soars overhead in an undertone
these violet autumn days inflict their madness
driving you out of your senses and books
tumors, dead ants
chills and shivers cover me
curiosity
is the genesis of a revolutionary
and above me in an undertone fly
cancer, begonia, death.

White gauze behind the windowpane
and eyes plucked out
real human eyes heavy like rocks
a mother who endures all the agony
and the dust stirred up by her corpse,
you warden of anguish, you autumn days.

Under the rain of the rebel leader
I clobber my own scorched and paltry beauty
Saturday afternoons pierce like a cramp
my hope
is a ferocious animal
which keeps toppling the bank notes and mass meetings
and chokes the houses we live in
with the aroma of cinnamon and with weariness
curiosity
is the genesis of a revolutionary
in the bazaars some coppersmiths wash
and women who knead dough are dragged with clangs
in their mortars they pound their stubborn streak
and their vile hopes too.

I cannot love a girl secretly
a thousand curiosities prick me all over
those gloomy smells of incense, our mothers
craving food in pregnancy must eat dirt
untie the ropes of my heart against the moon
my heavenly pain throbs in my wrists
sawdust convulsing sawdust
sawdust of the sledge that beats on my temples.

Kemal Özer

Fringe

Translated by Ayhan Sümer

his eyes are an open sleep on the table
the chart that the boy looks at
nearly vomiting of fear
if he wouldn't hold his mother's nearest hand

they have died now their lines are drawn
they have died now ignoring death
their lines are drawn and of girls
when their eyes disappear of weeping of sleep

is it the blood which passed it is so white
clothes and stones they are so white
is it the blood which passed through streets' brightness
it has so spilled on children's hands

every child is the clock tower of a town
in which acrobats swing to death
the horrible tower of minutes of death
one of his feet to mother and one to death

All the King's Men

Translated by Talat Sait Halman

you were a king how can I help recall
who could not find a place to put his hands
except the sagging shoulders of his subjects
you were the king this was certainly your right

the sea was yours the sea of plunges and hugs
when the moon stood on one side of the night
and while hairs almost reached the other hairs
yours was the night of sleeping side by side

blood is more valiant than all we have known
you reached it as if your hands had put it there
how can I help recall you were the king
your men poured out of the city's fountains

Ali Püsküllüoğlu

Oh, Winter Came Again

Translated by William Fielder and Dionis Coffin Riggs

A gentle snow is falling
Past the door to the courtyard
Where sparrows are searching for grain.
So there we are: another winter
And again the snow.
But the sun follows.

Someone is passing
(Don't ask who—people
Are always walking the streets)
Plunged in thought,
Collar raised,
In love perhaps.
He has a carnation in his hand.

Your body is warm
It does not know the cold.
Night falls early
The light in your room
Is like a low, fluttering street lamp
And birds sing all night long
In the blackness of your hair.

Oktay Rifat

Perçemli Sokak

Translated by Talat Sait Halman and Taner Baybars

This long poem, originally published as a single book in 1956, is almost impossible to translate. The title itself has posed many problems because it is not a proper street name, and yet any attempt at translating it would have been futile. It could have been "Street with Forelocks," "Scalplock Street," and so on, but these would not have conveyed the symbolic significance the poet intended. In my opinion, the title suggests a wilderness (the shaved part of the head, scalp) from which emanates a ray of consciousness and awareness (the tuft, the lock). As such the title should have been, in English, "Life in a Derelict Street," or, better still, "Life-force in a Derelict Street." Thus, the title remains as it is in Turkish.

The entire work is heavily loaded with related and unrelated images, but the image of the sea recurs throughout in conjunction with darkness and death, beauty and love looming in the background (see the last line). This is not the proper place for a critique of the poem, but it would be useful, I think, to quote from the poet's introduction to the book. He says that

Language is a tool for communication. If we want to tell somebody that a ship is cruising, we bring together the signs of the two concepts as words in the language, ship and cruise. It is the duty of the words in a language to make us visualise reality. But, when we talk we are not aware that by using words we are trying to probe into reality, trying to visualise. To use a language is to communicate through words which evoke in us what we call "images." The meaning of a word, most of the time, is no more than what it evokes as a visual image. Take the sentence, "Ahmet fell down as he was walking." The image of Ahmet falling while walking is the meaning which is real and acceptable. But if we said, "I'll see you when the fish has climbed the poplar tree," we perceive an image which leads to another one and that is, "I shall not see you at all".... "Ahmet fell" has a meaning, because Ahmet *may* fall. "The hair of the lamp is wet" has no meaning because a lamp has no hair. The art of using words which is poetry and hence the art of using images, cannot be restricted to images which are possible in reality and therefore meaningful.

Taner Baybars

I

In the bundle of clouds
The fragrant pigeons of heaven
Drive the human-eyed cats insane
Barefoot moonrise in the wells
Hulk carcasses on telegraph wires

II

There the mulberries of the sun
And the stained glass of daisies
Earcorn tops of houses
Blood-cheeked children with no pigtails
Under the diminutive trees
On the warped twisted railway line
Appear the rooftop-cutting scissors

Come lean on cloudless tables
Hold my hand make it grow
Look me in the face
Make my inward clock chime
On the return route in embrace
Let the ships sail between us

III

Cheerful as the children of the poor
Like the jagged edge of a tumbler
The rabid weeds of Istanbul

IV

Toward the five thousand meters of ships
My hands and feet stretch
Men tied to flaming masts
Tiny and with eyes of bone
They spin like weathercocks in the wind

V

The night of the unwound clock
Slouches in the table's shadow
Spreads starless as the sun strikes
Gazes at the bird flying in a blond light
Its hands are few
Its eyes uncombed

Along the familiar roads
Which never let go once they hold
Are lanterns laid flat in ditches
Ours for the mere glance
Lost to us on our mere thought
The wind of weeds that burn with violent cries

VI

Against multitudes of horses
The sun-scented girl
Feeds the lions on her childhood
Among the reeds taller than her
Through the sand covering her chest

VII

These are the streets of joyful days
These are the people of joyful days
Or else you could neither stop nor walk

VIII

A rug a table a lemon
A tree
A child linear
A cat empty inside
An ear one-fifth

IX

As the fish flogs the dark
The sky gently lifts
Toward aged tattered seagulls
The hermit's cloak of the sun bleeds
From wear and tear

X

Bees have eaten my sun I am nightless
On rectangular stones
Green olives at the sea's bazaar
Fish have gone by blowing their whistles
I started to live again where they left off
Hidden behind the lichen-covered gates
To seek out the twin gulls

XI

In the lame clockmaker's room
A table with wooden legs
Pitiful inkwell and pen
And the blue ink of our love
From the night we distilled hand in hand

XII

Light trails her like her shadow
Above the waist upon the roofs
At a wave of her hand sparrows fly
In the wake of naked trees
The candles of her eyes melt as they gaze

Such are the hours of this city
In the dark where these panes float
I wave my handkerchief with screams
Roads begin with you and end with you
Before they flow into the wide seas

XIII

To gather roses from this padlock
Distant as houses as rooms
In the vast hall of the brass bedstead

To see the bird crying for the dragonfly
On the trees with smashed windows
Wait for the rain of onions and salad
For April showers to make things green
In gardens impatient with blinkered horses.

XIV

From the fountain of grapes
Spills the green parrot's blood
Grass-haired, grape-eyed

Writhes as it dies in my pocket
The street in evenings house by house
A district larger than a marble bead

The night of wolves with white teeth
I suck the feather and down of the minaret

XV

The seagull speaks the language of the sky
She speaks the language of the sea
Citizen, speak Turkish!

XVI

Light all the lamps
As if you're off to bed
Go into the garden if you're thirsty
May it pour down all night
Sleep and become like the sea
Whiter than flour in the mill of sheets

XVII

No sooner the crimson-horned bullock of the
sleepless windowpanes licks my hands, than I start
turning green all over. Birds of my brow begin
to fly. Inside out, I have become visible to the
naked eye. What's the use if other people watch me
engrossed; I melt away in the solitude of seals and
sigils.

XVIII

The forest of the windowpane on which you lean, grows
with the joy of my fingertips, and your cities flow
in my veins. Spread the ink of our burning lamp all
over your face. See the daybreak on the furniture,
behind doors, upside down, fearless. The sun digs lacunae
in your face. Lower your eyelids halfway down, just
enough to feel the rain fall on your hands. This
false sky belongs to all of us.

XIX

The day I first saw you in the street the downpour
of houses had not yet ceased. Tiles were flying in the
air, and, as the walls came tumbling down, quiet ants
rained on us. Like the sky, like the mountains, like
the sea, you had something indefinable about you. You
smiled. A human being without scorpions could have been
no lovelier than that.

XX

The indolent wings in the blueness of inaudible sounds,
at noon, the timeless signal of joyful days, brand new
in the sun of the surf in spite of the presence of goat-
footed fish, the city with its exhausted streets, moldy
clouds pressing against coils of hawser, useless, easily
torn into innumerable pieces.
The sky, that unquiet rattle.

XXI

Flowing away like water
The sun's green
The truest rose
Our steel bench on the sea's edge
Fluttering its wings, the street
Slips out of sight behind the roofs
Who cares

XXII

One-half of the cup is day, the other night
Smaller than a carnation
Slender in the moonlight
Dips and flows in the brook of thought
Runs runs runs

XXIII

Neither the moss of glass
Nor the wind of mattresses
More ancient than daylight
Identical with its dress
Same age as its legs
Shattered with lamps
The woman was running to the sea
To the ship anchored at the door

XXIV

The aftermath of man too
The whiteness of the box held between teeth
For us against us
The telegraph wires of doors
That ugly devil's kite
The rain cloud rustling rustling
The hand we quietly lost
And obliviously left within the wall.

XXV

A dark wind raged
Night fell
The sea crept into its nest on roofs
Now the fish in its tent is alone

XXVI

Look at the sea its depth visible
Look
Look

XXVII

Chimneys too have birds
More virginal than pins
In the house of rains
The twin mirrors of kids

They sleep on the mattress of lamps
Berries of terebinth in their hands
Their long-haired eyes
Undulate as cities in the wind

XXVIII

The plaster of your hair crumbles
Down your shoulders on tattered pavements
Torrential rivers gush forth
From the windows of your skirt

As if boats shops float in streets
Anchored in your eyes
The gulls of the awnings flutter
Your hundred-fingered hands
In the sunny scabbard of my palms

Your legs are as many as my steps
Get closer and closer to the lighthouse
Suckle the cobblestones
That we found along streets
To babies forgotten in moonlight

XXIX

Days pass black above our heads
Up the helpless walls of baskets
Still that ship still that fish
Things they net within my eyes
Are junk like huge cupboards
From a window painted with sunlight

These are the old habits of the sea
To lean on the forest and the sun
Hairbreadth close to waters
From within glittering pitchers
Closed to all the stairways
In the spinning circle of my hand

XXX

In the house of ancient songs
A white-feathered table
In the splash and babble of doors
Uncorks its bottles in the window
The flag of warm loaves
Drifts from mirror to mirror

XXXI

Lilac scent holds the street corner
Let go of my collar let me walk on

XXXII

Where night turns into day, trees are younger and roads
longer. Either from the salt of the palms or the bounty
of the earth.

Tomorrow, the white dove of the swords, the shortest
distance between two points

Rather than stand with hands tied in the rain,
I drink water, read the papers, lean out of the window
into the sea.

Never mind if that nickel-plated watch, attached to one
end of a fishing rod, reads nine thirty! Catching baby
mackerel depends on the chimes of the vendor of sweets.

I wonder where my old hands are now?

XXXIII

The carpenter star on the roof
Bites into the crust of rancid moments
On the steps of a padlock a child smiles
Rain bursts out from its hands
Into the fields tied to my eyes

XXXIV

Hold the day by the end that whirls with the tree.
Radiance is the falling rock of your eyes. My hands
are blood-drenched with milk of your wind-breasts.
Your face is the mirror of houses. Water, higher than
us. Road, whatever leads to you.

XXXV

Easily caged the breakwater child
Lonely from one end to the other
Tirelessly thinks of the pyre
In the field of incomprehensible waves
Falls down gets up paints the stones

The sideway well of the night
Submerge it with salt before cracks mend
A bottle hangs out of the sea
Towards us
And we towards the morning.

XXXXVI

The balcony of sleep
Come on scratch yourself
March in the night of whips
Come on let's see

XXXVII

Finger-sized men
The beakless birds of solitude
Inside their boxes

XXXVIII

These are the mirror birds
In mirrors they fly
At night on most pointed roofs
The slender sun of your blonde hair
Sets feather by feather

Filthy it is even to think
Of the green of your palms
Tiny birds they are like dots

XXXIX

The cat of barefoot pines
When it appears screaming in the window
The knotted roads become even at once
The sun-armed chandelier
Of checkered poles and masts reeks
Deliriously from the stones of antique times.

XL

The fish flies not showing its leaf
How can it know the rattle in the mirror
Or the trees at our dinner table
Or the water flowing from the girth swing
Hill and rock and stone

It can't know for it has no sea nor night
It can't know the light for it has no hand
Clad with the bloody lichen
Beyond the sheep and the goat
Not showing its eyes the fish flies

XLI

There were white handkerchiefs in the sky
Musical ships on balconies half-dressed
There was a girl so lovely as if she wasn't
Not on earth not in the sky may be in salt
In bread's agony slice by slice in its steam

Houses have roofs their own steamboats
In the clash and clang of chimneys at night
Flowerpots divans and the pigeon of planks
The foster-mother to five children
Should sit pull up its socks and stop begging

Parsley gardens of crooked shapes
The knotted fish of long await
Do not delay beloved drop in on me
The core of this light is me me
Mine is this jug
Mine is the tap draining the incomplete love.

Freedom

Translated by Talat Sait Halman

Get off it will you
You traitor
You filthy beast
We've got freedom in this country
Freedom at Yenişehir
Freedom at Kavaklıdere
Freedom inside out
Here there and everywhere
Blue-eyed freedom in the street of love
Rip apart a watermelon
Freedom will pop out
Bite into a luscious apple
Freedom will lick your tongue
Freedom on your nose
Your ears are free aren't they
Freedom in the ears
Freedom in birds and hens and flies
The flies of this land
The flies of this land are free
The intellectuals of this land
The intellectuals of this land are free
Look at Mr. Citizen
He can go to any barber he chooses
And get a jolly good haircut and shave
Who dares interfere
The son of a gun is free

Free and how
Now take our Black Memiş
You don't even have to mention his name
That rascal too is free
There see the guy is free
Free with his lice
Free with his malaria
He harnesses his young bride to the plough
So he is free on the cracked soil
Free under the blue skies

Dearly beloved blue skies
This freedom is too much for us
Send us freedom with your mercy
Malaria-free and lice-free
Fleshy as our landlord's oxen
Succulent as a bride's breasts
Send us the freedom
We deserve
The freedom that's meant for us

Stones

Translated by Feyyaz Kayacan

All night tightly in my hands I held
My shivering stones.
Waking in the morning, I saw
Everything in its place:
The pigeon on the eaves, the cat on the threshold,
The cloud on the roof.
My loneliness was spilled across a mirror.
Waking in the morning, I saw it standing
With its sun, with its trees.

In a Sleep

Translated by Feyyaz Kayacan

I found it in a sleep. It was
Standing in the green of the grass.
Scant and sad, like the face of a child,
Small endlessly,
It was looking at a bygone part of me;
A swallow softly brushing it
Flew over, singing.
Oh I loved it so, tears singing in my eyes.

Then, like the others, it disappeared.

Self-Revelation

Translated by Bernard Lewis

How hard is my ordeal!
I know no arithmetic
And I'm employed as a bookkeeper
My favorite dish is fried eggplant
And it upsets me
I know a freckled girl
I love her
She doesn't love me.

Thanksgiving

Translated by Bernard Lewis

I must give thanks
To my boots and my coat.
I must give thanks to the falling snow
To this day, to this joy...
Thanks for having trodden the snow
Thanks to the sky and the earth
To the stars whose names I don't know
Praise be to water and fire!

A Docile Dog

Translated by Nermin Menemencioğlu

The plain, like a docile dog, slumbers
Crouching low at my feet, while I
Swing in a cradle between night and day
Run within a measureless mirror
Reflect under a tree in the garden
Wait for a ship delayed at the quayside
Strange visitor inside myself
Resembling, in my fear, those passing by
Insignificant, tired, one of the crowd.
Bottles are emptied, jars burst open
The plane tree changes its leaves
Like yellow snakes changing their skin
A dog plays with the children, now here, now gone.
Vineyards are tainted, roses bloom, roses
Disperse, infinitesimal, in the wind
The sail was waiting for. The sail burgeons
Is ripped from end to end before it swells.
Even the stars hurtle out of the sky!
Upon the dark, unquiet, boundless sea
Your hands are like a distant island
Drunk with wild smells, to which one cannot go.
The rotting cupboards in the attic
Fashioned in beautiful days but not forgotten
Grow dim, no longer turned toward the light.

Autumn Song

Translated by Nermin Menemencioğlu

I came upon a key
which I tried in every lock.
I found windmills with long locks
a giant ship in a tiny box.

I whittled the silent hours
guileless among obscene reeds
but the two ends of the pan never met
the pain that began in fire and water.

What is so mortal in the alien sky
which made me think of immortality?
Then another day shone upon
a pair of lost gloves
that hang from branches without leaves.

Arrival

Translated by Nermin Menemencioğlu

He appeared with the town, dangling a village from
His little finger, a few stars in his pocket.
Arabic script, prayer beads, wild apricots
Spilled like kittens from his saddlebag.
Creaking hands, like the wooden wheels of an ox cart,
His feet in primitive night, his lice bloodless.

There, chained to ferocious slumbers,
Parched fields and oxen smoking like oil lamps.
Here, clouds of flies, ragged memories,
Broken sweetmeat dishes, lively songs;
His cheeks were bulging with large morsels.
Stepping barefoot upon a bygone age,
Close to his old and hairless goat,
He did not think, he chewed. If loved, he'd smile,
If pruned, burst into leaf from top to toe,
If combed, spread his thick locks over the seas.

Angry, I reached to catch a flying crane,
To rip his face out of its yellow triangle.
I tore at sun-dried bricks in a mighty earthquake.
Facing me were the crooked, soot-lined walls
Against which we crouch in the sunlight, or piss,
Or line up for a photograph, in a row.

Girls

Translated by Feyyaz Kayacan

Girls are green and sometimes blue,
They point toward the sky the streets
Of our towns. Girls are our sailing clouds
We look at, crouched at the bottom of walls.
Without thinking we think of a port, we make
Our way through trees, there comes the sound of the sea,
A pomegranate shows us her breasts.
Through the door half-open
We see in the house
The staircase helping out a lovely carpet.

Girls are green and sometimes blue.

Underdeveloped

Translated by Nermin Menemencioğlu

To fall behind; in science, in art, leafless
Unflowering in the spring; an aching star
      Imprinted on the forehead.

To fall behind; doomed to the wooden plough
When you could cut through steel like paper
      Vanquished by time.

To fall behind; sunk in the caves od dogma
Hands to your flanks and starved, against the torrent
      Against the others.

To fall behind; sunk in the caves of dogma
Where one could live in brotherhood, to grasp
      At snakes instead.

To fall behind; ignorant and louse-ridden
Taut as a bow within a somber gorge;
      To break loose with that impetus!

Poem

Translated by Feyyaz Kayacan

In the evening breeze in the parish
Time is like a birdcage: slowly
And gently it sways in the window
Over the back garden of the red-painted house,
The house smelling of tobacco, of bread.
And the birds sing: chipet, chipet, chitalinya.
The sun goes down, we withdraw to our rooms,
The trees, our house, the world, together we gravitate.

Earth

Translated by Feyyaz Kayacan

I stepped on the wet earth. Suddenly
I was tree, I was bud, I was knot.
Toward the sun I turned
My leaf-drawn face. I heard that breeze
In the headlong sky. Come close,
Lovely girls, come close and with linked hands
Dance a circle around me.

Flower Shop

Translated by Feyyaz Kayacan

I fed them with the milk of trees
I made them grow this high.
They are my orphans, my near ones,
They wave hands from afar, fret about.
In voiceless smells
Their world dwindles.

Ziya Osman Saba

Acceptance

Translated by Talat Sait Halman

I accept the life for which I came into the world.
I accept my white hands and the tint of my eyes;
Man and woman, married or bachelor or widowed;
Above ground I accept roving around
And death and decay in the ground.
I accept all forms of life:
The face that frowns and the tongue that is angry,
I accept the miserable and the hungry.
Chattel to men
And serf to God.
Continents and oceans, domeful of skies:
I accept I accept I accept.

Mehmet Salihoğlu

Smoke-upon Smoke

Translated by Talat Sait Halman

At dawn,
with the shadows of solitude
engulfed in color,
suddenly night broke out,
you with your body and I—
we gathered clouds
in the peace of stars.

We came alive
like steel tempered with water
in the same fire—
so I can't tell you we died.
Purple smoke,
sizzling fumes smolder overhead.

When the pigeons of our love
took wing one by one,
leaving the violet and the blue,
the river we bathed in
suddenly turned dry...

Gültekin Samanoğlu

Come So Far As You Can Feel

Translated by Talat Sait Halman

Your eyes lit up with that gleam
When you said: "I'm fond of green eyes."

I am now daunted, defeated, full of regret
After years of search for that age-old dream.
Yearning for green eyes, my heart cries,
But my hopes are shattered—slain.

Your hands held a shadow-ridden plea:
"I've never tried loving, don't come."

Then I turned against longing and began to fret
With the pain that locks up all glee;
I kept smiting my desire and delirium;
All things I marvel at lie riddled like a net.

Your hair is caught in the wind's swagger and threat:
"The world," you say, "isn't worth living in."

And I am an echoless scream awaited in vain,
As if poking fun at those who drink and bet.
In all my beckonings you shall always remain:
Come so far as you can feel. Come, come again!

Tahsin Saraç

Through the Ages

Translated by Talat Sait Halman

In the deaf caves of oblivion,
The dead, having lost their graves,
Wander in the warmth of bewilderment.

The mossy slumber of dry wells stirs
Over the dangling beards of chiseled stone,
And time cracks out of an Assyrian night.

The lions at the gates of tyrant kings
Break loose from the fetters of ages all of a sudden
To pounce on naked captives
Whose bronze bodies are tattooed.

Then, with the eye of the storm raging beside them,
Torrential soldiers march on cities,
Led by the most masterful reapers of death.

A painful sky spreads over all the nests
The milk fountain of mothers' breasts are smothered with sand
At dinner every bite gets stuck in the throat
Immaculate brides smelling of apples, with the look
Of mountain mornings find their warm beds cold.

Suddenly darkness shivers with terrifying shrieks
The black blood of truth gashed by a lightning sword
Is inscribed on black marble—
And then, in a dense smoke reeking of human bones,
In full view, the loftiest monument arises
Where it was erected for a noble triumph.

To an Immortal Solitude Where We Now Pitch Our Stately Tent

Translated by Talat Sait Halman

Our first love that glows in the quiet blue
Is drenched in a forest rain now, far away.
It will perhaps endure alone against all my darkness,
Just this warm night in which my sleep is you.

A chill like the first breath of the universe
Sprinkles from beyond the prime of ages over our desert,
We have vaulted over so many deaths just to arrive here
To an immortal solitude where we now pitch our stately tent.

Cemal Süreya

Country

Translated by Murat Nemet-Nejat

The clock chimed like a Chinese jar.
Bending my brim hat over my misery,
Out of my white insomnia, I,
Exiled to your face,
You woman,
You were in every secret corner,
Your shadow nettled on the dark street,
A child sang
Lullabies endlessly, and a violin
Lengthened the blue smile of a young mother,
And you gave birth in me to a love, with tender beauty,
To a hope, my reprisal on loneliness.

A lover possesses only his love,
And losing is harder than not finding,
Exile to your face, my woman!
I have not forgotten
Your eyes who are my brother,

Your forehead who is my child,
Your mouth who is my lover,
I have not forgotten your fingers
Who are my friends,
Your belly who is my wife,
Your front, your harlot's sides,
And your back,
And all these, all these, all these
I have not forgotten, how can I forget?

Strike a match, your voice flamed in blue,
Toward the forests echoing, your voice, the sound of your face,
Into my mouth you poured, thickly,
The secret thoughts
Of this dour-skinned, this strange, this Asiatic love,
In your poisoned forest, gasping,
I lived your short, terrifying reign,
And my heart, throbbing
In the tide of your hair, mixed
With the Black Sea,
Then with the Mediterranean,
Then with wider waters.

At night, the moon resurrects
The minarets,
In the streets where Koran pages are sold
Death flies with a somewhat beauty,
Death flies over child-soft faces,
I have passed so many times through those streets,
Your tongue's taste in my palate like seaweed,
Now misty, now glittering clear, now misty again,
Like some sea creatures echoing some rabbits,
Echoing Sundays, echoing the other days,
Echoing Mondays, Tuesdays, Thursdays, Fridays, and Saturdays.

A stalk bursts out in miniature a city,
Down this stalk, round these streets, I press for you,
I tie each thing in the world around you,
The gold standard, and the half-cut coins,
And the coins stamped without gold value,
And the right to press all these coins,
The Euphrates,
And its surrounding mountains,
The wide plains of Babylon and its hanging gardens,
The sea of Antalya,
And the depths of that water, the sea crabs,

The land crabs, the sand crabs, the louse crabs,
Circling love crabs, the hermits, stoned barnacles
All make toward you.

I who am a master in the art of dejection,
I feed with my life these falcons of sadness,
You whose alchemy I grasp and lose in the crowd,
Your absence has moved
From here, to there,
In your land where once joyful banquets reigned,
Now big beaks of lonely hours are circling,
Now please, once again, begin to undress
From your mouth,
Unleash, once again, all your beasts upon me,
Once again, come rising from the ruins,
Come to me, once again, and disperse me.

Teasing

Translated by Ayhan Sümer

They have cut the cloud, cloud into three
My blood spilled, cloud into three
Face of a woman out of van Gogh
And two sailors hee hee hee.

Face of a woman small as my palm
With both eyes I saw it clearly
There were stars and I was drunk
Whose tavern is this hee hee hee.

This is Ali's tavern, and this a table
I take this rope for no one to see
I was hanged once in my childhood
Masts were on the ship hee hee hee.

Face of a woman out of van Gogh
And two sailors passed running by me
I never fell in love, love I never knew
Excluding Süheylâ hee hee hee.

Rose

Translated by Talat Sait Halman

Seated at the core of the rose I weep
As I die in the street each night
Ahead and beyond all unmindful
Pang upon pang of dark diminution
Of eyes upheld blissful with life

Your hands are in my caress into dusk
Hands forever white forever white
Cast into my soul icicles of fright
A train a while at the station
A man who lost the station me

On my face I rub the rose
Fallen forlorn over the pavement
And cut my body limb by limb
Bloodgush doomsday madmusic
On the horn a gypsy is reborn

The Yellow Heat

Translated by Murat Nemet-Nejat

My breath is a red bird
In the fair-brown of your hair,
As I embrace you
Your legs grow long endlessly.

My breath is a red horse,
The burning on my cheeks tell me;
We are alone, our nights short,
Let us make love at full tilt.

Song about Executioners

Translated by Nermin Menemencioğlu

Since the Bourgeois Revolution
One hundred and fifty years ago
Monsieur Guillotine, a Parisian lawyer
Reads of suicides in the morning paper
With tears in his eyes

Senor Bullet in Spain
Your glance could wander off
Towed by some cloud
Unless of course you were blindfolded
Like Lorca

And what's to be said about
Mr. Electric Chair
Credit investments apart
A better symbol
Than William James

The gushing blood is a salute
To Cain, to Ezra Pound
In parentheses to Raskolnikov
The head misunderstanding continues
To order the feet about
But Herr Axe's job is done

Citizen condemned to die
When the chair is pulled from under you
If you can husband your breath
You will live a short span longer
For death as proferred by Rope Effendi
Is one of polite delay

A Butt Cast in the Sea

Translated by Talat Sait Halman

Share now a pigeon's flight
Bluebound along the ancient skies,
Its women forever hair and mammal,
A Mediterranean town may arise
If you rip apart a pigeon's heart.

Time for you to love and to hug
Time to hold your hand, time for you
But which hand, my love, which hand:
One has clutched you, pure odd peevish,
One was anointed with an adult aurora,
One in freedom's endless exodus,
And one, unvanquished, breaks bread
With men toiling in mud and dust and smoke.

Such is our soul's rapture as of old:
A cloud, if in motion, is in our ken,
The minaret if joyful unto God,
And a man if gallant against misery.
Whenever we cast a butt in the sea
In the name of liberty, peace, and love
It keeps glowing till daybreak.

Hasan Şimşek

What's in the Ground?

Translated by Talat Sait Halman

When a man is dead
and gone
—ask God—
is he the scent of a flower
a grain
a rock
or water?

Down below
lower than the roots can go
every night
there's a whir—
is that our plea?

What's there in the ground?

Ülkü Tamer

Guillotine

Translated by Nermin Menemencioğlu

I LADY GUILLOTINE

Small silver guillotine on a wellborn lady's table
A delicate finger reaches toward you before dinner
Touches a button and down comes your knife
Between the yellow taffeta and the yellow wig
Upon the neck, brilliant with cream of a china doll.
Blood flows; perfumed blood,
Like that which stirs a distant crowd to roar,
But perfumed.
Aristocratic hands stretch lace handkerchiefs
Dip them in crimson,
Dab the blood-perfume behind their earrings.
Then lackeys take the guillotine away
Place bowls, range glasses
Around the severed doll's head.
At just that moment, two cities further
An applauded executioner, hands unwashed
Sits in his hut to eat and drink

The toy makers sleep by day and make guillotines by night,
To chop off lovingly the heads of chaffinches,
They make miniature guillotines for children;
Jewelers encase guillotines in snuffboxes;
Engrave the Avenger of the People on brooches,
The National Knife, the Patriotic Shortener, Guillotine,
Everyone's favorite, Lady Guillotine.

One can make love to you in dim-lit rooms, as in public places,
Bite your walnut elbow even when alone.
In the dank chateau rooms your body
Is a vertical bed, its velvet covers slowly come off,
Religion, death, turn to gay love beneath them.
You are the mistress of aristocrats
And the neckline of assassins, Lady Guillotine.

II SAINT GUILLOTINE

As of now, no one will be hanged,
No death by fire, no rack, no axe;
Who was it poured on a bandit's wounds
Burning fat, molten lead?
As of now, no such executioner,
There will be no differences in death
For criminals, or for classes.
No easy death for aristocrats,
Difficult death for the people.
As of now killing shall be performed
Without torture.

The first guillotine was made to order by a pianomaker,
So the blade makes the sound of piano keys as it falls.

First the heads of dead men were used for practice,
The public prosecutor, the judges, the deputies
Ate venison as they pronounced the knife satisfactory.
Then they drank wines from a priceless cellar.

And guillotines were made for the state at a handsome price,
The piano makers and certain ministers grew rich.

Someone had stolen a cow
On market day in the city
The cow was made to pull the guillotine cord

The wooden heads of saints were chopped off.

A dog trained to bark at the words of the prime minister
Had his head cut off, together with his master's.

Spectators ran to the market place, singing songs.
To show that the punishment was just
The death deserved so far as they were concerned
They all pulled the guillotine cord.
Suddenly the revolution came
Heads rained like confetti from the sky.

III PATRIOTIC SHORTENER

The platform was slowly erected; the knife was swift to fall.
A revolution is slow to ripen, then it comes abruptly.
No doubt these aristocrats will manage to enjoy death,
Looking at the multitudes in the square
They will find pleasure in philosophizing on revolution.
They do not shoot as they die
Not wishing to devalue the locks of their hair
Which will later be sold as souvenirs.

Here they come in their carriages, dressed as they wish,
Come across streets paved with a thin legality
Past empty houses echoing with usury
Past the pleasant gambling table of commerce
To a place where facing them the sun
Sharpens its blade.

Soon we shall dip our fingers in their blood
So as to be able to tell our children some day
What was the color of aristocratic blood.
And for some months the adult sons of the judges
Will discuss the cloth their shirts were made of
In the tribunal corridors.

Here they come to the white glove of the executioner
They had appointed him themselves
Only two weeks ago;
A snobbish fellow—
But this too is a matter for pleasure
For surely it is better to be killed by him
Rather than by some provincial novice.

IV NATIONAL KNIFE

You are past master of the art of killing,
At the age of seven, you were already a master
When they made you executioner in the square.

Delicate son of a poor carpenter,
Nephew of an executioner remembered before every sleep,
Yes, you were seven
When they placed the hilt of a sword in your hand,
You were seven
When you made other children dream of white necks
And scattered splinters across the city's silence.

Years passed, came the guillotine, the revolution,
They dressed you in bright clothes, a bright hat,
That you might sever the king's head with fitting panache.

You were carried on shoulders that evening
You found a gilt-embossed scabbard
For your sword with its patches of red
And you had an eagle painted on your front door.

But one day there were no aristocrats left to kill,
The revolution had ended with success.
The usurers, the extortioners, the lawyers replaced
The supply of aristocrats you had exhausted.
You did not build the platform in the square,
Death had middlemen now.

You paid
For your own drinks each night;
Mornings you slaughtered chickens for the doctors,
You slaughtered sheep for architects,
You sold your neighbors homemade drugs.
At last you had to take your guillotine,
Moldy and blunt-edged, to a pawnshop.

You were past master in the art of killing,
But there were other masters of other crafts
Those who placed you outside the monetary system
Gave you a metal spoon with a long handle
That your dishonored fingers might not touch
The foodstuffs when you went shopping in the market.

You were past master of all fears,
Came a day when you remembered this;
You gave the eagle on the door a coat of varnish,
Made plans for an aristocratic surprise attack,
And with a grindstone in your apron's pocket
Headed for the pawnshop in the middle of the city.

V AVENGER OF THE PEOPLE

This day of death is gnawing at your breast.
Sit here.
First I shall tear open the collar of your shirt,
Then shear your hair, level with your neck,
The knife dislikes delays about the neck,
It wants a swift freedom from a dead man.

Well-known judge of a while ago, sit down,
Even you cannot pass judgment as well as I
On a man's grudge whose defense was hatred.
One scale of your balance was weighted down with gold,
I weigh the other down with curses and phlegm,
I equalize you with your own blood.
And down the dusty steps which you are climbing
I bring my own judges into the square.
For now the favorite, the well-blown instrument
Of before the revolution
Shall cut its way through the accumulation of rancors.

You hold a diamond, but my guillotine
Can slit your diamond as a scythe might.
Kneel down, jeweler, and think of a necklace
Out of the blue, to the measure of your neck
That can pull you into the rainless clouds.
Now is the time for my goldsmith
To hammer enormous trays in the marketplace.

Stretch your necks
Engineers who make rivers flow
With the pus from our wounds
Then build hasty bridges across the rivers
I shall prolong the life of your necks a little
Then hold you up by the ears
To show you your severed bodies, with insatiable revengefulness.

This day of death is gnawing at my breast, too.
The strong guillotine of my hands, my muscles
Has become a ghost of mother of pearl.
It frightens the night
And spreads the first tidings of joy across the land.

A Sunday on the Meadows

Translated by Murat Nemet-Nejat

They set a small windmill
over the gallows.
As the bandit gasps, the mill turns;
the blood rising in the bandit's lungs
mingles with the brush
of old daddy painter
who is searching for a nice red
to paint the windmill.

Right at this moment
beavers run away.

The Dagger

Translated by Talat Sait Halman

Back in the fall we had buried our dagger
In this courtyard covered with square tiles.
That dagger was both precious and sharp.
Its handle must have melted away by now
Looking like the mossy hair of the herdsmen.

The blood of worms and hawks must be clinging
Onto its skeleton lying in the ground.
Spilling all over the blood-tiles of the yard
The blood of the hawks that sent their flight
Deep down in the form of a disheveled line.

The sea has lit the lamps on its streets.
The dagger received its only defeat from us.
Out of the land of its spout it gazes at night,
At birds that cling to their wings as they fall.
We received our final defeat from the dagger.

For some reason it frightens the gray silence
Of a beggar's voice and the mountaineers' sky,
It frightens the faces of rope-hearted seamen
Who cross the seas each with a panther on his back:
That noise which the dagger makes while rusting.

Ahmet Hamdi Tanpınar

Fear

Translated by Talat Sait Halman

I have the fear of all the things that end,
I am the Blue Eagle who drags the dawn
Along his iron beak...
                              And life is caught
Within my claws like dangling emeralds
And deathlessness along my lovely swoop
Now bites the thirsty antelope of time.

Morning

Translated by Bernard Lewis

Open your window to the cool fresh wind
And see the color of the whitening skies
Let slumber flicker from your tipsy eyes.

Come, let the breezes frolic in your hair
And do not hide your body that is fair
Its silver nakedness another spring.

Ethereal lips adore you with caresses
All of you, neck and breast and tresses
For you are fairer even than the dawn.

Oğuz Tansel

Knot

Translated by Talat Sait Halman

You sang a song chilling my spine—
Care dripped into my heart like venom
When the moment of farewell
Tapped on the door.

Just to think of travel
Gives me the shivers:
Knots come apart all of a sudden,
Light flickers in our clasped hands—
Who remains behind dies.

With heaves and sighs
The loving heart swells like the sea.
We refuse to believe in the bitter truth.
With the voyager gone
The world comes to an end.
The train glides away on the rails—
The earth crumbles under our feet.

Clutching the wind's hand and the ashen clouds,
I must take the road to the big city
—a watermill with all the water gone—
For a new life of faint memories.

Cahit Sıtkı Tarancı

I Want a Country

Translated by Bernard Lewis

I want a country
Let the sky be blue, the bough green, the cornfield yellow
Let it be a land of birds and flowers.

I want a country
Let there be no pain in the head, no yearning in the heart
Let there be an end to brothers' quarrels.

I want a country
Let there be no rich and poor, no you and me
On winter days let everyone have house and home.

I want a country
Let living be like loving from the heart
If there must be complaint, let it be of death.

Today

Translated by Talat Sait Halman

Today is not a tale,
Indeed it's more beautiful.
Today I'm in the world,
Standing right here
Vertical to the asphalt road,
Parallel to the acacia,
Rubbing shoulders with men,
Sharing the fate of bird and beast,
As mortal as a rose or tulip,
As sad as everyone else
And as hopeful,
Glad to be alive at any rate.
I take strides in life
As if living is a drinking bout

Or kissing my sweetheart
Or sleeping out and out.
Who can tell me, I'd like to know,
If the clouds are passing overhead,
Or if I'm walking under them?

Inevitable End

Translated by Talat Sait Halman

Since a solemn chant comes this way
From the minaret of the Grand Mosque
Although it's not Friday,
Someone in our neighborhood must have passed away.

There,
This is where we shall all end up: this coffin
Passing in the avenue in a proud and plain array
Upon shoulders like waves that sway.

Poem at Thirty-five

Translated by Talat Sait Halman

Age thirty-five: that means half the course,
Like Dante, we stand midway in life;
All our youthful vigor and resource
—Wanton is our plea, in vain our strife—
Drift away blind to tears of remorse...

Look at my temples, are they snow-clad?
O my God, is this wrinkled face me?
These eyes rimmed with rings purple and sad?
Why are you now my arch enemy,
Mirrors, the best friends I ever had.

All this change is more than I can bear:
None of my pictures here could be mine.
Where did all those days of joy go, where?
Can't be me, this man smiling, benign.
It's a lie that I am free of care.

Our first love looks hazy, far away,
A memory driven from our heart.
Friends who set out with us on life's way
Took separate paths and strayed apart.
Now our loneliness grows day by day.

Odd, I now find that the sky can turn
Into other hues, that stone is hard,
That the waters drown and the flames burn,
And each new day brings a painful load—
All these at thirty-five I could learn.

Autumn, quince yellow, pomegranate red;
Each year I feel it's closer to me.
Why do these birds circle overhead?
And these ravaged gardens that I see?
What funeral is this? Who is dead?

Immutably death is all men's fate.
"Slept, never woke," will be the story,
And who knows where or why or how late?
You shall have but one prayer's glory
On your stone-bier throne lying in state.

Terror

Translated by Talat Sait Halman

Gently daylight recoiled from the windowpane
Baring all the mirrors desolate and stark;
Now in the gardens the voices of silence reign
And the dome of the sky is a blotch of dark.

From fountains and springs water has ceased to pour
So our empty glasses may be filled no more;
Where narcissus had bloomed now a minotaur
Forbids passage to the birds that flee in vain.

Scylla is precious and so is Charybdis,
I fear the night and its dark-ridden abyss:
My trusted hills may suddenly go amiss
And beyond them dawn may never break again.

After Death

Translated by Talat Sait Halman

With many hopes about death we perished,
But the charm was broken in a vacuum.
Our song of love we cannot help exhume,
A view of the sky, tuft of twigs, bird's plume;
Living was a habit we had cherished.

No news comes from the world now or ever;
No one misses us, no soul cares to know,
The darkness of our night is endless, so
We might just as well do without a window:
Our image has faded from the river.

Closing Time

Translated by Orhan Burian

Time is up, no more of madness!
Mirrors begin to take on harsh tones.
Enough have I run after love;
Drinking and gambling have ruined me.
How could I deny that I was unwise?
I have wasted my youth myself
And lost the finest ship I was to sail
For the waves don't return what they get.
Drinking dens and all-night bars,
Friends, poets, painters, bums:
If you no longer see me at your revels,
Don't think that I quit on you.
Years advance, you know. Our turn is over.
A man should start a family before it's too late:
At least he can be sure then
That his dead body will not be left on the ground.

Suat Taşer

Going Gone on the Auction Block

Translated by Talat Sait Halman

Snow
dark
red wine
a huge book in the dark
man
is free
man shivers in his fears

It's an old song
a decrepit song
in the snow
in the dark
in red wine
in the book in the dark
man
is free
man suffers in his fears

Our tears are counterfeit
death
beloved is death
if man heroically faces it

Tears salty warm stale
man
going gone on the auction block
with his freedom and all
man
up for sale

Ahmet Kutsi Tecer

Rain-rimmed Horizons

Translated by Talat Sait Halman

Rain-rimmed horizons seal off the dry ground
Where a fretful light scuttles here and there;
As mad thunderbolts rattle and resound,
Might and rage and fear mingle together.

Like a feudal lord, God paces around
In his mansion—alone and defiant;
And suddenly the most savage bloodhound
Begins to chase a bloodcurdling giant.

All Too Clear

Translated by Talat Sait Halman

My death, it's all too clear, shall come at dawn
With the first fearful light through the window,
Let the drapes by my bedside remain drawn;
Don't put out last night's candle, let it glow.

In slippers, run to City Hall and say:
"One of my lodgers died early today."
They'll send in a hearse to take me away.
Also, let a few of my buddies know.

When strong shoulders carry my coffin through,
Forget my name as all others will too;
Keep my door ajar for a day or two
So that my few items may watch me go.

Ömer Faruk Toprak

After One O'Clock at Night

Translated by Manfred Bormann

The wharf is dark the hour very late a ship in the open
With its nearsighted eyes a lazy record looks from a distance
Up against me Vietnam rain after one o'clock
Through its open window I enter a hut
Noontime silence of the village of Hue is among us
In their mouths the tangy taste of some familiar tea
The moonlight below stands without speaking
An Asian newspaper wet on the floor
Hearts of stone against the use of napalm bombs
Over yellow fields passes endlessly
A jet-black cloud rocklike hatred
Before daylight spreads we have to reach shore
Those fiery poems live on our lips
None is forgotten patience in the apples of our eyes
A heavy tank passes the earth under us shakes
Were it not for your eyes for the spring in your eyes
For your blue open seas washing on my shores
This heart would not stay in the Congo could not live in Spain

Now every evening a Mediterranean vessel takes off
From our eyelids full sail with our hopes
On my desk sheets of my unpublished poems
At night your hair flies around me in waves
In your face my first lights go on and off
In your hair shines my Peruvian sun
Yet broken in Asia lies my happiness broken in Africa

Do you know the sleeplessness of Algeria in 1960
As if sliding into a well when stretching out on dry grass
With the sleep of a Javanese sailor in my eyes
A little later I suddenly awaken as if falling
Distilled through memories I find your face next to me
Wherever you go with you far away Congo's warm morning
Starts unhappier for me
A river from the night its humming sound in my ears
In the south as I move out in the sea I hesitate
Further on a face familiar from Budapest will appear
On its lips a slow Khachaturian concerto

Güven Turan

Autumn, a Wild Shore

Translated by Frederic Stark

Sound makes night sweat:
A huge—
Hard by, dull water
where fish drift:
Wait
in a tenderness of smells.

Song, slow-unfolding, joins
strummed string and wood.

      Mean, wild like river swelling surges
through all nature, the sky, sea, fields:
wild following storm after waters
        recede.
Each step we take, nature clings behind.

The sky
work / scorched soot:
Smell / to weary us. Cold,

      and dawn tones.

Osman Türkay

The Mediterranean Light

These vine leaves are as sacred as our first temples
And these flowers are a massive fire mixed with blood,
    Burns the rocks when this waterfall
      Roars with a concrete love:
    Here is the place where the Reality
    Unites the Beauty and the Infinity,
    Here are the monuments of summits

And the shrines of Immortality.
A deep voice echoes—you hear it eternally—
To the sleeping waves
From the kisses of seagulls
With the masts of the ships in horizon;
And recovering from an ecstatic dream
Broken off from worn-out yellow stones,
You look upon the mountains
From behind the time;
The peaks are so godlike and so green
You plunge yourself in the intimate water
With indistinct images:
The sea sleeps in your palms
And the waves are so intensely blue.

You don't know what it is
This Mediterranean light, do you
My friend? This sea looks different.
How can you get into the great episodes
Of those eternally youthful generations
Through the monuments of picturesque lights
Chipped into shape, by shapeless fingers,
If your skin with palm trees, marbles, and vulgar sunbeams
Was not burned in that stout salt even once?

Eyes and hands. Heart and brain.
The lips perpetually touching the sources of the streams.
Eyes looked, brain worked, heart beat
And the hands grasping a handful of colored earth
With the clumsy fingers painted in caves
This first picture on the granite rocks.

Eyes and hands. Heart and brain.
What is this endless song within us?
All its warmth sprang
From universal love and knowledge;
Catching fire, still burns
Our fingertips with unending torches.
The smiles are as resplendent as marble stones
And the glances as smooth as daylight;
Closing a vault of heaven, run toward the other
Artist shepherds together with the children
Of a saline sea and bare mountains.

On a warm summer day, at noon, with concrete reflections
I stretched myself upon the uncultivated soil absolutely alone;
The whole universe melted from Kyrenia range to Taurus in my palms.
Only you were in my mind, an unsolved question,
Only you were, my continuation, my restless god, ages before
In the long-forgotten miracles of lost moments
Your pictures yet unframed, your monuments unfinished.
Only you were...and how timelessly majestic were
Your city, your temples
And your prayers.

Turgut Uyar

And Came the Tailors

Translated by Talat Sait Halman

And came the tailors. With nooks and crannies that resembled big broken things
on darker colors and over wider links
With nooks and crannies that frighten a city and put it to shame.
Fabrics were provided and the sleeping cats were patted. Then
the endless music of joylessness.
In late afternoon some went out for tea and some to the parks
Conformity shortened their days with a grief which neither grew nor diminished.
Tired and pale, they found the fabrics and filled the city
Carrying here the ten-thousand-year-old wreath
Having buried their dead ones, they came in a crowd without brushing off their dust
All the avenues were suddenly vacated, everybody made way,
     "Devout women and republicans
     sweepstakes sellers and flower buyers
     fishermen gathered their nets and seines and hooks and
     hoods and bags and scoops.
     Smokers threw their cigarettes on the ground and put them out."
Under thick fabrics that never warmed up, there was something they cut and measured
Making out patterns and matching them
They cut out the end of an unbearable sleep

And broke into a requiem for a horse now dead
They did not put down their scissors
They had been expected.
      "The horse now dead—they said—
      How lovely was your folly within reach!
      You opened up
      The solitary source of thirty-three thousand breeds.
      Dark sparkling mane. Your harness
      —rubbed and shined with aromatic oils—
      went so well with your rumps and the sky.
      Your endless shape gave the sky a new grandeur.
      We rubbed your hoofs with filaments
      And your gallop, painted black,
      Awakened all the lands and all the seas.
      Next to infinity we heard your frenzied neigh
      Black horse, you had such lovely eyes.
      Thousands of people
      —children, men, women, everyone—
      in splendid or slovenly clothes
      blindmen and lepers
      and the whole crowd of the holy books
      the seer and the accursed and the sinner
      pregnant women and preachers
      ice-cream vendors and acrobats on horseback
      traders and royalists and seamen
      atheists and pawnbrokers
      and apostles...
      hailing from forests and seashores and barren places
      they filled your merry meadows
      and shouted
      Amid colossal sounds you galloped by..."
And came the tailors. The suns went out of the rooms now.
In the houses everyone was trembling and fidgety, trembling and fidgety
No dailies carried the news. We had embarked on an age of shops
Hundreds of tailors shut their windows in hundreds of rooms
Their fingers, slender, withered, their faces pale and old from a standstill
Lost watch chains, trembling and fidgety, their legs tired
They acquiesced with the standstill that directed all they had
they felt pleased and smiled.
      "The horse now dead—they said—
      Your saddle was so pretty.
      Made out of a she-goat's skin, adorned with the gold of Ophir
      It went so well with the noble curves of your torso
      With you reflected beyond.
      Beyond the sensitivity of fava beans and beets
      The unattainable personality that the cat arrived at

On a sunny roof.
You spurred the ships to set sail from our souls
So we freshened your waters with vast rites
You became our festivity. Your saddlebows
Sagged with coriander seeds and almonds.
Now the world is narrow
And death's mad speed has slackened."
And came the tailors. They did not bring fire and blood.
Yet their sorrows were blood and fire. A tumultuous thing
Express trains stranded in stations and drugs going mad
I roamed the city from one end to the other, not a click
They dispersed into all the rooms. Tumblers dusty, shoes shriveled up
On the floors bits and clips of fabric,
> "scooped up lapels, leftovers of sleeves
> shoulder pads, crossed strips and hooks,
> buttons and loops
> bits of thread, pieces of fabric,
> dark evenings and mornings
> shop˙signs and business cards…"

all the way up to the grains, there is not even the tiniest death.
A neutral love kept purling over their pallor
They locked up their kitchens and cut out huge horse outfits,
> "The horse now dead—they said—
> Your gallop once expanded the world.
> Your frenzied lunge forward
> While we lay down south you galloped on
> If any horse was pretty you were prettier
> At one bright spot your tail split
> The sky into black
> and exulted it with your fine embroidered crupper strap.
> Your reins made lovely sounds
> in your lovely mouth
> and everyone shouted for joy.
> Your head went so well with our thoughts
> and we looked into your eyes with deep respect…"

And came the tailors. A standstill was what they wore half-naked and tardy
They were left incomplete. And remained so. They loved their dusty rooms.
Passing death with sorrow, they worshipped fire.
The city stood at their threshold and they heard its wail
They cut and measured, but neither sewed nor went off
Having put thread through the needles they waited;
> "The horse now dead—they said—
> That was the loveliest of all, the tentacle
> between your face and the war
> An out-and-out resistance, balance
> and a willful diminution. We knew that.

That tree fed upon our blood
which fed all of us.
Our bafflement before you re-created
a country,
destroyed by trading and the alphabet and leftovers of thread
and the attempt to set everything straight..."

Everyone

Translated by Feyyaz Kayacan

They were caught unprepared, they had long voices,
Long arms, long beards.
Whoever is woken from such sunken sleep
Has to rub his eyes
Like a black rabbit
In a field of carrots.
But this rabbit
Had no carrots.
This black-eyed boy
Had, with janissaries, dismissed Byzantium,
Had donated his blood to conquests.
This boy had a forelock,
This boy had none.
And they, soldiers by boot and uniform discarded,
They who had never worn glasses,
Surgical belts,
With hunger swollen like doughnuts in their guts,
Their hearts rattling with the pain of death,
They were all caught unprepared.

I know an evening tasting like an exhibition
In the midst of garrulous mouths and expensive flowers.
His love should go well with the sun,
With days gone by,
In the midst of urgent wheat and oats.

New bar of soap,
Give up, for God's love, tarring my heart,
I walk barefoot in rice fields.
Many remembered the old days,
Many their old fathers.
Many, more or less many
Were caught unprepared.

O death, with eyes bigger than graves,
You cannot take us in full.
Some things are bound to stay with us,
Things that none can wear out:
A ripe summer evening, a how are you,
A rising with the sun like a raised cup.
The day veered from the Mediterranean, from Çukurova,
It veered into a feast till morning celebrated.
But the waters stopped, the evening grew long,
And everyone, oh how lovely, everyone
Was caught unprepared.

Old Broken Glasses

Translated by Ayhan Sümer

Now I am alone with these my hands, look you now
With these my hair, my nice clothing, these my nickels now
There is you and you are not enough for times
Are you away, is it you, you do not tell
Are your glances missing, or your lips, I do not see
I remember those men, dark and huge men
Those ships—of fallen sails and rudders
The swallow birds I forgot and broken glasses
If I know not that in summer in a wooden house
If I know not that in a courtyard from a jug
Do waters cold and cold ooze, if I know not
I can endure not.

This situation blames me only
I am with myself through the day, see you now.

This is the sun which breaks down now and then
And this the snake which strikes without cause
And these the broken glasses in rubbish heaps
To go to the easiest of love, of poetry, of death
And the streets which I lost in women I loved not
I know the reason, I know them all
So easy itself, so easy to be saved and to tell
That I get bored of its easiness
That I cannot save myself.

Blood Cities

Translated by Talat Sait Halman

Out of houses with dark-ridden windows gushes blood
Over the corpses of women and over the roof tiles
In the radiant and pearl-studded sea's blue exile
Athwart blood timorous are the fairest of wild fish
This is blood we pour in the tedious Sunday bazaars
Cascades over heaven and earth over casks of liquor

Their hands their gluttonous fingers blood-drenched
Not Bosnian those children at the ice-cream vendor's
At Eyüps of the sarcophagi and by the seashores
Children fair-haired with mothers and fathers though
From frame houses into streets and avenues pours blood
Over the short pants whose blue realms remain dull

Blood gushes from the spouts such profuse blood
That the Thursday of sunken vessels is painted red
And a rosary and a puncheon and a typewriter
While horses drag away the assassin kings
Horses their harnesses black their rumps salted
As blood awakens as the love of dead women awakens

On the trees and in the ships' wake and in restaurants
Looms the patch of blood upon blood of the cities
And the birth to dead women of fondled infants
In rooms without birds without fish with console
Were there no desert or the most female of melons
That sun that sun of the children of antiquities
Beyond the sandstone roofs of Malta over there

The Night of the Stag

Translated by Nermin Menemencioğlu

Yet there was nothing visible to fear
Everything was as though of nylon
And when we died it was in tens of thousands against the sun
Even so before we found that Night of the Stag
We were frightened as little children are

You must all know the Night of the Stag
In the distant forests green and untamed
When the sun sets slowly at the end of the asphalt
It will deliver us all from time

On one side we ploughed the land
And on the other we disappeared
Concealing it from the gladiators and the sharp-toothed
And from the big cities
Or fighting them for it
We have delivered the Night of the Stag

We were alone yes but not without hope
Three houses seemed to us a city
Three pigeons made us think of Mexico
Evenings we liked to wander on the streets
To watch the women looking for their husbands
Afterwards we drank wine red wine or white
Whether we knew it or not because of the Night of the Stag

Behind the Night of the Stag are the trees
Where its hoofs touch the water there is a sky
On its branching horns the cold light of the moon
Willingly or not one is reminded of love
Once there were splendid women and splendid loves
And there are now I know

If you but knew how happy I am at the thought
Up in the mountains during the fairest of Nights
Nothing at all matters I tell myself
Except for love and hope
Three cups and three new songs and in one moment
The Night of the Stag is furry-soft in my mind
Ships cannot carry it away I know nor

Neons and theories illumine its angles
Thus two of us used to drink in Manastır*
Or else make love in bed a man and a woman
Slowly our kisses seemed to grow warmer
Slowly our armpits sweeter
In the dark of the Night of the Stag

That we were misled was not important
Only that we remembered what others had forgotten
We did not love silver samovars and other old things
The better to reject them
Was it because we were evil you will ask
We were neither evil nor good
If we began and ended in separateness
It was because we were separate at beginning and end

But everything was in the Night of the Stag
If you but knew our palms were damp with excitement
We looked and evening fell upon the pavements
The crystal chandeliers and women's bare shoulders
We felt like strangers outside the great hotels
So easy was our helplessness to come by
Nor were we sad because of mighty reasons
For instance three cups of wine could set us free
Or sticking a knife into a man
Or spitting into the street
But best of all we simply went away
Into the Night of the Stag and there we slept

The eyes of the Stag shine luminous in the night
Timid and restless like fires of distress
Like royal daggers in the light of the moon
On one side of the Stag rock piles on rock
And on the other side I
But you are pitiful and I am pitiful
Outworn things do not suffice to distract us
Domino chips and cold afternoons
Alien crowds in flowered garments
Our shadow coils at our feet
Though we rejoice we know the end in sight
I have forgotten loans and bonds and sureties
The premiums of the world are not for me
At the first session I was pronounced innocent
Now I bathe a dark woman for myself
I do not dry her hair very well
I drink a glass of wine for myself

*Pun on the name of the Balkan town and a monastery.

Yet the Night of the Stag is in the forest
Intensely blue and filled with rustling sound
I cross into the Night of the Stag

And I lean forward to kiss myself on the cheek.

Nevzat Üstün

The Gate of the Lost

Translated by Mina Urgan

Look, we are going through the street where we found our five senses.
You begin to cry where you left off
Do not cry

I put forth my hands
They are about to touch you
Two joined creatures together
Become two different worlds
The waters of rain pour from my eyes
These are not my eyes
An ocean, tied to the shore
That's their way of life
I choose to look at myself
I look at my heart
Exhausted
I was love itself in the days of the past
Life loved me
There was no daylight

There was no time
Now there is
There is your
Way of coming
Do not cry
I can cry as well
January the first nineteen fifty-nine
You open the door
That's fine

I give up myself
I give you up
A woodenheaded man is roaring with laughter
No more tricks in life
Let me see you
Come and see me
Convulsed with laughter he looks at me
He almost sees me
If he only could I won't mind
But he will not see me
He is shaking his finger
A finger full of authority
Ideas get linked in my mind
A chain

I want to break all chains
And I break them
This idiot is positive
Pain is not easy
And
I caught fish three times in my life

I tell you, take the streets
And here you are taking all the streets of my sensations
There are days when I look only at what is everlasting
It's good in a way
I grow up slowly

It is beautiful to share the daylight
Kiss me
And here you are again
You are kissing my flesh
Anyone can kiss my flesh
Kiss me
Come and kiss the real me
It is easy to love with your eyes
It is a cigarette
A cheap cigarette
I give up myself
Let them give me up

Who should give you up
The clever people of course
The frightened infants the world
In the likeness of soap operas
In the likeness of capitalism

And whose darkness is this
Is it Fear,
Is it Enlightenment
Is it Love
Or is it Friendship

I want none of these
I am closing the gate
This is my gate
The Gate of the Lost

If my hand is not with me
It cannot be with you
I am riding a horse
A good full-blooded horse
I bury my face in its mane
It has a happy smell of its own
I lay my neck on its neck
Blood is flowing I can see it
A blue blood
You see the skin you see the hair
We laugh
A strident laughter

You stay in yourself
I just go
This is the way off, this is the broken glass
Sooner or later it reaches the Gate of the Lost
This is the street where I am registered
I came back I washed, tired, the stars, to love me,
near the dreams
I closed the gates
Anyone can open them

I have died so many times by myself
If only they could knock me down
If only they could kill me decently
I won't mind

News Bulletin

Translated by Talat Sait Halman

Nine killed and three wounded
Apricot trees are in blossom
The inmost leaf is green
They shot a girl in Urfa
Meanwhile
At the United Nations
An impeccable gentleman
Declared: "Human value is limitless."
Same day at midnight
Two thousand nine hundred ninety-six people in Asia
Were massacred assured of going to heaven
The reason
The reason is very serious
The ruffian who was executed last, for instance—
His buggy
Unmindful of the need for a passport
Crossed the border
What that gentleman
At the United Nations proclaimed
Is correct

What the hell do I care
In the year nineteen hundred and fifty-two
In a spring month

Our news bulletin for the day ends here, sir.

Halim Yağcıoğlu

Anzelha

Translated by Talat Sait Halman

I

Anzelha
Did you ever walk in streets
Six-feet wide
Twenty-five-feet long
Where walls
Barren walls
Stretch all along
And did you ever suffer
The agony of women prisoners
Behind those walls?

Humanity is cleanliness, Anzelha
Friendship and brotherhood
Did you ever walk in garbage dumps
Or hear your own countrymen talk some other tongue
In the heart of your homeland
Did you ever search your land?

I live in a land of phantoms, Anzelha
Where the nights of Ancient Ur still glow
And my brothers still wear druggets
Where Kurdish chiefs swagger out of tales

Did your people live in such lairs, Anzelha
Did trachoma burn out their eyes too
Were their faces riddled like sieves
And did the nights last eternally?

This land unawakened and unstirred
Still lives in the fifth century, Anzelha
And you live in the twentieth century
Is this how you absorbed civilization
Shame

434

Shame on you, Anzelha
In endless thoughts
Nights torture the sleep
Is this where the East starts, Anzelha
Is this Islam
Steeped in filth so deep?

II

Along the street of infinite shame
I saw the grime and the gutters, Anzelha
And the people who survive by chance
Gordian knots in tales

I have embraced you as a grief alive
You are my land, Anzelha
If I don't cry out your woes
My mother's milk would damn me now
And venom would smother whatever I eat

Anzelha
Believe me I awoke from a long dream
That Izmir and Bursa alone
Should be cherished in this land
Provokes anger and agony in me, Anzelha
Should Urfa, the city of millennia, come to this?

Urfa is ossified in time
But change is inevitable
Nimrod's city will come alive some day
Its womb will give birth to cherubic tomorrows
And a garland will be placed on your head

III

Anzelha
A fierce wind blazed from the desert
Ruthlessly
Driving us mad
I was drenched in sultry sweat
My lips were parched
And caravans of camels trudged far away

Then the muezzin's voice burst, Anzelha
Past the endless filth of this Muslim city
Past its public baths and graves and brothels
Transcendent, it reached out to God

Suddenly I heard a tumult
As in a revolt
Men and women and children
Wailing and snarling
In the dark of the night I ran toward the hubbub
And I saw a corpse carried away on shoulders

For a nickel, Anzelha, they had shot a man
For a head of lettuce five cents worth
That is heroism in our times
I have seen this town's valor too

Anzelha Anzelha
Abraham who destroyed Nimrod's idols
Was misguided
And perverse
Yet he never broke a man's heart, Anzelha
Nor shot a man for a head of lettuce
Shame, Anzelha, shame on you

Nevzat Yalçın

The Corpse on the Beach

Translated by Talat Sait Halman

I am a dead man lying stark naked on the beach,
Staring at the sky off the tips of my feet.
My soles are shored up on the sun at nightfall.
When waves tickle my limbs with foam and spray,
I laugh as I never have before...
I died so young and strong,
But I can't tell what for.

Fellow corpses, this is not a complaint, don't get me wrong!
I broke out of the vicious cycle. Come and see
No more multiple equations...no more,
Nor shackles around my ankles, heavy and sore.

The sky resembles a strange sieve:
Through one pore, I fell on the beach, all wet,
I am a moon-betrayed poet.

On the beach, where I lie stark naked,
I gaze at the sky through the wheel of fate.

Hilmi Yavuz

Hilmi's Childhood

Translated by Richard McKane

Hilmi says that oaths
remind me of fountains
A coffin is a thick bound book
And is there a walnut coffin of your childhood
gently leaving for the sea?

Hilmi says I
rented sadness on the cheap
from a crimson cheeked puppetman
The sky was made up of a thousand blue caps
And was your cap blue
in those days?

Hilmi says my mother
was flower-embroidered lantern
In the nights a blackout
And did you understand the seas
before you got into bed?

Can Yücel

Poems from Marmaris

Translated by Richard McKane

That eye was blue as a pimp's
turning to the sun second on the right
Where there is morning there is the evening house
swept clean by the afternoon rains

It's not easy to sprinkle clouds
there are poets, boors, green boys,
the bird-lime grasses swaying gently, beautifully,
there is a road guarding the custom

Ha, back from a shopping trip in the skies?
It could be Sunday it could be a holiday it could be a weekday
Fresh flying news was brought
and instructed the Phoenician winds

Captain Piri drew taut sails
my heart is an age-old map
These blue dots are where we loved
this is the day when eye met eye

Last night I dreamed of a circus
After the shaggy ponies came the thoroughbred mares
they circled before the audience on my left breast
and children balancing on crimson balls

A girl went by on a bicycle from open country
The day looked out at a son on the roof with the clothesline
It's fated who this song will hit,
a goat path between the stars.

Heretic

Translated by Talat Sait Halman

Mosques could do without minarets
Our world could revolve without God
So long as you got a loudspeaker there

A Parable

Translated by Murat Nemet-Nejat

I saw Christ in a vision last night
He was the same when alive, half-dead
He is standing like a specter on the raft
If you say this is the sea, it is not, it is the Sea of Galilee
The cross is around his neck like a hanged man
As the raft rolls he sways too.
On the shore a herd of wise fishermen
Staring at the cross they get swayed too.

As you know, prophecy is also a craft
It also has a science, an art.
At first occasion, he must push forward his ware
So that the demand increases, the market widens.
What is Christ's craft? Miracles of course.
The ones who know the New Testament remember it:
The Good Lord caught fish with his cock.
Look all of you at the power of faith.

As he entered my dream, I said to myself, "Now,
Is he going to challenge nature again?
In fact, opening his breeches doesn't
Christ hang his cock into the waters?"
Of course, we got exhausted waiting a long time,
But wasn't it worth it for such an event?
But finally what did he fish out of the water?
A dried fig turned purple in the cold.

A heavenly music began to play then.
The Messenger of God delivered an angry note:
The biggest fault was with the Turkish police.
When it poured Marx and Engels into the sea
The bane of Dialectical Materialism passed
From the books into the fish...
"They don't swallow now, either miracles or nets
Or hooks," he complained.

History Lesson at the Flea Market

Translated by Talat Sait Halman

If you recline into this brocaded couch
And if I go sit on that shelf of turbans,
Do you think we might upset the venerable dust?
If we take a pinch out of this snuffbox,
Which probably belonged to some Grand Mufti,
Do you think it might drum up a sneeze,
The parable of the snuff long since gone?

Is this the end of the auction or just about?
After all, no more bids are to be heard.
Before the gavel sounded to annouce Mr. N.
The owner of a full-length gold-leaf mirror
And before he could even say, "It's all done,"
Before his new piece jibed with the new features,
Mr. N., his mirror, his comb, and his auburn locks
All turned to dust and were scattered to the wind.
Is this the end of the auction or just about?

Were you ever, while sitting at a train window,
By the drifting trees and the earth and the rocks,
Deep in thought, watching the images of your face
With the twitches on your mouth and whatnot,
Jabbed and jostled by the rude elbow
Of some guy breezing through the corridor?

Did you then wish you were the only passenger?
Dismissing all that you wistfully watched—
The trees, the earth, the rocks, and yourself
Out of the window of the speeding train,
Did you wish you were left behind there
Where you had seen your image reflected?

Surely you have wished for that, haven't we all?

How about me buying you a mirror,
A full-length mirror with a gold-leaf frame
With the inscription on top "Here lies the deceased"?
And then we'll have your body washed clean
And in your memory we'll send out trays of fritters.

Surely you have wished for that, haven't we all?

Mr. N. had the urge to get off before the train stopped.
Yet these are venerable secondhand mirrors
And venerable mirrors fall into disuse,
With dust upon dust, and dust inside dust,
Venerable mirrors have fallen into disuse.

No one may get off while the train is moving.
If you do, they won't wash you the right way,
But they'll bury you at the flea market before you rot.

Surely you have wished for that, haven't we all?

Whatever remains after you are gone
Or whatever has remained after Mr. N. was gone
In a handful of dust,
Was it the unlived portion of his life?
Or whatever has remained after Mr. N. was gone
In a handful of dust,
Was it his death in defiance of dying?

They won't let you get off while the train is moving;
If you do, they won't wash you the right way,
They'll bury you at the flea market before you rot.

They won't allow you to mellow like wine
Or become an old man in the shade of a plane tree;
You shall remain idle in the midst of the mirrors
With dust upon dust, a passenger on the train,
Neither within the entrance nor without,
A flea market shopper with flea market items for sale.
If you live, you shall live with the dead at best,
Neither within the entrance nor without,
If you die, you shall die with death itself.

If you recline into this brocaded couch
And if I go sit on that shelf of turbans,
Do you think we might upset the venerable dust?
If we take a pinch out of this snuffbox,
Which probably belonged to some Grand Mufti,
Do you think it might drum up a sneeze,
The parable of the snuff long since gone?

Cahit Zarifoğlu

Tigerish

Translated by Talat Sait Halman

A wall is driven by your hair your eyes have a beast's glare
Brazenly you flash your sex putting countless nooses around my neck

I wish to let your twinkling dimples pour into my rooms
The way I bang the doors and turn into dungeons in houses

Now I shall release a scream of love into the wide open air
They will say this man presses rebellions into the veins

Notes on Contributors

Writers of Fiction

SAİT FAİK ABASIYANIK (1906-1954) is regarded as one of the most important short-story writers of modern Turkey. He studied briefly at Istanbul University, then at Grenoble. In addition to thirteen collections of short stories, he published a book of poems and two novels. A large selection of his short stories will be published under the title *A Dot on the Map*.

OKTAY AKBAL (b. 1923) is a prolific short-story writer and columnist for the influential Istanbul daily *Cumhuriyet*. He has won two of Turkey's major awards for fiction. In addition to many novels and collections of short stories, he has published books containing his diaries, essays, and memoirs.

SABAHATTİN ALİ (1907-1948) was one of the early figures of socialist realism in Turkish fiction. He studied at the Teachers College in Istanbul and later in Germany. He taught German at various schools and served as a drama consultant for the State Conservatory, which he left because of his leftist views. After working for numerous socialist periodicals in Istanbul, he was jailed for three months in 1948. He was shot and killed in April of the same year near the Bulgarian border while attempting to flee Turkey. Between 1934 and 1948 he published nine books of fiction and poetry.

ÇETİN ALTAN (b. 1926) is one of Turkey's most famous columnists. He holds a law degree from the University of Ankara, and served as a Member of Parliament from Istanbul from 1965 to 1969. In addition to many collections of his journalistic articles, he has published several major novels some of which have enjoyed critical acclaim in France, Sweden, and other countries as well. He is also a playwright.

FAKİR BAYKURT (b. 1929) is one of the principal figures of Turkish village fiction. He has received his country's major literary awards. A graduate of an Institute for Village Teachers, he taught in various parts of Turkey for some years. He has also served as president of the Teachers Union of Turkey.

KEMAL BİLBAŞAR (b. 1910) has published novels and collections of short stories since the late 1930s. Some of his works have won Turkey's top awards. After teaching for more than thirty years, he retired in 1961 to devote all of his time to writing.

TARIK BUĞRA (b. 1918) has published many collections of short stories, novels, essays, and travel impressions. He is a columnist for the Istanbul daily *Tercüman*, which enjoys one of Turkey's largest circulations. He has won a major award for one of his plays.

CENGİZ DAĞCI (b. 1920) is a Crimean Turk who became a POW in a German camp in 1941. After World War II, he settled in London. He has published ten novels, most of which deal with the plight of Crimean Turks and with the tragic events of World War II.

FERİT EDGÜ (b. 1936) is known for his short stories about ennui and disquietude written in the stream of consciousness style. He studied at the Academy of Fine Arts in Istanbul, and did further work in Paris for six years. He is also an essayist.

NAZLI ERAY attended the British High School and an American college in Istanbul, and later studied law and philosophy at the University of Istanbul. She writes fiction in Turkish and English. For one year she attended the International Writers' Workshop at the University of Iowa.

FÜRUZAN (b. 1935) has published one novel and three collections of short stories. She has won Turkey's two major fiction awards.

HALİKARNAS BALIKÇISI (literally, "The Fisherman of Halicarnassus") (1886-1973) is the pen name of Cevat Şakir Kabaağaçlı. After graduating from Robert College in Istanbul, he earned a degree in modern history at Oxford University in 1908. In 1924 he was banished to Bodrum, ancient Halicarnassus, where he settled after he was pardoned a year and a half later. In addition to fiction, he published numerous books on classical mythology and approximately one hundred books that he translated from various languages.

ORHAN HANCERLİOĞLU (b. 1916) holds a law degree from Istanbul University. He has worked as an administrator in several provinces, served as director of the City Theater of Istanbul, and was most recently the legal advisor for Istanbul electricity and transportation agency. After publishing eight novels and a collection of short stories, he devoted his energies to the history of philosophy. In 1956 he won the fiction prize of the Turkish Language Society.

YAKUP KADRİ KARAOSMANOĞLU (1889-1974), after serving as a member of Parliament, had ambassadorial posts in Tirana, Prague, The Hague, and Bern. Later he was the lead editorial writer for the Ankara daily *Ulus,* following which he served another four-year term in Parliament (1961-65). His books include major novels, collections of short stories and essays, two volumes of prose poems, and his memoirs in several volumes.

BİLGE KARASU (b. 1930) is a graduate of the University of Istanbul, where he studied philosophy. He has won awards for his collections of short stories and for his D. H. Lawrence translation.

REFİK HALİT KARAY (1888-1965) was a prolific writer of novels, short stories, newspaper articles, essays, and satirical pieces.

FEYYAZ KAYACAN (b. 1919) studied political science and economics in France and England and worked for many years as a BBC broadcaster. Most recently he was the chief of BBC's Turkish Desk. In addition to five collections of short stories, he has published a play and a book of poems. His stories about London during World War II won the award of the Turkish Language Society.

ORHAN KEMAL (1914-1970) was one of Turkey's major fiction writers. After working in factories, textile mills, and so on, he earned his living as a journalist and independent writer. He published more than forty books, which include novels, short-story collections, an autobiography, and two plays. Some of the plays adapted from his works have been very successful on the Turkish stage. He won several major awards.

YASHAR KEMAL (b. 1922) is frequently mentioned in the world press as a strong candidate for the Nobel Prize. His fiction has been translated into more than twenty-five languages. Among his books available in English are *Memed, My Hawk; Wind from the Plain; Iron Earth, Copper Sky; Anatolian Tales; They Burn the Thistles; The Legend of Ararat; The Legend of the Thousand Bulls; The Undying Grass; The Lords of Akchasaz: Murder in the Ironsmiths Market;* and *Seagull.* In Turkey he is also well known for his essays and journalistic writing. In the late 1960s he served as a member of the Executive Committee of the Turkish Labor Party.

SAMİM KOCAGÖZ (b. 1916) holds a degree in Turkish literature from the University of Istanbul. For three years he studied art history at the University of Lausanne. He has published many novels and collections of short stories and won the award of the Turkish Language Society in 1968.

MAHMUT MAKAL (b. 1930) achieved nationwide fame in 1950 with the publication of *Bizim Köy* (Our Village), a collection of vignettes and random notes from the village where he served as a teacher. This book, together with a subsequent one, was translated into English by Sir Wyndham Deedes and published under the title of *A Village in Anatolia.* Makal has written many volumes about Anatolian villages and the social, economic, and educational problems of Turkey.

AZIZ NESIN (b. 1915) has published more than seventy books. He is Turkey's most popular satirist. After serving as a career officer for several years, he became a columnist in 1944 and edited a series of satirical periodicals. He was jailed several times for his political views. Many of his plays have been staged. He has won numerous awards in Turkey, Italy, Bulgaria, and the Soviet Union. The first volume of his autobiography, *Istanbul Boy,* is available in English.

ERDAL ÖZ (b. 1935) holds a law degree from Ankara University. For some years he ran his own book shop and currently works as an editor of children's books. He has published two novels and two collections of short stories.

O. ZEKI ÖZTURANLI (b. 1926) is an attorney who holds a degree from the University of Istanbul. In addition to four collections of short stories, he has published a play which had a successful production in Istanbul in the late 1960s.

FETHI SAVAŞCI (b. 1930) was forced to cut his schooling short to support his family. He has been a worker in West Germany since the mid-1960s. He has published numerous collections of short stories and poems.

ZEYYAT SELIMOĞLU (b. 1922) is a graduate of the Faculty of Law at the University of Istanbul. Recipient of two of Turkey's top awards, he has published four books of stories. He has also won prizes for a newspaper article and for a radio play.

SEVGI SOYSAL who emerged as a major fiction writer in the 1970s died of cancer in 1976 at age 40. She was a graduate of the Department of Classical Philology at the University of Ankara, and had done further graduate work in West Germany.

KEMAL TAHIR (1910-1973) spent twelve years in prison because of his ideological views. After his release in 1950, he earned his living through his books. He won widespread fame, critical acclaim, and several major awards for his novels and short stories.

HALDUN TANER (b. 1915) is a major playwright whose works have enjoyed success in Turkey and abroad, most notably in West Germany, England, and Czechoslovakia. He has also been a columnist for several major newspapers, most recently for *Milliyet.* He studied political science at Heidelberg and holds a degree in German Literature from the University of Istanbul. He has won several awards.

ILHAN TARUS (1907-1967) wrote five novels, three plays, and six collections of short stories. After obtaining a law degree from Ankara University, he worked as a public prosecutor, judge, and legal consultant. He spent twenty years of his life as a journalist.

BEKIR YILDIZ (b. 1933) is an award-winning writer of fiction about Turkish workers at home and in West Germany, where he spent four years working at factories and printing plants. Following his return from Germany, he set up his own press in Istanbul and produced many works of fiction.

TAHSIN YÜCEL (b. 1933) holds degrees in French literature. His dissertation on Bernanos was published in Paris in 1969. His publications include six collections of short stories, one novel, a study of language reform in Turkey, and scores of translations from the French. Currently, he is a professor of French literature at the University of Istanbul, and President of the Turkish PEN Centre.

Poets

NAHIT ULVI AKGÜN (b. 1918) holds a degree in philosophy from the University of Istanbul and he has taught at lycées since the late 1940s. He has published six poetry books, one of which won the award of the Turkish Language Society in 1967.

NAZMI AKIMAN (b. 1929) is a poet-diplomat who has served as Turkey's deputy permanent representative at the United Nations. He holds degrees from the University of Istanbul and Columbia University. He is currently Turkey's ambassador in Cuba.

GÜLTEN AKIN (b. 1933) is an award-winning woman poet. She holds a law degree from Ankara University. In addition to six collections of poems, she has published several short plays.

SABAHATTİN KUDRET AKSAL (b. 1920) is a graduate of Department of Philosophy at the University of Istanbul. After teaching for several years, he worked for the city of Istanbul. His books include six collections of poetry, five plays, and two collections of short stories. He has won awards for his poetry, drama, and short stories.

FERİHA AKTAN (b. 1924) holds a degree in literature from the University of Istanbul. She worked for Turkey's Maritime Bank for some years. She has published five collections of poetry.

MELİH CEVDET ANDAY (b. 1915) is a leading poet, playwright, novelist, essayist, and translator. In 1971 UNESCO honored him as one of the world's major literary figures. His works have won many awards. Since 1954 he has taught phonetics, diction, and dramatic literature at the Conservatory of Istanbul. He is a weekly columnist for the Istanbul daily *Cumhuriyet*. His selected poems in English translation are in *Rain One Step Away*.

TALİP APAYDIN (b. 1926) graduated from an Institute for Village Teachers and worked for many years as a teacher in villages and cities. He is the author of many books of poetry and fiction dealing mainly with villagers. He has also written a play, children's books, and a book of essays.

ORHON MURAT ARIBURNU (b. 1918) is an actor, director, and scriptwriter of Turkish films. He has published two books of poems.

AHMET ARİF (b. 1925) is a best-selling poet; a collection of poems he published in 1968 reportedly sold close to twenty-five thousand copies.

ÖZDEMİR ASAF (1923-1981) is a poet, translator, and aphorist. He worked as a translator for several Instanbul newspapers. For some years he ran his own printing press.

ARİF NİHAT ASYA (1904-1975) taught literature for many years and served as a member of Parliament for one term. His books include fifteen volumes of poetry, many of which are in the form of the *Rubaiyat* stanza.

M. SAMİ AŞAR (b. 1932) has published three collections of poems.

OĞUZ KÂZIM ATOK (b. 1912) is a retired general who has published four poetry books and hundreds of essays.

ECE AYHAN (b. 1931), a graduate of the Faculty of Political Science in Ankara, worked as a provincial administrator before becoming an editor. One of Turkey's most controversial experimental poets, he has published four collections.

M. BAŞARAN (b. 1926) graduated from an Institute for Village Teachers and worked as a teacher in villages and cities. He has published many books of poetry, short stories, essays, and recollections.

SEYFETTİN BAŞCILLAR (b. 1930) is a veterinarian by profession. He has lived in the United States since 1966. He has published four collections of poetry.

ATAOL BEHRAMOĞLU (b. 1942) holds a degree in Russian language and literature from Ankara University. He has worked as a play-reader for the City Theater of Istanbul and has edited a literary magazine. His poems have been collected in three volumes.

CENGİZ BEKTAŞ (b. 1934) is an award-winning architect. He has published three books of poems. He holds a degree in architecture from the Technical University of Munich.

ŞEMSİ BELLİ (b. 1929) is a graduate of the faculty of Law at the University of Ankara. He is currently the editor-in-chief of an Istanbul newspaper.

SÜREYYA BERFE (b. 1943) studied literature at the University of Istanbul. He has published two collections of poems.

İLHAN BERK (b. 1916) has been a modernizing force in Turkish poetry for nearly three decades. He has published fourteen volumes of poetry and has compiled several major anthologies. He is also a leading essayist.

EGEMEN BERKÖZ (b. 1941) was one of the most talked about younger poets of the 1960s.

SALÂH BİRSEL (b. 1919) is a versatile writer who has published poetry, essays, translations, a novel, and treatises on poetry and painting. A graduate of the Department of Philosophy at the University of Istanbul, he has been a teacher of French, a labor inspector, and editor-in-chief of the publications division of the Turkish Language Society. He is one of Turkey's most successful essayists.

EDİP CANSEVER (b. 1928) is a recipient of the poetry prize of the Turkish Language Society. He has published eleven collections of poems. He owns and operates an antique shop in Istanbul's famous Grand Bazaar.

ARİF COŞKUN (b. 1928), who lives and works in Hatay, has published five books of poems.

NECATİ CUMALI. (b. 1921) is a prolific writer of novels, short stories, essays, and plays. He is a major poet. After graduating from the Faculty of Law at the University of Ankara, he practiced law for a few years. Since the late 1950s he has been an independent writer, and has lived in Paris, Israel, and Istanbul. He is the recipient of Turkey's most prestigious literary prizes.

ASAF HALET ÇELEBİ (1907-1958) was one of the earliest and most controversial modernists in Turkey. In addition to poetry, he wrote scholarly works and also did translations from Persian into Turkish and from Turkish into French.

MEHMET ÇINARLI (b. 1925), a graduate of the Faculty of Political Science in Ankara, is a judge of the Constitutional Court. He was for many years the editor of the influential literary monthly *Hisar* (1950-1980).

FAZIL HÜSNÜ DAĞLARCA (b. 1914) was honored by a panel of distinguished Turkish men of letters as "Turkey's leading living poet" in 1967 and received the Award of the International Poetry Forum (Pittsburgh, Pa.). He has published more than sixty books of poetry. Dağlarca books in translation have been published in English, French, Macedonian, Estonian, Hungarian, and Dutch. In 1974 he received Yugoslavia's Golden Wreath Award, which was previously given to W.H. Auden, Pablo Neruda, and Eugenio Montale et al. In 1977 he was the poet of the year at the Rotterdam Poetry International.

ARİF DAMAR (b. 1925) has published seven collections of poems, one of which won an important prize.

ZEKİ ÖMER DEFNE (b. 1903) was a teacher of literature at Turkish lycées until his retirement in 1969.

HASAN İZZETTİN DİNAMO (b. 1909) is the author of many novels about the Turkish War of Independence, and has published five volumes of poetry. In 1977 he won one of his country's major poetry awards.

AHMET MUHİP DRANAS (sometimes spelled DIRANAS) (1909-1980) was one of Turkey's major lyric poets. He held various posts, including those of director of the Children's Aid Society and member of the Executive Board of İş Bankası) Turkey's largest bank. He was also a well-known playwright.

REFİK DURBAŞ (b. 1944) has worked for several Turkish newspapers. He has published two collections of verse.

METİN ELOĞLU (b. 1927) is an innovative poet and painter. He won the award of the Turkish Language Society for one of his books of poetry.

MÜŞTAK ERENUS (b. 1915) is a graduate of the Faculty of Law at the University of Istanbul and practices law.

ABDULLAH RIZA ERGÜVEN (b. 1925) is a graduate of the Department of Turkish Literature at the University of Istanbul. He now lives in Sweden, and teaches Turkish at the University of Stockholm.

NÜZHET ERMAN (b. 1926) holds degrees from the Faculty of Political Science and the Faculty of Law in Ankara. For many years he has been a governor.

BEDRİ RAHMİ EYUBOĞLU (1913-1975) was one of Turkey's leading painters, who had numerous one-man shows in Europe and America. He published many books of poetry, essays, and travel impressions. For many years he was a professor of painting at Istanbul's Academy of Fine Arts.

İLHAN GEÇER (b. 1917) has held posts at the Directorate of Press, Broadcasting, and Tourism, Radio Ankara, and Social Security Administration. In the 1950s he served as the editor of the literary monthly *Hisar*.

ENVER GÖKÇE (b. 1920) is a graduate of the Department of Turkish Literature at the University of Ankara. He works as a journalist. In addition to his poetry he has published a book of Neruda translations.

SITKI SALİH GÖR (b. 1934) is a graduate of the Faculty of Forestry, University of Istanbul. Currently he is a consular official in West Germany. He has published four poetry books.

NEDRET GÜRCAN (b. 1931) has published four collections of poetry. He is one of the principal partners of a flour mill.

FEYZİ HALICI (b. 1924) is a chemical engineer who became a businessman and later served as a member of the Turkish Senate. He has published seven books of poems and compiled numerous anthologies.

NAZIM HİKMET (1902-1963) was Turkey's best-known Communist. Internationally, he is more famous than any other Turkish poet. His books have been translated into all major and many minor languages. Since 1954, five collections of his poetry in English translation have appeared. In addition to a vast body of lyric and epic poetry, he wrote numerous plays and novels. He spent many years in Turkish jails because of his ideological poems and died in self-imposed exile in Moscow.

AYHAN HÜNALP (b. 1927) holds a degree in Turkish literature from the University of Ankara. For many years he worked as a journalist. He has published poetry, short stories, and two novels.

RİFAT ILGAZ (b. 1911) was a teacher for many years. Since the late 1940s he has earned a living from his plays and journalistic writing. He has published many books of poems, short stories, and satires.

CAHİT IRGAT (1916-1971) was well known not only for his poems but also as an actor of the stage and screen.

TÜRKÂN İLDENİZ is a popular woman poet. Her poems have been collected in two volumes.

ATTİLÂ İLHAN (b. 1925) is a major figure of Turkish literature. He has achieved distinction with his poems, novels, and essays. Winner of several top awards, he is also well known as a newspaper columnist and as a scenarist.

ÖZDEMİR İNCE (b. 1938) has published three volumes of poetry and an anthology of Bulgarian poetry. After teaching for several years, he joined the staff of Turkish Radio and Television Administration, where he has served as program director.

A. KADİR (b. 1917) has published four collection of poems. His Rumi and Hayyam translations are famous. His *Iliad* translation, done in collaboration with the prominent classicist Azra Erhat, has won two awards.

ORHAN VELİ KANIK (1914-1950) was a major innovator and remains one of the most popular Turkish poets. His translations from the French also enjoy wide fame. Translations of his selected poems have been published in West Germany and the United States (*I Am Listening to Istanbul*).

CEYHUN ATUF KANSU (1919-1978), a pediatrician by profession, was a prolific poet and an award-winning essayist.

MUSTAFA NECATİ KARAER (b. 1929) was a career officer until 1969 when he retired. In 1961 he obtained a law degree from Ankara University.

SEZAİ KARAKOÇ (b. 1933) is a graduate of the Faculty of Political Science in Ankara. After serving as an official of the Ministry of Finance, he became a columnist in Istanbul and has published several periodicals. In addition to six books of poems, he has written various monographs on literature and culture.

MEHMED KEMAL (b. 1920) is a well-known journalist and columnist.

AYHAN KIRDAR (b. 1936) is a graduate of the Academy of Fine Arts in Istanbul and teaches painting and history of art at a lycée. He has published five collections of poetry.

NECİP FAZIL KISAKÜREK (b. 1905) studied at various graduate schools and held numerous jobs. He has published dozens of books of poetry, essays, historical studies, religious treatises, short stories, memoirs, and monographs. He is also the author of many plays, some of which had successful productions.

CAHİT KÜLEBİ (b. 1917) taught literature, served as Turkey's educational attaché in Switzerland, and was an assistant under secretary for Cultural Affairs. He has published eight books of poetry. Currently, he serves as editor-in-chief and secretary general of the Turkish Language Society.

ERCÜMENT BEHZAT LÂV (b. 1903) studied drama in Berlin, and was for many years an actor and director in Istanbul. In addition to five books of poetry, he has written two plays.

YUSUF MARDİN (b. 1916) holds a law degree from the University of Istanbul. In the late 1940s he was a member of Parliament. Later he served as Turkey's Press and Information attaché in London, Washington, and Bonn. He has published five collections of poetry.

MUAZZEZ MENEMENCİOĞLU (b. 1929) is known for her interviews with major literary figures in addition to her reputation as one of Turkey's principal woman poets.

İBRAHİM MİNNETOĞLU (b. 1920) owns and operates a book store in Istanbul. Through the years, he has been a columnist for several dailies. He has collected his poems in four volumes.

BEHÇET NECATİGİL (1916-1979) was one of the major poets of Turkey. He taught literature for thirty years until his retirement in 1972. He published thirteen books of poetry and thirty books that he translated from the German. In 1964 he received the award of the Turkish Language Society. He compiled a mythology dictionary and the *Who's Who in Turkish Literature*.

ÜMİT YAŞAR OĞUZCAN (b. 1926), who has published more than fifty books, is one of Turkey's most popular poets. Until his retirement in 1977, he was director of the book-publishing subsidiary of Turkey's largest bank, İş Bankası. Currently he owns and operates an art gallery in Istanbul.

AHMET OKTAY (b. 1933) is an award-winning poet who has published three books of poetry and some important literary essays and articles. A journalist, Oktay has also written a play, which was produced in 1974.

İSMET ÖZEL (b. 1944) has published three collections of poems.

KEMAL ÖZER (b. 1935) has been the editor of several literary journals and once operated his own book shop in Istanbul. He has published five volumes of poetry.

ALİ PÜSKÜLLÜOĞLU (b. 1935) is on the staff of the Turkish Language Society. He has published five volumes of poetry and compiled several anthologies. He now publishes one of Turkey's best poetry journals.

OKTAY RİFAT (b. 1914) has been in the vanguard of modern Turkish poetry since the late 1930s. He is also well known for his plays and translations. An attorney by profession, he was for many years a legal counsel for the Turkish State Railways.

ZİYA OSMAN SABA (1910-1957) wrote three books of poetry and two collections of short stories.

MEHMET SALİHOĞLU (b. 1922), an engineer, has held major positions in the Turkish Ministry of Reconstruction and Resettlement, including that of undersecretary. He has published four poetry books and four books of essays.

GÜLTEKİN SAMANOĞLU (b. 1927) is the Director General of the Publishing and Advertising Board in Istanbul.

TAHSİN SARAÇ (b. 1930) worked many years as a teacher of French. He has translated many Turkish poets and playwrights into French, and has compiled a major French-Turkish dictionary. He has published four collections of his poems.

CEMAL SÜREYA (b. 1931) held various positions in the Turkish Ministry of Finance after his graduation from the Faculty of Political Science. His poems have been collected in four volumes, two of which received major awards. Between 1960 and 1970 he served twice as editor-in-chief of the influential literary journal *Papirüs*. He enjoys fame as an essayist, anthologist, and translator as well.

HASAN ŞİMŞEK (b. 1918), an official of the Turkish Office of Agricultural Products, has published two collections of poetry.

ÜLKÜ TAMER (b. 1937) was educated at Robert College and the Journalism Institute of the University of Istanbul. He has won awards for his poetry and for his translation of Edith Hamilton's *Mythology*. In addition to seven collections of his own poems, he has published more than a hundred books in translation. Currently, he is the director of a major publishing house in Istanbul.

AHMET HAMDİ TANPINAR (1901-1962) was a professor of Turkish literature at the University of Istanbul, who wrote a very impressive history of nineteenth-century literature and many critical essays and monographs. He was also a major novelist, short-story writer, and poet.

OĞUZ TANSEL (b. 1915) was a teacher for many years. In addition to two poetry books, he has published six collections of children's stories.

CAHİT SITKI TARANCI (1910-1956) was a very popular poet in the 1940s and 1950s. In 1946 his poem entitled "Age Thirty-Five" won Turkey's top award.

SUAT TAŞER (b. 1919) was an actor with the Turkish State Theater until his retirement. In addition to several volumes of poetry, he has published a book of travel notes and collections of articles on the theater. He is also the author of two plays.

AHMET KUTSİ TECER (1901-1967), after graduation from the University of Istanbul and further study in Paris, became a teacher. Later he served as an educational attaché abroad. From 1942 to 1946 he was a member of Parliament. Besides poetry, he wrote several major plays.

ÖMER FARUK TOPRAK (1920-1979) published a novel, an autobiography, and a collection of short stories, in addition to several volumes of poetry.

GÜVEN TURAN (b. 1944), holds a degree in English literature from Ankara University and currently teaches English.

OSMAN TÜRKAY (b. 1927) is a Cypriot Turkish poet and critic who lives in London. In addition to five volumes of poetry, he has published many translations from English into Turkish and from Turkish into English.

TURGUT UYAR (b. 1927) is one of the most important modern poets of Turkey. He has published seven collections of poetry. He is also well known for his critical essays and translations.

NEVZAT ÜSTÜN (1924-1979) published many volumes of poetry, essays, short stories, and travel notes.

HALİM YAĞCIOĞLU (b. 1919) has held numerous teaching posts and has been an official of the General Directorate of Libraries in Ankara. He has published four volumes of poetry and several children's books and anthologies.

NEVZAT YALÇIN (b. 1926) is a graduate of the Department of Turkish Literature at Ankara University. Since the late 1960s he has been living in West Germany, where he teaches English literature. He has published two collections of poetry.

HİLMİ YAVUZ (b. 1936) studied philosophy at the University of London while he worked as a Turkish broadcaster for the BBC. In addition to two collections of verse, he has published a book of essays and a study of the novel.

CAN YÜCEL (b. 1926) studied classical literature at Ankara University and later at Cambridge University, and worked for the BBC. He is regarded as one of Turkey's most accomplished translators. He has published three volumes of poetry.

CAHİT ZARİFOĞLU (b. 1940) holds a degree in German literature from the University of Istanbul. He edits a literary magazine called *Mavera* which presents a fusion of traditional Turkish-Islamic values and a modern style.

The following were either originally written in English or translated from Turkish into English by their authors:

"Monte Kristo" by Nazlı Eray

"The Resurrection of the Unknown Soldier" by Halikarnas Balıkçısı

"The Shelter" by Feyyaz Kayacan

"Lullaby" by Yusuf Mardin

"The Mediterranean Light" by Osman Türkay

Biographical Notes

Translators

NAZMİ AKIMAN (See his biography as a Poet.)

ÖZCAN BAŞKAN is a Professor of Linguistics in the English Language and Literature Department of the Faculty of Letters, University of Istanbul.

TANER BAYBARS has published a collection of poems entitled *To Catch a Falling Man,* a novel, *A Trap for the Burglar,* and an autobiographical work *Plucked in a Far-off Land* (all in English) in addition to three volumes of his translations of Nazım Hikmet's poems. His latest book of poems is entitled *Narcissus in a Dry Pond.*

ESİN BİLBAŞAR is the daughter of Kemal Bilbaşar.

ÜNAL BODUROĞLU is a poet who holds a degree from Robert College (Istanbul).

MANFRED BORMANN holds degrees from Robert College and Syracuse University. He is currently an executive with the Atlantic Recording Corporation, and has staged several off-Broadway plays.

ORHAN BURİAN died in 1953 at the age of thirty-nine while serving as Professor of English Literature at Ankara University. He was a leading critic, anthologist, and translator (mainly of Shakespeare).

LARRY V. CLARK holds degrees from Indiana University where he specialized in Turkish language and literature. He has also translated Nazım Hikmet's poems into English.

GÜNGÖR DİLMEN is one of Turkey's leading playwrights. He is a graduate of the University of Istanbul, and has done further studies at Yale Drama School and the University of Washington.

ELLEN ERVIN has taught Turkish at the University of Pennsylvania and Columbia University. She is currently teaching at New York University.

AHMET Ö. EVİN holds a PhD in Comparative Literature from Columbia University. After teaching at Columbia, Harvard, and Hacettepe University (Ankara), he joined the faculty of the University of Pennsylvania where he gives courses in Turkish language and literature.

WILLIAM FIELDER is with the U.S. State Department.

ROBERT P. FINN holds a PhD in Turkish literature from Princeton University.

NIKI GAMM holds a PhD in Turkish literature from the University of Chicago.

DAVID GARWOOD was a professor at Robert College where he also served as Dean. He died in 1973.

PETER JENSEN did his graduate work in Near Eastern studies at Princeton University.

FEYYAZ KAYACAN (See his biography as a writer of fiction.)

THIILDA KEMAL is the translator of most of Yashar Kemal's works including *The Wind from the Plain; Anatolian Tales; Iron Earth, Copper Sky; The Legend of Ararat; The Legend of the Thousand Bulls; The Undying Grass; The Lords of Akchasaz: Murder in the Ironsmiths Market;* and *Seagull.*

APTUALLAH KURAN was President of Boğaziçi (Bosphorus) University. He is a well-known architectural historian who has published books on Ottoman architecture in Turkish and English.

452

BERNARD LEWIS is a distinguished historian of Islam. His many books include two highly acclaimed works on Turkish history. He is professor of Near Eastern studies at Princeton University and a co-editor of the *Encyclopaedia of Islam*.

RICHARD McKANE has published his translations of Osip Mandelstamm's poems and of Turkish poetry.

NERMİN MENEMENCİOĞLU is a prominent translator of Turkish literature. She is the editor of the *Penguin Book of Turkish Verse*.

ANIL MERİÇELLİ is a Turkish poet and translator.

ADAIR MILL holds a degree from St. Andrews University and teaches in the Department of English Philology at the University of Istanbul.

LOUIS MITLER holds a graduate degree from the University of Istanbul, and has done further work at Indiana University.

TATIANA MORAN is a professor of English language and literature at the University of Istanbul and at Boğaziçi (Bosphorus) University.

YIILDIZ MORAN is the translator of Özdemir Asaf's selected poems, *To Go To*.

MURAT NEMET-NEJAT holds degrees from Robert College and Amherst College, and has done graduate work at Columbia University. His first book of poetry was published in England in 1978 under the title of *The Bridge*.

A. TURAN OFLAZOĞLU is one of Turkey's leading playwrights. He holds a degree from the University of Istanbul, and has done further studies at the University of Washington. He is also well known as a translator (Shakespeare, Nietzsche, Rilke, et al.).

NİLÜFER MİZANOĞLU REDDY holds degrees in Psychology from the Department of Philosophy at the University of Ankara and from Columbia University where she also did postgraduate work. She is a painter and lives in New York City.

DIONIS COFFIN RIGGS is an American poet who has lived in Turkey. She is the author of *Seaborn Island*.

EDOUARD RODITI is a prominent translator and author. Among his many books is a collection of his versions of Turkish tales, *The Delights of Turkey*. He is the translator of Yashar Kemal's *Memed, My Hawk*.

FREDERIC STARK has lived in Ankara for many years. He has published numerous translations in U.S. literary journals.

CÖNÜL SUVEREN is one of the most productive translators in Turkey. She is a graduate of the American College for Girls (Istanbul).

AYHAN SÜMER is a graduate of Robert College.

BRIAN SWANN holds a PhD from Princeton University where he has also taught. Currently he is a professor at Cooper Union in NYC. He is a well-known poet and translator.

İLHAN TAYAR is an orthodontist who briefly taught at Columbia University in the early 1950s.

BEDİA TURGAY-AHMAD has published many articles and translations in Turkey and the United States.

OSMAN TÜRKAY (See his biography as a poet.)

DOĞAN TÜRKER is a graduate of Robert College. He has published two books of poetry.

MİNA URGAN is a retired professor of English literature at the University of Istanbul. She is well known as a translator. She has also published scholarly treatises on Shakespeare's *Macbeth* and on clowns in the Elizabethan theater.

ÖZCAN YALIM is a Turkish poet and translator.

TUNÇ YALMAN is a director of plays whose credits in the United States have included five years as the Artistic Director of Milwaukee Repertory Theatre as well as Broadway and off-Broadway work. A graduate of the Yale Drama School, he currently teaches drama in North Carolina.

JAMES LEE YARRISON has a PhD from the Department of Near Eastern Studies at Princeton University.

NURAL YASİN is a graduate of the Middle East Technical University (Ankara).

ALİ YUNUS is the joint pen name of two woman translators who published their versions of Nazım Hikmet's selected poems in book form in New York in 1954. They are Nilüfer Mizanoğlu Reddy (see her biographical note under REDDY) and Rosette Avigdor Coryell who is a professional translator in Paris.